STO

YO-BWS-093

G

University of Cambridge
Department of Applied Economics
OCCASIONAL PAPER 7

GROWTH, PROFITABILITY AND VALUATION
A Study of United Kingdom Quoted Companies

University of Cambridge

Department of Applied Economics

Occasional Papers

Growth, Profitability and Valuation

A Study of United Kingdom Quoted Companies

by A. SINGH and G. WHITTINGTON

in collaboration with H. T. BURLEY

CAMBRIDGE

AT THE UNIVERSITY PRESS

1968

PUBLISHED BY

THE SYNDICS OF THE CAMBRIDGE UNIVERSITY PRESS

Bentley House, 200 Euston Road, London, N.W.1.

American Branch: 32 East 57th Street, New York, N.Y. 10022

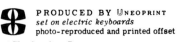
PRODUCED BY Uneoprint
set on electric keyboards
photo-reproduced and printed offset
at The Gresham Press
UNWIN BROTHERS LIMITED
Old Woking   Surrey   England

(U 2547)

Contents

II Analysis   1439136

Appendices

List of Tables

10

List of Figures

Preface

This book is a study of the relationship between the size, profitability, growth and other economic and financial attributes of the individual firm, with growth as the subject of main interest. The firms included in this study are public companies whose stocks or shares were quoted on United Kingdom stock exchanges during the period 1948 to 1960. The main source of data for the study is the standardized series of individual company accounts first produced by the National Institute of Economic and Social Research and continued by the Statistics Division of the Board of Trade. We are grateful to both of these bodies for the use of the data and for their help in answering the many detailed questions which we have put to them in the course of our work. We also owe a considerable intellectual debt to Professor Brian Tew and Dr. Ronald Henderson, the editors of Studies in Company Finance, which was the first major analysis, on the level of the individual firm, of the data prepared by the National Institute.

The unique feature of the present project is that we have transferred the data in a standardized form to magnetic tape for use on a high speed electronic computer. The difficulties involved in this process have meant that we have had to confine the quantity of data studied in the present work to four industries, amounting to something less than a fifth of the data available. On the other hand, we have been able to do far more statistical analysis and to study these industries in greater depth – at least in relation to the issues discussed here – than was possible in earlier studies.

Although this book is based on data for nearly 500 individual companies, it must be regarded as a preliminary study whose conclusions may be revised when, in subsequent work, the analysis is extended to cover further industries and a more recent time period. We should feel that our efforts have been amply rewarded if, in the view of the reader, we have succeeded in sifting and clarifying various issues and putting forward precise testable hypotheses.

Data processing on this scale has proved to be a difficult task. Thanks to the programming work of Mr J. N. Christie, we developed a computer program which would process the data on the TITAN computer at the Cambridge University Mathematical Laboratory. However, the input and output facilities there proved to be inadequate to handle the quantity of data involved. Our computer problems were resolved by the use of the I. B. M. 7090 computer at Imperial College, London, and by the programming efforts of Mr H. T. Burley, without whom the project would undoubtedly have failed. Mr Burley has displayed quite exceptional ingenuity and accuracy in programming the very complex process of testing and standardizing the data in a form which is readily available for further analysis, and it is in recognition of this that his name appears on the title page. We should also like to thank the Computer Unit of Imperial College, London, and the Cambridge University Mathematical Laboratory for the use of their facilities.

We are grateful to Mr Ian Fairbairn and his co-trustees of the Esmée Fairbairn Trust for their encouragement and faith in the ultimate success of the project. They financed the work throughout the difficult early stages when the pioneering data processing was done and even extended their grant for an additional year to enable us to complete this stage of the work. The more sophisticated analysis embodied in Chapters 4 to 8 of the book was carried out while we were in receipt of a grant from the Social Science Research Council, who have made a further grant to enable us to extend the analysis. Mr Singh also wishes to acknowledge a research grant from the National Economic Development Office, and a travel grant from the University of California, Berkeley. Mr Whittington held a research fellowship at Fitzwilliam College, Cambridge, during the period in which this book was written.

We owe an enormous debt to the Director of the Department of Applied Economics, Mr W.B. Reddaway, who has most unselfishly given advice, encouragement and perceptive criticism at all stages of the project, despite his heavy commitments elsewhere and despite the fact that he was theoretically on leave during the last stages of our work. We are conscious that this book still retains many shortcomings and errors, for which we take full responsibility, but these would have been much greater and more numerous were it not for Mr Reddaway's remarkable capacity for detecting the plausible but false step in an argument and separating the essential from the irrelevant.

We have also benefited from the advice of a number of our colleagues, including the members of an Advisory Committee which was set up to assist the project. Among those who have read and commented upon various chapters of the first draft of the book, we should like particularly to thank Mr K.D. George, Dr G.C. Harcourt, Mr R.L. Marris, Mr R.E. Rowthorn, and Professor Tew.

Work of this type inevitably involves assembling innumerable tables, sorting out and interpreting computer output, filing, checking and recording information on a very large scale. All of this has been done for us efficiently, intelligently and cheerfully by Mrs Joan Morrision, who has acted as our statistical assistant and without whom this book would never have reached the press.

Apart from Mrs Morrison, we have been helped in many ways by most of the assistant staff of the Department of Applied Economics, who have prepared data on punched cards or paper tape for the computer, carried out tedious calculations on desk calculators, provided us with books and journals for our innumerable references, and last, but not least, typed our unreadable manuscripts.

Cambridge,   A. Singh
September, 1967.   G. Whittington

PART I

DESCRIPTION

1 Introduction

1. Subject of the study

In the post-war period the attention of many economists has turned to the processes of economic growth and development. In general, the focus of attention has been on aggregate phenomena. However, in the last ten years a small number of important theoretical and empirical works on the growth of the individual firm have appeared both in the United States and in this country. These works concern the determinants of the growth of the firm, and the relationship of growth to the firm's profitability and to the sources of its finance, to mention but a few of the more important questions which have been posed.[1]

This book also is concerned with growth on the level of the individual firm. It is an empirical study of the relationship between the growth, size, and profitability of the firm — growth being the main dependent variable. Apart from size and profitability, the relationship of growth to other attributes of the firm, particularly its stock market valuation and the financial policy choices facing it, is also considered. The main financial policy variables discussed are the dividend pay-out ratio, gearing, outside finance, liquidity, and trade credit.

The basis of this study is accounting and stock market data for approximately 450 U.K. public quoted companies, belonging to four industries. These firms existed over a part or the whole of the period 1948-60. The nature and limitations of this data are discussed briefly in Section II, and in greater detail in Appendix A.

Part I of the book is mainly descriptive. The concepts used to measure growth, profitability, size, and other attributes of firms are discussed in Chapter 2. Frequency distributions of the firms studied, classified by each of these measures are also presented in that chapter. A preliminary analysis of the inter-relationship between the various characteristics of these firms is attempted in Chapter 3 where matrices of simple correlation coefficients between each pair of variables are given. Part I of the book thus gives, inter alia, a detailed profile of a part of the company sector of the U.K. economy on a micro-economic level for the period 1948-60. This micro-economic description complements the aggregate ones given in the National Income Blue Book and the Annual Abstract of Statistics.

Part II is the main analytical core of the book.

On one level it attempts to answer a number of elementary questions concerning the relationship between growth, size, and profitability of the firm. Do large firms grow faster than small firms or medium-sized firms? Are large firms more profitable than firms of smaller size? Is there a greater dispersion in the growth rates or the profit rates of the small firms as compared with the larger ones? As for the relationship between growth and profitability: How close is this relationship? Does it vary between industries? Does it remain stable over time?

On another level slightly more complex questions may be asked. For the firms of the same size and level of profitability, is there any relationship between growth and stock market valuation, or between growth and financial policy variables? From a practical point of view a more useful, although, indeed, more complex issue is the extent to which future growth of the firm can be predicted on the basis of its past economic and financial record.

However, it must be noted that all of these questions have been discussed here within a particular analytic framework. We start our analysis of the growth of the firm in Chapter 4 by asking whether the distribution of the growth rates can be regarded as the outcome of the simple stochastic process, known as the Law of Proportionate Effect. It is within this context that the relationship between size and growth is discussed. In the following chapter we consider two further aspects of the growth process of the firm which are linked to the Law of Proportionate Effect, and which are of considerable economic interest. First we discuss the internal mobility of firms, i. e., how firms change rank in the size distribution over time. Next we discuss the question of the persistency of growth rates – whether or not firms which have above-average growth in one period also display above-average growth in succeeding periods.

In Chapter 6 we explore the parallel relationship between size and profitability of the firm, as well as the question of the persistency of profitability over time. Finally in Chapter 7 the hypothesis that the growth of the firm is an entirely random phenomenon is discarded. We analyze the effect of certain systematic influences on growth, particularly that of profitability. Once the effect of these systematic factors is removed, we analyze the nature of the residual growth rates to determine to what extent they can be regarded as the outcome of some simple stochastic process and to what extent they are related to other financial variables.

However, for those readers who are not interested in stochastic processes or other theoretical issues raised in this approach, but who would nevertheless like to know the answers to some of the questions posed above, we have summarized the main conclusions at the end of each chapter and in Chapter 8. Such readers may, therefore, prefer to read only the concluding sections of Chapter 4 to 7 and go straight from Part I to Chapter 8. They may also like to look at Appendix F which eschews other than the most elementary statistical analysis.[1] This appendix gives the average value of each of the other variables for given ranges of each variable in turn.

Lastly, we must emphasize that this study is not only a preliminary one in the sense of coverage of data. It is also very much a preliminary study with respect to the limited range of issues it discusses. Several pertinent questions relating to the variables included in this study have not been discussed. In particular we should like to mention that we have not tested the empirical validity of some of the most recent and

most comprehensive theoretical models of the growth of the firm.[1]
In these models the equilibrium growth of the firm is simultaneously
determined with the equilibrium profitability and equilibrium values
of other financial policy variables. There are still a number of unre-
solved theoretical and statistical difficulties in testing these models
with the kind of data used in this study. Also we should like to emphasize that we have discussed only simple stochastic models of the growth
process of the firm. As this study is concerned only with continuing
firms, the more complicated stochastic models which require detailed
information on the birth and death processes of the firms have not been
discussed. These questions will be taken up in subsequent work.

2.   Sources and nature of the data

The firms studied here are public companies quoted on United Kingdom
stock exchanges.[2] They tend therefore to be the larger firms in their
respective industries because they found it expedient to gain access
to the capital market to finance their growth. Access to the capital
market also usually implies a wider distribution of share ownership
than would be found in a non-quoted company, and introduces a greater
likelihood that ownership will be divorced from control.

Within the quoted company population, we have confined ourselves to
four industries, Shipbuilding and Non-Electrical Engineering, Food,
Clothing and Footwear and Tobacco. All quoted companies in these
industries are covered by the data available to us, but we have limited
our analysis to companies which continued in existence throughout at
least one of the two 6-year sub-periods studied. The two sub-periods
cover the years 1948 to 1954 and 1954 to 1960 respectively. The full
period covers the years 1948 to 1960.

The population analysed is described in detail in Appendix A (pp. 203-37
and Tables A.1-A.4). The picture which emerges is that the industries
chosen include something short of one fifth of all quoted companies in
the manufacturing and distribution industries. The Engineering industry
is bigger than the remaining three together, but not by a great margin,
so that we can say that a little more than half of the population produces
capital goods and somewhat less than half consumer goods. Within
the industries chosen the continuing companies studied here are approximately two-thirds of the total quoted companies in these industries at
some time during the period, and a greater proportion of those in
existence at any given time.

Table 1.1 below shows the number of continuing companies in the four
industries. Our data cover all of these companies.

Table 1.1. Number of continuing companies, by industry and period

	Clothing and Footwear	Food	Tobacco	Total Consumer goods	Ship-building & Non-Electrical Engineering	Total
Sub-period 1	86	108	11	205	259	464
Sub-period 2	79	91	7	177	262	439
Whole period	70	73	7	150	214	364

The sources of data

The major source of data for the present analysis was the standardized series of the annual accounts of each quoted company prepared by the Statistics Division of the Board of Trade, in collaboration with the National Institute of Economic and Social Research. The other source was an estimate of the stock exchange valuation of each company's quoted share capital, and this was calculated from the data on Moodies cards and in the Stock Exchange Yearbooks.

Full details of the two sources of data, together with description of their limitations and the data processing methods used, will be found in Appendices A, B and C at the end of this book. The serious reader is advised to study these appendices carefully as they explain some severe limitations of the basic data which must not be forgotten when considering the significance of the results reported here. Where the limitations are serious, we have tried to point them out in presenting the results. The most obvious defect in the basic accounting data is, of course, the accounting convention for the valuation of assets which encourages caution at the expense of accuracy and which may differ between firms. This is particularly important in the case of fixed assets which are often valued at historic cost, less depreciation, even in a period of persistent inflation such as that examined here. For these and other conceptual problems relating to our data, the reader is once again referred to the appendices.

2 Frequency Distributions of the Main Indicators

Introduction

In this chapter, we describe the variables used to indicate the various economic and financial characteristics of the firms studied in this book. We also present distributions of the values of these indicators for different time periods, classified by industry. Precise definitions of the indicators will be found in Appendix D.

Fourteen indicators were calculated for each firm. Apart from the Valuation Ratio (Indicator 14), a separate set of indicators was computed for each of the two sub-periods (1948-54 and 1954-60 respectively) and for the whole period (1954-60). Each indicator was calculated for each individual firm continuing over the relevant sub-period or period. Thus a firm which continues over the whole period (1948-60) will have two sets of fourteen indicators for each of the two sub-periods (1948-54 and 1954-60). In addition, it will have a set of 13 indicators for the whole period (1948-60), since Indicator 14 has not been calculated with reference to the latter period.

Apart from Opening Size, Closing Size, and the Valuation Ratio (Indicators 1, 2, and 14 respectively), the indicators are averaged over the period or sub-period for which they are calculated. They are thus long-run indicators in which year-to-year fluctuations would be expected to cancel out, and it is hoped that they will reveal the more permanent aspects of the economic behaviour and financial structure of companies, rather than their short-run reaction to the vicissitudes of the economic environment. It must, however, be borne in mind that we are dealing with a historical period in which companies were subject to environmental constraints unique to that period. Examples which spring to mind are the differential profits tax and capital issues control, both of which were removed during our second sub-period.

The basic method of calculating the indicators is similar to that of Tew and Henderson[1], and many of our indicators are drawn from their work. We have used less indicators than our predecessors, in part because of the different focus of this work and partly due to the fact that this is a preliminary study of a longer period and a wider range of data (for instance, average market valuation of ordinary shares has been calculated for each company). Where we have altered indicators used by Tew and Henderson, or introduced new ones, we explain the reasons below, but we do not attempt to justify the omission of a wide range of possibly interesting indicators (e. g. investment in fixed tangible assets) which must await a more detailed analysis of the data.

Measures of Size

The first three indicators measure the size of the firm at different points of time.

The balance sheet or the book value of 'net assets' is used as a measure of the size of the firm in this study.[1] 'Net assets' of the firm represent its share capital, plus reserves, plus long-term liabilities. Alternatively, net assets may be defined as total fixed assets, plus current assets net of current liabilities.[2] Assets are usually valued in balance sheets at historic costs net of depreciation.

The book value of net assets is, therefore, a measure of the long-term capital employed in the firm, whether owned by the shareholders or borrowed from outside. The imperfections in its use as a measure of size, in the context of this study, arise from the problems connected with the valuation of assets in company accounts which are discussed in detail in Appendix A.[3] However, to the extent that the firms belonging to a particular industry have similar accounting conventions, the differences between firms in the value of net assets will tend to represent genuine differences in size.[4]

Indicator 1: Opening Size

This indicator classifies the respective populations of continuing firms according to their opening size at the beginning of the relevant period. As the main feature of the three distributions (two for each of the sub-periods and one for the whole period) are essentially the same, only the whole period (1948-60) distribution is given below in Table 2.1.[5] The table shows the opening size distribution of firms to be uni-modal (single-peaked) and positively skewed in each of the three individual industries. The bi-modal distribution in the 'All Industries' column arises from the aggregation of separate industries.

Indicator 2: Closing Size

Indicator 2 classifies firms according to size at the end of the relevant time period. Again it is only necessary to give the whole period (1948-60) table below. Even allowing for the effects of inflation, there is a very appreciable increase in the size of firms by the end of the period. For instance, the average size of the firm in the Food industry increased from nearly $2\frac{1}{2}$ million pounds in 1948 to nearly 7 million pounds in 1960, which is a high rate of growth notwithstanding the continuous inflation over the period.

Indicator 3: Average Size

Indicator 3 measures the average size of each firm for each of the three periods. For each firm, it is the simple arithmetic average of mid-year assets over the relevant time period, where mid-year assets are calculated on the assumption that the change in assets from one balance sheet to the next balance sheet date is linear.[6]

22

Table 2.1. Percentage frequency distribution of firms classified by Indicator 1 (OPENING SIZE)*

Whole period (1948-60)

Range (£'000's)	Clothing and Footwear	Food	Consumer Goods Industries, including Tobacco	Non-Electrical Engineering	All Industries
< 250	33	27	29	18	23
< 500	23	26	23	19	21
< 1,000	26	11	18	26	23
< 2,000	10	10	10	19	15
< 4,000	6	10	8	12	10
< 8,000	-	8	4	3	4
< 16,000	3	4	5	2	4
< 32,000	-	4	2	0·5	1
> 32,000	-	-	1	0·5	1
Total (%)**	101	100	100	100	102
No. of observations	70	73	150	214	364
Mean (£'000's)	893	2,486	2,645	1,578	2,018
Standard Deviation (£'000's)	2,035	4,863	10,209	4,252	7,350

* Size. The book value of net assets is used as a measure of the size of the firm. Net assets are equal to share capital, plus reserves, plus long term liabilities. Alternatively, net assets may be defined as total fixed assets, plus current assets net of current liabilities. Assets are valued at historic costs net of depreciation.

Opening size (Indicator 1), therefore refers to the book value of net assets in the firm's balance sheet at the beginning of the relevant period.

** The totals may not add up to 100 because of rounding errors.

Table 2.2. Percentage frequency distribution of firms classified by Indicator 2 (CLOSING SIZE)*

Whole period (1948-60)

Range (£'000's)	Clothing and Footwear	Food	Consumer Goods Industries, including Tobacco	Non-Electrical Engineering	All Industries
< 250	21	8	14	7	10
< 500	9	22	15	7	10
< 1,000	31	16	23	14	18
< 2,000	21	14	17	20	18
< 4,000	7	11	9	20	15
< 8,000	6	5	6	18	13
< 16,000	1	8	5	8	7
< 32,000	1	8	6	5	5
> 32,000	1	7	5	1	3
Total (%)**	98	99	100	100	99
No. of observations	70	73	150	214	364
Mean (£'000's)	2,263	6,959	6,799	4,997	5,740
Standard Deviation (£'000's)	.6,180	4,294	21,121	11,164	16,059

* Closing Size (Indicator 2), refers to the book value of net assets in the firm's balance sheet at the close of the relevant period.

** The totals may not add up to 100 because of rounding errors.

Growth

Indicator 4: Rate of growth of net assets

This indicator classifies the respective populations of continuing firms by the rate of growth of net assets, compounded annually over the relevant time period.[1] It must be remembered that growth is measured here in money terms rather than real terms.

Tables 2.3a, 2.3b and 2.3c show that relative to the size distribution of firms, the distribution of growth rates in the individual industries is more symmetrical for each period although its shape is not that of the normal distribution. The tables also show a great deal of variation between the growth rates of individual firms, but only a small part of this appears to be due to differences among industries.[2]

As far as the growth of firms is concerned, Engineering appears to be the best industry. Not only is the growth rate of the average firm in this industry higher than in other industries, the relative dispersion of growth is also lower in this industry than in the others.

The two sub-period tables show that the average growth of net assets was somewhat lower in sub-period 2 (1954-60) than in sub-period 1 (1948-54).

Rates of return

The next three indicators refer to rates of return of various kinds.

Indicator 5: Rate of return on net assets

This indicator gives the average pre-tax rate of return on Net Assets, expressed as a percentage.[3] This indicator tends to overstate the actual profitability of the firm, for two reasons. Firstly, as fixed assets tend to be under-valued in company accounts in a period of inflation, the denominator of the rate of return (net assets) is understated, and the numerator (profits) is over-stated because depreciation charges are too low. Secondly, stock appreciation is included in profits.

Tables 2.4a, 2.4b and 2.4c show that firms in the Engineering industry performed best of all not only in terms of growth, but also in terms of pre-tax profitability. The average profitability of Engineering firms was higher, and the relative dispersion of profitability lower, than in the other two major industries.

Just as average growth in sub-period 1 (1948-54) was generally higher than in sub-period 2 (1954-60), average profitability was also higher in the former period as compared with the latter. A difference in the average rate of return over time can arise from a variety of factors, but the magnitudes involved in this case are small and may be largely due to the more realistic accounting valuation of fixed assets in the second sub-period as compared with the first. It has been argued by some writers that fixed assets tended to be relatively more undervalued in the first few years after the introduction of 1948 Companies Act than in the middle and late '50s.[4]

Table 2.3a. Percentage frequency distribution of firms classified by Indicator 4 (Growth of net assets*)

Whole period (1948-60)

Range (%)	Clothing and Footwear	Food	Consumer Goods Industries, including Tobacco	Non-Electrical Engineering	All Industries
< -5.0	4	1	3	0.5	1
< -2.5	3	1	2	0.5	1
< 0	6	3	5	0.5	2
< 2.5	17	11	13	5	8
< 5.0	24	18	21	11	15
< 7.5	19	23	21	22	22
< 10.0	10	19	14	18	16
< 15.0	13	15	13	30	23
< 20.0	4	7	6	8	7
> 20.0	-	1	1	4	3
Rejects**	-	-	-	0.5	0
Total (%)[+]	100	99	99	100	98
No. of observations	70	73	150	214	364
Mean (%)	4.5	7.1	6.0	9.3	7.9
Standard Deviation (%)	6.0	5.2	6.1	5.0	5.7

* <u>Growth</u>. Indicator 4 gives the compound annual rate of growth of net assets over the relevant time period. Growth of assets has been measured in such a way as to mitigate the influence of revaluation of fixed assets by some firms. Growth is measured in money terms rather than in real terms.

** The rejects refer to cases where the firms had negative net assets at the end of the period.

+ The totals may not add up to 100 because of rounding errors.

Table 2.3b. Percentage frequency distribution of firms classified by Indicator 4 (Growth of net assets)

Sub-period 1 (1948-54)

Range (%)	Clothing and Footwear	Food	Consumer Goods Industries, including Tobacco	Non-Electrical Engineering	All Industries
< -5.0	6	1	3	2	2
< -2.5	-	3	1	1	1
< 0	12	9	11	0	5
< 2.5	17	13	14	5	9
< 5.0	13	15	14	8	11
< 7.5	26	10	18	17	18
< 10.0	13	15	14	21	18
< 15.0	8	19	14	28	22
< 20.0	2	11	7	12	9
> 20.0	2	5	4	6	5
Rejects	-	-	-	-	-
Total (per cent)*	100	101	100	100	100
No. of observations	86	108	205	259	464
Mean (%)	4.7	7.3	6.0	9.9	8.2
Standard Deviation (%)	7.5	6.9	7.2	6.5	7.1

*   The totals may not add up to 100 because of rounding errors.

Table 2.3c. Percentage frequency distribution of firms classified by Indicator 4 (Growth of net assets)

Sub-period 2 (1954-60)

Range (%)	Clothing and Footwear	Food	Consumer Goods Industries, including Tobacco	Non-Electrical Engineering	All Industries
< -5.0	6	4	5	1	3
< -2.5	4	2	3	0	1
< 0	8	10	10	5	7
< 2.5	22	13	17	10	13
< 5.0	16	15	16	16	16
< 7.5	10	20	15	19	18
< 10.0	14	13	13	15	14
< 15.0	8	8	7	21	15
< 20.0	9	9	8	7	8
> 20.0	4	5	6	5	5
Rejects	-	-	-	0	0
Total (per cent)*	101	99	100	99	100
No. of observations	79	91	177	262	439
Mean (%)	5.3	6.6	6.3	8.0	7.3
Standard Deviation (%)	10.1	8.2	9.3	6.2	8.0

*   The totals may not add up to 100 because of rounding errors.

Table 2.4a. Percentage frequency distribution of firms classified by Indicator 5 (Rate of return on net assets*)

Whole period (1948-60)

Range (%)	Clothing and Footwear	Food	Consumer Goods Industries, including Tobacco	Non-Electrical Engineering	All Industries
< 0	6	3	4	1	2
< 5	4	3	4	1	2
< 10	14	7	11	8	9
< 15	31	25	27	17	21
< 20	16	34	27	23	25
< 25	17	11	13	22	19
< 30	7	11	9	14	12
< 35	3	4	3	7	6
< 40	1	3	2	3	2
> 40	-	-	-	2	1
Total (%)**	99	101	100	98	99
No. of observations	70	73	150	214	364
Mean (%)	14.7	17.6	16.0	20.3	18.5
Standard Deviation (%)	9.4	8.0	8.8	9.2	9.3

* Rate of return on net assets: Indicator 5 is used as an indicator of pre-tax profitability of the firm. It gives the average returns on average net assets of each firm for the relevant time period. In line with the definition of net assets, the returns include trading profits and investment and other income of the firm. They are net of depreciation and charges for current liabilities (e.g. bank interest), but are taken before taxation, long term interest payments and payments to minority interests in subsidiaries.

** The totals may not add up to 100 because of rounding errors.

Table 2.4b. Percentage frequency distribution of firms classified by Indicator 5 (Rate of return on net assets)

Sub-period 1 (1948-54)

Range (%)	Clothing and Footwear	Food	Consumer Goods Industries, including Tobacco	Non-Electrical Engineering	All Industries
< 0	3	2	3	1	2
< 5	7	6	7	2	4
< 10	16	14	15	4	8
< 15	16	12	15	17	16
< 20	21	19	20	18	19
< 25	13	17	15	18	17
< 30	12	12	11	17	15
< 35	6	9	7	9	8
< 40	3	1	2	7	5
> 40	2	7	5	7	6
Rejects*	–	–	–	–	–
Total (per cent)**	99	99	100	100	100
No. of observations	86	108	205	259	464
Mean (%)	17.1	20.2	18.4	23.2	21.1
Standard Deviation (%)	11.5	12.8	12.2	11.7	12.2

*   The rejects are mostly cases where the firms had negative net assets.

**   The totals may not add up to 100 because of rounding errors.

Table 2.4c. Percentage frequency distribution of firms classified by Indicator 5 (Rate of return on net assets)

Sub-period 2 (1954-60)

Range (%)	Clothing and Footwear	Food	Consumer Goods Industries, including Tobacco	Non-Electrical Engineering	All Industries
< 0	5	6	5	2	3
< 5	9	3	7	3	4
< 10	14	14	15	12	13
< 15	25	20	22	20	21
< 20	19	25	23	21	21
< 25	16	16	16	21	19
< 30	4	11	7	13	11
< 35	3	1	2	5	3
< 40	3	2	2	3	3
> 40	1	1	1	1	1
Rejects*	1	-	1	-	0
Total (per cent)**	100	99	101	101	99
No. of observations	79	91	177	262	439
Mean (%)	14.2	15.9	14.9	18.3	16.9
Standard Deviation (%)	10.7	9.3	9.9	9.2	9.7

*   The rejects are mostly cases where the firms had negative net assets.

**   The totals may not add up to 100 because of rounding errors.

Indicator 6: Post-tax rate of return on equity assets

From the point of view of an individual investor the rate of return on total net assets of the firm is not as important as the post-tax return he can obtain on the assets attributable to the ordinary shares of the firm.[1] This measure suffers from the same shortcomings, arising from the accounting conventions used in a period of inflation, as the previous one.

Not surprisingly Tables 2.5a, 2.5b and 2.5c, which give the distribution of this indicator show a similar pattern as between the three major industries to that observed for the rate of return on net assets. However, the pattern as between different time periods is not similar for the two indicators. Unlike the pre-tax rate of return on net assets, the post-tax rate of return on equity assets is not noticeably higher in the first sub-period (1948-54) than in the second sub-period (1954-60). This is probably due to the lower level of company taxation during the latter period.

Indicator 7: Dividend return on equity assets

Another variable which is important from the point of view of the individual investor is the dividend which is paid out to the shareholders.

This indicator expresses dividends before deducting income tax, as a percentage of the average equity assets of the firm during the relevant time period. It therefore has a different meaning and significance from the ordinary usage of the term 'dividend yield' which expresses dividends as a percentage of the market value of ordinary shares. Tables 2.6a, 2.6b and 2.6c give the distribution of this indicator over the three periods.

The most striking feature of these tables is that both the average dividend return and its dispersion are much the same in different industries and over different time periods. It is also worth noting that the dispersion of dividend return between firms is relatively much lower than the dispersion of profitability or growth between firms. It would, therefore, appear that in spite of the very considerable differences in average profitability, firms try to maintain a similar dividend on equity assets.

Another point of interest is that whereas Engineering was the 'best' industry both from the point of view of profitability and of growth, it performs worst of all in relation to the dividend return on equity assets. The average dividend return in this industry is lower, and its dispersion higher, than in the other two industries in each period.

Long-term financial indicators

Indicator 8: Retention ratio

The retention ratio is defined as retained profits (excluding capital profits and losses), divided by the sum of retained profits and ordinary dividends paid during the period. All of the items included are net of tax.

32

Table 2.5a. Percentage frequency distribution of firms classified by Indicator 6 (Post-tax rate of return on equity assets*)

Whole period (1948-60)

Range (%)	Clothing and Footwear	Food	Consumer Goods Industries, including Tobacco	Non- Electrical Engineering	All Industries
< 0	6	3	5	1	3
< 2.5	9	4	6	2	4
< 5.0	11	7	9	4	6
< 7.5	24	14	19	18	18
< 10.0	17	25	21	20	20
< 12.5	14	27	22	24	23
< 15.0	10	11	10	17	14
< 17.5	3	5	4	7	6
< 20.0	1	3	2	3	3
> 20.0	1	1	1	3	2
Rejects**	3	-	1	-	1
Total (%)+	99	100	100	99	100
No. of observations	70	73	150	214	364
Mean (%)	7.5	8.6	7.6	10.3	9.2
Standard Deviation (%)	5.6	8.4	8.9	5.0	7.0

* Average post-tax rate of return on equity assets. Indicator 6 gives the average post-tax rate of return for the relevant time period on assets of the firm owned by ordinary shareholders. Equity assets are derived from net assets by deducting from the latter debentures, minority interests and preference capital. Corresponding returns on equity assets are obtained from the profit and loss account.

** Rejects are mostly firms with negative equity assets.

+ The totals may not add up to 100 because of rounding errors.

Table 2.5b. Percentage frequency distribution of firms classified by Indicator 6 (Post-tax rate of return on equity assets)

Sub-period 1 (1948-54)

Range (%)	Clothing and Footwear	Food	Consumer Goods Industries, including Tobacco	Non-Electrical Engineering	All Industries
< 0	9	6	8	2	4
< 2.5	8	5	6	2	3
< 5.0	8	12	10	4	6
< 7.5	19	8	15	14	14
< 10.0	17	18	17	22	19
< 12.5	15	19	18	20	19
< 15.0	8	16	12	18	15
< 17.5	5	7	6	10	8
< 20.0	7	5	5	4	5
> 20.0	2	6	4	5	5
Rejects*	1	-	1	0	0
Total (per cent)**	99	102	102	101	98
No. of observations	86	108	205	259	464
Mean (%)	7.1	9.7	8.4	11.1	9.9
Standard Deviation (%)	9.7	7.9	8.8	6.0	7.5

*   The rejects are mostly cases where the firms had negative equity assets.

**   The totals may not add up to 100 because of rounding errors.

34

Table 2.5c. Percentage frequency distribution of firms classified by Indicator 6 (Post-tax rate of return on equity assets)

Sub-period 2 (1954-60)

Range (%)	Clothing and Footwear	Food	Consumer Goods Industries, including Tobacco	Non-Electrical Engineering	All Industries
< 0	9	5	7	2	4
< 2.5	8	5	7	5	5
< 5.0	9	8	8	8	8
< 7.5	18	12	15	15	15
< 10.0	19	21	19	19	19
< 12.5	14	23	19	24	22
< 15.0	13	15	14	13	13
< 17.5	4	3	3	7	5
< 20.0	-	4	2	5	4
> 20.0	5	1	3	2	3
Rejects*	3	1	2	-	1
Total (per cent)**	102	98	99	100	99
No. of observations	79	91	177	262	439
Mean (%)	7.8	8.6	8.2	9.8	9.2
Standard Deviation (%)	8.4	6.9	7.6	5.5	6.5

*   The rejects are mostly cases where the firms had negative equity assets.

**   The totals may not add up to 100 because of rounding errors.

Table 2.6a. Percentage frequency distribution of firms classified by Indicator 7 (Dividend return on equity assets)*

Whole period (1948-60)

Range (%)	Clothing and Footwear	Food	Consumer Goods In- dustries, including Tobacco	Non- Electrical Engineering	All Indus- tries
0	-	-	-	-	-
< 2.5	4	5	6	6	6
< 5.0	27	22	23	26	25
< 7.5	30	32	31	40	36
< 10.0	20	14	16	14	15
< 12.5	9	16	14	8	10
< 15.0	7	8	7	3	5
< 17.5	-	1	1	1	1
< 20.0	-	1	1	1	1
> 20.0	-	-	-	1	1
Rejects**	3	-	1	-	1
Total (per cent)[+]	100	99	100	100	101
No. of ob- servations	70	73	150	214	364
Mean (%)	6.9	7.4	7.2	6.8	6.9
Standard Deviation (%)	3.1	3.8	3.4	4.7	4.3

* Dividend return on equity assets. Indicator 7 expresses dividends before tax as a percentage of average equity assets of the firm during the relevant time period. This is not to be con- fused with the Dividend Yield which expressed dividends as a percentage of market value of ordinary shares of the firm.

** The rejects are mostly cases where the firms had negative equity assets.

+ The totals may not add up to 100 because of rounding errors.

Table 2.6b. Percentage frequency distribution of firms classified by Indicator 7 (Dividend return on equity assets)

Sub-period 1 (1948-54)

Range (%)	Clothing and Footwear	Food	Consumer Goods Industries, including Tobacco	Non-Electrical Engineering	All Industries
0	1	2	1	2	2
< 2.5	9	8	9	4	6
< 5.0	19	24	22	37	30
< 7.5	34	24	27	31	29
< 10.0	15	18	17	13	14
< 12.5	10	11	11	4	7
< 15.0	6	6	5	5	5
< 17.5	3	5	4	3	3
< 20.0	-	2	1	1	1
> 20.0	1	1	1	2	1
Rejects*	1	-	1	-	0
Total (per cent)**	99	101	99	102	98
No. of observations	86	108	205	259	464
Mean (%)	7.1	7.4	7.2	6.8	7.0
Standard Deviation (%)	4.4	5.2	4.8	6.1	5.6

*   The rejects are mostly cases where the firms had negative equity assets.

**   The totals may not add up to 100 because of rounding errors.

Table 2.6c. Percentage frequency distribution of firms classified by Indicator 7 (Dividend return on equity assets)

Sub-period 2 (1954-60)

Range (%)	Clothing and Footwear	Food	Consumer Goods Industries, including Tobacco	Non-Electrical Engineering	All Industries
0	4	2	3	1	2
< 2.5	10	5	8	6	7
< 5.0	20	19	20	23	22
< 7.5	29	31	29	38	34
< 10.0	15	19	17	19	18
< 12.5	10	14	12	8	10
< 15.0	6	5	6	2	3
< 17.5	-	2	1	1	1
< 20.0	1	1	1	1	1
> 20.0	1	-	1	1	1
Rejects*	3	1	2	-	1
Total (per cent)**	99	99	100	100	100
No. of observations	79	91	177	262	439
Mean (%)	6.7	7.3	6.9	6.7	6.8
Standard Deviation (%)	4.0	3.8	3.8	4.4	4.2

*   The rejects are mostly cases where the firms had negative equity assets.

**   The totals may not add up to 100 because of rounding errors.

This type of ratio appears to be more interesting than the Thrift indicator used by Tew and Henderson, because it shows retentions as a proportion of disposable income, i.e. income after tax and after fixed dividend and interest obligations have been met. It thus concentrates attention on the area where the Company has an actual choice between retention and distribution, whilst our gearing measure (Indicator 10) concentrates on the magnitude of fixed interest obligations relative to income. Our indicator also has the incidental advantage that it avoids having to classify the share of post-tax profit attributable to minority interests as either retention or distribution, either of which is arbitrary.

The retention ratio, as defined here, has one obvious defect. For the period during which the differential profits tax was in force (i.e. until April 1958, the end of our year 9), it does not accurately show the relative choice between distribution and retention of post-tax income, from the company's point of view, because distribution would entail an additional tax burden. It might therefore be more appropriate to add to the denominator of the ratio the additional tax burden incurred by distribution, if the information were readily available. This refinement is not, however, necessary when making inter-company comparisons, because the tax system applies equally to all companies, producing the same proportionate under-statement of the cost of dividends in each case.

Tables 2.7a and 2.7b show the values of the retention ratio, classified by industry and sub-period. Negative ratios occur where the company concerned made insufficient profits to cover the dividend, so that the dividend was paid partly out of past retentions. The negative ratios are often less than minus one and sometimes very large indeed because the drawing on past retentions is deducted from the positive part of the denominator (the dividend paid) and can make it extremely small. These negative ratios are therefore eliminated, together with the "rejects", in calculating means and standard deviations. The "rejects" are cases where the denominator is negative, because an actual loss was incurred after meeting fixed interest and preference dividend obligations, so that the ordinary dividend, if any, is exceeded by the drawing on past retentions. In this case, as with some negative ratios, the arithmetic value of the ratio is of doubtful significance.

Examination of the tables shows that the retention ratio tended to be higher in Engineering (Industry 04) than in the consumer goods industries (11, 12 and 14) particularly in the first sub-period. The ratio tended to be lower in the second period than in the first, more than half of the observations being in the range 50% to 80% in sub-period 1 and in the range 40% to 70% in sub-period 2. The removal of the differential profits tax in 1958 and capital issue controls in February 1959 may have encouraged the lower retention ratios in the second period.

Indicator 9: Internal finance of growth[1]

This indicator shows the total addition to the company's reserves (i.e. retained profits not appropriated to meet a known liability) as a proportion of total growth of net assets. It therefore treats additions to minority interests as an external source of funds, together with the

Table 2.7a. Percentage frequency distribution of firms

Indicator 8, retention ratio

Sub-period 1, 1948-1954

Range (%)	Clothing and Footwear	Food	Consumer Goods Industries, including Tobacco	Non-Electrical Engineering	All Indus-tries
< 0	5	6	5	2	3
< 20	8	6	6	1	3
< 30	4	2	3	2	2
< 40	8	3	6	3	4
< 50	14	14	14	8	11
< 60	16	18	18	11	14
< 70	25	19	22	22	22
< 80	15	20	17	31	26
< 100	5	12	9	18	14
= 100	-	-	-	2	1
Total %	100	100	100	100	100
No. of observations	76	104	189	255	444
No. of rejects	10	4	16	4	20
Total no. of observations	86	108	205	259	464
*Mean (%)	53.6	59.5	56.9	67.4	63.1
*Standard Deviation (%)	19.5	19.2	19.4	15.9	18.2

*   Means and standard deviations exclude negative values.

Table 2.7b. Percentage frequency distribution of firms

Indicator 8, retention ratio

Sub-period 2, 1954-1960

Range (%)	Clothing and Footwear	Food	Consumer Goods Industries, including Tobacco	Non-Electrical Engineering	All Industries
< 0	3	3	4	1	2
< 20	6	6	6	3	4
< 30	7	6	6	3	4
< 40	16	13	14	6	9
< 50	14	13	13	10	11
< 60	14	18	17	22	20
< 70	26	26	25	34	31
< 80	7	10	9	17	14
< 100	4	5	4	4	4
= 100	3	-	2	-	1
Total %	100	100	100	100	100
No. of observations	70	85	161	255	416
No. of rejects	9	6	16	7	23
Total no. of observations	79	91	177	262	439
*Mean (%)	52.8	52.4	52.9	58.3	56.2
*Standard Deviation (%)	19.8	18.3	19.1	19.7	17.6

*   Means and standard deviations exclude negative values.

more obvious cases of issues of shares and debentures. Bank credit is left out of the denominator, although it clearly is an external source of funds, because this indicator is intended to measure growth of the company's long-term financial resources. Some bank loans may be for long periods and secured, so that they are almost the same as debenture stock, but such cases are an unknown proportion of the very large volume of bank credit, so we chose to ignore them. This is a serious but unavoidable limitation of the internal finance indicator.

Tew and Henderson's Indicator 14, 'Self-financing' was similar to our internal finance of growth indicator. The main difference in the numerator is that we, unlike Tew and Henderson, have treated increases in the future tax reserve as an internal source of finance, because this item is, in fact, a reserve for tax which will be incurred in future years, not for any present liability. In the denominator, we differ from Tew and Henderson in that we exclude changes in bank loans, current tax liabilities and dividend and interest liabilities. As explained above, we have excluded such items because we are attempting to measure the sources and growth of long-term finance.

This indicator incorporates the basic limitations of our indicator 4 (growth). It is therefore a mixture of growth in real terms and in money terms, and the measurement of its internal components, particularly retentions, is made difficult by the well-known problems of inflation in relation to accounting conventions.

The distributions of the values of the internal finance indicator for each sub-period are given in Tables 2.8a and 2.8b. The most common value in all cases is 100%, and this is the median value in most cases. This occurs where a company has grown by retaining profits but has not issued shares or debentures or increased minority interests (if any) in the group. The distributions for Industries 11 and 12 (Clothing and Footwear and Food) have a second peak in the range 40 to 60%, but Industry 04 (Engineering) is less consistent in this respect. Values less than zero occur when a company has made losses (after paying dividends) but has still managed to grow by issuing shares or debentures or increasing minority interests. Conversely, values of over 100% occur when the company has repaid shares or debentures, or reduced minority interests, but has grown by retaining profits. Rejects are companies which did not grow, i.e. for which the denominator is negative.

There is a distinct tendency for the proportion of internal finance to be lower in the second sub-period. All the means are lower, as are the lower quartiles. The higher proportion of external finance must, like the lower retention ratios, be largely explained by the removal of capital issue controls, the removal of the differential profits tax and the buoyant stock market conditions during the second sub-period. The distributions are similar as between industries, except that, as mentioned above, Non-electrical Engineering (Industry 04) does not have a minor peak in the range 40 to 60%. Engineering is also peculiar in that it has an exceptionally low proportion of companies which did not grow (rejects) in the second sub-period.

Table 2.8a. Percentage frequency distribution of firms

Indicator 9, internal finance

Sub-period 1, 1948-1954

Range (%)	Clothing and Footwear	Food	Consumer Goods Industries, including Tobacco	Non-Electrical Engineering	All Industries
< 0	3	3	3	-	1
< 20	4	1	2	2	2
< 40	6	4	7	6	6
< 60	10	13	12	10	11
< 80	3	10	8	12	11
<100	11	14	12	16	14
= 100	49	44	45	40	43
<120	13	8	9	10	10
<140	1	1	1	2	1
>140	-	2	1	2	1
Total %	100	100	100	100	100
No. of observations	70	93	171	251	422
No. of rejects	16	15	34	8	42
Total no. of observations	86	108	205	259	464
*Mean (%)	84.8	82.9	82.6	85.6	84.0
*Standard Deviation (%)	30.6	33.8	32.8	26.0	29.4

*   Means and standard deviations exclude values < -100 and > 200.

Table 2.8b. Percentage frequency distribution of firms

Indicator 9, internal finance

Sub-period 2, 1954-1960

Range (%)	Clothing and Footwear	Food	Consumer Goods Industries, including Tobacco	Non-Electrical Engineering	All Industries
< 0	-	5	3	3	3
< 20	8	6	8	3	5
< 40	8	9	9	12	11
< 60	15	10	12	8	10
< 80	5	4	5	10	8
< 100	8	12	10	15	13
= 100	41	36	37	39	38
< 120	11	12	11	8	0
< 140	1	3	2	1	1
> 140	3	3	3	1	2
Total %	100	100	100	100	100
No. of observations	65	76	146	241	387
No. of rejects	14	15	31	21	52
Total no. of observations	79	91	177	262	439
*Mean (%)	80.5	74.7	76.7	77.3	77.1
*Standard Deviation (%)	33.8	22.7	38.4	34.2	35.9

*   Means and standard deviations exclude values < -100 and > +200.

44

Indicator 10: Gearing

The gearing ratio is the sum of interest on long term loans and preference dividends, both net of tax, divided by the sum of interest on
long-term loans, preference dividends, ordinary dividends, and retained
profits, all net of tax. In other words, it shows the proportion of post-
tax income which is allocated to fixed interest and dividend payments.
It differs from this strict definition, and from Tew and Henderson's
otherwise identical Indicator 13, in that it omits from the denominator
the share of post-tax profits which is attributable to minority interests.
We have omitted minority interests because they consist partly of preference dividends and partly of ordinary dividends and retentions.
Strictly, therefore, a proportion of the income attributable to minority
interests should be in the numerator and the total in the denominator,
but since the relevant break-down is not available, we chose to omit
minority interests altogether.

The gearing measure, like the retention ratio, is wrongly measured
to the extent that companies' profits, and therefore their post-tax
retentions, are wrongly measured, but it is the best estimate available
to us, and often to the companies themselves.

Tables 2.9a and 2.9b give the values of the gearing ratio for the population studied. The ratio cannot, by definition, fall below zero. The
rejects are cases where the denominator was negative, i.e. the company made a loss even before charging fixed dividend and interest
obligations. Zero is the most common value for every industry in
every period. Apart from this, the most striking feature of the tables
is the low gearing ratio in the Engineering industry. The consumer
goods industries have a secondary peak in their distribution of gearing
ratios somewhere between values of $2\frac{1}{2}\%$ and 10%. The Engineering
industry, on the other hand, has a more marked concentration of zero
values and the distribution tails away rapidly above zero, the next most
common value being between 0 and $2\frac{1}{2}\%$. The lower gearing ratios in
Engineering may be due to the more pronounced cyclical nature of
demand and profits in the industry, which makes heavy fixed interest
obligations inadvisable.

Over time, the tendency seems to have been for gearing ratios to even
out. Those in the consumer goods industries (other than Tobacco, which
is too small to be really significant) fell, on average, but those in the
Engineering industry rose slightly.

Current financial indicators

These three indicators require a common explanation because they
are all averaged over the relevant periods. Tew and Henderson used
indicators similar to 11 and 12 but calculated them at a single point
in time. Since we are comparing them with long-run indicators, we
decided to average these indicators over the full period, so that they
would reflect the character of the companies during the period rather
than at an arbitrarily chosen point in time. The three indicators are
all concerned with current assets and liabilities, which are by definition
subject to short-run fluctuations as well as more permanent patterns
imposed by the character of the individual company, and we hope that
our averaging procedure will eradicate the former and emphasise the

Table 2.9a. Percentage frequency distribution of firms

Indicator 10, gearing

Sub-period 1, 1948-1954

Range (%)	Clothing and Footwear	Food	Consumer Goods Industries, including Tobacco	Non- Electrical Engineering	All Industries
0	20	21	21	31	26
< 2.5	3	9	6	16	12
< 5.0	5	11	9	16	13
< 7.5	16	8	11	12	11
<10.0	1	11	7	9	8
<15.0	15	12	13	7	10
<20.0	10	7	9	3	6
<30.0	14	8	10	4	7
<40.0	1	6	4	1	2
>40.0	15	7	10	1	5
Total %	100	100	100	100	100
No. of observations	80	104	193	255	448
No. of rejects	6	4	12	4	16
Total no. of observations	86	108	205	259	464
Mean (%)	21.6	13.8	16.9	5.4	10.4
Standard Deviation (%)	33.0	25.0	28.4	7.7	20.3

Table 2.9b. Percentage frequency distribution of firms

Indicator 10, gearing

Sub-period 2, 1954-1960

Range (%)	Clothing and Footwear	Food	Consumer Goods Industries, including Tobacco	Non-Electrical Engineering	All Industries
0	25	23	24	24	24
< 2.5	3	9	6	19	14
< 5.0	12	16	14	18	16
< 7.5	7	10	10	11	11
< 10.0	7	12	9	8	8
< 15.0	12	12	12	8	9
< 20.0	10	3	7	4	6
< 30.0	12	5	8	1	4
< 40.0	6	5	5	4	4
> 40.0	6	5	5	3	4
Total %	100	100	100	100	100
No. of observations	72	86	164	257	421
No. of rejects	7	5	13	5	18
Total no. of observations	79	91	177	262	439
Mean (%)	15.9	10.3	13.2	7.8	9.9
Standard Deviation (%)	31.3	17.9	25.4	14.7	19.7

latter. Lest it should be thought that the short-run fluctuations, which we are eliminating, are the only important feature of current asset and liability ratios, it should be mentioned that analyses of variance carried out by Barna[1] on a similar population and by the present authors on the Clothing and Footwear industry (Industry 11) show that the variance between companies is usually much greater than that between years, i.e. inter-company differences are greater than inter-temporal differences.

All three indicators use net assets as a denominator. This is open to criticism, firstly because of the defects of net assets as a size measure, which were discussed earlier, and secondly because the ratio can be extremely large in the case of firms which have abnormally low net assets in relation to total assets. Firms with negative net assets are rejected completely in calculating these indicators, as the resulting ratio is of dubious significance, but equally misleading values for firms with low net assets may remain in the population.

Indicator 11: Liquidity

Our definition of Liquidity is identical with that used by Tew and Henderson for their Indicator 12, except that we have adopted an averaging procedure, as explained above. The indicator consists of average net liquid assets (cash, tax reserve certificates, and marketable securities, less bank overdrafts and loans, dividend and interest liabilities, and current tax liabilities), divided by average net assets, as defined for Indicator 1. The definition is arbitrary, especially with regard to the deduction of bank loans (as opposed to overdrafts), which may not affect the short-term availability of cash, and dividend and interest liabilities and taxation, which in many cases do not become due for payment until several months from the balance sheet date. If anything, the definition is likely to understate liquidity, in the sense of immediate access to cash, because the deductions are over-stated.

However, we are satisfied that our definition of average liquidity is as good, if not better, than any of the many alternatives. Its object is to show the access to cash which the firm enjoys, apart from its power to run down stocks or take net trade credit.

The ranges of liquidity ratios obtained are given in Tables 2.10a and 2.10b. The greatest concentration of firms is in the range 0 to 5% in the first sub-period and 0 to -5% in the second. The remaining firms are, however, widely scattered, a considerable proportion being out of the range +20% to -20%. In both periods, more than half of the companies are in the ranges < -10% or >10%, which Tew and Henderson defined as being "highly illiquid" or "highly liquid".

Indicator 12: Net trade credit given

This is the average of net trade credit given (trade and other debtors less trade creditors), divided by average net assets. It is not a pure trade credit ratio because the debtor and creditor figures include such items as provisions for prepaid or accrued expenses.

Tables 2.11a and 2.11b show the distributions of this indicator.

Table 2.10a. Percentage frequency distribution of firms

Indicator 11, liquidity

Sub-period 1, 1948-1954

Range (%)	Clothing and Footwear	Food	Consumer Goods Industries, including Tobacco	Non-Electrical Engineering	All Industries
< -20	22	14	21	13	16
< -10	17	7	11	15	13
< - 5	7	7	6	6	6
< 0	9	8	8	8	8
< 5	11	5	7	15	11
< 10	11	8	9	9	9
< 20	8	20	14	10	12
< 30	7	12	10	9	10
< 40	6	7	6	7	7
> 40	2	12	8	8	8
Total %	100	100	100	100	100
No. of observations	86	108	2C5	2£9	4£4
No. of rejects	-	-	-	-	-
Total no. of observations	86	108	205	259	464
Mean (%)	-4.5	10.2	1.5	3.6	2.7
Standard Deviation (%)	23.9	24.5	27.5	27.8	27.7

Table 2.10b. Percentage frequency distribution of firms

Indicator 11, liquidity

Sub-period 2, 1954-1960

Range (%)	Clothing and Footwear	Food	Consumer* Goods Industries	Non-Electrical Engineering	All Industries
< -20	20	11	17	10	14
< -10	13	11	13	11	11
< - 5	11	10	10	10	10
< 0	18	14	15	12	13
< 5	8	10	8	11	10
< 10	5	11	8	13	11
< 20	8	11	9	14	12
< 30	10	12	11	12	11
< 40	4	5	5	3	4
> 40	3	5	4	4	4
Total %	100	100	100	100	100
No. of observations	78	91	176	262	438
No. of rejects	1	-	1	-	1
Total no. of observations	79	91	177	262	439
Mean (%)	-4.0	4.6	-0.4	2.9	1.6
Standard Deviation (%)	23.5	21.4	23.0	22.2	22.6

*   Including Tobacco.

Table 2.11a. Percentage frequency distribution of firms

Indicator 12, net trade credit given

Sub-period 1, 1948-1954

Range (%)	Clothing and Footwear	Food	Consumer* Goods Industries	Non- Electrical Engineering	All Industries
< -20.0	6	1	3	3	3
< -10.0	10	7	8	6	7
< - 5.0	14	7	10	3	6
< - 2.5	7	12	9	5	7
< 0	14	10	11	3	7
< 2.5	12	9	10	3	6
< 5.0	7	21	14	9	11
< 10.0	16	19	17	24	21
< 20.0	13	10	12	29	21
> 20.0	1	4	6	15	11
Total %	100	100	100	100	100
No. of observations	86	108	205	259	464
No. of rejects	-	-	-	-	-
Total no. of observations	86	108	205	259	464
Mean (%)	-2.3	2.0	1.4	8.5	5.4
Standard Deviation (%)	15.8	11.7	14.8	15.4	15.5

*   Including Tobacco.

Table 2.11b. Percentage frequency distribution of firms

Indicator 12, net trade credit given

Sub-period 2, 1954-1960

Range (%)	Clothing and Footwear	Food	Consumer* Goods Industries	Non-Electrical Engineering	All Industries
< -20.0	5	4	5	2	3
< -10.0	9	10	9	4	6
< - 5.0	7	9	7	3	5
< - 2.5	7	4	5	4	5
< 0	5	10	7	3	5
< 2.5	15	11	12	5	8
< 5.0	7	9	8	7	7
< 10.0	25	22	23	17	19
< 20.0	15	12	15	39	29
> 20.0	5	9	9	16	13
Total %	100	100	100	100	100
No. of observations	78	91	176	262	438
No. of rejects	1	-	1	-	1
Total no. of observations	79	91	177	262	439
Mean (%)	1.2	1.8	2.1	9.9	6.7
Standard Deviation (%)	15.3	15.4	15.9	13.7	15.1

*   Including Tobacco.

Although gross trade credit usually forms the greatest proportion of current assets and liabilities, net trade credit seems to vary within fairly stringent limits. The degree of dispersion is fairly consistent both between industries and over time, and is much less than that for liquidity (Indicator 11). There is a marked tendency in both periods for these companies to give net trade credit rather than to receive it, but there are differences between industries: Engineering firms gave most credit, followed by Food. Clothing and Footwear firms, which were mainly small, tended to receive net credit in the first period, and were the smallest givers in the second. These inter-industry differences are not surprising, because the giving and receiving of trade credit is bound up with the customs and structure of the particular industry.

Over time, there is no striking change in the pattern of net trade credit given. The average for the whole population is slightly lower in the second sub-period, but the individual industries do not show any uniform trend.

Indicator 13: Stocks

This is the ratio of average stocks to the average net assets of the company. Stocks include work-in-progress, and progress payments are deducted. This means in the case of some shipbuilding firms (a subgroup of the Engineering industry) that there are negative stocks, because progress payments on ships are often very large. Stocks and work-in-progress are usually valued on a cost basis (or market value if that is lower) which can give rise to large differences of practice between companies, e.g. in the allocation of overheads.

The distribution given in Tables 2.12a and 2.12b show marked differences between industries. Most of the distributions are fairly strongly concentrated around a single peak, but the peak occurs at strikingly different levels in different industries. Tobacco has the highest average stockholding, followed by Clothing and Footwear, Engineering, and Food. These marked inter-industry differences in the average level of stockholding are to be expected, because stockholding is likely to depend very much on the technological nature of the industry. Food, for example, tends to be perishable, whereas clothing and footwear are more durable, and the seasonal nature of the tobacco crop means that very high stocks will be held at certain times of the year. The stocks and work-in-progress of heavy engineering firms would be expected to be high, because of the relatively long time lag in production, but the existence of progress payments, as mentioned above, reduces the amount of unpaid-for stocks.

Between sub-periods, the pattern of stockholding remains very constant. There is a slight lowering of the general level and evening-out of differences, but the marked inter-industry differences remain.

Stock market valuation of the firm

Indicator 14: Valuation ratio

As was indicated in the first chapter, one purpose of this study is to

Table 2.12a. Percentage frequency distribution of firms

Indicator 13, stocks

Sub-period 1, 1948-1954

Range (%)	Clothing and Footwear	Food	Consumer* Goods Industries	Non-Electrical Engineering	All Industries
< 0	-	-	-	1	1
<10	1	8	5	2	3
<20	-	19	10	10	10
<30	2	28	16	6	10
<40	9	13	11	15	13
<50	18	11	13	21	18
<60	18	8	12	13	13
<70	14	3	8	13	11
<80	10	4	7	7	7
< 90	12	4	7	5	6
> 90	16	2	11	7	8
Total %	100	100	100	100	100
No. of observations	86	108	205	259	464
No. of rejects	-	-	-	-	-
Total no. of observations	86	108	205	259	464
Mean (%)	67.5	33.7	50.6	50.2	50.4
Standard Deviation (%)	30.7	22.1	32.3	26.5	29.2

*   Including Tobacco.

54

Table 2.12b. Percentage frequency distribution of firms

Indicator 13, stocks

Sub-period 2, 1954-1960

Range (%)	Clothing and Footwear	Food	Consumer* Goods Industries	Non-Electrical Engineering	All Industries
< 0	-	-	-	-	-
< 10	-	5	2	4	3
< 20	3	15	9	6	7
< 30	5	31	18	9	12
< 40	10	20	15	22	19
< 50	13	15	14	21	18
< 60	28	3	14	17	16
< 70	13	6	9	10	10
< 80	11	3	9	5	7
< 90	9	-	5	3	4
> 90	8	2	5	3	4
Total %	100	100	100	100	100
No. of observations	78	91	176	262	438
No. of rejects	1	-	1	-	1
Total no. of observations	79	91	177	262	439
Mean (%)	59.1	34.5	47.0	46.2	46.6
Standard Deviation (%)	22.6	21.2	25.5	21.7	23.3

* Including Tobacco.

analyze the relationship between growth and the stock-market valuation of the firm.[1] However, in order to compare in a meaningful way the stock-market valuation of different firms on an inter-firm basis, it is essential to remove the effect of size of the firm on its market valuation.[2] We have attempted to do this here by introducing the concept of a 'valuation ratio', which is the ratio of stock-market valuation of a firm's ordinary shares to the book value of its equity assets. Average valuation ratios for the calendar year 1954 (not for the period 1948-54) have been computed for every continuing firm in sub-period 1; average valuation ratios for the calendar year 1960 have similarly been computed for every continuing firm for sub-period 2. The methods of computation and the data used are discussed in Part II of Appendix A.

Apart from being a convenient statistical device to normalize share prices[3], the ratio of the market value to the book value of the ordinary shares of the firm is also a meaningful concept in its own right.[4] Although it is not called the valuation ratio, the ratio is calculated and discussed in the academic literature on the theory of finance.[5] It is not mentioned as such in the financial press, but comparisons of market value to book value are frequently made there in relation to take-over bids, portfolio selection, etc. In fact, for a large number of big firms, Moodies cards give historical series of the market price, per ordinary share of the company and the corresponding book value of assets per share, from which the valuation ratio can easily be calculated.

Our interest in the valuation ratio also derives from its economic meaning and the recent theoretical speculations concerning its behaviour by several economists.[6] Under the usual rarified assumptions of a 'golden age' in pure economic theory, including those of perfect markets, complete certainty, and, consequently, equilibrium prices, the denominator of the valuation ratio, i.e. the book value of assets, would – at least if accounting conventions conformed to economic principles – reflect the value of the economic resources embodied in the firm. The numerator of the valuation ratio represents the market's valuation of the firm as a going concern, i.e. its valuation of the earning power of these resources. Under certain assumptions, in a golden age, the two coincide and the valuation ratio will be equal to unity. However, in the real world of imperfect markets, rapidly changing conditions and uncertainty about the changes, the valuation ratios of most firms will almost certainly be different from unity.

Tables 2.13a and 2.13b give the distribution of the valuation ratios of firms in 1954 and 1960 respectively. The tables reveal the following interesting features:

1. The generally low level of magnitude of the valuation ratios, especially in 1954, in all industries, is very striking. The average valuation ratio is below unity in Clothing and Footwear and in Engineering, and only slightly above unity in Food. Interpreted literally, Table 2.13a indicates that more than 50% of the firms in all the three industries had a book value greater than the value of the firm as a going concern as reflected by the market price of its ordinary shares.

It is not possible to argue that the low valuation ratios in 1954 are due either to unrealistic accounting valuation placed on assets in the balance

Table 2.13a. Percentage frequency distribution of firms classified by Indicator 14 (Valuation ratio)* for 1954

Range	Clothing and Footwear	Food	Consumer Goods Industries, including Tobacco	Non-Electrical Engineering	All Industries
.20- .39	5	4	6	7	6
.40- .59	21	15	17	17	17
.60- .79	28	19	23	23	23
.80- .99	7	18	13	22	18
1.00-1.24	19	19	18	16	17
1.25-1.49	8	3	6	7	7
1.50-1.74	8	10	10	3	6
1.75-1.99	3	4	3	3	3
2.00-2.49	1	4	3	2	2
2.50-2.99	-	2	1	-	-
3.00-3.99	-	-	-	-	-
4.00-	-	-	-	-	-
Total (%)**	100	98	100	100	99
No. of observations	75	93	176	226	402
Mean	.89	1.05	.98	.91	.94
Standard Deviation	.44	.52	.49	.47	.48
co-ef. of variation	49.11	49.72	50.52	51.82	51.55

* Valuation ratio. Indicator 14 is defined as:

$$V = \frac{\text{Stock Market valuation of a firm's ordinary shares}}{\text{Book value of the firm's capital owned by ordinary shareholders}}$$

Average valuation ratios for the calendar year 1954 (not for the period 1948-54) have been computed for every continuing firm in sub-period 1 for which the necessary data were available.

** The totals may not add up to 100 because of rounding errors.

Table 2.13b. Percentage frequency distribution of firms classified by Indicator 14 (Valuation ratio) for 1960*

Range	Clothing and Footwear	Food	Consumer Goods Industries, including Tobacco	Non-Electrical Engineering	All Industries
.20- .39	1	-	1	2	1
.40- .59	10	5	8	13	11
.60- .79	15	17	15	11	13
.80- .99	13	16	15	19	17
1.00-1.24	15	23	19	17	18
1.25-1.49	7	9	9	15	13
1.50-1.74	13	12	12	8	10
1.75-1.99	6	4	5	5	5
2.00-2.49	13	6	9	6	7
2.50-2.99	3	2	3	2	2
3.00-3.99	3	4	3	1	2
4.00-	-	1	1	1	1
Total (%)**	99	99	100	100	100
No. of observations	68	77	149	232	381
Mean	1.33	1.35	1.34	1.20	1.26
Standard Deviation	.69	.81	.75	.74	.74
co-ef. of variation	51.75	60.32	55.72	61.57	58.40

* Average Valuation Ratios for the calendar year 1960 have been computed for every firm which continued over the period (1954-60) and for which the necessary data were available.

** The totals may not add up to 100 because of rounding errors.

58

sheets of the firm, or that they arise from the exclusion of preference shares in our definition of the valuation ratio. More realistic valuation of assets would have lowered the valuation ratios even more, since fixed assets, especially buildings and land, tended to be considerably under-valued in the balance sheets during this period.[1] The inclusion of preference shares, whose market value tended to be below par value at this time, could conceivably have raised the valuation ratios if they were very low, but it could not have raised them to unity.[2]

The low valuation ratios in 1954 are entirely due to the relatively depressed state of the stock market during this period.[3] As Wright has suggested,[4] share prices during the period failed to value businesses adequately even on the basis of achieved earning power, because shareholders had no confidence that the increased earnings would be reflected in increased dividends. In the specific institutional environment of various controls and fiscal discrimination against distributed profits, even where retained earnings were being profitably re-invested, it seems that shareholders had no confidence that they would ever be allowed to benefit.

It is interesting to compare the figures for 1954 with the figures for valuation ratios for 1955 for the American firms on the New York Stock Exchange given by Cottle and Whitman.[5] Although, owing to the nature of the sampling procedure used by them, Cottle and Whitman's figures are not exactly comparable to ours, they are still revealing. They found the following average valuation ratios in 1955 for firms in different groups of industries: Consumers' durable goods, 2.62; Consumers' non-durable goods, 1.53; Producers' capital goods, 2.11; Producers' raw material and supplies, 1.80; and composite for all industries, 1.79. These figures are much higher than the figures for U.K. firms given in Table 2.13a.

2. In spite of the fact that in the opinion of some writers,[6] the accounting valuation of assets in the balance sheets may have become comparatively more realistic, i.e. higher, in 1960 than in 1954, there was an appreciable all round increase in the magnitude of valuation ratios in 1960. The valuation ratio of the typical firm in 1960 is more than a third higher than in 1954. The explanation lies in the generally higher share prices in the late '50s and especially in the share price boom of 1959 and 1960.[7] Moodies Industrial Share Price Index which only went up from 100 to 116.9 from 1947 to 1954, climbed from the latter figure to 251.6 in the period 1954 to 1960. It is interesting to note however, that notwithstanding the higher share prices and generally higher level of valuation ratios in 1960, nearly 40% of the firms still had a valuation ratio of less than unity.

It may appear surprising that the valuation ratios and share prices in 1960 are higher than in 1954, even though as we saw earlier, the rates of return, the dividend returns on equity assets and the growth rates were on the whole lower in sub-period 2 (1954-60) than in sub-period 1 (1948-54). The explanation is in fact quite simple: although dividend returns in 1954-60 were somewhat lower than in 1948-54 they were higher in 1959-60 than in 1953-54. Table 2.14, which is based on the Board of Trade aggregate figures,[8] makes the point clear. The post-tax

Table 2.14. Dividend return on equity assets and post-tax rate of return on equity assets in 1953-54 and 1959-60*

	1953-54	1959-60
Food: Dividend Return	7.55	9.16
Post Tax Rate of Return	14.41	13.61
Clothing and Footwear: Dividend Return	8.65	11.23
Post Tax Rate of Return	13.44	15.66
Non-Electrical Engineering: Dividend Return	9.23	10.17
Post Tax Rate of Return	15.73	13.47
All Manufacturing Industries: Dividend Return	7.88	9.29
Post Tax Rate of Return	13.46	14.48

*The source of this table is the aggregate figures given in Board of Trade, Income and Finance of Public Quoted Companies, Summary and Industrial Group Tables, 1949-60.

The discrepancy in the magnitude of the average dividend return and the average rates of return in the above table and tables for these indicators for sub-period 1 and sub-period 2, given earlier can arise from two other sources. First, the latter tables are based on companies which continued over a six year period whereas the table above is based on companies which continued over a two year period, i.e. either in 1953-54 or in 1959-60. Secondly, it is not strictly accurate to compare the average based on aggregate figures which give unequal weight to different firms, with the one based on figures of individual firms where equal weight is given to each firm.

rates of return in 1959-60 are not always higher than in 1953-1954, but probably as a result of the abolition of differential profits tax in 1958, which discriminated in favour of retentions, the dividends went up sharply. The share price boom of 1959-60 reflected not only higher dividends but changed expectations about the future.

3. The inter-industry pattern of the valuation ratios is different from that observed for the rates of return or the growth rates. It may be recalled that the Engineering industry performed 'best' of all with respect to both profitability and growth. It not only had the highest average growth and profitability; the dispersion of growth and profitability in this industry was also lower than in the other two major industries. However, we also saw that with respect to dividend return on equity assets, the Engineering industry performed worst of all in that it had both lower dividends on average, and a higher dispersion of dividends than in the other two industries. In the case of valuation ratios, the pattern is not clear for 1954, but for 1960, the Engineering industry again performs worst of all. The average valuation ratio of Engineering firms is lower, and its dispersion higher, than in the other two major industries.

3   Simple Correlation Matrices

The first obvious question to be asked about the fourteen variables
described in the preceding chapter is 'what is the degree of association
between each pair of variables?' A preliminary answer to this question
will be provided in this chapter by computing simple correlation coefficients between each pair of variables.

It may perhaps be appropriate to recall that the simple (zero-order)
correlation coefficient r, is a summary measure of association between
any two variables based only on linear dependence. A perfect positive
linear association will yield a value of r of exactly +1.0; a perfect
negative linear correlation will yield a value of -1.0, and in cases
where there is absolutely no linear relationship between the variables,
r will be zero. In general, the lower the absolute value of r, the lower
is the degree of linear relationship between the variables.[1]

The values of r in the following tables (Tables 3.1-3.3) must, therefore,
be interpreted with particular care. A low value of r for any two variables may arise, not because the two variables are not related, but
because the relationship between them is non-linear. Conversely, a
high value of the simple correlation coefficient does not necessarily
indicate that there is an intrinsic or independent association between
the variables. The observed value of r may be entirely due to the
relationship of the variables to a third variable even where there is
little intrinsic association between the former variables. Lastly, it
should be noted that the existence of a high degree of correlation implies
no relationship of cause and effect between the variables. The consideration of cause and effect, as well as a more detailed analysis of
the degree of independent association between the variables is left to
later chapters.

Tables 3.1 to 3.3 present matrices of correlation coefficients (i.e.
r, not r^2) for firms in all industries together, for each of the two sub-
periods (1948-54 and 1954-60) and for the whole period (1948-60). Each
row and each column gives the correlation coefficient between the
indicator named at the head of the row and the indicator named at the
end of each successive column. Thus, the correlation coefficients
along the diagonal of each table represent the correlation of each indicator with its own value, which must always yield a perfect positive
correlation, r = +1.00. Each table is symmetrical about the diagonal,
e.g. the correlation between Opening Size (Indicator 1) and Valuation
Ratio (Indicator 14) appears in both the bottom left-hand corner and
the top right-hand corner. The number of companies observed is given
at the foot of each table. It will be noted that correlations relating to
Retention Ratio, Internal Finance, Gearing and Valuation Ratio, involved
the exclusion of a number of companies.[2] Average Size (Indicator 3)
is omitted from all of the tables because it does not yield correlations

Table 3.1. Correlation coefficients

Industries 04, 11, 12, 14

All industries

Sub-period 1 (1948-54)

Indicators	1 Opening Size	2 Closing Size	4 Growth	5 Rate of Return (Net Assets)	6 Rate of Return (Equity Assets)	7 Dividend Return	8 Retention Ratio	9 Internal Finance	10 Gearing	11 Liquidity	12 Trade Credit	13 Stocks	14 Valuation Ratio
1. Opening Size	1.00	0.99	-0.01	-0.06	-0.02	-0.02	-0.02	-0.13	0.02	-0.05	0.05	0.02	0.03
2. Closing Size	0.99	1.00	0.04	-0.04	0.00	-0.02	-0.00	-0.15	0.01	-0.04	0.05	0.02	0.05
4. Growth	-0.01	0.04	1.00	0.72	0.66	0.34	0.22	-0.30	-0.31	0.11	0.09	-0.06	0.30
5. Rate of Return (Net Assets)	-0.06	-0.04	0.72	1.00	0.73	0.71	0.00	0.30	-0.41	0.19	0.12	-0.07	0.54
6. Rate of Return (Equity Assets)	-0.02	0.00	0.66	0.73	1.00	0.46	0.12	0.23	-0.27	0.09	0.08	-0.09	0.36
7. Dividend Return	-0.02	-0.02	0.34	0.71	0.46	1.00	-0.51	0.04	-0.22	-0.01	0.04	0.04	0.60
8. Retention Ratio	-0.02	-0.00	0.22	0.00	0.12	-0.51	1.00	0.20	-0.25	0.10	0.04	-0.08	0.08
9. Internal Finance	-0.13	-0.15	-0.30	0.30	0.23	0.04	0.20	1.00	-0.25	0.29	0.05	-0.17	0.11
10. Gearing	0.02	0.01	-0.31	-0.41	-0.27	-0.22	-0.25	-0.25	1.00	-0.18	-0.09	0.04	-0.16
11. Liquidity	-0.05	-0.04	0.11	0.19	0.09	-0.01	0.10	0.29	-0.18	1.00	-0.04	-0.72	0.07
12. Trade Credit	0.05	0.05	0.09	0.12	0.08	0.04	0.04	0.05	-0.09	-0.04	1.00	-0.32	-0.01
13. Stocks	0.02	0.02	-0.06	-0.07	-0.09	0.04	-0.08	-0.17	0.04	-0.72	-0.32	1.00	-0.02
14. Valuation Ratio	0.03	0.05	0.30	0.54	0.36	0.60	0.08	0.11	-0.16	0.07	-0.01	-0.02	1.00

Number of observations: Indicators 8 & 9 = 358; Indicator 10 = 421; Indicator 14 = 402; Other indicators = 464.

Table 3.2. Correlation coefficients

Industries 04, 11, 12, 14

All industries

Sub-period 2 (1954-60)

Indicators	1 Opening Size	2 Closing Size	4 Growth	5 Rate of Return (Net Assets)	6 Rate of Return (Equity Assets)	7 Dividend Return	8 Retention Ratio	9 Internal Finance	10 Gearing	11 Liquidity	12 Trade Credit	13 Stocks	14 Valuation Ratio
1. Opening Size	1.00	0.96	0.01	-0.03	0.01	-0.01	0.00	-0.10	0.03	-0.05	0.03	0.02	0.00
2. Closing Size	0.96	1.00	0.12	-0.00	0.05	0.00	0.04	-0.17	0.03	-0.06	0.02	0.02	0.05
4. Growth	0.01	0.12	1.00	0.50	0.57	0.27	0.31	-0.52	-0.07	-0.04	-0.03	-0.01	0.43
5. Rate of Return (Net Assets)	-0.03	-0.00	0.50	1.00	0.93	0.72	0.17	0.33	-0.47	0.31	0.12	-0.17	0.47
6. Rate of Return (Equity Assets)	0.01	0.05	0.57	0.93	1.00	0.66	0.28	0.18	-0.38	0.25	0.11	-0.14	0.35
7. Dividend Return	-0.01	0.00	0.27	0.72	0.66	1.00	-0.45	0.12	-0.29	0.15	-0.03	-0.02	0.58
8. Retention Ratio	0.00	0.04	0.31	0.17	0.28	-0.45	1.00	0.12	-0.12	0.07	-0.02	-0.06	0.08
9. Internal Finance	-0.10	-0.17	-0.52	0.33	0.18	0.12	0.12	1.00	-0.21	0.39	0.18	-0.18	0.06
10. Gearing	0.03	0.03	-0.07	-0.47	-0.38	-0.29	0.12	-0.21	1.00	-0.28	-0.07	0.11	-0.23
11. Liquidity	-0.05	-0.06	-0.04	0.31	0.25	0.15	0.07	0.39	-0.28	1.00	-0.04	-0.65	-0.01
12. Trade Credit	0.03	0.02	-0.03	0.12	0.11	-0.03	-0.02	0.18	-0.07	-0.04	1.00	-0.29	-0.06
13. Stocks	0.02	0.02	-0.01	-0.17	-0.14	-0.02	-0.06	-0.18	0.11	-0.65	-0.29	1.00	0.01
14. Valuation Ratio	0.00	0.05	0.43	0.47	0.35	0.58	0.08	0.06	-0.23	-0.01	-0.06	0.01	1.00

Number of observations: Indicators 8 & 9 = 324; Indicator 10 = 380; Indicator 14 = 381; Other indicators = 439.

Table 3.3. Correlation coefficients

Industries 04, 11, 12, 14

All industries

Whole period (1948-60)

Indicators	1 Opening Size	2 Closing Size	4 Growth	5 Rate of Return (Net Assets)	6 Rate of Return (Equity Assets)	7 Dividend Return	8 Retention Ratio	9 Internal Finance	10 Gearing	11 Liquidity	12 Trade Credit	13 Stocks
1. Opening Size	1.00	0.94	-0.01	-0.06	-0.01	-0.03	-0.00	-0.08	0.01	-0.05	0.04	0.02
2. Closing Size	0.94	1.00	0.13	-0.02	0.05	-0.01	0.05	-0.16	-0.01	-0.06	0.04	0.01
4. Growth	-0.01	0.13	1.00	0.64	0.59	0.34	0.25	-0.35	-0.32	0.10	0.12	-0.14
5. Rate of Return (Net Assets)	-0.06	-0.02	0.64	1.00	0.79	0.72	0.03	0.39	-0.53	0.32	0.18	-0.21
6. Rate of Return (Equity Assets)	-0.01	0.05	0.59	0.79	1.00	0.51	0.09	0.27	-0.50	0.22	0.10	-0.14
7. Dividend Return	-0.03	-0.01	0.34	0.72	0.51	1.00	-0.51	0.13	-0.26	0.06	0.04	-0.02
8. Retention Ratio	-0.00	0.05	0.25	0.03	0.09	-0.51	1.00	0.21	-0.44	0.15	0.03	-0.13
9. Internal Finance	-0.08	-0.16	-0.35	0.39	0.27	0.13	0.21	1.00	-0.22	0.44	0.11	-0.23
10. Gearing	0.01	-0.01	-0.32	-0.53	-0.50	-0.26	-0.44	-0.22	1.00	-0.32	-0.09	0.20
11. Liquidity	-0.05	-0.06	0.10	0.32	0.22	0.06	0.15	0.44	-0.32	1.00	-0.05	-0.70
12. Trade Credit	0.04	0.04	0.12	0.18	0.10	0.04	0.03	0.11	-0.09	-0.05	1.00	-0.27
13. Stocks	0.02	0.01	-0.14	-0.21	-0.14	-0.02	-0.13	-0.23	0.20	-0.70	-0.27	1.00

Number of observations: Indicators 8 & 9 = 300; Indicator 10 = 340; Other indicators = 364.

greatly different from those for Opening Size and Closing Size (Indicators 1 and 2).

These tables contain a vast amount of interesting information about the economic behaviour of quoted companies during the period. As they will constitute an important source material to students of company finance, the correlation matrices for each of the major individual industries, for each time period, are presented in Appendix G. The results for individual industries have been relegated to an appendix because, broadly speaking, there are not very great inter-industry differences in the correlation coefficients, as an examination of Appendix G will show.

To the extent that the simple correlation coefficients give at least some idea of the way in which the variables are inter-related, the zero-order correlation matrices are also a necessary prelude to the more sophisticated statistical analysis undertaken in the later chapters. A valuable supplement to this information is given in Appendix F, which presents tables of the average values of each indicator, associated with each range of each other indicator in turn. The Appendix F tables give a more detailed picture of the relationship between each pair of variables than that given by the correlation coefficients, although this picture is necessarily less precise. However, even an impressistic glance at these tables is quite often sufficient to warn the reader of the possible non-linearity in the relationship between any two variables.

In view of all the limitations of the simple correlation coefficients given above, we must therefore again stress the preliminary nature of the analysis of this chapter. In interpreting the tables, it must also be remembered that weight must be given to the number of observations in assessing the relative significance of correlation coefficients derived from different populations, although all of the populations covered by the tables are large by the usual statistical standards.[1] Furthermore, some of the highest correlations obtained are those where there is an almost tautological relationship, e.g. between Opening Size and Closing Size (Indicators 1 and 2) or between the two rates of return (Indicators 5 and 6). On the other hand, the absence of correlation can be as important from an economic point of view as the existence of a significant association between the variables. An example of this is the relationship between size and growth, which is discussed in the next chapter.

Turning to the relationships which are meaningful from an economic point of view, an inspection of Tables 3.1-3.3 and Appendix G reveals that the positive correlations between the rates of return (Indicators 5 and 6) and the growth of net assets (Indicator 4) are consistently fairly high for each industry and each time period. It is worth noting, however, that the highest value of the coefficient of correlation between growth and profitability is of the order of 0.7, indicating that the latter explains less than 50% of the variance of growth rates. This statement, insofar as it implies that growth is caused by profitability, is not strictly accurate. A priori, these are good reasons to believe that profitability of a firm depends as much on its growth, as growth depends on its profitability. This particular question, among others, requires further analysis which is done in Part II of the book.

The valuation ratio (Indicator 14) is most highly correlated with dividend return (Indicator 7), but is also positively correlated with the rates of return and growth.[1] The relationship between growth and the valuation ratio can arise from the fact that growth is positively correlated with profitability which in turn is related to the dividend return as well as the valuation ratio. On the basis of simple correlation coefficients, it is impossible to say whether growth is independently related to valuation ratios or whether the observed association is entirely due to the relationship of the former to profitability or the dividend return. The answer to this and related questions can only be given by further statistical analysis attempted in Chapter 7.

There are also other interesting features of the data which may be briefly noted here. The tables show an apparent lack of any correlation between the two size measures and any of the other variables.[2] The zero-order correlation coefficients between size and all the other variables are so small that it is unlikely that size will have an appreciable influence on the rate of growth, profitability, valuation ratio, etc., even in multiple regression models. The implications of this relationship for growth and profitability are discussed in the next three chapters but it is particularly surprising that there is no relationship between size and the valuation ratio. One would expect that, other things being equal, bigger firms which are better known, and in whose shares there is a much more active market, will have higher share prices than the smaller, less known firms. There is some evidence that this in fact is the case, e.g. size has an influence on valuation ratio for firms on the New York Stock Exchange,[3] but it seems not to be so for the British firms which are being considered here.[4]

The correlation coefficient between size and internal finance of growth (Indicator 9) is also in most cases near to zero, but it is worth noting that in every case it is negative. This suggests that although size is not the most important influence on the extent of internal financing, there may be some systematic tendency for large firms to look rather more to external finance.

A number of financial policy variables, particularly retention ratio (Indicator 8), gearing (Indicator 10), internal finance of growth (Indicator 9) and liquidity (Indicator 11) show some degree of association with the growth of the firm. Whereas liquidity is in some cases positively, and in other cases negatively, related to growth, retention ratio is always positively related to growth, whilst internal finance and gearing are always negatively related to it. At one level, this means that the firms with above average growth tend not only to retain an above average proportion of their profits, but they require so much more finance that they also tend to raise an above average proportion of it from outside sources. At this level, since we use an income measure of gearing, it also means that growing firms tend to pay a below average proportion of their income to service fixed interest securities.

However, the tables show that all of the above financial policy variables are also related to the profitability of the firm which as we know is significantly related to its growth. Therefore, it is not possible to say whether there is any independent association between growth and financial policy variables, apart from the association of both of them to profitability. For instance, the observed negative association between gearing and growth could entirely be due to the fact that there is a negative association between gearing and profitability,[1] which in turn is positively associated with growth. This whole subject is investigated further by means of first order correlation coefficients in Chapter 7.

Another consistently high correlation shown in the tables is the negative correlation between average stocks (Indicator 13) and average liquidity (Indicator 11). This indicates that companies which normally hold high stocks find it less necessary to have a large amount of other liquid assets,[2] presumably because their reserves of liquid assets can always be replenished by running down stocks. The fact that this is a relationship between the averages of the two variables over a fairly <u>long</u> period (6 to 12 years) tends to invalidate an alternative explanation, that firms which hold abnormally high stocks, will be abnormally illiquid in the <u>short</u> run because the short-run source of finance for stock-building is to run down balances of liquid assets. An equally persistent but lower negative correlation is that between average net trade credit given (Indicator 12) and average stocks. This shows a tendency for firms with high stocks to take more trade credit from their suppliers, and, possibly, to give less to their customers. Thus, suppliers of stocks may finance other people's stockholding through giving trade credit, whilst the stockholder's customers may also help to finance it by taking less trade credit and paying more promptly in exchange for the more rapid delivery dates and wider choice offered by a firm which holds large stocks.

Table 3.4 gives the correlation coefficients for correlations between the value for each company of an indicator in the first sub-period and its corresponding value in the next sub-period, i.e. it shows to what extent an above-average value of a particular indicator for a particular company in the first sub-period could be used to predict an above- or below-average value of the same indicator for the same company in the second sub-period. In calculating inter-period correlations, we had in mind, particularly, the possibility that a measure of the consistency of relative profitability, growth and dividend yields, might throw further light on the recent work of Barna and of Little.[3]

The results given in Table 3.4 show that, apart from the size measures, none of the indicators has a particularly stable pattern of variation between different companies, and it is exceptional for more than 50% of the variance in the second sub-period to be explained by values in the first (i.e. $r^2 = 0.5$). Rates of return are more consistent over time than growth and it may seem surprising that the most stable indicators, apart from size measures, are the three which measure current assets and liabilities (Indicators 11, 12 and 13), which might <u>a priori</u> be expected to be the most variable of all items in a company's accounts. It should, however, be noted that these indicators are based on the <u>average</u> over several years of the various current assets and liabilities so that year-to-year fluctuations tend to be removed. Furthermore, the stability itself is a stability of the pattern of <u>variation</u> between companies not of the <u>average</u> level for all companies. As was described in the last chapter, there were variations between periods in the average

Table 3.4. Inter-period correlation coefficients (1948-54 correlated with 1954-60)

Indicators	1	2	4	5	6	7	8	9	10	11	12	13
	Open-ing Size	Clos-ing Size	Growth	Rate of Return (Net Assets)	Rate of Return (Equity Assets)	Divi-dend Return	Reten-tion Ratio	Inter-nal Finance	Gear-ing	Liqui-dity	Trade Credit	Stocks
Industries												
Ind. 04: Non-electrical engineering	0.98	0.97	0.35	0.73	0.46	0.59	0.52	0.46	0.70	0.79	0.67	0.80
Ind. 11: Clothing & Footwear	0.97	0.91	-0.05	0.46	0.14	0.52	0.31	0.54	0.31	0.79	0.67	0.72
Ind. 12: Food	0.99	0.98	0.05	0.40	0.42	0.67	0.38	0.28	0.43	0.68	0.72	0.71
Ind. 11 + 12 + 14: Con-sumer goods industries	1.00	0.96	0.01	0.44	0.27	0.61	0.42	0.39	0.35	0.74	0.69	0.78
Ind. 04 + 11 + 12 + 14: All industries	0.99	0.96	0.18	0.63	0.38	0.59	0.51	0.43	0.45	0.77	0.69	0.79

Number of observations

	Indicators 8 & 9	Other indicators
Ind. 11: Clothing & Footwear	35	70
Ind. 12: Food	38	73
Ind. 11 + 12 + 14: Consumer goods industries	78	150
Ind. 04: Non-electrical engineering	151	214
Ind. 04 + 11 + 12 + 14: All industries	229	364

levels of all these indicators. The relative instability of the pattern of variation between companies of indicators 4 to 10 inclusive may be partly due to the fact that they all depend to some extent on profitability. Even, if there were no other determining factors, given that the relative rates of return (Indicators 5 and 6) of different companies change over time, one would expect some instability in the pattern of relative dividend returns (Indicator 7), retentions (Indicator 8), internal finance (Indicator 9) and gearing, measured on an income basis (Indicator 10). Growth (Indicator 4) also is highly correlated with the rates of return, so this too is likely to reflect any instability in the pattern of profitability between companies.

PART II

ANALYSIS

In the first part of this book, we have described the main features of our data. The second part of the book is more analytical in character and explores more deeply the relationship between some of the variables described in Part I.

The next two chapters explore several aspects of the growth of firms by regarding growth as a random phenomenon. In Chapter 6, we discuss some parallel issues in relation to the profitability of firms. Finally in Chapter 7, the assumption that growth is a completely random pheno- menon is dropped and we discuss growth in deterministic terms, parti- cularly in terms of profitability. For a fuller preview of the basic analytical scheme of these chapters, the reader is referred back to section 4 of Chapter 1.

The main conclusions of Chapters 4 to 7 are summarized at the end of each of these chapters. Those conclusions of our analysis which are of general interest are summarized in Chapter 8, where the practical implications of these conclusions are also discussed.

4 Size and Growth: The Law of Proportionate Effect

The preliminary correlation analysis in the last chapter showed that there is no linear relationship between the rate of growth of the firm and its size. In the next two chapters we propose to look more closely, and from different points of view, into the relationship between size and growth, in order to distinguish some important economic features of the growth process of firms.

In studying the relationship between size and growth of firms, the simplest hypothesis to start from would seem to be the Law of Proportionate Effect,[1] which has received a great deal of attention in recent investigations of the growth of firms both in the U.K. and the U.S.A.[2] In its simplest and strongest form, the law of proportionate effect asserts that the probability of a firm's growing at a given rate during any specified period of time is independent of the initial size of the firm. In other words, a large firm (say, with assets worth a hundred million pounds) has as much chance of growing during any period of time at a given rate, as a medium sized firm (say, with assets worth a million pounds), or a small firm (say, with assets of only £50,000). The underlying motivation for this law may be expressed as follows: The proportionate change in the size of a firm during any period of time is a stochastic phenomenon which results from the cumulative effect of the chance operation of a large number of forces acting independently of each other. The chances of growth or shrinkage in the sizes of individual firms will depend on their profitability as well as on the financial policy and other decisions of their respective managements. Profitability in turn will depend on a number of factors such as the quality of the firm's management, the range of its products, availability of particular inputs, general economic climate, political conditions and so on. During any particular period of time, some of these factors would make for an increase in the size of the firm, others for a decline, but their combined effect would yield a probability distribution of the rates of growth (or decline) for firms of each given size. The law of proportionate effect assumes that this probability distribution is the same for all size-classes of firms.

Apart from its intrinsic interest as an explanation of the growth process of firms, this hypothesis has several important economic implications. First, the law implies that there is no optimum size of the firm.[3] Secondly, it suggests that the rate of growth of the firm in one period has no influence on its growth in the subsequent periods. Thirdly, depending upon the form it takes, it also has some important consequences for changes in industrial concentration over time. In the strong form stated above, the law implies increasing industrial concentration over time. This is because if the large firms as well as the small firms have the same chance of growing by a given proportion during any period of time, the dispersion in the size of firms will keep on increasing.[1]

Furthermore, it should be noted that the law of proportionate effect also lies at the heart of several stochastic processes which are put forward to explain the observed size distribution of firms. As is well-known, the size distribution of firms from widely different populations has been observed to approximate to Pareto-type or log-normal distribution.[2] Whereas the static theory of the firm is unable to account for these observed distributions, the law of proportionate effect, with suitable modifications, does generate distributions of this type.

In view of all these implications, it is of some importance to examine the validity of the law. We must, however, emphasize that our interest in this law derives chiefly from its ability to explain the <u>growth</u> process of firms. The explanation of <u>size</u> distributions of firms, which raises a number of other issues, is not our objective in this book.

The main burden of this chapter will, therefore, be to test directly the validity of the Law of Proportionate Effect. This will be done for continuing firms only, within individual industries. Now, if the law is valid, and the probability distributions of growth rates are the same for firms of different sizes, the following two essential requirements must hold:[3]

(a) That firms of different size-classes have the same average proportionate growth rate.

(b) That the dispersion of growth rates about the common mean is the same for all size-classes.

In the rest of this chapter we test each of these implications in various ways for our population of companies for the period 1948 to 1960. Since all these populations consist of continuing companies only, we also discuss in a later section the size distributions of births and deaths of companies. A further section analyzes companies which revalued their assets and assesses the possible impact of revaluations on growth in different size classes. Finally, we summarize the main conclusions of our analysis.

Those readers who do not wish to examine the statistical logic behind these conclusions can pass straight to the final section, but they will probably find that a number of tables contain information which is useful for other purposes besides establishing the conclusions. In particular, Tables 4.1-4.3 (which give the distribution of growth rates by the size of the firm), Tables 4.7-4.9 (which give the size distribution of non-growing firms) and Table 4.11 (which gives the size distribution of firms which revalued their assets) will be of interest to many readers.

1 Regression of growth on size

A simple way to test the first essential requirement of the law of proportionate effect, that average proportionate growth rates are the same for all size classes, is by the regression of growth on size. If the

74

average growth rate were systematically different for different size classes, then size would explain at least part of growth.

We give below the results of the regression of growth on size. Two simple relationships were tested:

$$G = a + b S + \epsilon \tag{1}$$

$$\log_e G = a + b \log_e S + \log_e \epsilon \tag{2}$$

Where: G = Percentage annual growth of Net Assets (Indicator 4).[1]

S = Opening Net Assets (Indicator 1), in £'000.

a and b are parameters, and ϵ is the error term.

The first equation implies that percentage growth changes by the same amount (given by the coefficient 'b') for any given change in size, for all sizes of firms. The logarithmic equation (2), on the other hand, asserts that the proportional change in percentage growth is the same for any given proportional change in size, for all sizes of firms. It should be noted that the latter equation was tested for only those firms which had positive growth.

Each equation was tested for each of the three larger industries separately, for the three consumer goods industries together, and for the four industries together, over each of the two sub-periods and over the period as a whole, making, in all, fifteen tests of each of the equations. For both equations (1) and (2), r^2 and the parameter b were not significantly different from zero at the 5% level,[2] with the possible exception of the Food industry in sub-period 2 (1954-1960), for which the parameter b in the logarithmic equation was barely significant.

These regression results are a fairly conclusive rejection of the two simple equations tested. This is, however, a rather negative achievement. The existence of a simple linear or log-linear relationship between size and growth would have been a fairly conclusive refutation of the Law of Proportionate Effect, but the non-existence of such a relationship does not establish the working of the Law, since there could be a more complex non-linear relationship between size and growth. The possibility of such a non-linear relationship is tested in the next section, which presents the means of the growth rates of different size classes.

2   **Distribution of growth rates by size of firm**

In this section, we present the mean and standard deviation of the growth of companies for five different size classes (Tables 4.1 to 4.3 inclusive). The means are a further test of implication (1) of the Law of Proportionate Effect, that average growth rates will be the same for all sizes of firm. The standard deviations test proposition (2), that the dispersion of growth rates about the mean is the same for all size classes.

a Average growth rate by opening size-class

Tables 4.1 to 4.3, which refer to the populations of continuing com-

Table 4.1. Growth (Indicator 4) by opening size class (Indicator 1)

Sub-period 1: 1948-1954

Industry	Clothing and Footwear			Food			Engineering			All (including Tobacco)		
Opening Size	n	m	s	n	m	s	n	m	s	n	m	s
1 < £250,000	31	3.3	7.6	32	7.7	9.4	51	10.7	6.3	117	7.6	8.1
2 < £500,000	19	6.5	11.8	29	6.8	7.5	55	8.5	6.2	103	7.7	7.8
3 < £1,000,000	20	4.5	13.5	13	7.6	6.5	68	9.8	8.1	102	8.4	7.5
4 < £2,000,000	9	4.0	3.2	11	6.5	3.2	45	10.8	5.4	67	8.9	5.6
5 > £2,000,000	7	7.6	3.4	23	7.8	4.4	40	9.9	5.0	75	8.8	4.6
All Sizes	86	4.7	7.5	108	7.3	6.9	259	9.9	6.5	464	8.2	7.1

n = number of companies

m = arithmetic mean growth rate (% per annum)

s = standard deviation, corrected for degrees of freedom

Welch-Aspin test:

Significant differences between means, at the 10% level

Industry groups		Size classes significantly different
Industry 11, Clothing and Footwear	:	1 < 5, 4 < 5
Industry 12, Food	:	None
Industry 04, Engineering	:	1 > 2, 2 < 4
All four industries, including Tobacco	:	None

Each pair of means was tested for each industry grouping, making a total of 10 tests for each group.

Table 4.2. Growth (Indicator 4) by opening size class (Indicator 1)

Sub-period 2: 1954-1960

Industry	Clothing and Footwear			Food			Engineering			All (including Tobacco)		
Opening Size	n	m	s	n	m	s	n	m	s	n	m	s
1 < £250,000	19	4.7	15.5	16	6.6	13.8	29	6.0	5.5	64	5.8	11.4
2 < £500,000	16	5.5	12.7	24	4.6	7.7	39	7.4	7.1	79	6.2	8.4
3 < £1,000,000	26	4.7	5.5	13	8.6	5.5	55	8.4	6.3	94	7.4	7.7
4 < £2,000,000	10	4.6	4.5	16	4.7	6.3	53	7.8	6.3	81	7.3	8.9
5 > £2,000,000	8	8.9	7.1	22	9.0	7.1	85	8.8	6.3	120	8.8	6.3
All Sizes	79	5.3	10.2	91	6.6	8.3	261	8.0	6.2	438	7.3	8.1

n = number of companies

m = arithmetic mean growth rate (% per annum)

s = standard deviation, corrected for degrees of freedom

Welch-Aspin test:

Significant differences between means, at the 10% level

Industry groups	Size classes significantly different
Industry 11, Clothing and Footwear :	None
Industry 12, Food :	2 < 5, 3 > 4, 4 < 5
Industry 04, Engineering :	1 < 3, 1 < 5
All four industries, including Tobacco :	1 < 5, 2 < 5, 3 < 5

Each pair of means was tested for each industry grouping, making a total of 10 tests for each group.

Table 4.3. Growth (Indicator 4) by opening size class (Indicator 1)

Whole period: 1948-1960

Industry	Clothing and Footwear			Food			Engineering			All (including Tobacco)		
Opening Size	n	m	s	n	m	s	n	m	s	n	m	s
1 < £250,000	23	2.6	7.4	20	6.6	6.4	39	9.5	5.4	82	6.8	6.8
2 < £500,000	16	6.2	6.7	19	6.1	6.2	40	8.1	5.1	75	7.2	5.8
3 < £1,000,000	18	3.9	3.2	8	6.8	4.9	55	10.0	4.8	82	8.6	5.6
4 < £2,000,000	7	4.5	3.4	7	6.4	2.6	40	9.8	5.2	55	8.5	5.2
5 > £2,000,000	6	9.1	5.5	19	8.8	3.7	39	8.9	4.7	69	8.8	3.2
All Sizes	70	4.5	6.0	73	7.0	5.3	213	9.3	5.0	363	7.9	5.5

n = number of companies

m = arithmetic mean growth rate (% per annum)

s = standard deviation, corrected for degrees of freedom

Welch-Aspin test:

Significant differences between means, at the 10% level

Industry groups	Size classes significantly different
Industry 11, Clothing and Footwear :	1 < 5, 3 < 5
Industry 12, Food :	4 < 5
Industry 04, Engineering :	2 < 3
All four industries, including Tobacco :	1 < 3, 1 < 5, 2 < 5

Each pair of means was tested for each industry grouping, making a total of 10 tests for each group.

panies in sub-period 1 (1948-54), sub-period 2 (1954-60) and the whole period (1948-60) respectively, show that as far as the individual industries are concerned, the average growth rate does not, on the whole, vary in any systematic way with the opening size of the firm. The tables also indicate that in the All Industries column, there is a tendency in each period for average growth rate to increase with the size of the firm. However, since the 'All Industries' results arise from the aggregation of firms in the individual industries which have very different average growth rates and very different size distributions, these results cannot be regarded as a reliable guide as to how growth varies with the size of the firm.

Turning to the consideration of individual tables, Table 4.1 (1948-54) shows that although there is no systematic pattern in the relationship between average growth rate and size-class in the individual industries, there are some noticeable differences in the average growth rates of firms of different sizes. This is particularly true of an industry such as Clothing and Footwear, in which there is a difference of more than 4 percentage points between the average growth rates of the largest (£2 million size-class) and the smallest (less than £$\frac{1}{4}$ million size-class) firms. It is also worth noting that in each individual industry, the highest average growth rate occurs in one of the two largest size classes.

However, as these results can arise from the chance inclusion of particular firms in particular size-classes, it is important to ask how significant are the observed differences between average growth rates. Since there was reason to believe that there were important differences between the variability of growth rates of firms in the different size-classes (see below) the Welch-Aspin Test was used to test the significance of differences between average growth rates.[1] This test, whose results are given at the bottom of Tables 4.1 to 4.3, does not assume equal variances of growth rates for the sets of firms whose average growth is being compared. It shows that, in the first sub-period (1948-54), differences between the average growth rates of firms of various sizes were rarely significant at the 10 per cent level.

Table 4.2 (1954-60) shows an essentially similar pattern of average growth rates to that of Table 4.1. The only difference is that there appears to be a tendency for growth to increase with the size of the firm, in that in each of the individual industries, the highest growth rate occurs in the largest size-class. However, the results of the Welch-Aspin test shows that this is a very weak tendency. Of the thirty possible differences in the average growth rates, between size-classes, in the three individual industries, there are only 5 differences which are significant at the 10% level.

The results of Table 4.3, pertaining to the whole period (1948-60) are not different from those of Tables 4.1 and 4.2 and do not require any special comment. The overall conclusion must, therefore, be that although, we have found a few significant differences between the average growth rates of firms in different size-classes, the average growth rates are on the whole very similar to each other. There are not a sufficient number of cases of significant differences to warrant the conclusion that the growth process of our populations of firms over the period 1948-60, was in conflict with the first necessary requirement of the Law of Proportionate Effect.

b Dispersion of growth by size-class

Tables 4.1 to 4.3 also show how the dispersion of growth rates varies with the size of firms. The following points are worth noting.

Firstly, unlike the case of average growth rates, the dispersion of growth rates displays considerable differences between different size-classes in almost every industry in each period. For instance in sub-period 1 (1948-54), the standard deviation of growth rates of firms in the Clothing and Footwear industry in the middle size-class (£500,000 to £1,000,000) is well over thirteen per cent, and in the next highest size-class, it is just over three per cent.

Secondly, the tables show that on the whole in each of the individual industries, the standard deviation of growth declines with the size of the firm. However, it must be noted that in the case of individual industries, the standard deviation does not decline regularly with the size of the firm; it is not the case that in each successive larger size-class the standard deviation of growth is lower than in the size-class below it. It is for example, quite often true that the standard deviation of growth in the largest size-class is higher than in the size-class below it. Nevertheless, the tables clearly show that firms above a certain size (for example firms with net assets of more than £1 million in the first sub-period, and with assets of more than £$\frac{1}{2}$ million in the second sub-period and the whole period) have an appreciably greater uniformity of growth rates than that of firms below this size.

Thirdly, the tables show that for all industries together, the standard deviation of the growth rates declines fairly consistently with the size of the firm. However, for reasons similar to those given above in the case of average growth rates, the aggregate results cannot be considered reliable.[1]

The differences in the dispersion of growth rates between size-classes were also found to be statistically significant[2] at a high level in almost every industry in every period.[3] We must, therefore, conclude that the second necessary requirement of the Law of Proportionate Effect that the dispersion of growth rates should be the same for firms of various sizes, is comprehensively contradicted by the data relating to the populations of firms being studied here.[4]

3.   Logarithms of the ratio of closing size to opening size

In order to make our study comparable with others for the United Kingdom, such as those by Hart and by Samuels,[5] we decided also to test whether the means and standard deviations of the logarithms of proportionate growth vary systematically with size. The use of logarithms of proportionate growth would be necessary if a peculiarly restricted form of Gibrat's Law held, namely that the birvariate frequency distribution of opening size and closing size represented a log-normal surface, so that any section across it would be log-normally distributed, e.g. the closing size of companies in a particular opening size class, the opening size of companies in a particular closing size class, or the proportionate growth of all companies, should all be log-normally distributed.[1] This assumption seems to us to be unduly restrictive, but for comparability with earlier studies, we repeated the analysis of Tables 4.1 to 4.3 for the logarithms of proportionate growth, and, on this occasion, measured growth as the ratio of closing size to opening size. Hart and Samuels have used this ratio, which is different from our measures of growth.[2]

The means and standard deviations derived from using the logarithm of the re-defined growth measure are remarkably consistent with those originally given in Tables 4.1 to 4.3, so they are not reproduced here. However, the results of the Welch-Aspin test on these results are reported in Table 4.4. It will be seen that the revised data yield all the cases of significant differences between means which occurred in the earlier data, plus a few new instances, particularly in the first sub-period, but the number of significant cases is still small.

Thus we conclude that Hart's restricted version of the Law of Proportionate Effect also does not hold. The means of the logarithms of proportional growth in the individual industries are on the whole very similar to each other for firms of different sizes. However, the variance is significantly heterogeneous at a high level between size classes. These conclusions differ from those of Hart,[3] who used a very different kind of data from ours, as well as Samuels who used similar data.[4]

4   Regressions of logarithms of closing size on logarithms of opening size

Another way of testing directly the validity of the restricted version of the Law of Proportionate Effect used by Hart and Samuels is to study the relationship between the logarithms of firm sizes at the beginning and the end of a period. If the Law is valid, there will be a systematic relationship between the two variables, which would be reflected by the parameters of the equation:

$$\log S_{t+1} = a + b \cdot \log S_t + \log_\epsilon$$

where: S_{t+1} = closing size

S_t = opening size

a and b are parameters

$\log_\epsilon$, the random error term is normally distributed with zero mean and constant variance.

When b = 1 and the variance of ϵ is in fact constant, this will mean that for all firms, irrespective of size, the average and the variance of the logarithms of proportionate growth are the same, i.e. the two basic requirements of this version of the Law of Proportionate Effect are fulfilled. If b > 1, the large firms will grow proportionately faster, and the dispersion of the size of firms will increase. If b < 1, the

Table 4.4.   Significant differences between means of
$\log \dfrac{\text{opening size}}{\text{closing size}}$ **for different size classes**

	Industry groups	Size classes* significantly different
Sub-period 1, 1948-1954		
	Industry 11, Clothing & Footwear	: 1 < 5, 3 < 5, 4 < 5
	Industry 12, Food	: None
	Industry 04, Engineering	: 2 < 4
	All four industries, including Tobacco	: 1 < 4, 1 < 5
Sub-period 2, 1954-1960		
	Industry 11, Clothing & Footwear	: 3 < 5
	Industry 12, Food	: 2 < 5, 4 < 5
	Industry 04, Engineering	: 1 < 5
	All four industries, including Tobacco	: 1 < 5, 2 < 5, 3 < 5, 4 < 5
Whole period, 1948-1960		
	Industry 11, Clothing & Footwear	: 1 < 2, 1 < 5
	Industry 12, Food	: None
	Industry 04, Engineering	: 2 < 3, 2 < 4
	All four industries, including Tobacco	: 1 < 3, 1 < 4, 1 < 5, 2 < 3, 2 < 4, 2 < 5

Each pair of means was tested for each industry grouping making a total of 10 tests for each group.

*   Size classes are those used in Tables 4.1 - 4.3.

smaller firms grow proportionately faster, thus reducing the degree of dispersion.[1]

The parameter "a" is a constant term which is independent of size, and the properties of logarithms are such that its effect on the second term in the equation is multiplicative. When b = 1, "a" is the logarithm of a multiple by which all firms' closing sizes exceed their opening sizes, e.g. if a = 0.6931 (which is $\log_e 2$) then all firms will have a closing size exactly double that of their opening size.

The study by Hart (1962) based on stock market value of firms in the period 1950-1955 produced evidence in favour of Gibrat's Law, obtaining values of b which were not significantly different from unity. Samuels (1965), on the other hand, produced evidence based on similar data to ours, and also using net assets as the size measure, which suggested that b was significantly greater than unity during the period 1950 to 1959, i.e. the larger firms tended to grow faster. He concluded, in the light of Hart's evidence, that the larger firms must have started to grow faster during the second part of his period (1956-9).

Our results for various industries and time periods are given in Table 4.5. For the whole period, 1948-1960, our estimate of b for the four industries together is 1.043 ($\pm$ 0.025). This is lower than that obtained by Samuels (b = 1.07 $\pm$ 0.02) for a similar but shorter period (1950 to 1959), and it is significantly different from unity at the 10% level. A striking feature of the table is that all of the values of b are greater than unity indicating that larger firms tended to grow faster than smaller ones. On the other hand, it should be emphasized that, in the individual industries, this tendency is never significant at the 10% level (i.e. b is not significantly greater than 1).

The regressions over sub-periods show a tendency for b to be higher in the second sub-period than in the first, i.e. the tendency for bigger firms to grow faster was more marked between 1954 and 1960 than in the earlier period. The values of b obtained for the first sub-period (1949 to 1954) are higher than those of Hart for the period 1950 to 1955 (b = 1.025 $\pm$ 0.016 for the four industries combined, as compared with 0.99 $\pm$ 0.02 for Hart's data) but are very close to unity. They are not significantly different from unity at the 10% level. Having regard to the different measures of size used and the differences between the samples, the similarity to Hart's results is as striking as the differences. During the second sub-period for all industries together, our estimate of b is significantly greater than unity at the 5% level. This greater value of b in the second sub-period agrees with Samuels' conclusion that the tendency for larger firms to grow faster (regression away from the mean) appeared or became more pronounced after 1955. However, in the individual industries the 'b' coefficients are still not significantly greater than unity at the 10% level. This confirms our own results reported in the preceding sections of this chapter.[2]

An interesting indication of the source of the tendency for the largest firms to grow slightly faster than the smaller firms is given in Table 4.6. This gives the results of fitting the same regression equations as for Table 4.5 to a slightly more restricted population. The main restriction (amounting to 90% of the companies excluded) was that com-

Table 4.5. Regression results

Equation: Log_e Closing size $= a + b.\ \text{Log}_e$ Opening size $+ \text{Log}_e\ \epsilon$

Tested on all companies in each group

	R^2	a	b
Sub-period 1: 1948-1954			
Industry 11: Clothing & Footwear	0.85	0.13 ($\pm$0.28)	1.026 ($\pm$0.047)
Industry 12: Food	0.92	0.36 ($\pm$0.19)	1.007 ($\pm$0.029)
Industries 11 + 12 + 14: Consumer Goods Industries	0.91	0.20 ($\pm$0.15)	1.023 ($\pm$0.023)
Industry 04: Engineering	0.90	0.49 ($\pm$0.13)	1.014 ($\pm$0.020)
All Four Industries: Industries 04 + 11 + 12 + 14	0.90	0.32 ($\pm$0.10)	1.025 ($\pm$0.016)
Sub-period 2: 1954-1960			
Industry 11: Clothing & Footwear	0.83	0.13 ($\pm$0.35)	1.032 ($\pm$0.055)
Industry 12: Food	0.92	0.22 ($\pm$0.22)	1.027 ($\pm$0.032)
Industries 11 + 12 + 14: Consumer Goods Industries	0.89	0.17 ($\pm$0.19)	1.032 ($\pm$0.027)
Industry 04: Engineering	0.92	0.28 ($\pm$0.12)	1.029 ($\pm$0.017)
All Four Industries: Industries 04 + 11 + 12 + 14	0.91	0.21 ($\pm$0.11)	1.033 ($\pm$0.015)
Whole period: 1948-1960			
Industry 11: Clothing & Footwear	0.79	0.06 ($\pm$0.43)	1.090 ($\pm$0.070)
Industry 12: Food	0.87	0.67 ($\pm$0.32)	1.028 ($\pm$0.048)
Industries 11 + 12 + 14: Consumer Goods Industries	0.84	0.38 ($\pm$0.25)	1.057 ($\pm$0.038)
Industry 04: Engineering	0.83	0.99 ($\pm$0.21)	1.017 ($\pm$0.032)
All Four Industries: Industries 04 + 11 + 12 + 14	0.82	0.68 ($\pm$0.17)	1.043 ($\pm$0.025)

Table 4.6. Regression results

Equation: Log_e Closing size = $a + b$. Log_e Opening size + $\text{Log}_e \epsilon$

Excluding non-growing companies

	R^2	a	b
Sub-period 1: 1948-1954			
Industry 11: Clothing & Footwear	0.92	0.65 ($\pm$ 0.21)	0.962 ($\pm$ 0.034)
Industry 12: Food	0.94	0.73 ($\pm$ 0.16)	0.967 ($\pm$ 0.025)
Industries 11 + 12 + 14: Consumer Goods Industries	0.95	0.63 ($\pm$ 0.12)	0.975 ($\pm$ 0.018)
Industry 04: Engineering	0.93	0.64 ($\pm$ 0.11)	0.997 ($\pm$ 0.017)
All Four Industries: Industries 04 + 11 + 12 + 14	0.94	0.64 ($\pm$ 0.08)	0.987 ($\pm$ 0.012)
Sub-period 2: 1954-1960			
Industry 11: Clothing & Footwear	0.87	0.84 ($\pm$ 0.30)	0.945 ($\pm$ 0.047)
Industry 12: Food	0.94	0.48 ($\pm$ 0.22)	1.002 ($\pm$ 0.030)
Industries 11 + 12 + 14: Consumer Goods Industries	0.93	0.57 ($\pm$ 0.16)	0.988 ($\pm$ 0.023)
Industry 04: Engineering	0.94	0.46 ($\pm$ 0.12)	1.009 ($\pm$ 0.017)
All Four Industries: Industries 04 + 11 + 12 + 14	0.93	0.51 ($\pm$ 0.10)	1.000 ($\pm$ 0.014)
Whole period: 1948-1960			
Industry 11: Clothing & Footwear	0.85	0.73 ($\pm$ 0.34)	1.005 ($\pm$ 0.055)
Industry 12: Food	0.88	0.93 ($\pm$ 0.31)	1.000 ($\pm$ 0.045)
Industries 11 + 12 + 14: Consumer Goods Industries	0.88	0.78 ($\pm$ 0.22)	1.013 ($\pm$ 0.033)
Industry 04: Engineering	0.84	1.03 ($\pm$ 0.21)	1.016 ($\pm$ 0.031)
All Four Industries: Industries 04 + 11 + 12 + 14	0.85	0.93 ($\pm$ 0.15)	1.015 ($\pm$ 0.023)

panies which did not grow (i.e. having growth of net assets, Indicator 4, < 0) were excluded. The effect of this is to reduce the estimated value of b in every case so that it rarely exceeds unity. The apparent tendency for the larger firms to grow relatively faster in the full population must therefore be due to the asymmetrical size distribution of the excluded companies, i.e. the companies which did not grow. In other words either smaller companies appear proportionately more often in the category of those which do not grow, or the smaller companies which do not grow have the highest negative growth rates. Either or both of these possibilities must hold to explain the lower observed value of the coefficient b for the populations of firms which do not include non-growing companies. Tables 4.7 to 4.9 give evidence that at least the first of these possibilities holds, i.e. a larger proportion of small companies have negative growth. This is not consistent with the Law of Proportionate Effect, which predicts that the probability of negative growth should be independent of size.

5   Births and deaths

We have shown that the first requirement of the Law of Proportionate Effect holds approximately with respect to continuing companies. The remaining question is whether it holds for the full population, including those which have been recently 'born' into the population or are about to leave it by 'death'. This problem is outside the scope of the present study, which deals specifically with continuing companies, but this section attempts to give some indication of the size and impact of the birth and death processes. It should also be noted that the data given in Table 4.10 refer to a limited range of births and deaths, i.e. companies which were born in 1948-54 and subsequently continued throughout the period 1954-60, and companies which died in 1954-60 and had previously continued throughout the period 1948-54. In fact, our analysis of births and deaths is very restricted and only claims to give a general impression of the magnitude and impact of the two processes.

Table 4.10 gives information about this restricted range of births and deaths for the four industries which we have studied. It will be observed that the size in 1954 of companies which were born during the previous six years and of companies which would die in the next six years was on the whole much less than the size of the companies which continued in existence over the full twelve years. 70% of the deaths come in the lower three size classes, compared with 78% of the births and less than 50% of the continuing companies.[1] The average size of companies which 'died' was £1,033,000, of those which were born £1,327,000, and of continuing companies £3,376,000.

The conclusion to be drawn from this is that the birth process tends to add a supply of smaller companies to the population but this is counterbalanced by the fact that death also tends to affect the smaller companies most. The net effect of the birth and death process is given in the third column of the table. This shows that a net loss of companies by death was the general rule for all groups except the largest and one class of small companies, but it should be remembered that births in an earlier period are being compared with deaths in a later period.

Table 4.7. Size distribution of non-growing companies

Sub-period 1, 1948-1954

Opening Size (£)	Non-growing companies as a percentage of all continuing companies				Number of non-growing companies
	Industry 11, Clothing and Footwear	Industry 12, Food	Industry 04, Engineering	All four industries including tobacco	All four industries including Tobacco
< 250,000	22.6	18.8	-	12.8	15
< 500,000	26.3	20.7	3.6	12.6	13
< 1,000,000	10.0	15.4	7.4	8.8	9
< 2,000,000	22.2	-	2.2	6.0	4
> 2,000,000	-	4.3	-	1.3	1
Total	18.6	13.9	3.1	9.1	42

Table 4.8. Size distribution of non-growing companies

Sub-period 2, 1954-1960

Opening Size (£)	Non-growing companies as a percentage of all continuing companies				Number of non-growing companies
	Industry 11, Clothing and Footwear	Industry 12, Food	Industry 04, Engineering	All four industries including tobacco	All four industries including Tobacco
< 250,000	21.1	37.5	16.7	23.1	15
< 500,000	31.3	29.2	23.1	26.6	21
< 1,000,000	19.2	-	3.6	7.4	7
< 2,000,000	10.0	12.5	3.8	7.4	6
> 2,000,000	-	-	2.4	2.5	3
Total	19.0	16.5	7.6	11.8	52

Table 4.9. Size distribution of non-growing companies

Whole period, 1948-1960

Opening Size (£)	Non-growing companies as a percentage of all continuing companies				Number of non-growing companies,
	Industry 11, Clothing and Footwear	Industry 12, Food	Industry 04, Engineering	All four industries including tobacco	All four industries including Tobacco
< 250,000	26.1	10.0	-	9.8	8
< 500,000	6.3	10.5	7.3	7.9	6
< 1,000,000	5.6	-	1.8	2.4	2
< 2,000,000	14.3	-	5.0	7.3	4
> 2,000,000	-	-	-	-	-
Total	12.9	5.5	2.8	5.5	20

Table 4.10. Births and deaths in all four industries

Size in 1954 (£'000)	(1) Deaths 1954-1960	(2) Births 1948-1954	(3) Net change (Births minus deaths)	(4) Continuing 1948-1960	(5) Deaths Col.(1) as % of col.(4)	(6) Births Col.(2) as % of col.(4)
< 250	24	16	- 8	49	49.0	32.7
< 500	20	25	+ 5	54	37.0	46.3
< 1,000	26	18	- 8	76	34.2	23.7
< 2,000	18	11	- 7	70	25.7	15.7
< 4,000	7	1	- 6	53	13.2	1.9
< 8,000	4	2	- 2	36	11.1	5.6
< 16,000	1	1	-	15	6.7	6.7
< 32,000	-	-	-	7	-	-
> 32,000	-	1*	+ 1	4	-	25.0
Total	100	75	-25	364	27.5	20.6
Mean (£'000)	1,033	1,327		3,376		
Standard Deviation	1,328	4,378		11,080		

* Reckitt and Coleman (Holdings) Ltd.

Notes.　(1) Deaths are confined to those of companies which had survived from 1948 to 1954.

(2) Births are confined to those of companies which subsequently survived from 1954 to 1960.

(3) The Net Change (Col. (3)) is the difference between the number of continuing companies in 1948-1954 (sub-period 1) and the number continuing in 1954-1960 (sub-period 2).

This pattern of births is contrary to that assumed by the Yule distribution, which is one alternative to the lognormal as a description of the size distribution of companies. The simplest Yule process assumes a constant birth of companies in the lowest size class.[1] The wide range of size of 'births' is due partly to our definition of 'birth' (see note 1, page 86) and partly due to the nature of quoted companies, which are usually in existence as unquoted companies for a number of years before achieving a quotation and so being 'born' into our population.

It will be observed that whilst births are not confined to any single size class, the net birth and death process leads to a proportionate loss of companies which is spread fairly evenly over the different size classes. In view of the high proportion of births and deaths relative to continuing companies, the net impact of the birth and death process is remarkably small both in number and size distribution of companies.

However, we are unable to say without further investigation what effect the inclusion of companies which were 'born' or 'died' during any period would have had on the relative growth of companies in different size classes.[2] If, as is possible, death removes a stream of slow or non-growing firms, whilst birth adds a stream of fast-growing firms, the concentration of both processes in the lower size classes will tend to increase the rates of growth in these classes over what they would otherwise be. In other words, the birth and death processes could work in such a way as to eliminate the slight tendency for larger firms to grow faster observed mainly in the second sub-period. On the other hand, the effect could be the reverse.

6   Revaluations

A possible source of bias in studies of growth based on the ratio of opening net asset size to closing size is the revaluation of fixed assets.[3] If revaluations are confined to a particular size-class of firms, then firms in this class will apparently grow faster than firms of others which do not revalue, when their actual growth is otherwise identical.

Table 4.11 presents evidence relating to revaluations by companies in the four industries studied here. It shows that in both periods some companies in all size-classes revalued. The proportionate distribution of revaluations between size-classes was fairly even in the first sub-period, but in the second sub-period there was a pronounced tendency for a higher proportion of large firms to revalue. A much higher proportion of all firms revalued in the second sub-period. This suggests that revaluations could cause a systematic bias in such analyzes as that of Samuels[4] and of sections 3 and 4 of this chapter. It will be recalled that Samuels found that the parameter b, relating the log of opening size to the log of closing size, was greater than unity due to some new factor in the period 1955 to 1960. Our analysis reported in Table 4.7 also found this to be the case for the period 1954-60 (sub-period 2). We eliminated most of the cases of b > 1 when we excluded non-growing companies from the population (Table 4.6), but even in this case the value of b was higher in the second sub-period than the first, suggesting that the larger companies were now growing relatively

Table 4.11. Revaluations

Four Industries: continuing companies only

Opening Size Range (£)	1948-1954			1954-1960		
	(1) Number of continuing companies	(2) Number of companies which revalued	(3) Col.(2) as % of col.(1)	(4) Number of continuing companies	(5) Number of companies which revalued	(6) Col.(5) as % of col.(4)
< 250,000	117	10	8.5	65	11	16.9
< 500,000	103	5	4.8	79	10	12.7
< 1,000,000	102	8	7.8	94	11	11.7
< 2,000,000	67	5	7.5	81	10	12.3
< 4,000,000	42	1	2.4	54	7	13.0
< 8,000,000	14	2	14.3	38	6	15.8
<16,000,000	13	1	7.7	16	6	37.5
<32,000,000	4	1	25.0	7	2	28.6
>32,000,000	2	1	50.0	5	1	20.0
Total	464	34	7.3	439	64	14.6

faster. The tendency for larger companies to 'grow' more by revaluing would explain this, and this explanation is further supported by the fact that the Clothing and Footwear industry (Industry 11), which had the lowest value of b in both periods (Table 4.6) and was the only industry for which b was lower in the second period than in the first, had the lowest proportion of companies which revalued.

We conclude, therefore, that the tendency for a higher proportion of the larger companies to revalue during the period 1954-1960 is a systematic bias which will tend to make larger companies appear to grow faster (where growth is the ratio of closing balance sheet value to opening balance sheet value) than smaller companies. This may partly explain Samuels' observation that there appeared to be significant regression away from the mean (b > 1) and may also explain why our results, using the alternative measure of growth as closing size divided by opening size, as reported in section 3, showed a slightly more significant tendency for larger firms to grow faster.

Summary and conclusions

In this chapter, we have tested the Law of Proportionate Effect within individual industries by testing whether two necessary requirements, that both the mean and the dispersion of growth rates are independent of the size of the firm, are fulfilled.

The first of these requirements has not been rejected by our data. We have found very few statistically significant differences between the average growth rates for different size-classes of companies, although there is a very slight tendency for average growth rates to increase with the size of firms, particularly in the second sub-period (1954-1960) where the highest size-class (companies with net worth of more than £2 million) has a higher average growth rate than those of the lower size classes in each of the three industries. We have also found that this tendency for the very largest companies to grow faster is probably exaggerated by the effects of revaluations when growth is measured as the ratio of closing balance sheet figures to opening balance sheet figures. However, the tendency still persists when revaluations are excluded. It has also been found that the concentration of negative growth rates among the relatively small companies is an important component of the slightly lower average growth rate of these companies when compared with the largest ones. Our limited analysis of births and deaths showed that they are more frequent among the smaller companies, but we have not investigated their effect on the distribution of growth rates.

The second requirement of the Law of Proportionate Effect, that the dispersion of growth rates is the same for all size-classes of firms, has not been found to hold for the companies analyzed in this study. The variances of growth rates in different size-classes are different from one another at a high level of statistical significance in all but one of the populations of companies studied. The variances tend to be heterogeneous in the smaller size classes, but for companies above a certain minimum size, the variance of growth rates tends to be lower than for smaller companies. In other words, although the variance does not decline consistently with size, companies above a certain size (Net Worth of £1 million in sub-period 1 and £$\frac{1}{2}$ million in sub-period 2) have more uniform rates of growth than firms below this size.[1] Since we would expect the largest firms to be more diversified and to operate in a number of different product and geographical markets, it is not at all surprising that they should have more uniform growth rates. For a diversified firm an adverse growth rate in one market may be offset by better than average performance in another. Similarly, the management of large firms may tend to be more uniform than that of small firms. (These issues are considered further in Chapter 8.) However, our analysis in this chapter has shown that it is only firms which are above a certain minimum size are able to achieve more uniform growth rates.[2]

In an earlier section we noted some important differences between our findings and those of some British studies which have tested a particularly restricted version of the Law of Proportionate Effect. When these results are compared with those of leading American studies in this field, which have in fact tested the Law of Proportionate Effect in the form considered by us, we find that there are some important differences with respect to some of the studies, but only apparent differences with respect to others. Our findings of no significant differences in the means of growth rates between size-classes and of heterogeneous variances are obviously in conflict with those of Simon and Bonini who found that for the 500 largest American manufacturing companies for the period 1954-1956 (a much shorter period than ours), the means and variances of the growth rates were the same for different size classes. Our results are also apparently in conflict with those of Hymer and Pashigan[3] who found that although means were the same and variance was heterogeneous between size-classes, variance declined regularly with size. We find, on the other hand, that the variance is heterogeneous in the lowest size-classes, but above a certain minimum size the variance of growth rates is lower than for firms below this size. As the study by Hymer and Pashigan was confined to large firms, the apparent conflict between our results and theirs could well be due to the fact that it is only amongst the largest firms that the variance of growth rates falls inversely with size.[4]

Our final conclusion with respect to the Law of Proportionate Effect is that, in its simplest and strongest version which we have tested in this chapter, it does not explain the growth of quoted companies in the United Kingdom from 1948 to 1960. It is possible that the observed distribution of growth rates, with broadly homogeneous means but heterogeneous variances for different size-classes, is compatible with a mere complicated stochastic process based on a weaker version of the Law of Proportionate Effect.[5] However, since this study is concerned with continuing companies only, the more complicated stochastic processes which require a detailed analysis of the birth and death processes, cannot be considered here. In later chapters we shall examine the growth of firms in deterministic terms, i.e. in terms of economic factors such as profitability and the financial structure of firms, rather than regarding it as a wholly chance phenomenon.

5 Size and Growth: Internal Mobility and Persistency of Growth

The relationship between size and growth was investigated in the last chapter by comparing the distribution of growth rates for firms in different size classes. The same information can be rearranged in somewhat different forms to reveal other important aspects of the growth process of firms. In this chapter, we propose to look at two of these aspects which are of considerable economic interest.

We shall first study the question of the internal size mobility of firms in different industries and in different time periods, i.e. how surviving firms in various industries change ranks in their size distribution over time. The usual methods of studying concentration in terms of some kind of index of concentration focus attention on the static aspects of industrial structure. However even if two industries appear to have the same degree of concentration in terms of one or more of the usual indices of concentration, their condition may be different from an economic point of view. Prais and Hart have put this point succinctly in the following words:[1] "In one industry it may be that the largest firm at present was also the largest firm a century ago, and so on all along the size range; but in the other industry or country, the state of competition and rate of innovation may be such that no firm holds its rank in the size distribution for very long. One may thus speak of industries that have a rigid structure and those that have a mobile structure; industries that have both a high degree of concentration and a rigid structure are those in which one may suspect the existence of monopoly elements." The study of mobility, by enquiring into the amount of 'mixing' or reordering that takes place in the size ranks of individual firms over time, thus, focuses on the dynamic aspects of the industrial structure. It deals with a different, and perhaps a more relevant set of issues than do the static measures of concentration, particularly in comparing industrial structures which are in any case highly concentrated in the static sense.[2]

The second aspect of the growth process of firms studied in this chapter is the question of persistency of growth rates, i.e. whether the rate of growth of a firm in one period raises any presumption about its subsequent growth rate. It may be recalled that one of the implications of the law of proportionate effect is that the rate of growth of a firm in a particular period is independent of its growth rate in previous periods. Since the law of proportionate effect has not been found to be valid, there is a possibility that there is some relationship between growth rates in consecutive time periods.[3] Here we shall investigate directly the strength of this relationship; we shall find out the extent to which firms which have a high (or low) growth rate in one period also have a high or low growth rate in the following period. We shall also see whether the relationship between the growth rates of firms in the two successive six-year periods is the same for different industries and for firms of different sizes.

In what follows, the problem of internal mobility in the size distribution of firms is studied in the first two sections, and that of the persistency of growth rates in the third one. The main conclusions of the chapter are summarized in the last section.

1.   Transition matrices and internal mobility

Transition matrices for firms in all four industries taken together are given below (Tables 5.1 to 5.3) for sub-period 1 (1948-54), sub-period 2 (1954-60) and the whole period (1948-60). These matrices show the proportion of firms in different size classes at the beginning of the period which have gone into various size classes at the end of the period. For instance in sub-period 1, of the 103 firms in the size class £250,000 to £500,000 at the beginning of the period, 30% remained in the same size class, 57% went up one size class, 9% went up two size classes and 4% went down one or more size classes at the end of the period. Since the upper limit of each size class is double that of the preceding one, going up or down one size class means, for the typical firm in that class, doubling or halving of size, and going up or down two size classes similarly means quadrupling or being reduced to one quarter of the initial size at the end of the period.

The general picture which emerges from these tables is that in both sub-period 1 and sub-period 2 most of the surviving firms either remained in the same size class or went up one size class. This can be seen most clearly from the summary under each table. In sub-period 2 (1954-60), proportionately more firms remained in the same size class and proportionately less went up one or more size classes than in sub-period 1 (1948-54), reflecting no doubt the lower average growth rate of firms in the second sub-period. For the twelve year period as a whole (1948-60) most of the surviving firms, as one would expect, went up one or more size classes, and only fifteen per cent still remained in the same size class.

The transition matrices, apart from being another way of looking at the growth of firms,[1] also give some indication of the internal size mobility of firms. We shall use the transition matrices for the individual industries[2] to compare the relative mobility in the three major industries for the whole period. Now it is obvious that there will be some connection between the amount of mobility in an industry and the distribution of growth rates in that industry, but what is perhaps not so obvious is that there is also a relationship between mobility and the initial size distribution of firms in the industry. If the distribution of growth rates is identical in two industries, then, barring exceptions of the type mentioned below, the amount of mixing that takes place in the size ranks will be greater in the industry with a less dispersed initial distribution of firm sizes than in the industry with a greater variation in initial sizes. In other words, the more closely packed together are the initial firm sizes, the greater will be the change in the distribution

Table 5.1 Sub-Period 1: 1948-1954 All Four Industries

Indicators 1 & 2: Opening Size and Closing Size

Opening Size (£)	Closing Size (£) <62,500	<125,000	<250,000	<500,000	<1,000,000	<2,000,000	<4,000,000	<8,000,000	<16,000,000	<32,000,000	<64,000,000	<128,000,000	>128,000,000	Total number of firms
<62,500	40.0	40.0	20.0	—	—	—	—	—	—	—	—	—	—	5
<125,000	5.7	40.0	45.7	5.7	2.9	—	—	—	—	—	—	—	—	35
<250,000	1.3	2.6	36.4	50.6	9.1	—	—	—	—	—	—	—	—	77
<500,000	1.0	1.9	1.0	30.1	57.3	8.7	—	—	—	—	—	—	—	103
<1,000,000	—	—	1.0	2.0	34.3	52.0	10.8	—	—	—	—	—	—	102
<2,000,000	—	—	—	—	—	37.3	55.2	7.5	—	—	—	—	—	67
<4,000,000	—	—	—	—	—	2.4	28.6	69.0	—	—	—	—	—	42
<8,000,000	—	—	—	—	—	—	—	42.9	57.1	—	—	—	—	14
<16,000,000	—	—	—	—	—	—	—	—	61.5	38.5	—	—	—	13
<32,000,000	—	—	—	—	—	—	—	—	—	50.0	50.0	—	—	4
<64,000,000	—	—	—	—	—	—	—	—	—	—	—	100.0	—	1
<128,000,000	—	—	—	—	—	—	—	—	—	—	—	—	100.0	1
>128,000,000	—	—	—	—	—	—	—	—	—	—	—	—	—	—
Total number of firms	6	21	46	74	102	88	60	40	16	7	2	1	1	464

Proportionate Growth

Size in 1954/Size in 1948	1/8	1/4	1/2	1	2	4	8	Total number of firms
Number of firms	1	4	8	163	252	35	1	464
Proportion of firms	0.2	0.9	1.7	35.1	54.3	7.5	0.2	

Table 5.2 Sub-Period 2: 1954-1960 All Four Industries

Indicators 1 & 2: Opening Size and Closing Size

Opening Size (£)	Closing Size (£)													Total number of firms
	<62,500	<125,000	<250,000	<500,000	<1,000,000	<2,000,000	<4,000,000	<8,000,000	<16,000,000	<32,000,000	<64,000,000	<128,000,000	>128,000,000	
<62,500	50.0	33.3	—	16.7	—	—	—	—	—	—	—	—	—	6
<125,000	11.8	41.2	23.5	17.6	5.9	—	—	—	—	—	—	—	—	17
<250,000	2.4*	4.8	47.6	35.7	9.5	—	—	—	—	—	—	—	—	42
<500,000	1.3	—	3.8	45.6	39.2	8.9	1.3	—	—	—	—	—	—	79
<1,000,000	—	—	—	—	47.9	44.7	7.4	—	—	—	—	—	—	94
<2,000,000	—	—	—	—	4.9	42.0	44.4	7.4	—	1.2	—	—	—	81
<4,000,000	—	—	—	—	—	—	33.3	59.3	3.7	3.7	—	—	—	54
<8,000,000	—	—	—	—	—	—	—	31.6	57.9	7.9	2.6	—	—	38
<16,000,000	—	—	—	—	—	—	—	—	18.7	68.8	12.5	—	—	16
<32,000,000	—	—	—	—	—	—	—	—	—	42.9	42.9	14.3	—	7
<64,000,000	—	—	—	—	—	—	—	—	—	—	66.7	33.3	—	3
<128,000,000	—	—	—	—	—	—	—	—	—	—	—	—	100.0	1
>128,000,000	—	—	—	—	—	—	—	—	—	—	—	—	100.0	1
Total number of firms	7	11	27	55	85	83	62	50	27	20	8	2	2	439

* Includes company with opening size <250,000 and closing size <0

Proportionate Growth

Size in 1960/Size in 1954	1/8	1/4	1/2	1	2	4	8	16	Total number of firms
Number of firms	1	1	11	184	200	35	6	1	439
Proportion of firms	0.2	0.2	2.5	41.9	45.6	8.0	1.4	0.2	

Table 5.3 Whole Period: 1948-1960 All Four Industries

Indicators 1 & 2: Opening Size and Closing Size

Opening Size (£)	Closing Size (£) <62,500	<125,000	<250,000	<500,000	<1,000,000	<2,000,000	<4,000,000	<8,000,000	<16,000,000	<32,000,000	<64,000,000	<128,000,000	>128,000,000	Total number of firms
<62,500	20.0	40.0	20.0	20.0	—	—	—	—	—	—	—	—	—	5
<125,000	8.3	20.8	41.7	12.5	8.3	8.3	—	—	—	—	—	—	—	24
<250,000	3.8	1.9	15.1	39.6	34.0	3.8	1.9	—	—	—	—	—	—	53
<500,000	2.6*	—	2.6	17.1	39.5	28.9	9.2	—	—	—	—	—	—	76
<1,000,000	—	—	—	—	14.6	42.7	30.5	9.8	1.2	1.2	—	—	—	82
<2,000,000	—	—	—	—	3.6	10.9	32.7	43.6	7.3	1.8	—	—	—	55
<4,000,000	—	—	—	—	—	—	10.8	37.8	37.8	10.8	2.7	—	—	37
<8,000,000	—	—	—	—	—	—	—	7.7	38.5	46.1	7.7	—	—	13
<16,000,000	—	—	—	—	—	—	—	—	15.4	53.8	23.1	7.7	—	13
<32,000,000	—	—	—	—	—	—	—	—	—	25.0	50.0	25.0	—	4
<64,000,000	—	—	—	—	—	—	—	—	—	—	—	—	100.0	1
<128,000,000	—	—	—	—	—	—	—	—	—	—	—	—	100.0	1
>128,000,000	—	—	—	—	—	—	—	—	—	—	—	—	—	—
Total number of firms	7	8	21	38	64	67	55	47	26	20	7	2	2	264

* Includes company with opening size <500,000 and closing size <0

Proportionate Growth

Size in 1960/Size in 1948	1/8	1/4	1/2	1	2	4	8	16	32	Total number of firms
Number of firms	2	2	7	53	145	118	3C	6	1	364
Proportion of firms	0.5	0.5	1.9	14.6	39.8	32.4	8.2	1.6	0.3	

of size ranks at the end of the period for an identical distribution of growth rates.

Similarly, for the same initial size distribution of firms in two industries, the one with the greater variation in growth rates (e.g. a higher standard deviation of growth rates) will also tend to have greater mobility. There are, however, important exceptions to this type of argument. For example, it is possible that, in a particular industry, the greater dispersion of growth rates is simply due to the fact that the larger firms in the industry tend to have a more or less equal, but much bigger growth rate than that of the smaller firms which also have more or less similar growth. In this case, the mixing of size ranks in the industry may be less than in an industry with a lower dispersion of growth rates, but a different distribution of growth rates by size of firm, even though the initial size distribution of firms is identical in both industries. A parallel argument applies to the case of two industries with identical distribution of growth rates, but with different dispersion of initial sizes.

Thus, to sum up, relative mobility in an industry, in general, is not just a simple function of the mean and variance of growth rates and of initial sizes; it depends in a complex way on the parameters of the bivariate distribution of size and growth. In the particular case where the law of proportionate effect is valid and the distribution of growth rates are identical for firms of different sizes in each industry, there does obtain a simple relationship between relative mobility and the two univariate distributions of growth and size respectively, provided that the distributions are 'well behaved'. Relative mobility in this case varies directly with the average growth rate and the variation in growth rates and inversely with the relative variation in the initial size distribution of firms in the industry.[1] However, this simple relationship does not hold in general.

Keeping in view these general considerations, we should like to assess and compare the degree of mobility in the different industries. One way of doing this is to compute a measure of relative mobility for each industry based on transition matrices. The measure which we have chosen gives the probability that a typical (randomly selected) firm in any size class in a particular industry will catch up with or overtake any (randomly selected) firm in the next higher size-class by the end of the period.[2] Since, as noted earlier, the upper limit of each size-class in our transition matrices (Tables 5.1 to 5.3 and Appendix E) is double that of the previous one, this measure of mobility has the following very simple intuitive meaning. Suppose that a firm is selected at random of size X and another firm is similarly selected of size 2 X from the same industry. Then the measure of mobility given above amounts to asking the question: what is the probability of the initially smaller firm (of size X) catching up with, or becoming bigger than the initially larger firm (of size 2 X) at the end of the period? It must be remembered that the initially smaller firm need not necessarily double or more than double in size for it to overtake the larger firm. In fact it can remain the same size or even decline, but the larger firm in that case must decline more than it by the end of the period. All that is necessary for catching up, or an interchange of relative positions,

is that the initially smaller firm should have a higher rate of growth
(or lower rate of shrinkage) than the larger firm. A probability measure
of this kind[1] will give some notion of the relative amount of switching
between size ranks that has taken place in the different industries.

The transition matrices for the whole period (1948-60) revealed the
following probabilities of catching up or switching of size ranks (in the
sense described above) in the three major industries:

Food Industry	.38
Non-Electrical Engineering Industry	.32
Clothing and Footwear Industry	.36

The relative orders of magnitude indicate that the Food industry is most
mobile followed in that order by the Clothing and Footwear industry and
the Engineering industry. If it is assumed that all firms belonging to
a particular size-class in the transition matrices have the same size
(say, the average of that size class), then the above figures show that
the probability of a randomly selected firm which was initially double
the size of another firm chosen at random, being caught up with or
being over-taken by the latter at the end of the 12-year period, was 38%
in the Food industry, 36% in the Clothing and Footwear industry and
32% in the Engineering industry.

Before we can accept these conclusions with respect to relative mobility in different industries, it must be noted that the above measure of
mobility is somewhat arbitrary, particularly in relation to the pair of
firms chosen for comparison. There is no reason for instance why
one should examine the catching up or the switching of a firm which
is initially half the size of the larger firm, rather than .7 or .8 the
size of the latter. In principle, it is possible to compute the latter
probabilities in the same way as we computed the former, but the
clerical work involved in doing this becomes prohibitive.

Fortunately, this particular defect of the measure of mobility used
above does not affect the comparisons of the Engineering industry with
either of the other two industries. However, it renders doubtful any
conclusion with respect to the comparison between the degree of mobility in the latter industries. As far as the Engineering industry is concerned we would have obtained the same results with respect to relative
mobility in this industry as compared with the other two industries,
had we chosen a higher than .5 cut-off point for the initially smaller
firms. This is because a low cut-off point, other things being equal,
tends only to discriminate against an industry which has a relatively
lower average growth rate. Since the Engineering industry has a higher
average growth rate (9.3%) than either the Food industry (7.1%) or the
Clothing and Footwear industry (4.5%), it is most probable that we
would have still found Engineering to be least mobile had we chosen
the initially smaller firm to be .6 or .7 or .8 the size of the larger.
This argument, however, cannot be applied to the comparisons of
relative mobility in Food and Clothing and Footwear since the latter
has a lower average growth rate than the former. As far as these two

industries are concerned, it is quite possible that we would have found Clothing and Footwear to be more mobile than Food, rather than the other way round, if the initially smaller firm had been taken to be more than half the size of the larger firm.

Thus, on the basis of the measure of mobility used in this section, we conclude that although Engineering was relatively less mobile than either Food or Clothing and Footwear, it is not possible to say which of the latter two industries displayed the highest degree of internal mobility in the period 1948-60. This question will be explored further by means of rank correlation analysis in the next section, which supplements the measure of mobility used in this section.

2. Mobility and rank correlation analysis

Kendall's rank correlation coefficient between the size ranks of surviving firms at the beginning of the period and their ranks at the end of the period is given in the first row of Table 5.4 below for each of the three major industries and for each time-period. As is well known, such a coefficient has a simple meaning as a coefficient of disarray. If the firms are ranked in their natural order at the beginning of the period, then the more the corresponding size ranks are in 'disarray' at the end of the period, the smaller will be the magnitude of the rank correlation coefficient. 'Disarray' is greater, the greater the proportion of actual inversions between pairs of closing ranks to the maximum number which could have taken place.[1]

The main difference between the measure of mobility used in the previous section and this one is that whereas the former gives the probability of catching up or inversion between firms of a particular kind (i.e. those which are approximately half the size of other firms at the beginning of the period, the latter is based on the probability of all possible inversions in the size-ranks of firms. The measure of mobility used in section 1 ignores any inversions or catching up in the size ranks of firms which are close to each other in size. However, although the rank correlation coefficient, to the extent that it considers all possible inversions of size ranks is a more refined measure than the one used in the previous section, it is not in every respect superior to the latter. It is, for instance, much more likely to be influenced by 'spurious' mobility, which, as discussed earlier, can arise simply from the initial 'packing' of size ranks. The measure of mobility used in section 1, by restricting itself to a particular category of inversions, is much less sensitive to the differences in the dispersion of initial sizes in various industries.

However, as the earlier discussion showed, it is very difficult to construct one single measure of relative mobility which is meaningful from an economic point of view, except in the special case where the law of proportionate effect holds.[2] We must, therefore, rely on both the rank correlation coefficient and the measure of mobility used in Section I to draw conclusions about relative mobility in different industries.

Table 5.4. Kendall's rank-correlation coefficients, coefficients of variation of growth and coefficients of variation of opening sizes for the major industries*

	Sub-period 1 (1948–54)			Sub-period 2 (1954–60)			Whole Period (1948–1960)		
	Non-Electrical Engineering	Food	Clothing and Footwear	Non-Electrical Engineering	Food	Clothing and Footwear	Non-Electrical Engineering	Food	Clothing and Footwear
Kendall's r_k	.818	.796	.793	.837	.811	.771	.725	.717	.693
Standard Deviation (%) of growth rates	6.5	6.9	7.5	6.2	8.2	10.1	5.0	5.2	6.0
Average Growth Rate (%)	9.9	7.3	4.7	8.0	6.6	5.3	9.3	7.1	4.5
Coefficient of variation of opening sizes	277.1	213.2	220.8	259.5	207.3	220.7	269.5	195.7	227.9

* It can be argued that from some points of view, Spearman's rank correlation coefficient is a more suitable measure of disarray for our purposes than r_k. Our experiments with different industries over some of the time periods showed that in fact the same pattern of relative mobility is observed when Spearman's coefficient is computed as when r_k is used. As the discussion in the last part of this section will indicate, there are also good a priori reasons which suggest that this would be the case. The rank correlation coefficient is a major tool of analysis in the rest of this book and for most of the problems considered, r_k seemed to be very much the better measure to use.

The rank correlation coefficients in Table 5.4 show that the relative mobility is greatest in Clothing and Footwear, followed in order by Food and Engineering. The same pattern of relative mobility emerges in all the three time periods.[1] However, from an economic point of view there is a 'spurious' element in the greater relative amount of stability revealed by the rank correlation analysis in the Engineering industry. Since the opening size ranks of firms are less closely packed together in the Engineering industry (as shown, for instance, by the greater size of the coefficient of variation of opening sizes), it can be argued that the rank correlation coefficient indicates less 'mobility' in this industry even though there is just as much 'tendency' for firms in this industry to change size ranks as there is in the other two industries. This argument is valid as far as it goes, and we cannot draw any conclusions about the degree of relative mobility in the Engineering industry on the basis of rank correlation coefficients alone.

The comparisons of relative mobility between Clothing and Footwear and Food are not marred by this argument. The coefficients of rank correlation indicate greater mobility in Clothing and Footwear than in Food in spite of the fact that the opening size ranks are in every case more closely packed together in the latter industry. It may also be recalled that the analysis of the last section, based upon a measure of mobility which is much less sensitive to the problem raised by the 'packing of size-ranks', did show that Food is more mobile than Engineering. We may, therefore, conclude by noting that even when the spurious element of mobility in the rank correlation analysis is taken into account, the Clothing and Footwear industry is more mobile than the Food industry, which is most likely more mobile than the Engineering industry.

Comparisons of relative mobility over time

Table 5.4 also enables us to compare the relative mobility of firms in the different time periods. It shows a greater degree of mobility for the Food and Engineering industries in sub-period 1 (1948-54) than in sub-period 2 (1954-60), in spite of the fact that there is less relative dispersion of opening sizes for both industries in the latter period. It is interesting to note that the Food industry shows greater relative stability in the second sub-period, even though in this industry, not only is the relative dispersion of initial sizes lower in this period, but also both the absolute and relative dispersion of growth are higher than in sub-period 1. Thus although the growth rates are more variable and the initial size ranks are more packed together in the period 1954-60, a smaller proportion of Food firms change their position in their respective size rankings than in the period 1948-54. In view of our previous discussion, this result is not surprising. A lower average growth rate in the second sub-period, or different distributions of growth by size in the two time periods, or both, would be able to account for the observed differences in relative mobility in the two periods.

As the variability of growth rates in the Clothing and Footwear industry in the period 1948-54 is substantially lower than in the period 1954-60, and the relative dispersion of initial sizes is much the same in both periods, it is not unexpected that relative mobility in this industry is greater in the latter period. It is also not surprising that for all the three industries there is greater mobility in the whole period (1948-60) than in either of the two sub-periods. Proportionately more firms are likely to change their position in the size ranking over a twelve-year period than over a six-year period.

Relative mobility of firms of different sizes. Table 5.5 below indicates the relative mobility of firms of different sizes in the three industries. First of all, it is worth noting that within each industry firms of different sizes appear more mobile than the firms in the industry as a whole. This suggests that, as is to be expected, most of the changes in size rankings in any industry occur among the firms which lie in a particular size group rather than among the firms which lie in different size groups. Large, medium-sized or small firms interchange ranks much more within their own size groups than between other size groups.

Secondly, we may note that, generally speaking, relative mobility declines with size, but not uniformly. Although the largest firms are on the whole less mobile than the medium-sized or the small firm, the very largest firms are not always relatively more stable. For instance, in the Engineering industry the 10 largest firms, exhibit much greater mobility over the period 1948-60 than the 14 largest firms (each of which had initial assets of greater than £4 millions) or the firms with initial assets of greater than £2 million. It is possible that the observed greater relative stability of the large firms is due to the 'spurious element' mentioned earlier. Large firms are likely to have more dispersed initial sizes than the medium-sized or small firms. But the lower variance of growth rates for larger firms, and at least the casual observation of other characteristics of the joint distribution of growth and size for firms in different size classes, do not warrant the interpretation that the lower relative mobility of the larger firms is entirely due to their being initially more 'spread out' in size.

Thirdly, it is interesting to note that, whereas the relative mobility is highest in the Clothing and Footwear industry, followed in that order by the Food and Engineering industries, the pattern is exactly the reverse when only the largest firms are considered.

Mobility of largest firms: all industries together

Tables 5.6a, 5.6b and 5.6c show how the very largest firms in all industries taken together (including the Tobacco industry) have changed their size ranks over sub-period 1 (1948-54) and sub-period 2 (1954-60). The thirty-two largest firms, in Table 5.6a, each had net assets of greater than 4 million pounds in 1948. In Table 5.6b, 28 of the 32 largest firms which continued over the period 1954-60, had net assets of greater than 8 million pounds in 1954. In Table 5.6c, each of the 60 largest firms had net assets of greater than 4 million pounds in 1954.

The bivariate frequency distributions of opening and closing size ranks show in an intuitive way how immobile the very largest firms tended to be in size rankings over time. They also show that, as far as the largest firms were concerned, there was greater relative mobility in sub-period 2 (1954-60) than in sub-period 1 (1948-54).[1]

104

Table 5.5. Kendall's rank correlation coefficients between opening size ranks and closing size ranks for firms of different sizes*

	Sub-Period 1 (1948-54)			Sub-Period 2 (1954-60)			Whole Period (1948-60)		
	Ind.04 Engineering	Ind.12 Food	Ind.11 Clothing and Footwear	Ind.04 Engineering	Ind.12 Food	Ind.11 Clothing and Footwear	Ind.04 Engineering	Ind.12 Food	Ind.11 Clothing and Footwear
All firms	.818	.796	.793	.837	.811	.771	.725	.717	.693
10 largest firms	.644	.644	.778	.644	.733	.733	.289	.511	.733
Firms > 4 million	.736	.744	-	.541	.789	-	.604	.667	-
" > 2 million	.692	.787	-	.657	.714	-	.501	.614	-
" > 1 million	-	-	.869	-	-	.833	-	-	.744
" > 500,000-<2 million	.585	.667	-	.595	.497	-	.599	.276	-
" > 500,000-<1 million	-	-	.413	-	-	.458	-	-	.138
" < 500,000	.601	.517	.663	.655	.434	.540	.463	.293	.515
" < 250,000	.565	.402	.512	.536	.218	.523	.483	-.042	.356

* In the Food and Engineering industries, firms with net assets of more than £2 millions may be regarded as the 'large firms', firms with net assets lying between £500,000 and £2 million may be regarded as the 'medium-sized firms', and firms with net assets below £500,000 way be regarded as 'small firms'. In the Clothing and Footwear industry, where the average opening size is appreciably smaller than in the other two industries, firms with net assets of more than a million pounds are regarded as the 'large firms', firms with net assets lying between £500,000 and £1 million are regarded as the 'medium sized' firms and firms with assets below £500,000 are regarded as the small firms. There is a further breakdown of large firms and small firms in the above table.

Table 5.6. Distribution of opening size ranks by closing size ranks for the largest firms in all industries combined

Table 5.6a. Top 32 continuing companies: sub-period 1 (1948-54)*

Rank in 1948	Rank in 1954					
	1-8	9-16	17-24	25-32	>32	Total
1 - 8	6	2	-	-	-	8
9 - 16	2	3	2	1	-	8
17 - 24	-	3	4	1	-	8
25 - 32	-	-	2	2	4	8
Total	8	8	8	·4	4	32

* Coefficient of Rank Correlation between Opening and Closing Size Ranks = .738.

Table 5.6b. Top 32 continuing companies: sub-period 2 (1954-60)*

Rank in 1954	Rank in 1960					
	1-8	9-16	17-24	25-32	>32	Total
1 - 8	6	2	-	-	-	8
9 - 16	2	3	3	-	-	8
17 - 24	-	1	3	3	1	8
25 - 32	-	2	-	2	4	8
Total	8	8	6	5	5	32

* Coefficient of Rank Correlation between Opening and Closing Size Ranks = .633.

Table 5.6c. Top 60 continuing companies: sub-period 2 (1954-60)*

Rank in 1954 \ Rank in 1960	1-8	9-16	17-24	25-32	33-40	41-48	49-56	57-60	>60	Total
1 - 8	6	2	-	-	-	-	-	-	-	8
9 - 16	2	3	3	-	-	-	-	-	-	8
17 - 24	-	1	3	3	-	1	-	-	-	8
25 - 32	-	2	-	2	2	1	1	-	-	8
33 - 40	-	-	-	-	2	1	1	2	2	8
41 - 48	-	-	1	1	1	-	2	2	1	8
49 - 56	-	-	-	-	3	1	1	-	3	8
57 - 60	-	-	-	-	-	1	-	-	3	4
Total	8	8	7	6	8	5	5	4	9	60

*   Coefficient of Rank Correlation between Opening and
      Closing Size Ranks = .665.

3.   Persistency of growth

The purpose of this section is to find out whether the rate of growth of a firm's net assets in one 6-year period (1948-1954) is of any value in predicting the rate of growth in the next 6-year period (1954-1960), relative to that of other firms. If there were a direct correlation between the relative growth of companies in different periods, this would be a further refutation of the simple version of the Law of Proportionate Effect, which we tested in the preceding chapter.

The results of this section cannot be related directly to the recent work of Little and Rayner,[1] who have found that the relative growth of earnings per ordinary share shows little persistency between different periods. Growth of earnings per share is a totally different concept from growth of net assets.[2] However, it is interesting to test whether Little's discovery of apparent randomness in the temporal pattern of growth of earnings is part of a more general pattern of randomness in company growth.

Tables 5.7 and 5.8 show that there is a significant but not a strong relationship between relative growth rates of firms in the two periods. The regression analysis (Table 5.7) shows that growth in the first period gives a 2% explanation of the variance of growth in the second period ($r^2 = 0.02$) for the four industries together, and 11.5% ($r^2 = 0.115$) for the Non-Electrical Engineering industry. The parameter b, relating growth in sub-period 1 (1948-54) to growth in sub-period 2 (1954-60), is significant at a very high level (1%) in Engineering and at an acceptable level (5%) for the aggregate of all four industries, of which 60% are Engineering companies. The value of b (= 0.37) in Engineering indicates that a growth rate of 10 percentage points above average in the first sub-period tended to be associated with a growth rate 3.7 percentage points above average in the second sub-period. There is a non-significant negative value of b for the Clothing and Footwear industry, and an even less significant positive value for the Food industry.

The conclusion to be drawn from the regression analysis is, therefore, that, in the Engineering industry, there is a significant tendency for above-average growth of individual firms to persist throughout both sub-periods. In the other industries our analysis has shown no tendency for growth to breed growth. It should, however, be noted that even for the Engineering industry, this is no more than a tentative conclusion. Engineering is a large group composed of fairly homogeneous sub-groups such as Shipbuilding, and the apparent persistency of relative growth rates may be due to the persistency of high or low growth rates for such sub-groups, rather than for individual firms within these groups. This is investigated later.

Regression analysis is, however, a crude tool of analysis for the present purpose, for two reasons. Firstly, it is extremely sensitive to the effect of a few extreme values of the variables, which may contribute a large proportion of the variance from the mean even though they represent a minute proportion of the total number of observations. Secondly, the regression equations which we have fitted have all been linear ones, and there is no reason why the relationship between past

Table 5.7. Results of regression of growth (Indicator 4) in 1954-60 (Sub-period 2) on growth in 1948-54

Industry	a	b	r^2	number of companies
Clothing and Footwear (11)	6.48 ± 1.58	-0.26 ± 0.20	0.025	68
Food (12)	6.18 ± 1.63	0.07 ± 0.16	0.003	72
Non-electrical Engineering (04)	4.26 ± 0.86	0.37 ± 0.07	0.115	211
Total (including Tobacco)	5.77 ± 0.75	0.19 ± 0.07	0.022	357

Regression equation: $G_{t+1} = a + b\, G_t$

Where :
    a, b = constants
    G = growth (indicator 4)

Subscripts: t = sub-period 1 (1948-54)
    t+1 = sub-period 2 (1954-60)

Table 5.8. Kendall rank correlation coefficients of companies ranked by growth in 1948-54 and in 1954-60

Industry		r_k	number of companies
Clothing and Footwear	(11)	0.18***	70
Food	(12)	0.03	73
Non-electrical Engineering	(04)	0.25****	214
Tobacco	(14)	0.43*	7

r_k is the Kendall rank correlation coefficient.

*   Significantly different from zero at the 15% level.

**   Significantly different from zero at the 10% level.

***   Significantly different from zero at the 5% level.

****   Significantly different from zero at the 1% level.

(See Biometrika Tables for Statisticians, Volume I, edited by E.S. Pearson and H.O. Hartley, Cambridge University Press, 1954, pp. 87-89).

growth and future growth should follow this simple pattern. A more powerful test of the persistency of growth, which overcomes these two limitations for our purposes, is provided by rank correlation, which has already been described and used in section 2 of this chapter (see particularly note 1, page 103).

Kendall rank correlation coefficients, relating the rankings of companies by rate of growth for each of the two sub-periods, are given in Table 5.8. The rank correlation coefficient for the Food industry is not significantly different from zero, at an acceptable level of statistical significance. This indicates that companies which had an above average rank in terms of growth in the first sub-period (1948-54) did not tend to have a significantly higher-than-average ranking, of growth in the following sub-period (1954-60). The coefficient for Clothing and Footwear is significant at the 5% level, and that for Engineering is the highest and most significant (significant of 0.1%). This confirms the result of regression analysis that there is some persistency in the pattern of growth rates among Engineering firms. With respect to Food, it confirms the previous conclusion that there is little association between growth rates in the two periods. The result with respect to Clothing and Footwear reverses the earlier result. An insignificant negative association is replaced by a significant positive one. This is less surprising when the limitations of regression analysis described in the preceding paragraph, are borne in mind. There are two cases of extremely high growth in the second sub-period associated with negative growth in the first. These two observations carry great weight in the regression analysis and explain a large part of the difference between the results of regression and of rank correlation, in the case of the Clothing and Footwear industry.[1]

Table 5.9 extends the rank correlation analysis by dis-aggregation in two different ways. Firstly (sections (a) and (b)) the two industries which showed persistency of ranking by growth are split into their sub-groups to reveal whether the correlation was due to the effect of aggregating sub-industries which had persistently different growth rates. The third major industry, Food, is also split into sub-groups (section (c)) to discover whether the apparent lack of rank correlation between growth rates of different periods was due to the masking of correlation within sub-groups by the effects of aggregation.[2] Secondly (section (d)) the largest size class in each industry is tested for persistency of ranking by growth to see if the persistency was greater or less for the largest, and in terms of assets the most important, companies.

The results for industry sub-groups (sections (a), (b) and (c) of Table 5.9) do not suggest that the results previously reported were due merely to aggregation. In the case of the Engineering industry, only two of the five sub-groups have rank correlation coefficients which are not statistically significant at an acceptable level,[3] and one of these groups is extremely small (only six continuing companies).[4] For Clothing and Footwear, the rank correlation coefficient of the Clothing group is significant at the 15% level, but that for the small Footwear group is not, although it is slightly higher than that for the whole industry. In the Food industry, it appears that the low overall rank correlation coefficient is partly due to the fact that in some of the sub-groups,

110

there is a positive relationship between growth rates of firms in the two periods, and in the others there is a negative relationship. However, apart from Baking (sub-group 2), which is significant at the 10% level, the size of the rank correlation coefficients in the sub-groups is too small to indicate a significant association between the growth rates in the two periods.

The dis-aggregation by size class (Table 5.9, section (c)) shows no really significant deviations from the general industry pattern. The largest Engineering firms have highly significant positive rank correlation between growth in the two periods, very similar to that for the industry as a whole. For the Clothing and Footwear industry, the highest size class has a greater rank correlation between growth rates in the two periods than is the case for the whole industry, but the coefficient is obtained from only six observations and is not, therefore, very significant. The upper size classes of the Food industry show hardly any deviation from the pattern for the whole industry.

Our conclusion, therefore, is that the rate of growth of net assets of a firm, relative to that of other firms in the same industry, tended to persist to a significant extent between the two sub-periods in the Engineering industry and in the Clothing and Footwear industry, but not in the Food industry. Our tests on industry sub-groups do not suggest that the significant positive rank correlations of growth between periods in Engineering and in Clothing and Footwear are due merely to the effect of aggregating sub-groups which have persistently different growth rates. The tests on the upper size classes of various industries have shown that the persistency of growth rates within the largest size class is always similar to that in the industry as a whole.

On the other hand, although we have found a significant tendency for growth to persist between periods in two major industries, the actual degree of persistency was weak in these two industries and negligible in the third. Thus, we can refute the Law of Proportionate Effect which predicts that there will be no significant persistency of the relative growth of companies between different time periods, but we cannot draw the positive conclusion that relative growth in the first period could have been used to predict a substantial part of the pattern of relative growth of companies in the second period.

4.   Summary and conclusions

In this chapter two important aspects of the growth process of firms were investigated. First we discussed the question of internal size mobility, i.e. as firms grow, how much mixing or reordering takes place in the size ranks of surviving firms. A discussion of the theoretical issues involved showed that the amount of mobility in an industry is not simply a function of the mean and variance of either the growth or of size. In the general case, it depends in a complex way on the parameters of the joint distribution of growth and size.

The following main conclusions, regarding the relative mobility of firms in different industries and over different time periods, emerged:

Table 5.9. Kendall rank correlation coefficients of companies ranked by growth in 1948-54 and in 1954-60

		r_k	Number of companies
(a) Engineering sub-groups:			
Shipbuilding	(04.1)	0.22*	26
Machine tools	(04.2)	0.02	20
Textile machinery	(04.3)	0.07	6
Constructional Engineering	(04.4)	0.49***	13
Other	(04.5)	0.25****	149
(b) Clothing and Footwear sub-groups:			
Clothing	(11.1)	0.14*	54
Footwear	(11.2)	0.24	16
(c) Food sub-groups:			
Grain milling	(12.1)	-0.146	7
Baking	(12.2)	0.352**	15
Sugar	(12.3)	-0.167	4
Confectionery	(12.4)	-0.143	15
Fruit and Vegetable products	(12.5)	0.231	13
Other Food	(12.6)	0.123	19
(d) Upper size classes of various industries:			
Engineering:	> £2,000,000	0.29****	39
Clothing and Footwear:	> £2,000,000	0.47*	6
Food:	> £2,000,000	0.05	19

*   Significantly different from zero at the 15% level.

**   Significantly different from zero at the 10% level.

***   Significantly different from zero at the 5% level.

****   Significantly different from zero at the 1% level.

(a) Relative mobility is greatest in the Clothing and Footwear industry (which is the slowest-growing industry and has the fewest really large firms), followed in that order by Food and Non-electrical Engineering. The same pattern of relative mobility is observed for the two six year sub-periods and for the whole period (1948-60).

(b) The comparisons of relative mobility over time showed that for the Food and Engineering industries, relative mobility was greater in the first sub-period (1948-54) than in the second sub-period (1954-60) in spite of the fact that the variability of proportionate growth rates and relative variability of initial sizes was greater in these industries in the latter period. In the Clothing and Footwear industry on the other hand, relative mobility was greater in the period 1954-60.

(c) Generally speaking, the relative mobility of firms declines with size, although by no means uniformly. The larger firms are, on the whole, more likely to maintain their rank in the size distribution than the smaller-sized firms. However, the comparison between industries of the relative mobility of the largest firms reveals an entirely different pattern from that observed previously. The largest firms are consistently the least mobile in the Clothing and Footwear industry, followed in that order by the Food and Engineering industries.

As this study is confined to only three major industries, these conclusions with respect to relative mobility are only of limited practical interest. Our main purpose here has been to explore the methodological problems involved in the measurement of relative mobility in a way which is meaningful from an economic point of view. When, in subsequent work, this study is extended to the rest of the industries, we shall be in a position to generalize which type of industry is most mobile and what type of economic environment leads to the greatest degree of mobility. The question of 'external' mobility (i.e. the entry of new firms) which is just as important in studying industrial structures as internal mobility in the size ranks of continuing firms, will also be taken up in subsequent work.

The second aspect of the growth of firms discussed in this chapter is the question of persistency of growth rates, i.e. whether firms which have a high (or low) rate of growth in one period also tend to have a high (or low) growth rate in subsequent periods. Our main conclusion on this point is that there is a significant tendency for growth rates to persist in the Engineering, Tobacco and Clothing and Footwear industries, but not in the Food industry. We also found that there is no tendency for the largest firms in each industry to show a different persistency of growth from that observed for the industry as a whole.

These findings contradict an important implication of the Law of Proportionate Effect. Since growth is found to be a systematic function of past growth in two of the three major industry groups, it cannot be regarded as a purely random process. Secondly, although our conclusions, for reasons indicated earlier, do not relate directly to the recent work of Little and Rayner, it seems that growth is somewhat less higgledy-piggledy when measured in terms of net assets. On the other hand, even in the two major industries for which we discovered a significant persistency of growth between periods, the actual degree of persistency was very low.

6   Size and Profitability, and Persistency of Profitability

The object of this Chapter is to find out to what extent the two measures of profitability used in this study[1] are related, firstly to size and secondly to their own values in an earlier period. The first aspect has important implications for the theory of the firm, since it should show whether there is an optimal size of the firm in the sense of achieving maximum profitability.[2] The second aspect is particularly important for investment analysis since it shows how far past profitability can be regarded as an indicator of future profitability.

1.   Size and profitability

The relationship between size and profitability is an important one in the theory of the firm. If profitability increases on average with the size of the firm, this suggests that profitability is not constrained by size; in fact, in this case it is a positive inducement to future growth. If profitability does not vary systematically with size, it will not be a constraint on future growth, but neither will it then be a positive inducement to growth. In this case, however, we must not only consider the average profitability of firms of different size classes, but also its dispersion. The reason for this has already been considered in the context of growth in Chapter 4. Briefly, the argument is that large firms are usually diversified enough to operate in different product and geographical markets. They are, therefore, likely to display much less variability in their profits since each is in a position to offset abnormal losses in some areas of activity against abnormal profits in others. If this is the case, the greater certainty of the profits of large firms may make greater size more attractive, although the average profits are no greater. A priori, therefore, we would expect that a constant average profitability but a lower variability of profitability with respect to size would provide an inducement for firm to grow to a larger size. If average profitability declined with respect to size, this would provide a disincentive to future growth, but it would have to be offset against any tendency for profits to be more certain for larger firms, on the assumption that certainty is preferred to risk.

The analysis which follows is conducted largely on an industry basis. This is necessary for three reasons. First, it is quite probable that economies of scale[3] and monopoly power exist to different degrees in different industries, so that the most profitable size of the firm varies between industries. Secondly, the relative prosperity of different industries varies in different periods because of demand conditions which are independent of the size of the firms in the industry, so that aggregation of industries of varying degrees of prosperity can lead to a spurious relationship between size and profitability. Thirdly, the

114

errors in measurement of rates of return arising out of different depreciation and asset valuation conventions are likely to be greater between industries than between firms in the same industry.

It may be appropriate at this stage to recall the fundamental limitations of our rate of return measures, as described in Chapter 2 and in Appendices A and C. The greatest of these by far is the method of valuation of fixed assets, which varies between companies. Fixed assets are not only a major element in determining the denominator of a rate of return, but also affect the numerator, since depreciation is a charge against profits. If fixed assets are under-valued, the depreciation charge is low, and the numerator (a measure of post-depreciation profits) is large, whereas the denominator (an asset measure) is low. Thus the two biases reinforce one another, causing under-valuation of assets to inflate the rate of return and over-valuation to deflate it. It is impossible to quantify the effect of different methods of valuation on the rates of return of individual firms, but two of the main potential sources of bias can be examined. Firstly, revaluations of fixed assets will reduce rates of return below what they would otherwise be, and a later section will consider the extent to which the incidence of revaluation varies with the size of companies in our population. Secondly, it is clear that in a period of continuous inflation, a company with older assets is likely to under-value most, if it uses the customary historic cost method. The companies with older assets are likely to be those which grow at a slower rate. It is therefore fortunate for the present analysis that growth was not found to be a function of size. Otherwise the companies in the fastest growing size classes would tend to have a downward bias in their rates of return.[1]

2.   Distribution of rates of return by size classes

(a) Comparison of average rates of return on net assets between size classes

The simplest way of looking at the relationship between size and profitability is to compare the average profitability of firms in different size classes. Table 6.1, 6.2 and 6.3 show the means and standard deviations of Rate of Return on Net Assets for different opening size classes. Table 6.4 shows the ratio of the sum of the means of the lowest two size classes to the sum of the means of the highest two size classes. It is intended to provide a rough indication of the general trend of average profit rates in relation to size.

Table 6.1 shows that between 1948 and 1954 the average rate of return on net assets tended to decline with the size of firms in the largest industry, Engineering, and in all industries taken together, although the 'all industries' result is of dubious significance since it could arise from the effects of aggregation. The results for the other two industries, Clothing and Footwear, and Food, show no systematic tendency for profitability to vary with firm size, although Table 4 shows that the lower two size classes taken together were considerably more profitable than the highest two size classes in these industries, the smaller firms being roughly 18% more profitable in Clothing and Footwear (the

Table 6.1 Rate of Return [Net Assets] (Indicator 5) by Opening Size class (Indicator 1)

Sub-Period 1: 1948-1954

Industry / Opening Size	Clothing and Footwear			Food			Engineering			All (including Tobacco)		
	n	m	s	n	m	s	n	m	s	n	m	s
1 <£ 250,000	31	16.9	14.2	32	23.6	17.7	51	25.5	12.0	117	22.3	14.8
2 <£ 500,000	19	20.4	13.5	29	18.4	9.9	55	22.7	10.3	103	21.1	10.9
3 <£1.000,000	20	15.1	8.2	13	20.2	16.4	68	23.2	15.5	102	21.2	14.6
4 <£2,000,000	9	16.1	5.3	11	18.6	4.8	45	22.7	9.1	67	20.6	8.6
5 >£2,000,000	7	15.6	5.1	23	18.4	7.0	40	21.7	7.8	75	19.8	7.4
All companies	86	17.1	11.5	108	20.2	12.8	259	23.3	11.7	464	21.2	12.5

n = number of companies   m = arithmetic mean of Rate of Return [Net Assets] (% per annum)
s = standard deviation, corrected for degrees of freedom

Welch-Aspin Test

Significant differences between means, at the 10% level

Industry groups	Size classes significantly different
Industry 11, Clothing and Footwear	: None
Industry 12, Food	: None
Industry 04, Engineering	: 1 > 5
All four industries, including Tobacco	: None

Each pair of means was tested for each industry grouping, making a total of 10 tests for each group.

Table 6.2 Rate of Return [Net Assets] (Indicator 5) by Opening Size class (Indicator 1)

Sub-Period 2: 1954–1960

Industry / Opening Size	Clothing and Footwear			Food			Engineering			All (including Tobacco)		
	n	m	s	n	m	s	n	m	s	n	m	s
1 < £ 250,000	18*	10.7	13.0	16	11.2	11.5	30	18.9	10.9	64*	14.7	12.2
2 < £ 500,000	16	14.7	14.0	24	14.7	8.5	39	18.6	11.0	79	16.6	11.1
3 < £1,000,000	26	15.7	9.1	13	16.6	7.4	55	18.2	8.9	94	17.3	8.8
4 < £2,000,000	10	15.4	7.9	16	18.5	12.1	53	17.4	8.1	81	17.0	9.1
5 > £2,000,000	8	15.1	3.6	22	18.4	6.0	85	18.4	8.8	120	17.9	8.1
All companies	78*	14.2	10.7	91	15.9	9.4	262	18.3	9.2	438*	16.9	9.7

* excluding one company with negative denominator

n = number of companies   m = arithmetic mean of Rate of Return [Net Assets] (% per annum)

s = standard deviation, corrected for degrees of freedom.

Welch–Aspin Test

Significant differences between means, at the 10% level

Industry groups	Size classes significantly different
Industry 11, Clothing and Footwear	: None
Industry 12, Food	: 1 < 4, 1 < 5, 2 < 5.
Industry 04, Engineering	: None
All four industries, including Tobacco	: None

Each pair of means was tested for each industry grouping, making a total of 10 tests for each group.

Table 6.3 Rate of Return [Net Assets] (Indicator 5) by Opening Size class (Indicator 1)

Whole Period: 1948-1960

Industry / Opening Size	Clothing and Footwear			Food			Engineering			All (including Tobacco)		
	n	m	s	n	m	s	n	m	s	n	m	s
1 <£ 250,000	23	12.6	11.6	20	19.1	9.1	39	23.3	9.7	82	19.3	11.0
2 <£ 500,000	16	18.7	11.0	19	14.4	7.2	41	19.4	8.1	76	18.0	8.8
3 <£1,000,000	18	13.7	6.8	8	16.3	11.2	55	20.7	10.4	82	18.6	10.1
4 <£2,000,000	7	14.4	5.5	7	21.4	6.8	40	20.8	9.3	55	19.7	9.1
5 >£2,000,000	6	15.5	4.1	19	18.5	5.8	39	17.3	6.0	69	17.2	5.8
All companies	70	14.7	9.5	73	17.6	8.0	214	20.3	9.1	364	18.5	9.2

n = number of companies   m = arithmetic mean of Rate of Return [Net Assets] (% per annum)
s = standard deviation, corrected for degrees of freedom.

Welch-Aspin Test

Significant differences between means, at the 10% level

Industry groups	Size classes significantly different
Industry 11, Clothing and Footwear	: None
Industry 12, Food	: 1 > 2, 2 < 4, 2 < 5
Industry 04, Engineering	: 1 > 2, 1 > 5, 3 > 5, 4 > 5
All four industries, including Tobacco	: 4 > 5.

Each pair of means was tested for each industry grouping, making a total of 10 tests for each group.

value of the ratio being 1.18) and 14% in Food. The results of the Welch-Aspin test (Table 6.1) do not suggest that the differences between the means are significant, although it must be remembered that this test relies on the assumption of a normal distribution of the variables, which may not hold for some of the comparisons,[1] in the present case.

In the second sub-period, 1954 to 1960 (Table 6.2) profitability increases with the size of firm in the Food industry, and, to a lesser extent, in the Clothing and Footwear industry. Engineering, on the other hand, shows very small variations in profitability with respect to size, but the tendency is for profits to decline with size. These results are confirmed by reference to Table 6.4. The Welch-Aspin test suggests that the increase in profitability with respect to size in the Food industry is significant at the 5 per cent level, but the differences in the other two industries are not usually statistically significant.

Tables 6.3 and 6.4 show that the pattern of average profitability with respect to the opening size of companies continuing over the whole period 1948-60, is broadly consistent with that for the two sub-periods, there being no obvious systematic trend which holds for each major industrial group.

Our preliminary conclusion as to changes in average profitability with respect to the size of the firm must, therefore, be negative. There is no systematic tendency for average profitability to increase or decrease as the size of firm changes, and such variations as we have observed are not statistically significant.

(b) Comparison of dispersion of rates of return on net assets within different size classes

The dispersion of profitability within size classes is expressed by the standard deviations in Tables 6.1, 6.2 and 6.3. Table 6.1 shows that, in the period 1948-1954 (sub-period 1), there was a tendency for the degree of dispersion of profit rates to decline with the size of firms. This is the case in each industry group, although the tendency is consistent between all size classes only in the Clothing and Footwear industry. The crude significance test used in Chapter 4[2] suggests that the variances differ significantly between classes, at the 5% level, for each industry group.

The dispersion of rates of return also declines with size in the second sub-period (Table 6.2). There are exceptions, notably the second-largest size class in the Food industry, but, in general, the standard deviations are lowest in the higher size classes. The significance test suggests that these variations are significant at the 5% level, except in the Engineering industry.[3] Table 6.3 shows a similar tendency for the dispersion of profit rates to decline with the size of firms in the full period (1948-1960).

(c) Post-tax rate of return of equity assets

The analysis of profitability by size classes was repeated, using Post-tax Rate of Return on Equity Assets instead of Rate of Return on Net Assets. In general, the pattern of means and the standard deviations of Post-tax Rate of Return on Equity Assets with respect to opening size was very similar to that of Rate of Return on Net Assets. The Welch-Aspin test and the test of heterogeneity of variance also yielded very similar results. The only systematic difference between the distributions of the two rates of return was a tendency for the mean of Post-tax Rate of Return on Equity Assets to be relatively higher in the larger size classes. The reasons for this are examined in the next section, where the regression results indicate a similar pattern. Table 6.5 gives the means and standard deviations of Post-tax Rate of Return on Equity assets for different size classes. Only the aggregate figures for the four industries are given, because, apart from the difference just mentioned, the detailed results are otherwise very similar to those for the Rate of Return on Net Assets.

3.   Regression analysis

A further way of investigating the relationship between size and profitability is by the regression of profitability on size. The zero-order correlation coefficients presented in Chapter 3 showed little relationship between size and profitability, irrespective of which measure of profitability was used. However, as noted in the earlier discussion of this point, the low values of the simple correlation coefficients could be due to the fact that there is a non-linear relationship between size and profitability, or due to the disproportionate effect of particular kinds of observations (e.g. relating to non-profitable firms). These possibilities are investigated in this section by fitting a number of different regression models to various populations of firms. Two populations of companies were used for this purpose. One, referred to as the full population, consisted of all companies except the very small number which had negative opening net assets or average equity assets. The second, referred to as the log population, excluded companies with negative values for any of the first six indicators,[1] so that logarithmic transformations of the variables could be made.

The first regression equation tested was of the simple form;

$$P = a + b S + \epsilon \tag{1}$$

where;   P = Rate of Return on Net Assets

S = Opening Size

E = Error term

a, b = Parameters.

This is the linear form implicit in the simple zero-order correlations previously calculated. It postulates that profitability changes by a fixed amount (measured in percentage points) for any given change in size, e.g. if the coefficient b = 0.01, the rate of return on net assets increases by 1 per cent as opening size increases by £100,000. The results of fitting this equation to the full population are given in Table 6.6. It will be seen that only one of these results (for Engineering for 1948 to 1960) includes a statistically significant value of the regression coefficient b, relating Opening Size to Rate of Return, and that the degree

Table 6.4 Rate of return on net assets

Ratios of the sums of means of the lowest two size classes to the sums of means of the highest two size classes

	Industry 11 Clothing and Footwear	Industry 12 Food	Industry 04 Engineering	All four industries incl.tobacco
Sub-Period 1, (1948-1954)	1.18	1.14	1.09	1.07
Sub-Period 2, (1954-1960)	0.83	0.70	1.05	0.90
Whole Period, (1948-1960)	1.05	0.84	1.12	1.01

Table 6.5 Post-tax rate of return [equity assets]
(Indicator 6) by opening size class (Indicator 1)

All four industries, including Tobacco [industries 04+11+12+14]

Opening Size	Sub-period 1, 1948-1954			Sub-period 2, 1954-1960			Whole Period, 1948-1960		
	n	m	s	n	m	s	n	m	s
1 <£250,000	116[a]	10.5	12.6	63[b]	7.4	9.8	80[b]	9.8	5.7
2 <£500,000	103	9.9	6.4	79	8.5	7.2	76	8.6	6.1
3 <£1,000,000	102	9.8	9.3	93	9.6	5.1	82	9.1	8.1
4 <£2,000,000	67	10.1	5.1	80[a]	9.3	5.8	55	9.3	10.8
5 >£2,000,000	75	10.1	3.7	120	10.1	4.8	69	9.4	3.3
All companies	463[a]	10.1	8.6	435[c]	9.2	6.5	362[b]	9.2	7.0

[a]excluding one company with negative denominator

[b]excluding two companies with negative denominators

[c]excluding three companies with negative denominators

n = number of companies

m = arithmetic mean of Post-tax Rate of Return on Equity Assets

s = standard deviation of Post-tax Rate of Return on Equity Assets

Table 6.6. Regression results

<u>Equation</u>: Rate of Return [Net Assets] = Constant + b. Opening size.
Where Rate of Return is expressed in percentage points
and Size in £'000's.

Full population

	r^2	a(constant term)	b(regression coefficient)
Sub-Period 1; 1948-54			
Industry 11, Clothing and Footwear	0.01	17.81($\pm$1.36)*	-0.00069($\pm$0.00066)
Industry 12, Food	0.01	20.79($\pm$1.36)*	-0.00033($\pm$0.00030)
Industry 04, Non-Electrical Engineering	0.01	23.73($\pm$0.77)*	-0.00031($\pm$0.00019)
All four industries (including Tobacco), Industries 04+11+12+14	0.00	21.39($\pm$0.58)*	-0.00012($\pm$0.00009)
Sub-Period 2; 1954-60			
Industry 11, Clothing and Footwear	0.00	14.05($\pm$1.35)*	0.00025($\pm$0.00047)
Industry 12, Food	0.00	15.99($\pm$1.09)*	0.00005($\pm$0.00013)
Industry 04, Non-Electrical Engineering	0.01	18.81($\pm$0.60)*	-0.00014($\pm$0.00008)
All four industries (including Tobacco), Industries 04+11+12+14	0.00	17.23($\pm$0.47)*	-0.00003($\pm$0.00004)
Whole Period; 1948-60			
Industry 11, Clothing and Footwear	0.00	17.20($\pm$2.09)*	-0.00033($\pm$0.00093)
Industry 12, Food	0.01	17.96($\pm$1.06)*	-0.00013($\pm$0.00019)
Industry 04, Non-Electrical Engineering	0.02	20.85($\pm$0.65)*	-0.00030($\pm$0.00014)*
All four industries (including Tobacco), Industries 04+11+12+14	0.00	19.20($\pm$0.57)*	-0.00010($\pm$0.00008)

*   Significant at the 5% level

of explanation of Rate of Return by Size (represented by r^2) is very low. Nevertheless, it is significant that fourteen out of the sixteen values of b in the table are negative, indicating that profitability tended to decline slightly with size.

Regression analysis on the restricted population of growing and profitable firms (log population)

Table 6.7 gives the results of fitting the same equation to the log population. This population is restricted to growing and profitable companies, and, since non-growing and unprofitable companies are mostly small, their exclusion leads to an upward bias in the average growth and profit rates of the smaller companies. This is discussed further at the end of this section of the chapter.

This table shows that the exclusion of unprofitable and shrinking companies improves the significance of the equation in almost every case, and all values of the regression coefficient, b, are now negative. Amongst the profitable and growing firms, the regression coefficient relating size to profitability is significant at the 5% level for the Engineering industry and for all industries together in all the three periods. In the case of Food and Clothing and Footwear, the coefficient 'b' is significant only for sub-period 1 (1948-54). As an illustration of the quantitative significance of these results, a value of b equal to -0.00035 (as for Engineering in sub-period 1) means that if a firm A has an Opening Size £1,000,000 greater than that of another firm B, firm A's rate of return will be, on average, .35 percentage points lower than that of B. It must be noted that although the regression coefficient for this equation is significant for a number of different populations, the proportion of inter-firm variation explained by the equation is rather small because other factors are powerful and variable.[1]

The next stage of our analysis was to fit a semi-logarithmic equation of the form:

$$P = a + b \log_e S + \epsilon \tag{2}$$

The results of this, for the log populations, appear in Table 8. This equation tests the hypothesis that a given <u>proportionate</u> change in opening size causes the same <u>absolute</u> change in the Rate of Return for all sizes of firm.

It will be seen that in most cases the degree of explanation of the variance of Rate of Return (represented by r^2) is higher, and that the regression coefficient (b) is more significant, than was the case of the simple linear equation of Table 6.2. However, in the case of Clothing and Footwear (Industry 11) and Food (Industry 12) in the second sub-period and for the whole period, the results remain insignificant, despite the fact that these industries yield the greatest degree of explanation (9% and 10%, respectively, i.e. $r^2 = 0.09$ and 0.10) in the first sub-period. Apart from these indeterminate cases, the logarithm of size seems to provide a better explanation of profitability than the absolute value of size. In other words, absolute changes in profitability tend to be a direct function of proportionate variations in opening size rather than the absolute amount of such variations. An example of the quantitative significance of the relationships given in Table 6.8 is that where the regression coefficient (b) is - 1.90 (as for All Industries, sub-period 1), doubling the opening size of the firm tends to reduce the average profit rate by 1.3 per cent per annum. Again, it must be noted that the degree of explanation provided by the equation is small.

Finally, a fully logarithmic equation was fitted;

$$\log_e P = a + b \log_e S + \epsilon \tag{3}$$

In contrast to the semi-log equation, this equation embodies the hypothesis that a given percentage change in size leads to the same percentage change in profitability at all levels of size and of profitability. The regression results are reported in Table 6.9.

This table shows that the regression coefficient is significant at the 5% in all the three periods for the Engineering industry and in sub-period 1 for the Clothing and Footwear industry and is negative in all cases except one. Although the goodness of fit of this double-logarithmic equation cannot be compared directly with that of the two previous equations in terms of R^2,[1] it appears that the semi-logarithmic equation provides the best explanation of profitability in terms of size. The semi-logarithmic equation provides significant regression coefficients for more of the populations of growing and profitable firms than do the other equations. However, to keep the relationship between size and profitability as revealed by this equation in its perspective, it must be remembered that the proportion of inter-firm variation in profitability explained by the semi-log equation is on an average about 2% in sub-period 2 (1954-60) and in the whole period (1948-60), and about 4% in the first sub-period.

The regression analysis was then extended by fitting the following three equations to both the full population and the log population

$$P = a + b S + c S^2 + \epsilon \tag{4}$$

$$P = a + b S + c S^2 + d S^3 + \epsilon \tag{5}$$

$$P = a + b S + c S^2 + d S^3 + e S^4 + \epsilon \tag{6}$$

The following additional logarithmic equation was fitted to the log population;[2]

$$P = a + b \log_e S + c (\log S)^2 + \epsilon \tag{7}$$

The object of testing these equations was to ascertain whether a more complex curvilinear relationship could be found which would give a better fit. However none of them yielded better results than the simple semi-logarithmic equation given in Table 6.8.

Regression analysis; size and post-tax profitability

The regression equations of Tables 6.1 to 6.4 were then repeated, substituting Post-tax Rate of Return on Equity Assets for Rate of Return on Net Assets. The results obtained showed that the relationship between Rate of Return on Equity Assets and Opening Size was similar,

124

Table 6.7. Regression results

Equation: Rate of Return [Net Assets] = Constant + b. Opening Size.
Where Rate of Return is expressed in percentage points,
and Size in £'000's.

Restricted population

	r^2	a(constant term)	b(regression coefficient)
Sub-Period 1; 1948-54			
Industry 11, Clothing and Footwear	0.06	21.57(±1.26)*	-0.00115(±0.00055)*
Industry 12, Food	0.04	23.83(±1.35)*	-0.00055(±0.00027)*
Industry 04, Non-Electrical Engineering	0.02	24.62(±0.74)*	-0.00035(±0.00017)*
All four industries (including Tobacco), Industries, 04+11+12+14	0.02	23.35(±0.56)*	-0.00017(±0.00008)*
Sub-Period 2; 1954-60			
Industry 11, Clothing and Footwear	0.01	18.29(±1.11)*	-0.00019(±0.00034)
Industry 12, Food	0.01	18.75(±0.99)*	-0.00008(±0.00010)
Industry 04, Non-Electrical Engineering	0.02	20.16(±0.57)*	-0.00019(±0.00008)*
All four industries (including Tobacco), Industries, 04+11+12+14	0.01	19.33(±0.43)*	-0.00007(±0.00004)*
Whole Period; 1948-60			
Industry 11, Clothing and Footwear	0.01	19.11(±2.25)*	-0.00056(±0.00094)
Industry 12, Food	0.03	19.29(±0.97)*	-0.00023(±0.00017)
Industry 04, Non-Electrical Engineering	0.02	21.35(±0.64)*	-0.00032(±0.00014)*
All four industries (including Tobacco), Industries, 04+11+12+14	0.01	20.15(±0.56)	-0.00012(±0.00007)*

*   Significant at the 5% level.

Table 6.8. Regression results

Equation: Rate of Return(Net Assets) = Constant b.Log_e Opening Size. Where Rate of Return is expressed in percentage points, and Size in £'000's.

Restricted population

	r^2	a(constant term)	b(regression coefficient)
Sub-Period 1; 1948-54			
Industry 11, Clothing and Footwear	0.09	36.64(±6.24)*	-2.66(±1.01)*
Industry 12, Food	0.10	39.48(±5.48)*	-2.58(±0.82)*
Industry 04, Non-Electrical Engineering	0.03	34.79(±3.94)*	-1.65(±0.60)*
All four industries (including Tobacco), Industries 04+11+12+14	0.05	35.27(±2.73)*	-1.90(±0.41)*
Sub-Period 2; 1954-60			
Industry 11, Clothing and Footwear	0.02	23.95(±5.56)*	-0.92(±0.85)
Industry 12, Food	0.00	16.93(±4.11)*	0.20(±0.56)
Industry 04, Non-Electrical Engineering	0.03	28.10(±3.05)*	-1.20(±0.42)*
All four industries (including Tobacco), Industries 04+11+12+14	0.01	24.01(±2.16)*	-0.72(±0.30)*
Whole Period; 1948-60			
Industry 11, Clothing and Footwear	0.00	24.60(±11.48)*	-0.99(±1.84)
Industry 12, Food	0.01	21.85(±3.86)*	-0.48(±0.56)
Industry 04, Non-Electrical Engineering	0.04	30.39(±3.30)*	-1.46(±0.49)*
All four industries (including Tobacco), Industries 04+11+12+14	0.02	26.91(±2.74)*	-1.07(±0.41)*

*   Significant at the 5% level

Table 6.9. Regression results

Equation: $\text{Log}_e \dfrac{\text{Rate of Return[Net Assets]}}{\text{Opening Size}} = \text{Constant} + b.\text{Log}_e \text{Opening Size}$

Restricted population

	r^2	a(constant term)	b(regression coefficient)
Sub-Period 1; 1948-54			
Industry 11, Clothing and Footwear	0.07	6.02($\pm$0.36)*	-0.13($\pm$0.06)*
Industry 12, Food	0.04	5.79($\pm$0.26)*	-0.08($\pm$0.04)
Industry 04, Non-Electrical Engineering	0.02	5.76($\pm$0.16)*	-0.06($\pm$0.02)*
All four industries (including Tobacco), Industries, 04+11+12+14	0.03	5.76($\pm$0.12)*	-0.07($\pm$0.02)*
Sub-Period 2; 1954-60			
Industry 11, Clothing and Footwear	0.01	5.36($\pm$0.31)*	-0.04($\pm$0.05)
Industry 12, Food	0.01	4.92($\pm$0.25)*	0.03($\pm$0.03)
Industry 04, Non-Electrical Engineering	0.03	5.68($\pm$0.19)*	-0.07($\pm$0.03)*
All four industries (including Tobacco), Industries 04+11+12+14	0.01	5.40($\pm$0.13)*	-0.04($\pm$0.02)
Whole Period; 1948-60			
Industry 11, Clothing and Footwear	0.01	5.39($\pm$0.38)*	-0.05($\pm$0.06)
Industry 12, Food	0.00	5.22($\pm$0.23)*	-0.01($\pm$0.03)
Industry 04, Non-Electrical Engineering	0.03	5.65($\pm$0.16)*	-0.06($\pm$0.02)*
All four industries (including Tobacco), Industries 04+11+12+14	0.01	5.46($\pm$0.12)*	-0.04($\pm$0.02)*

*   Significant at the 5% level

but less strong, than that between Rate of Return on Net Assets and Opening Size. The simple linear equation (1), yielded no values of the regression coefficient (b) which were significant at the 5% level, and only seven of the twelve coefficients were negative. The highest r^2 obtained was only 0.01.

For equation (1) on the log population all of the regression coefficients (b) were negative and were generally more significant than for the full equation, although only two (out of twelve) were significant at the 5% level. The highest r^2 obtained was 0.03. The semi-logarithmic form (equation (2)) again yielded the best results. These are given in Table 6.10. The highest r^2 was 0.08 and eleven out of twelve regression co-efficients were negative with five of them significant at the 5% level. An idea of the orders of magnitude involved can be obtained from the fact that a value of the regression coefficient (b) of -5.9 (as for All Industries, sub-period 1) means that if firm A is twice as large as firm B, its Post-tax Rate of Return on Equity assets will, on average, be 0.4 percentage points lower than that of firm B.

We conclude, therefore, that for the population of growing and profitable firms the Rate of Return on Equity Assets is explained by Opening Size even less than the Rate of Return on Net Assets, although there seems again to be an inverse relationship between Size and Profitability. The reason for this must be in the differences between the two measures. The two main differences are that the Rate of Return on Equity Assets is post-tax, and that it is affected by gearing (i.e. it excludes fixed dividend and interest obligations from its numerator and the nominal value of preference shares and debentures from the denominator). Either or both of these factors could in principle account for the fact that the observed inverse relationship between size and post-tax profi-tability is less pronounced than that between size and pre-tax profita-bility.[1]

Comparison of regression results with earlier analysis of size and profitability

Finally, we must compare the results of the regression analysis of this section with those of the analysis of the preceding section. Both approaches yield the same result; that the average rate of profit is independent of the size of the firm if all companies are considered. This section has revealed, however, that the exclusion of non-growing and unprofitable firms gives rise to a weak, but statistically significant, tendency for profitability to decline with size, i.e., amongst growing and profitable firms, the smallest tend to have the highest rate of profit.

The reason for this is simply that non-growing and unprofitable firms tend to be smaller than average. Nine companies made losses in the first sub-period, fifteen in the second sub-period and nine in the whole period. In the first sub-period none of the companies which made losses had an opening size greater than £1,000,000. In the second sub-period and the whole period, none of the loss-making companies had an opening size of more that £2,000,000. Thus, the exclusion of loss-making companies would tend to increase the average rate of return of the lower size classes relative to the highest size class. It was shown

Table 6.10. Regression results

<u>Equation:</u> Equity Return = Constant + b. Log_e Opening Size
Rate of return is expressed in percentage points, and
size in £000's.

Restricted population

	r^2	a(constant term)	b(regression coefficient)
Sub-Period 1; 1948-54			
Industry 11, Clothing and Footwear	0.01	13.16(±3.06)	-0.49(±0.49)
Industry 12, Food	0.06	17.83(±2.65)	-0.99(±0.40)*
Industry 04, Non-Electrical Engineering	0.01	14.74(±1.84)	-0.48(±0.28)
All four industries (including Tobacco), industries 04+11+12+14	0.02	15.09(±1.29)	-0.59(±0.20)*
Sub-Period 2; 1954-60			
Industry 11, Clothing and Footwear	0.08	19.12(±3.77)	-1.32(±0.57)*
Industry 12, Food	0.01	9.03(±2.26)	0.21(±0.31)
Industry 04, Non-Electrical Engineering	0.02	13.95(±1.69)	-0.46(±0.23)*
All four industries (including Tobacco), industries 04+11+12+14	0.01	13.19(±1.24)	-0.37(±0.17)*
Whole Period; 1948-60			
Industry 11, Clothing and Footwear	0.00	9.82(±3.05)	-0.16(±0.49)
Industry 12, Food	0.00	14.58(±7.67)	-0.43(±1.12)
Industry 04, Non-Electrical Engineering	0.02	14.19(±1.70)	-0.52(±0.26)*
All four industries (including Tobacco), industries 04+11+12+14	0.06	12.91(±2.02)	-0.36(±0.30)

* Significant at the 5% level.

in Chapter 4 (Tables 4.7, 4.8 and 4.9) that non-growing companies are heavily concentrated in the lower size classes. Since growth has a strong positive correlation with profitability (as shown by the correlation coefficients in Chapter 3 and discussed at greater length in Chapter 7), the exclusion of negative growth would also remove a large number of low-profit firms from the lower size classes, thus reinforcing the tendency to raise the average profit rate of these size classes.

A final consideration concerning the relationship between size and profitability is the effect of revaluations. We have already shown in Chapter 4 (Table 4.11) that revaluation was more common in the larger companies. The effect of revaluation as explained in the first section of this chapter, is to introduce a downward bias into the rate of return. Furthermore, companies which revalued in earlier periods will have a larger opening size than they would otherwise have had. Thus, the incidence of revaluations may partly explain the tendency for larger firms to have lower rates of return. This is a further factor reducing the significance of those cases where we have found a statistically significant negative correlation between size and profitability and increasing the significance of those cases where we have found a tendency for profitability to increase with size, such as the Food industry between 1954 and 1960.

4.   The 'best' size of the firm for profitability and for growth

In section 2, we examined the size distribution of rates of return (Tables 6.1-6.4) to see how the latter vary with the size of the firm. Another interesting way of looking at Tables 6.1 to 6.4 is to try to find what is the 'best' size of the firm which achieves maximum profitability. It is also interesting to compare the 'best' size of the firm for profitability with the 'best' size from the point of view of achieving maximum growth as revealed by Tables 4.1 to 4.3. Table 6.11 summarizes this information for sub-period 1 (1948-54) and sub-period 2 (1954-60).

The table shows that as far as pre-tax profitability is concerned the smallest size classes tend to have the highest rates of return in sub-period 1. Post-tax profitability on equity is also highest in the smallest size classes for Food and Engineering, but it is highest in the largest size class in Clothing and Footwear.

In sub-period 2 (1954-60), we find that in Engineering, the maximum pre-tax profitability still occurs in the lowest size class. However, it is now the medium-sized firms which achieve the highest rate of return on net assets in Food and in Clothing and Footwear. As far as post-tax profitability on equity is concerned, the highest rates are achieved by the largest firms (with book value of opening net assets of greater than £2 million) both in Clothing and Footwear and in Engineering. In the Food industry, where it is still the medium-sized firms which show maximum post-tax profitability, it is interesting to note that the post-tax profitability of the largest firms is only slightly less (10.8% as against 10.9%).

130

Thus we find that in the period (1954-60), the 'best' size of firm from the point of view of post-tax profitability on equity is usually the largest size class whereas from the point of view of pre-tax profitability it is the small or medium-sized firm.[1] In this context, it must be noted that although the average pre-tax rate of return is highest in the smaller firms, its dispersion tends to be greater for these firms than for the larger firms. As was argued in section 1, the small or medium size may not, therefore, be the 'optimum' one. On the other hand, as far as post-tax profitability on equity assets is concerned the large size <u>is</u> likely to be the optimum one since for this size, the average return is higher and the dispersion is lower.[2]

It is interesting to note that from the point of view of growth, the best 'size' is almost always the large one. To the extent that the large firms also tend on the whole to have a lower dispersion of growth rates; it would also be the 'optimum' size, as defined in the first section of this Chapter, as far as growth is concerned. For the period 1954-60, as noted earlier, the post-tax rate of return also tends to be highest for the largest firms, but in sub-period 1 (1948-54) for the Food and Engineering industries we find that it is the smallest ($<250,000$) firms which achieve both the highest pre-tax and the highest post-tax profitability whereas it is the largest firms which achieve higher growth.

<u>Inter-industry similarities in the profitability and the growth of largest firms</u>

As a by-product of the investigation of Tables 6.1 to 6.4, we may note the interesting fact that the inter-industry differences in average pre-tax rates of return are much lower for the largest firms than for the smaller size classes. An examination of the size distribution of the post-tax rate of return on equity assets in the indivudual industries shows that the inter-industry differences in the average and the dispersion of post-tax profitability for the largest firms are almost negligible in <u>every period</u>. For instance, in the whole period (1948-60) the average post-tax profitability for the largest firms ($>£2$ million) was 9.6% in Clothing and Footwear, 10.6% in Food and 10.1% in Engineering. The corresponding figures for the average post-tax profitability for the smallest firms ($<£\frac{1}{4}$ million) in the three industries was as follows; Clothing and Footwear; 6.3%, Food; 9.9% and Non-Electrical Engineering; 11.6%. Similarly the standard deviation of post-tax profitability for the largest firms during this period was 3.1% in Clothing and Footwear, 3.5% in Food and 3.2% in Engineering.

Tables 4.1 to 4.3 show a similar picture of the rates of growth of the largest firms. The inter-industry differences in the average growth and its dispersion, for the largest firms, were negligible. These differences were also very small compared with the differences for firms of smaller size.

There are a number of <u>a priori</u> reasons which can account for the similarity in the growth and profitability experience of the largest firms in different industries. First, the large firms tend to be multiproduct firms with products straddling across different industries. This has already been suggested as a possible reason for the lower dispersion of

Table 6.11. 'Best' sizes* for profitability and growth

	'Best' Size for Rate of Return on Net Assets	'Best' Size for Post-Tax Rate of Return on Equity Assets	'Best' Size for Growth
Sub-Period 1; 1948-54			
Clothing and Footwear	$£\frac{1}{4}$ million to $£\frac{1}{2}$ million	$> £2$ million	$> £2$ million
Food	$> £\frac{1}{4}$ million	$< £\frac{1}{4}$ million	$> £2$ million
Engineering	$< £\frac{1}{4}$ million	$< £\frac{1}{4}$ million	$£1$ million to $£2$ million
Sub-Period 2; 1954-60			
Clothing and Footwear	$£\frac{1}{2}$ million to $£1$ million	$> £2$ million	$> £2$ million
Food	$£1$ million to $£2$ million	$£\frac{1}{2}$ million to $£1$ million	$> £2$ million
Engineering	$< £\frac{1}{4}$ million	$> £2$ million	$< £2$ million

*   The 'best' size is defined in terms of maximum average profitability of growth

profit and growth rates between large firms, relative to smaller firms, within the same industry.

Another possible reason is that large firms are relatively more subject to the discipline of the stock market. The zero-order correlation matrices in Chapter 3 showed that there was some evidence that large firms tend to raise a larger proportion of external finance than smaller firms. Furthermore, large firms have a more dispersed ownership of shares[1] so that, unlike family firms, they are more sensitive to the stock market's assessment of the value of their shares. From the investor's point of view what is important is not which industry a firm belongs to but the relative performance of the firm with respect to present and potential earnings. Therefore it would not be surprising to observe a relative similarity in the growth and profitability experience of large firms.[2]

However, we must note that our results so far pertain only to the three industries which we have examined here. It would be very interesting indeed, if the same results were obtained when our investigation is extended to other industries as well.

5.   Persistency of rates of return

In the last chapter we found that there was some tendency for the growth rates of firms to persist over time. In two of the three major industries (Engineering and Clothing and Footwear) there was statistically significant evidence that firms which had a relatively high (or low) rate of growth of net assets in the first sub-period, 1948-54, also tended to have a relatively high (or low) growth in the subsequent 6-year period 1954-60. We shall now examine the complementary question of the persistency of rates of return.

Is there any pattern in the profitability of firms over time? If profitability is to any degree a causal phenomenon, depending for instance on the quality of a firm's management, or on the monopoly power the firm enjoys or on both of these factors, we should expect to find some persistency in the profitability of firms over successive time-periods. Since there is usually some continuity of good managements and of monopoly power we should find that firms which have an above average profitability (relative to the other firms in the industry) in one period of six years will also have an above average profitability over at least a subsequent, comparatively short-run period of 6 years. On the other hand, it is quite possible that the profitability of a firm is a purely chance phenomenon and that, as is suggested by some writers, there is no such thing as a 'good' or 'bad' management.[3]

We shall test the validity of these propositions in this section by examining the relationship between the average rates of return on net assets (Indicator 5) in the periods 1948-54 and 1954-60 for the populations of firms which continued over the whole of the twelve-year period. We shall also see whether a different relationship between the rates of return in the two periods is obtained if instead of pre-tax profitability Indicator 5, the post-tax rate of return on equity assets (Indicator 6) is used. Lastly, we shall study the question of persistency of rates of return for the largest firms alone.

The relationship between the average rates of return on net assets (Indicator 5) in the two successive six-year periods for the three major industries is depicted in the scatter diagrams given in Figures 6.1-6.3. The results of the regression analysis (a simple linear regression model is fitted in each case) are summarized in Table 6.12. The regression results for the relationship between post-tax rates of return on equity assets (Indicator 6) in the two periods are given in Table 6.13.

The regression analysis shows that there is a fairly strong relationship between the rates of return in the two periods. For all industries together (including tobacco), the rate of return on net assets (Indicator 5) in sub-period 1 (1948-54) provides a 37% explanation of the inter-firm variation in the rates of return on net assets in sub-period 2 (1954-60). The regression coefficients are highly significant in each of the major industries and there is a particularly marked relationship in the large Engineering industry where the average rate of return on net assets in the period 1948-54, explains more than 50% of the variance of average rates of return in the period 1954-60. The scatter diagrams Figures 6.1-6.3 indicate that in Food and in Clothing and Footwear, the explanation provided would be higher if we had used a regression model which minimized the effect of certain extreme observations relating particularly to firms which were profitable in the first six year period, but unprofitable in the period 1954-60.

Table 6.13 shows similarly a strong persistency of the post-tax rates of return on equity assets (Indicator 6) in the Food industry, the Non-electrical Engineering industry and in all industries together. There is a slightly greater persistency of post-tax profitability than of pre-tax profitability in the case of the Food industry and a somewhat smaller persistency for the Engineering industry. However, in the case of Clothing and Footwear, both the coefficient of multiple correlation and the b coefficient are statistically insignificant at a high level implying that there is little relationship between the post-tax rates of return in the two periods. Nevertheless, in view of the fact that we have in each case fitted only a linear regression model, and that the regression analysis is rather sensitive to extreme values, this question must be investigated further.[1]

As explained in Chapter 5 the problems of extreme values, and those of possible non-linear relationship between the variables, are to a considerable extent ameliorated by the use of rank correlation analysis. The results of this analysis are given in Table 6.14. Kendall's co-efficients of rank correlation between the ranks of rates of return in the period (1948-54) and the corresponding ranks in the period (1954-60) are significantly different from zero at the 1% level in each of the major industries. Such high values of the rank correlation coefficient are most unlikely to arise purely from chance. For instance in the Clothing and Footwear industry, discussed above, the probability of getting a rank correlation coefficient of .32 between the post-tax rates of return in the two periods purely by chance, when in fact there is no relationship between the variables, is less than 1 in 100,000. We must therefore,

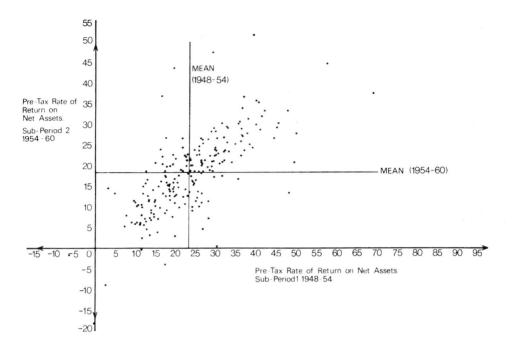

6.1.   Industry 04, Non-Electrical Engineering. Number of companies = 214

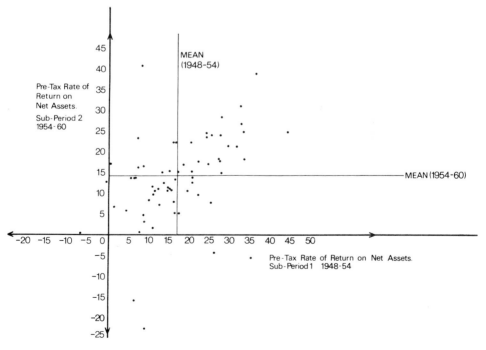

6.2.   Industry 11, Clothing and Footwear. Number of companies = 68

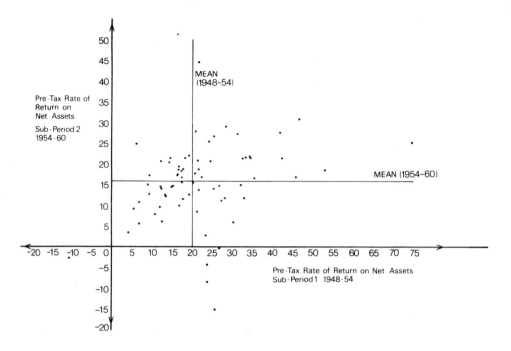

6.3.   Industry 12, Food. Number of companies = 72

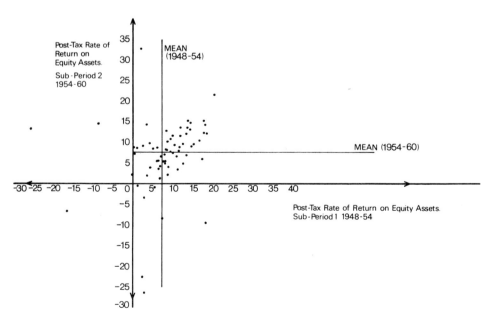

6.4.   Industry 11, Clothing and Footwear. Number of companies
= 68

Table 6.12. Results of regressions of rate of return [net assets] in sub-period 2, 1954-60 on rate of return [net assets] in sub-period 1, 1948-54.

Industry	a	b	r^2	Number of companies
11 Clothing and Footwear	5.64 ± 2.32	0.44 ± 0.11	0.18	68
12 Food	9.93 ± 1.93	0.26 ± 0.08	0.14	72
04 Engineering	3.96 ± 1.03	0.58 ± 0.04	0.53	211
All four industries, including Tobacco	5.52 ± 0.87	0.49 ± 0.03	0.37	357

Regression equation;

$$P_{t+1} = a + b\,P_t + \epsilon$$

where: a, b are constant, ϵ is the random error term.

p = profitability on net assets (Indicator 5), expressed in percentage points

Subscripts: t = sub-period 1 (1948-54)

$t+1$ = sub-period 2 (1954-60)

Table 6.13 Results of regressions of rate of return [equity assets], in sub-period 2, 1954-1960 on rate of return [equity assets] in sub-period 1, 1948-1954

Industry	a	b	r^2	Number of companies
11 Clothing and Footwear	6.44 ± 1.58	0.10 ± 0.15	0.01	68
12 Food	2.81 ± 1.47	0.52 ± 0.12	0.21	72
04 Engineering	1.89 ± 0.65	0.66 ± 0.05	0.46	211
All four industries, including Tobacco	3.65 ± 0.62	0.49 ± 0.05	0.21	357

Regression equation;

$$P'_{t+1} = a + b\ P'_t + \epsilon$$

where: a, b are constant, ϵ is the random error term.

P' = post-tax profitability on equity assets (Indicator 6), expressed in percentage points

Subscripts; t = sub-period 1 (1948-54)

t+1 = sub-period 2 (1954-60)

Table 6.14 Kendall's rank correlation coefficients for firms ranked by profitability on net assets in 1948-54 and in 1954-60 (Col. 2), and for firms ranked by profitability on equity assets in 1948-54 and in 1954-60 (Col. 3)

Industry	r_k between P_t and P_{t+1}	r_k between P'_t and P'_{t+1}	Number of firms
Clothing and Footwear (Industry 11)	.388***	.322***	70
Food (Industry 12)	.297***	.291***	73
Non-electrical Engineering (Industry 04)	.561***	.478***	214
Tobacco (Industry 14)	.293	.143	7

r_k is the Kendall rank correlation coefficient

P stands for Profitability on Net Assets (Indicator 5)

P′ stands for Post-tax Profitability on Equity Assets (Indicator 6)

Subscripts; t refers to sub-period 1 (1948-54)
t+1 refers to sub-period 2 (1954-60)

*** indicates significance at the 1% level

conclude that but for the possible effects of aggregation discussed later, profitability is not a random phenomenon; the relative profitability of a firm in the period 1948-54 is an important guide to its relative profitability in the period 1954-60.

Table 6.14 also shows that for every industry, there is a greater persistency of the pre-tax rate of return on net assets than of the post-tax rate of return on equity assets. The differences, however, are very small and could easily arise from the difference in the structure of company taxation and of company finance in the two periods. There was a major change in the structure of company taxation in the sub-period 2 (1954-60) as compared with sub-period 1 (1948-54). The differential profits tax which in the early and middle fifties discriminated heavily against distributed profits as opposed to undistributed profits, was in force throughout sub-period 1 and was abolished in March 1958.[1] The abolition of the differential profits tax, along with the fact as we saw in Chapter 3 that there is some positive association between the pre-tax rate of return on net assets and retention ratio particularly in the second sub-period, could probably by itself account for the observed lower persistency of post-tax profitability as opposed to pre-tax profitability.

The comparison of Table 6.14 with Table 5.7 shows that there is a greater persistency of rates of return than of growth. In fact in the case of the Food industry, we found that there was no persistency of growth, whereas we now find that there is some persistency in the rates of return. In the case of Engineering and Clothing and Footwear, we find that the profitability of a firm in sub-period 1 has a closer relationship with its profitability in sub-period 2, than does growth in sub-period 1 with its growth in sub-period 2. This again is not surprising since profitability is only one of the factors, albeit an important one, which affects the growth of demand for the industry's and the firm's products: the orientation of its management etc., also affect the firm's willingness and ability to grow.[2] It is not, therefore, necessary that there should be a similar degree of persistency in the rates of growth of firms as there is in the rates of return.

Before we can say that our conclusions with regard to the persistency of the rates of return in the major industries are firmly established, we must examine what is the effect of aggregation of more or less homogeneous sub-groups of firms within each industry. If there was no persistency in the rates of return within each sub-group, but there was persistency in the average rates of return of the sub-groups themselves, aggregation of these sub-groups would show persistency in the rates of return of the firms within the industry. In order to find out whether the results of Table 6.14 are entirely due to such effects of aggregation, we computed Kendall's rank correlation coefficients between the rates of return in the two successive time-periods for identifiable sub-groups within each industry. These coefficients are reported in Table 6.15. The table shows that although there is greater persistency of the rates of return in some sub-groups than in others, it is quite clear that our previous finding of persistency in the rates of return for each of the major industries does not arise merely from aggregating sub-groups within each industry. In most of the sub-groups, there is a significant[3] association between the profitability of firms in the two periods. The few sub-groups in which the rank correlation coefficients are not much different from zero do not usually contain more than a very small number of firms. We must therefore conclude that in general, the firms which had a relatively high (or low) profitability in one period to tend to have a relatively high (or low) profitability in the subsequent period.

Lastly, the rank correlation coefficients for the largest firms alone within each industry are reported in Table 6.15. The persistency of the rates of return for the largest firms alone is not much different from that observed for the industry as a whole in Engineering and in Clothing and Footwear.[1] It is, however, interesting to observe that in the Food industry, which shows the least persistency in the rates of return relative to other industries, the 10 largest firms have a much higher persistency than that of the industry as a whole or that of the largest firms in other industries.[2]

In conclusion, we must consider another type of objection which may be raised with respect to the observed persistency of profitability of firms. It can be argued that in fact, there is no persistency of profitability at all, and the observed persistency is a 'spurious' one arising either from the persistency of growth, or from the different accounting conventions used by various firms.[3]

This argument deserves to be examined in some detail since there are a number of considerations which are relevant here. First, it would appear that if all firms within an industry followed the same accounting conventions, and they all had the same rate of growth (or more accurately, the rate at which they acquired new fixed assets), there is no danger of observing spurious persistency in the profitability of firms arising from the persistency of growth. In the context of this study, this argument can be put in a stronger form. Since we have found that there is only a small degree of persistency in the growth of firms, as long as all firms within an industry follow the same accounting conventions, there is probably only a relatively small degree of spurious persistency of profitability arising from this source.

However, the danger of observing spurious persistency increases to the extent that it is assumed that the firms in the same industry may be following very different accounting conventions. It is very difficult to generalize as to what kind of firms within an industry may be following different conventions, but we have examined here separately the case of at least one identifiable group of firms, namely the larger firms, which could be expected to follow more uniform, but different accounting conventions than the firms in the rest of the industry. We have of course, found a similar degree of persistency in the profitability of large firms as of the industry as a whole.

Furthermore, we must also remember that there is the opposite danger of observing no persistency at all when in fact there is persistency of profitability. This could arise if some firms revalued their assets late in the first sub-period (1948-54) or early in the second (1954-60), as a number of firms did, particularly the larger firms (see Chapter 4, section 6). In such cases, the revaluation would lead to an understatement of the profit rate in the second sub-period (after revaluation)

Table 6.15 Kendall's rank correlation coefficients for firms ranked by profitability in 1948-54 and in 1954-60 (Col. 2), and for firms ranked by post-tax profitability in 1948-54 and in 1954-60; Industry sub-groups

Industry Sub-groups	r_k between P_t and P_{t+1}	r_k between P'_t and P'_{t+1}	Number of firms
(a) Engineering sub-groups;			
Shipbuilding (04, 1)	0.201	0.260*	26
Machine tools (04, 2)	0.347**	0.216	20
Textile machinery (04, 3)	0.333	0.067	6
Constructional Engineering (04, 4)	0.692***	0.740***	13
Other (04, 5)	0.629***	0.550***	149
(b) Clothing and Footwear sub-groups;			
Clothing (11, 1)	0.352***	0.252***	54
Footwear (11, 2)	0.667***	0.700***	16
(c) Food sub-groups;			
Grain milling (12, 1)	0.238	0.190	7
Baking (12, 2)	0.295·	0.410**	15
Sugar (12, 3)	0.000	0.167	4
Confectionery (12, 4)	0.325*	0.163	15
Fruit and vegetable products (12, 5)	0.359*	0.338·	13
Other food (12, 6)	0.258·	0.305	19

r_k is the Kendall correlation coefficient

P stands for Profitability on Net Assets (Indicator 5)

P' stands for Post-tax Profitability on Equity Assets (Indicator 6)

Subscripts; t   refers to sub-period 1 (1948-54)
　　　　　　t+1 refers to sub-period 2 (1954-60)

·　　 indicates significance at 15% level

*　　 indicates significance at 10% level

**　　indicates significance at 5% level

***　 indicates significance at 1% level

Table 6.16 Kendall's rank correlation coefficients for the largest firms in each industry ranked by profitability on net assets in 1948-54 and in 1954-60 (Col. 2), and for the largest firms in each industry ranked by post-tax profitability on equity assets in 1948-54 and in 1954-60 (Col. 3)

Industry	r_k between P_t and P_{t+1}	r_k between P'_t and P'_{t+1}	Number of firms
Engineering			
10 Largest Firms	0.404·	0.200	10
Above £4 million	0.420**	0.253	14
Above £2 million	0.424***	0.369***	39
Clothing and Footwear			
10 Largest Firms	0.244	0.289	10
Above £2 million	0.057	0.333	6
Above £1 million	0.348*	0.436**	13
Food			
10 Largest Firms	0.629**	0.674***	10
Above £4 million	0.382*	0.351*	12
Above £2 million	0.446***	0.453***	19

r_k is the Kendall correlation coefficient

P stands for Profitability on Net Assets (Indicator 5)

P′ stands for Post-tax Profitability on Equity Assets (Indicator 6)

Subscripts; t refers to sub-period 1 (1948-54)
t+1 refers to sub-period 2 (1954-60)

·   indicates significance at 15% level

*   indicates significance at 10% level

**   indicates significance at 5% level

***   indicates significance at 1% level

relative to those of the earlier period (before revaluation). For these reasons, we do not feel that the fairly high degree of observed persistency of the rate of profit of firms is a spurious one.

6.   Summary and conclusions

Two broad questions have been investigated in this chapter. The relationship between opening size and the two measures of profitability (pre-tax rate of return on net assets and the post-tax rate of return on equity assets respectively) were discussed in sections 1 to 4. On the whole the results of this analysis were negative, but for many purposes, negative results are important. The question of the persistency of rates return (i. e. whether firms which have an above (or below) average rate of return in one period also have an above (or below) average rate of return in a subsequent period) was discussed in section 5. Here, the results were positive.

Size and profitability

The relationship between size and profitability, which is of considerable importance in the theory of the firm, was first discussed considering the distribution of the two measures of profitability with respect to opening size. The following conclusions emerge from the comparisons of average profitability and its variability for firms in different size groups.

(a) Average profitability was on the whole (with some exceptions) lower, the larger the size of the firm, but the difference in average profitability of firms between size classes were not found to be statistically significant at the 5% level, by the usual tests, for most of the populations of firms considered.

(b) The dispersion of profitability for firms in different size classes was on the whole lower, the larger the size of the firm, but there was no rigid rule that it was always lower for a certain size-class than for any smaller one.

(c) The same conclusions with regard to average profitability and its dispersion hold when post-tax rate of return on equity assets is considered. The only important difference is that the slight tendency for profitability to decline with size is even less clear in relation to the largest size-class (i. e. for firms with assets of more than 2 million pounds) when this indicator is used than it is with the pre-tax rate. The relationship between size and profitability was next studied (in section 3) by means of regression analysis. A number of different regression models were fitted to various populations of firms. The more important results of the regression analysis are summarized below:

(a) There is no linear relationship of any importance between size and either measure of profitability when all firms are considered.

(b) There is a small inverse linear relationship between size and profitability when the non growing and non profitable firms are

144

excluded from the population. This relationship is statistically significant but very weak. The proportion of inter-firm variation in profitability explained by size is, on average, only of the order of 1 to $1\frac{1}{2}\%$, because there are other important factors which influence a firm's profitability and these vary greatly from firm to firm, independently of the size of the firm. Furthermore, revaluations, which lower the observed rate of return, are much more common among the larger firms than among the smaller ones. Our conclusion that there is a small negative association between profitability and size amongst growing and profitable firms, is, therefore, of dubious significance.

The 'best' size of the firm for profitability and for growth. In section 2, we discussed the question of what is the 'best' size of the firm, i.e. the size which on the average, achieved maximum profitability, or maximum growth. The size-classes, in each of the three major industries, were judged by the following criteria:

(a) Maximum profitability (taken as the average for firms in that size-class) (b) Smallest dispersion of profit rates. (c) Maximum average growth rates and (d) Smallest dispersion of growth rates.

Naturally, the optimum size-class need not be the same on each of the above tests – and, indeed, was not; and any test may give a different answer for different time periods. However, the following conclusion of this analysis deserve some notice;

(1) In almost every case, it was the largest firms (with assets of more than £2 million) which achieved maximum growth even when the maximum pre-tax and post-tax profitability of an industry was achieved by the smallest firms (with assets of less than £$\frac{1}{4}$ million).

(2) The 'best' size of the firm for pre-tax profitability on net assets in an industry was different from the 'best' size for post-tax profitability on equity assets in a number of cases. In particular, it was found that in the period 1954-60, it was the smallest firms (with assets of less than £$\frac{1}{4}$ million) or the medium sized firms (with assets lying between £$\frac{1}{4}$ million and £2 million) which achieved maximum pre-tax profitability on net assets, whereas it was, on the whole, the largest firms (with assets of more than £2 million) which achieved maximum post-tax profitability on equity assets.

The inter-industry differences in the profitability and growth of firms in the various size-classes were also examined in this section. There was found to be a remarkable similarity in the growth and profitability experience of large firms (as opposed to small or medium-sized firms) in different industries in every time period. The inter-industry differences in the post-tax profitability and rates of growth of large firms (with opening net assets greater than £2 million) were negligible in every period.

Although, there are good, a priori reasons for expecting this inter-industry uniformity in the experience of large firms, it must be remembered that our analysis is based only on three industries. It would be very significant, indeed, if this conclusion were to hold when our investigation is extended to more industries.

Persistency of the rates of return

As for the second major question asked in this chapter, our analysis yielded the following conclusions.

First we found that in every industry there was a fairly strong tendency for firms which had an above average profitability in the period 1948 to 1954 to have an above average profitability in the period 1954 to 1960. The tendency was strongest in the engineering industry for which more than 50% of the inter-firm variation in the pre-tax rates of return in the period 1954-60 could be explained by the variation in the pre-tax rates of return in the period 1948-54.

Secondly, it was found that, perhaps because of the abolition of the differential profits tax in 1958, the persistency of post-tax profitability on equity assets was somewhat less than that of pre-tax profitability on net assets. However, even with this measure the persistency of profitability was considerably greater than that observed for growth in the last chapter.

Thirdly, it was found that except for the food industry, which showed relatively smaller persistency in rates of return than the other industries, the persistency of profitability for the largest firms alone was not much different from that of the industry as a whole. In the case of the food industry, the largest firms, particularly the 10 largest firms, showed a considerably greater persistency of the average rates of return over the two periods.

The findings of this Chapter that there is a strong persistency in the profitability of firms and of the last one that there is some persistency in their growth, do not necessarily conflict with the work of Little and Rayner, mentioned earlier, since their conclusions only relate to the growth of earnings per share. The growth of earnings per share [or, loosely speaking, the growth of profitability] is a totally different concept from that of the level of profitability. However, these findings do cast doubt on one of the economic conclusions derived by Little and Rayner, from their statistical analysis. They believe that the fact that there is no persistency in the growth of profitability implies either that there is no continuity of good or bad management, or that there is no such thing as good or bad management.

It would seem that a more reasonable criterion of good management is the maintenance of an above average level of profitability rather than the maintenance of an above average growth of profitability. Surely if a management makes say a 30% per cent rate of profit in one period one would still regard it as good management if it is able to make the same or even a slightly lower rate of profit in the next period; conversely a managment which trebled the rate of profitability would deserve little credit if the movement were from 0.1% to 0.3%.

In terms of a criterion of this kind, which is surely the more relevant criterion, our results support the view that there is such a thing as good management and that there is an important amount of continuity of good management and bad management. However, we must hasten to add that, since the profitability of a firm can also be ascribed to the monopoly power which it enjoys, rather than to the quality of its management, the observed persistency of profitability may show nothing more than the continuity of monopoly power.

Our discovery of persistency of profit rates also has implications for the investor who wishes to maximize the future earnings yield of his portfolio. These implications are examined at some length in Chapter 8.

7   Profitability and Growth

In this chapter, we return to the study of the growth of firms. We shall study growth here in terms of systematic influences which may affect it, rather than regarding it as a wholly chance phenomenon, as was done in Chapters 4 and 5. The most important systematic influence on growth, especially in the context of the present data, is that of profitability. Since the relationship between growth and profitability is of considerable interest both from a theoretical and a practical point of view, we shall examine this relationship in some detail for different time periods, industries and size classes.

Once the influence of profitability on growth is removed, we shall examine the nature of the residual growth rates. We shall attempt to find out whether they are the outcome of a chance process, or of systematic influences other than that of the profitability of the firm. In the last part of the chapter, we shall also attempt to relate growth in one period to profitability and other financial indicators in the preceding period, i.e. we shall find to what extent it is possible to predict future growth from the past values of these variables.

The subject matter of this chapter can therefore be conveniently divided into three parts. In the first part (sections 1 to 3) we shall study the systematic influence of profitability on growth; the second part (sections 4 and 5) is devoted to an analysis of residual growth rates; and the third part (section 6) is concerned with the prediction of growth on the basis of past data. The main conclusions of the chapter are summarized in the final section.

1.   The profitability and growth of firms: some general considerations

What sort of relationship between the profitability and the growth of firms does economic theory lead one to expect? The traditional neoclassical theory of the firm is unfortunately not very helpful in this respect. Under it usual assumptions of perfect competition in all markets, given technology, tastes, etc., firms may grow only in order to achieve the 'optimum size' at which they maximize profits. Therefore in equilibrium, when all firms are at their optimum size, there will be no relationship at all between the profitability and growth of firms, simply because no firms will grow. If, for some reason, some or all firms are not in equilibrium at any moment of time, and are assumed to be moving towards equilibrium, there may well emerge some relationship between profitability and growth on a cross-section basis. However, the character, strength and nature of this relationship is in general indeterminate, depending as it does on the causes of disequilibrium and the speed of adjustment.[1]

Once we move away from this kind of essentially static theory, it becomes possible to put forward some very general considerations regarding the nature of the relationship which may be expected to hold between the profitability and growth of firms. |It is a commonplace to say that a firm's rate of growth depends both on its <u>ability</u> to grow and on its <u>willingness</u> to grow. Its ability to finance growth is closely related to its achieved profitability. The higher the level of its profitability, the more it would be in a position to grow from retained profits. Furthermore, a high achieved level of profitability will be taken by potential investors as a strong indication that the future level of profitability will be high, so that the company will be able to make new issues on favourable terms. This correspondence between a high ability to grow and a high level of achieved profitability is particularly close when growth is measured as growth of the long-term finance (i.e. net assets) of the business, as is the case with our measure of growth. |

However, a firm's willingness to grow does not depend so directly on its profitability. To be sure, profitability does provide an incentive for growth, but there are other factors such as the state of competition, the nature of management, the state of demand, and the technological opportunities, which are of greater relevance in this context. For instance, for the same rate of profit, a firm operating in an industry with a buoyant demand may be expected to grow more, by retaining profits or raising new issues, than the firm which operates in an industry with less buoyant prospects. Similarly, a firm which is run by a growth-oriented management may be expected to grow more than a firm, with the same level of profitability, which is run by, say, a profit-maximizing owner-manager. In the same way, it is possible that there are industries in which there is competition amongst the leading firms to increase their relative market shares, so that they have to grow at a faster rate for the same level of profitability than firms in a less competitive industry.

In an expanding economy, we should expect to find a positive association between the growth and profitability of firms, since profits do provide the <u>ability</u> to grow. However, the factors affecting the <u>willingness</u> to grow are such that they are likely to vary between different industries. They are also likely to vary within the same industry at different points in time, e.g. as demand for the product of the industry changes. This means that the magnitude and the precise form of the positive association between profitability and growth will be different in different industries at a particular time and in the same industry at different times. One of the purposes of the next section of this chapter is to examine the extent and significance of these differences.

Furthermore, the factors affecting the willingness to grow may be different for large firms as opposed to small firms in the same industry. In particular, a large firm is usually more diversified and may produce a range of products which could be legitimately classified as belonging to more than one industry, so that the firm's willingness to grow will probably be influenced by conditions in a range of industries rather than a single industry. It can also be argued that the largest firms in an industry would tend to be dominated by managers (as opposed to the shareholders) who for a number of well known reasons[1] are more interested in the growth of the firm rather than its profits. For both of these reasons, the nature of the relationship between profitability and growth for these management-dominated firms may be different from that for the smaller-sized firms. We attempt to assess the extent of these differences in Section 3 of this chapter.

To sum up, the above considerations suggest that, if we examined a cross-section of firms, we should expect to find, in general, a positive association between growth and profitability, although this association need not be a close one. Furthermore, we should not be surprised to find that the nature and form of this relationship vary between industries, vary over time for the same industry, and vary between firms of different sizes. Without making drastic simplifying assumptions, it is very difficult to deduce more precise a priori predictions about the nature of the relationship between profitability and growth.[2]

Lastly, we should like to remind the readers that growth is defined in terms of net assets in this study. Thus, we shall be relating the growth of the long-term finances of the business to its profitability. Since retained profits automatically lead to 'growth' in this sense, we should expect to find a closer positive association between growth and profitability than we would have observed if growth had been defined in terms of, for example, sales or employment.

2. The explanation of growth rate by profitability: empirical results

In this section, we explore the relationship between profitability and growth by means of regression analysis. As this is a relatively long section, we summarize the main results at the beginning in order to help the reader.

(a) Although a number of regression models were tried, the simple linear regression equation relating growth to profitability was found to be the most appropriate one. Of our two measures of profitability, the pre-tax rate of return on net assets (Indicator 5) and the post-tax rate of return on equity assets (Indicator 6), the latter provided the best explanation of growth.

(b) Growth and profitability, as one would expect, are positively associated with profitability explaining on an average about 50% of the variation of growth rates between firms. A one percentage point increase in the firm's post-tax profitability on equity assets led on average to a .7 percentage point increase in its growth rate.

(c) The regression coefficient 'b', relating growth to profitability in the linear regression equation varied significantly between industries and over time. The degree of explanation of growth (r^2) achieved in different industries and over different time-periods, also varied to a considerable degree.

(a) The choice of models

Three alternative regression models were tested:

$$G = a + bP + \epsilon \qquad (1)$$

$$G = a + b \log P + \epsilon \qquad (2)$$

$$\log G = a + b \log P + \epsilon \qquad (3)$$

where:

G = Growth rate

P = Profitability

ϵ is the error term

log indicates logarithms to the base e

a, b are parameters.

Equation (1) tests the simple hypothesis that growth rate is a linear function of profitability. Equation (2) tests the hypothesis that growth rate increases by a constant amount (e.g. one percentage point) as profitability increases by a given proportion (e.g. doubling). The double logarithmic equation (3) tests the hypothesis that a given proportionate change in profitability is associated with a constant proportionate change in growth rate (e.g. if b = 2, growth rate quadruples as profitability doubles).

Each of these three models was tested for each industry group for each of the three periods. Testing the logarithmic equations (2) and (3) required the exclusion of negative values of growth and profitability. This involved the exclusion of about 10 per cent of the companies.[1] For reasons of space, all the regression results and scatter diagrams for each industry and each period, cannot be given here. The most important ones, or the ones which illustrate particular points made in the following analysis are given in Tables 7.1 to 7.4 and Figures 7.1 to 7.4.

In the vast majority of cases,[2] equation (1) gave a better explanation (i.e. higher r^2) when applied to the full population rather than the restricted population used for the logarithmic equation. In other words, there was a close linear relationship between profitability and growth amongst companies which made losses or did not grow, and the exclusion of these companies leaves only the profitable and growing companies, amongst whom the correlation between profitability and growth did not conform so closely to the linear pattern. An examination of scatter diagrams of the joint distributions of profitability and growth (see, for example, Figures 7.1 to 7.4) shows that this is due largely to the existence of a considerable number of companies which had low positive profitability and negative growth. These are companies whose net assets declined as a result of paying dividends in excess of the very low profits, or of repaying debentures, which could not be replaced by new issues. The exclusion of these companies introduces an artificial non-linearity into the relationship between profitability and growth, because it raises the average growth of low-profit firms.[3]

151

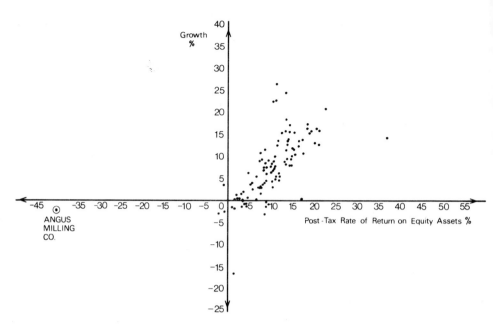

7.1.   Scatter diagram of Growth and Profitability:
        Industry 12 (Food): Sub-period 1 (1948-54)
        Number of companies = 108

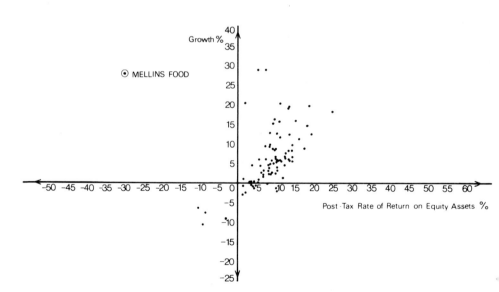

7.2.   Scatter diagram of Growth and Profitability:
        Industry 12 (Food): Sub-period 2 (1954-60)
        Number of companies = 91

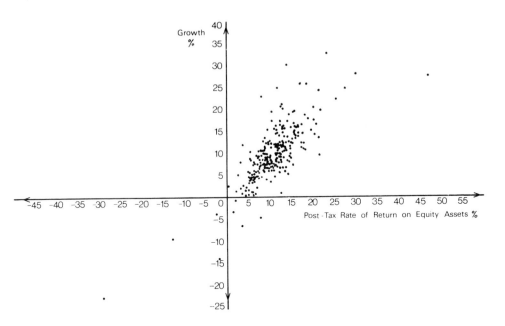

7.3.   Scatter diagram of Growth and Profitability:
        Industry 04 (Engineering): Sub-period 1 (1948-54)
        Number of companies = 259

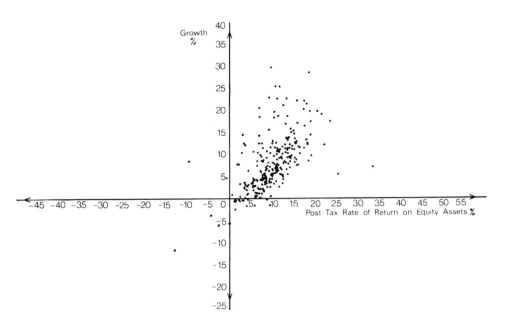

7.4.   Scatter diagram of Growth and Profitability:
        Industry 04 (Engineering): Sub-period 2 (1954-60)
        Number of companies = 262

Table 7.1. Regression results

Equation: Growth = a + b. Rate of return on Net Assets.

Full population

	r^2	a (constant term)	b (regression coefficient)
Sub-Period 1: 1948-1954			
Industry 11, Clothing & Footwear	0.44	-2.77($\pm$1.12)*	0.44($\pm$0.05)*
Industry 12, Food	0.45	0.05($\pm$0.94)	0.36($\pm$0.04)*
Industry 04, Non-Electrical Engineering	0.54	0.34($\pm$0.61)	0.41($\pm$0.02)*
All four industries (including Tobacco), Industries 04 + 11 + 12 + 14	0.52	-0.72($\pm$0.46)	0.42($\pm$0.02)*
Sub-Period 2: 1954-1960			
Industry 11, Clothing & Footwear	0.43	-3.22($\pm$1.46)*	0.61($\pm$0.08)*
Industry 12, Food	0.15	0.96($\pm$1.63)	0.35($\pm$0.09)*
Industry 04, Non-Electrical Engineering	0.28	1.28($\pm$0.75)	0.36($\pm$0.04)*
All four industries (including Tobacco), Industries 04 + 11 + 12 + 14	0.24	0.30($\pm$0.69)	0.41($\pm$0.03)*
Whole Period: 1948-1960			
Industry 11, Clothing & Footwear	0.20	2.10($\pm$0.91)*	0.16($\pm$0.04)*
Industry 12, Food	0.30	0.68($\pm$1.26)	0.36($\pm$0.06)*
Industry 04, Non-Electrical Engineering	0.39	2.19($\pm$0.66)*	0.35($\pm$0.03)*
All four industries (including Tobacco), Industries 04 + 11 + 12 + 14	0.29	2.58($\pm$0.52)*	0.29($\pm$0.02)*

*   Significantly different from zero at the 5% level.

Notes. (1) Both Growth and the Rate of Return are measured in percentage points in all tables in this chapter.

(2) All the significance tests used in this chapter, except for tables 9 and 13, are two-tailed 't' tests.

Table 7.2. Regression results

Equation: Growth = a + b. Post-tax Rate of Return on Equity Assets

Full population

	r^2	a (constant term)	b (regression coefficient)
Sub-Period 1: 1948-1954			
Industry 11, Clothing & Footwear	0.55	0.66($\pm$0.69)	0.57($\pm$0.06)*
Industry 12, Food	0.40	1.99($\pm$0.83)*	0.55($\pm$0.07)*
Industry 04, Non-Electrical Engineering	0.61	0.49($\pm$0.54)	0.84($\pm$0.04)*
All four industries (including Tobacco), Industries 04 + 11 + 12 + 14	0.55	1.27($\pm$0.37)*	0.70($\pm$0.03)*
Sub-Period 2: 1954-1960			
Industry 11, Clothing & Footwear	0.68	-2.07($\pm$0.88)*	0.98($\pm$0.08)*
Industry 12, Food	0.09	3.53($\pm$1.35)*	0.35($\pm$0.12)*
Industry 04, Non-Electrical Engineering	0.35	1.10($\pm$0.66)	0.70($\pm$0.06)*
All four industries (including Tobacco), Industries 04 + 11 + 12 + 14	0.33	0.72($\pm$0.56)	0.72($\pm$0.05)*
Whole Period: 1948-1960			
Industry 11, Clothing & Footwear	0.64	-1.19($\pm$0.69)	0.80($\pm$0.07)*
Industry 12, Food	0.05	6.25($\pm$0.72)*	0.08($\pm$0.04)*
Industry 04, Non-Electrical Engineering	0.48	1.84($\pm$0.59)*	0.72($\pm$0.05)*
All four industries (including Tobacco), Industries 04 + 11 + 12 + 14	0.19	5.40($\pm$0.39)*	0.27($\pm$0.03)*

*   Significantly different from zero at the 5% level.

Table 7.3. Regression results

Equation: Log Growth = a + b. Log Rate of Return on Net Assets

Restricted population (growing and profitable firms only)

	r^2	a (constant term)	b (regression coefficient)
Sub-Period 1: 1948-1954			
Industry 11, Clothing & Footwear	0.43	-1.09($\pm$0.72)	0.97($\pm$0.14)*
Industry 12, Food	0.48	-2.92($\pm$0.79)*	1.33($\pm$0.15)*
Industry 04, Non-Electrical Engineering	0.38	-0.84($\pm$0.43)	0.98($\pm$0.08)*
All four industries (including Tobacco), Industries 04 + 11 + 12 + 14	0.42	-1.59($\pm$0.34)*	1.11($\pm$0.06)*
Sub-Period 2: 1954-1960			
Industry 11, Clothing & Footwear	0.19	-2.34($\pm$1.66)	1.23($\pm$0.32)*
Industry 12, Food	0.25	-1.46($\pm$1.14)	1.07($\pm$0.22)*
Industry 04, Non-Electrical Engineering	0.24	0.01($\pm$0.49)	0.81($\pm$0.09)*
All four industries (including Tobacco), Industries 04 + 11 + 12 + 14	0.23	-0.65($\pm$0.46)	0.93($\pm$0.09)*
Whole Period: 1948-1960			
Industry 11, Clothing & Footwear	0.31	-2.15($\pm$1.16)	1.17($\pm$0.23)*
Industry 12, Food	0.28	-1.89($\pm$1.19)	1.16($\pm$0.23)*
Industry 04, Non-Electrical Engineering	0.37	0.27($\pm$0.38)	0.79($\pm$0.07)*
All four industries (including Tobacco), Industries 04 + 11 + 12 + 14	0.32	-0.98($\pm$0.42)*	1.00($\pm$0.08)*

*   Significantly different from zero at the 5% level.

Table 7.4. Regression results

Equation: Log Growth = a + b. Log Post-tax Rate of Return on
Equity Assets

Restricted population (growing and profitable firms only)

	r^2	a (constant term)	b (regression coefficient)
Sub-Period 1: 1948-1954			
Industry 11, Clothing & Footwear	0.47	-0.03(±0.53)	0.89(±0.12)*
Industry 12, Food	0.60	-2.31(±0.56)*	1.40(±0.12)*
Industry 04, Non-Electrical Engineering	0.41	-0.02(±0.34)	0.96(±0.07)*
All four industries (including Tobacco), Industries 04 + 11 + 12 + 14	0.47	-0.19(±0.26)	1.08(±0.07)*
Sub-Period 2: 1954-1960			
Industry 11, Clothing & Footwear	0.41	-3.32(±1.14)*	1.59(±0.25)*
Industry 12, Food	0.29	-1.13(±0.96)	1.13(±0.21)*
Industry 04, Non-Electrical Engineering	0.29	0.29(±0.40)	0.86(±0.09)*
All four industries (including Tobacco), Industries 04 + 11 + 12 + 14	0.30	-0.51(±0.37)	1.02(±0.08)*
Whole Period: 1948-1960			
Industry 11, Clothing & Footwear	0.44	-1.54(±0.78)	1.22(±0.18)*
Industry 12, Food	0.25	0.30(±0.81)	0.83(±0.18)*
Industry 04, Non-Electrical Engineering	0.47	0.52(±0.29)	0.85(±0.06)*
All four industries (including Tobacco), Industries 04 + 11 + 12 + 14	0.40	-0.27(±0.30)	0.99(±0.07)*

*   Significantly different from zero at the 5% level.

Amongst the restricted population of profitable and growing companies, the degree of explanation is not improved on the whole if equation (2) is substituted for equation (1). The strongest result for this population appears to be yielded by equation (3), i.e. in most cases, the best fit is obtained by assuming that the growth rate increases proportionately as profitability increases proportionately.[1] The results of fitting equation (3) are given in Tables 7.3 and 7.4. These results may be interpreted intuitively as follows: a value of b (the regression coefficient) greater than unity means that the higher profitability, the more growth rises for any given rise in profitability, i.e. plotted on a graph with growth on the vertical axis, the regression line is an upward sloping curve of increasing steepness. A value of b less than unity implies the converse, i.e. growth does not increase so much in response to a change in profitability at the higher levels of profit.

Although the logarithmic equation seems to provide a better fit than the simple linear equation for the restricted population of growing and profitable companies, most of the subsequent analysis is a closer investigation of the results of the simple linear equation (equation 1) applied to the full population. The latter has three advantages: first, it has the simplest intuitive meaning; secondly, it yields the best fit (highest r^2) in most cases, even when compared with the logarithmic equation for the restricted population (see Tables 7.2 and 7.4); thirdly, and most importantly, it is applied to the widest population of firms. The logarithmic equation can only be applied to a restricted population[2] which, as explained above, produces a misleading picture of the relationship between growth and profitability, particularly with respect to those companies which have low profitability.

(b) The choice of indicators of profitability

A comparison of the results given in Tables 7.1 and 7.2 shows that the Post-tax Rate of Return on Equity Assets gives a better explanation of Growth rate (i.e. a higher r^2) than does the pre-tax Rate of Return on Net Assets in Clothing and Footwear (Industry 11) and Non-electrical Engineering (Industry 04) but not in Food (Industry 12). The results for the Food industry are due to two extremely perverse cases of extreme negative profits where the equity rate of return is used, as can be seen in the scatter diagrams (Figures 7.1 and 7.2). An argument can be made for excluding one of these observations, which would mean that in sub-period 1, the post-tax equity return would give the better explanation even in the Food industry (see note 1, page 159).

The regression coefficients (b), are, as would be expected, higher when Post-tax Rate of Return on Equity Assets is used. This is due to the fact that this return is post-tax and therefore usually lower than the pre-tax net asset return. When the net assets return is used, for the 'all industries' group in 1948-54 and in 1954-60, a change of one percentage point in the Net Asset return was associated with a 0.4 percentage point change in growth rate (b = 0.42 and 0.41), whereas an equal change in the equity return was associated with a 0.7 percentage point change in the growth rate (b = 0.70 and 0.72).

As the post-tax rate of return on equity assets provides a much better explanation of growth than the pre-tax rate of return on net assets, and since there are no strong theoretical grounds for preferring one over the other (if anything, a stronger case exists for post-tax profitability), the subsequent analysis of the relationship between profitability and growth is based on the latter measure of profitability.

(c) Stability over time

Table 7.2 shows that, for each individual industry group, the regression coefficient b, relating post-tax rate of return on equity assets to growth, changed substantially between the two sub-periods. In the case of Clothing and Footwear, growth varied more in response to a given change in equity return in 1954-60, but in the case of Food and Engineering the regression coefficient was higher in 1948-54. All of these changes are high relative to the standard deviations of the estimates, but the result for Food is subject to some qualification, because it is very sensitive to the effect of the two freak values which carry high weight.[1] Changes in the constant term (a) over time were not usually very significant.

The actual degree of explanation (r^2) of variations in Growth Rate (Table 7.2) tends to be lower in the second sub-period than in the first, except in Clothing and Footwear. An examination of scatter diagrams suggests that this was due to the greater dispersion of growth rates of companies which were only moderately profitable during the period 1954-60, and this variability seems to take the form of an increase in the maximum rate at which a moderately profitable company can grow relative to a highly profitable company. A comparison of Figures 7.1 and 7.2 will provide an example of this. This tendency for moderately profitable companies to grow relatively faster in the period 1954-60 was probably due partly to the increased activity of the new issue market during this period. Internal growth must always depend ultimately upon the amount of profit actually available for retention, whereas external growth can be obtained by selling the prospect of future profits. The large number of take-over bids during this period, particularly in the Food industry, may have provided both the incentive and the means for much of this growth.

We conclude that the relationship between profitability and growth may change substantially over time within individual industries. These results are interesting in relation to the proposal by Marris[2] that an industry norm could be established for the level of profitability necessary to sustain a given level of growth of individual companies. Clearly, if there are significant changes over time in the relationship between profitability and growth, the establishment of such a norm from historical data is impossible.[3]

(d) Differences between industries

There are considerable differences between both the regression coefficients (b) and the degree of explanation of growth (r^2) obtained for different industries, which are also of interest in relation to the above proposals by Marris. When profitability is measured in terms of post-tax rate of return on equity assets (Table 7.2) the differences between the regression coefficients are generally large in comparison with the standard deviations of the estimates.

An alternative test of the existence of inter-industry differences is to estimate a regression equation of the following form on data for the three large industries together:

$$G = a_1 + b_1 P' + b_2 P' D_1 + b_3 P' D_2 + a_2 D_1 + a_3 D_2 + \epsilon$$

Where: G = Growth

P' = Post-tax Profitability

$$D_1 = \begin{cases} 1 \text{ for companies in Industry 04 (Engineering)} \\ 0 \text{ for other companies} \end{cases}$$

$$D_2 = \begin{cases} 1 \text{ for companies in Industry 12 (Food)} \\ 0 \text{ for other companies} \end{cases}$$

a_1, a_2, a_3, b_1, b_2, b_3, are parameters

The parameters relating to the dummy variables give an indication of the relative significance of inter-industry differences. The parameters b_2 and b_3 give an indication of how far the industry variable affects the slope of the regression line, whilst the parameters a_2 and a_3 show how the constant term is different in the relevant industry from that in Clothing and Footwear, which acts as the base industry. Table 7.5 gives the results of fitting this equation, using post-tax rate of return on equity assets as the measure of profitability. The effect of the dummy variable can be seen by comparing Table 7.5 with Table 7.2. If the second sub-period is taken as an example, it will be seen that the value of the regression coefficient b in Table 5 is the same as that for Clothing and Footwear in Table 7.2. Adding the values of the parameter b_2 from Table 7.5 gives the values of the regression coefficient for Engineering from Table 7.2. This can be repeated, using the parameters a_1 and a_2 from Table 7.5 to derive the constant term for the Engineering industry as given in Table 7.2. Adding b_3 to b_1 and a_3 to a_1 gives the corresponding results for the Food industry.

Table 7.5 shows that for the period 1954-60 the dummy variables were highly significant, indicating that Clothing and Footwear was significantly different from the other two industries both as regards the regression coefficient (b) and the constant element in growth (a). In the first sub-period (1948-54) Clothing and Footwear was significantly different from Engineering with respect to the regression coefficient, but inter-industry differences between the constant terms seem to be insignificant.

We conclude that inter-industry differences in the relationship between profitability and growth are statistically significant. They are also quantitatively important. For example, the value of the parameters b_1 and b_2 in the second sub-period indicates that a change of ten percentage points in the profit rate (on equity assets) led to an almost equivalent increase of 10 percentage points in the growth rate of a Clothing and Footwear firm, but only to a rise of about 7 percentage points in the growth of an Engineering firm.

160

Table 7.5 Regression Results

Equation: $\text{Growth} = a_1 + b_1 P' + b_2 P'D_1 + b_3 P'D_2 + a_2 D_1 + a_3 D_2 + \epsilon$

where P' is Post-tax Rate of Return on Equity Assets.
The other terms are explained in the text (page 160).

All Firms (except Tobacco)

	a_1	b_1	b_2	b_3	a_2	a_3	$\overline{R}^2$	Number of observations
Sub-Period 1 (1948-54)								
Value	0.66	0.58	0.27	-0.021	-0.18	1.3	0.57	451
Standard Error	0.62	0.052	0.071	0.077	0.87	0.9		
T	1.06	11.11*	3.78*	-0.27	-0.20	1.41		
Sub-Period 2 (1954-60)								
Value	-2.1	0.98	-0.29	-0.63	3.2	5.6	0.39	428
Standard Error	0.9	0.080	0.11	0.12	1.2	1.3		
T	-2.27*	12.33*	-2.71*	-5.27*	2.65*	4.16*		
Whole Period (1948-60)								
Value	-1.2	0.80	-0.087	-0.53	3.0	5.9	0.50	354
Standard Error	0.8	0.094	0.100	0.100	1.0	1.0		
T	-1.53	9.61*	-0.87	-5.34*	3.03*	5.82*		

* Significance at the 5% level.

Notes (1) The elements in the equation are explained in the text.
(2) $\overline{R}^2$ is R^2 adjusted for degrees of freedom.

3. The relationship between growth and profitability for the largest firms

We observed in Chapter 6 that there are certain common characteristics of the largest firms (defined as firms with book value of opening net assets of greater than two million pounds) which distinguish them in an important way from the smaller firms. In particular, the evidence presented there suggested that, in the analysis of growth and profitability of the largest firms, the industrial classification was not of much relevance; the inter-industry differences in the (univariate) distributions of growth rates and of profit rates for the three major industries were negligible. In this section, we shall discuss to what extent the relationship between growth and profitability for the largest firms is different from that observed for the smaller-sized firms. We wish particularly to find out to what extent, if at all, the inter-industry and the inter-temporal differences in the regression coefficients relating growth to profitability which exist for all firms, also exist when the largest firms alone are considered.

The following two linear regression models, used in the last section, were fitted to the populations of firms with book value of net assets of greater than two million pounds:

(i) Growth $= a + b$ (profitability) $+ \epsilon$

(ii) Growth $= a_1 + b_1 \, P' + b_2 \, P'D_1 + b_3 \, P'D_2 + a_2 D_1 + a_3 D_2 + \epsilon$

The results obtained by using the post-tax measure of profitability (P') for the above models are reported in Tables 7.6 and 7.7 respectively.[1] These tables reveal a number of interesting features of the relationship between growth and profitability for the largest firms considered by themselves.

First, it is worth noting from Table 7.6 that the intercept of the regression equation for the largest firms, like that for all firms together, is rarely significantly different from zero at the 5% level. Secondly, and more importantly, the tables show that there are few significant inter-industry differences (at the 5% level) between the regression coefficients relating growth to post-tax profitability for the largest firms. The only exception is for the Clothing and Footwear industry in sub-period 1 (1948-54), for which the slope of the regression line is significantly different at the 5% level from that for the Engineering industry. In every other case, in all three periods, it is not possible statistically to refute the hypothesis that the observed cluster of growth-profitability observations for the different industries in each period comes from the same population, or from the same 'structure' in the econometric sense.

It must, however, be emphasized that this is a weak conclusion. It arises from the high standard errors of the regression coefficients, despite considerable differences in the magnitude of these coefficients. Table 7.6 shows, for instance, fairly large differences between the slopes of the regression lines for the three industries in sub-period 2. The slope for the Engineering industry is .47, for Clothing and Footwear, it is 1.3 and for Food it is .86. However, the standard errors of these

Table 7.6. Regression results

Equation: Growth = a + b. Post-tax Rate of Return on Equity Assets

Firms with book value of net assets of greater than £2 million

	$\overline{R}^2$	a (constant term)	b (regression coefficient)
Sub-Period 1: 1948-1954			
Industry 11, Clothing & Footwear	0.07	3.3(±3.0)	0.45(±0.28)
Industry 12, Food	0.53	-0.6(±1.7)	0.86(±0.16)*
Industry 04, Non-Electrical Engineering	0.63	-2.0(±1.5)	1.13(±0.13)*
Sub-Period 2: 1954-1960			
Industry 11, Clothing & Footwear	0.10	-3.6(±7.7)	1.38(±0.82)
Industry 12, Food	0.29	-0.4(±2.9)	0.86(±0.26)*
Industry 04, Non-Electrical Engineering	0.13	4.0(±1.4)*	0.47(±0.12)*
Whole Period: 1948-1960			
Industry 11, Clothing & Footwear	0.03	-0.8(±6.9)	1.02(±0.69)
Industry 12, Food	0.59	-0.0(±1.7)	0.83(±0.15)*
Industry 04, Non-Electrical Engineering	0.29	1.3(±1.9)	0.85(±0.20)*

*   Indicates significance at the 5% level.

Note. $\overline{R}^2$ is R^2 corrected for degrees of freedom

Table 7.7 Regression Results

All firms with opening Net Assets greater than £2 million (except Tobacco)

Equation: Growth $= a_1 + b_1 P' + b_2 P' D_1 + b_3 P' D_2 + a_2 D_1 + a_3 D_2 + \epsilon$

where P' is Post-tax Rate of Return on Equity Assets.
(The meaning of the equation is explained in the text, page 160).

	a_1	b_1	b_2	b_3	a_2	a_3	$\bar{R}^2$	Number of observations
Sub-Period 1. 1948–54								
Value	3.3	0.45	0.68	0.41	−5.2	−3.9	0.60	70
Standard Error	2.9	0.27	0.30	0.32	3.2	3.3		
T	1.14	1.65	2.22*	1.28	−1.62	−1.16		
Sub-Period 2. 1954–60								
Value	−3.6	1.40	−0.91	−0.52	7.7	3.3	0.15	115
Standard Error	6.7	0.71	0.72	0.78	6.8	7.7		
T	−0.54	1.95	−1.27	−0.66	1.12	0.43		
Whole Period. 1948–60								
Value	−0.75	1.00	−0.18	−0.19	2.1	0.71	0.33	64
Standard Error	5.2	0.52	0.55	0.57	5.5	5.9		
T	−0.14	1.96	−0.32	−0.33	0.37	0.12		

* Indicates significance at the 5% level. Note $\bar{R}^2$ is R^2 adjusted for degrees of freedom

regression coefficients are so high that we cannot refute the statistical hypothesis that all the three regression lines are a part of the same statistical structure.

Thirdly, as far as the inter-temporal stability of the regression coefficients is concerned, Tables 7.6 and 7.7 show a stability of regression coefficients for the Food industry and for the Clothing and Footwear industry. The slope of the regression line for the Engineering industry in the period 1948-54 is significantly higher than in the period 1954-60.

Thus, as far as the largest firms are concerned, the main conclusion of this analysis is that there are very few significant inter-industry and inter-temporal differences between the regression coefficients relating growth to profitability. This suggests – although by no means proves – that for these firms, if we wish to predict growth for a given level of profitability, the best procedure might be to base the prediction on the regression line obtained from pooling all observations, across industries and over time.

However, in view of the relatively large standard errors of the regression coefficients for the largest firms, it should be noted that the above conclusions can be regarded as meaningful only if it can be established that there are structural differences in the relationship between growth and profitability for the largest firms as compared with the relationship which exists between these variables for the smaller-sized firms. In order to distinguish these structural differences, regression equation (ii) (with dummy variables) was fitted in each of the three periods, to firms with net assets of less than two million pounds. The results are reported in Table 7.8.

Comparisons of Tables 7.7 and 7.8 shows that the 'b' coefficients, relating growth to profitability, were considerably different as between large and small firms, but the direction of the differences was not consistently the same. For instance, in the period 1948-54, whereas a 1% increase in post-tax profitability led on average, to a .45 percentage point increase in growth rate for the largest firms in the Clothing and Footwear industry, it led to a .57 percentage point increase in the growth rate of smaller firms. Conversely, in the Engineering industry, a 1 percentage point increase in post-tax profitability of a firm in the period 1948-54, led on average to 1.13 percentage point increase in its rate of growth if it were a large firm, but only to a .82 percentage point increase in its growth rate if it were a smaller-sized firm. Therefore, although no generalization is possible, with respect to the 'b' coefficients for the large firms being always higher or lower than those for the small firms, there do exist important differences between these regression coefficients.

The remaining question is how significant are the differences between the regression coefficients of the large firms as compared with those of the small firms? One way of answering this question is to test the hypothesis that the regression equations estimated in Tables 7.7 and 7.8, relating to the largest and smaller sized firms respectively, belong to the same statistical structure for the same period.[1] The analysis of co-variance is used to test this hypothesis.[2] The results for each of the three periods are given in Table 7.9.

Table 7.8 Regression Results

Equation: $\text{Growth} = a_1 + b_1 P' + b_2 P'D_1 + b_3 P'D_2 + a_2 D_1 + a_3 D_2 + \epsilon$

where P' is Post-tax Rate of Return on Equity Assets.
(The meaning of the equation is explained in the text.)

All firms with opening Net Assets less than £2 million (except Tobacco)

	a_1	b_1	b_2	b_3	a_2	a_3	$\bar{R}^2$	Number of observations
Sub-Period 1. (1948-54)								
Value	0.55	0.57	0.25	−0.036	0.00	1.5	0.57	381
Standard Error	0.67	0.055	0.076	0.082	0.93	1.0		
T	0.82	10.44*	3.37	−0.43	0.004	1.45		
Sub-Period 2. (1954-60)								
Value	−2.2	0.97	−0.18	−0.69	2.1	5.8	0.44	313
Standard Error	0.9	0.082	0.12	0.13	1.3	1.4		
T	−2.36*	11.94*	−1.55	−5.45*	1.60	4.06*		
Whole Period. (1948-60)								
Value	−1.3	0.78	−0.066	−0.55	3.0	5.9	0.54	290
Standard Error	0.8	0.085	0.10	0.10	1.0	1.0		
T	−1.61	9.16*	−0.64	−5.38*	2.86*	5.62*		

* Indicates significance at the 5% level. Note $\bar{R}^2$ is R^2 adjusted for degrees of freedom.

Table 7.9. Analysis of covariance to test the hypothesis that the regression equations for large and small firms respectively, estimated in Tables 7.7 and 7.8, come from the same statistical structure

	Sub-period 1 (1948-54)		Sub-period 2 (1954-60)		Whole Period (1948-60)	
	Sum of Squares	Degrees of Freedom	Sum of Squares	Degrees of Freedom	Sum of Squares	Degrees of Freedom
Sum of Squared Residuals from Pooled Regression, Q_1:	95.469	m+n-2k = 439	146.033	416	51.726	342
Sum of Squared Residuals from Table 7.7 Regression for Large Firms	5.719	m-k = 64	32.089	109	7.556	58
Sum of Squared Residuals from Table 7.8 Regression for Small Firms	88.679	n-k = 375	109.767	307	42.298	284
Line 2 + Line 3 = Q_2:	94.398		141.856		49.854	
$Q_3 = Q_1 - Q_2$	1.071		4.177		1.872	
$F = \dfrac{Q_3/K}{Q_3/m+n-k}$	.83	6, 439	2.04	6, 416	2.14	6, 342
Critical Value of F at 5% level	2.12		2.12		2.13	
Critical Value of F at 10% level	1.80		1.80		1.81	

<u>Note.</u> 'm' is the number of observations in the Table 7.7 regression and n is the number of observations in Table 7.8 regression.

Table 7.9 shows that for sub-period 1 (1948-54), the hypothesis cannot be rejected since the F ratio obtained from the analysis of co-variance is not significantly different from zero. It may be recalled that for the period 1948-54, we also found some significant inter-industry differences in the regression coefficients for the largest firms. However, for sub-period 2 (1954-60) and the whole period (1948-60), the F ratios in Table 7.9 are significantly different from zero. Thus at least for the periods 1954-60 and 1948-60, we find that there are statistically significant structural differences in the relationship between growth and profitability for firms with net assets of greater than 2 million pounds, as compared with the relationship between growth and profitability for firms of smaller size.

4.   Analysis of residuals

Up to this point, we have studied the systematic influence of profitability on growth, in different industries, in different time-periods and for firms of various sizes. In the next two sections, we shall examine the nature of residual growth rates once the systematic influence of profitability on growth is eliminated. The analysis of residuals reveals some important features of the growth of firms.

It may be recalled that in Chapter 4, we found that the observed distribution of the growth rates of firms cannot be regarded as the outcome of a simple stochastic process, such as the law of proportionate effect. In particular, we saw that although the average growth rates of firms of different sizes were not significantly different from each other, the dispersion of growth rates was heterogeneous, with a general tendency for the dispersion to decline with the size of the firm. We should now like to find out whether, even though the crude distribution of growth rates is not generated by the law of proportionate effect, it is possible that the law applies when the systematic influence of profitability on growth is removed. It is worth noting that although profitability is an important influence on growth, it explains only about 50% of the inter-firm variance of growth rates. There is still a large residual element, and it is important to know whether this residual element is an outcome of a chance process, or of systematic influences, other than the profitability of the firm.

It seems reasonable to argue that, even if the probability of growing by a given proportion may not be the same for firms of all sizes, there may be the same chance of proportional growth for all firms for a given level of profitability. As suggested earlier, the growth of a firm depends on both its willingness and its ability to grow. Profitability provides the ability to finance growth, but the willingness to grow seems to depend on a number of different factors. The chance operation of all these factors, independent of each other, may generate a probability distribution of growth rates which is the same for all firms of given profitability. Thus we should now like to test the hypothesis that it is the residual growth rates, rather than the growth rates themselves which obey the Law of Proportionate Effect.[1]

168

The bivariate distribution of residual growth rates by size of firm is given in Table 7.10 for each of the three major industries for each time period. The residuals have been obtained from the equation, Growth = a + b Profitability + ϵ, where, as usual, a and b are the parameters and ϵ is the random error term. In order for the law of proportionate effect in this modified form not to be invalidated, the average residual growth rate and the variance of the residual growth rates should be the same in each size class.

The table shows that the means of the residual growth rates are not significantly different from each other for firms in the various size classes. In fact, in not a single one of the 9 different distributions of residual growth rates given in Table 7.10, is the mean residual growth rate significantly different from zero in any size class. However, it is also clear from the table that there is usually a significant heterogeneity of variances in different size classes, which invalidates the second major requirement of the law of proportionate effect. Much the same results are obtained when instead of the residuals from the simple linear equation above, the size distribution of the logarithms of the residual growth rates from the log-linear equation in growth and profitability is examined.

The univariate distribution of residual growth rates for each of the three periods, from the following regression equation fitted to firms in all the three major industries together, is given in Table 7.11:

$$\text{Growth} = a_1 + b_1 P' + b_2 P' D_1 + b_3 P' D_2 + a_2 D_1 + a_3 D_2 + \epsilon,$$

where, as before, the dummy variables D_1 and D_2 indicate whether or not a firm belongs to the Engineering industry or the Food industry respectively and where P' is Post-Tax Rate of Return on Equity Assets. The table shows that for each of the three periods, the distribution of the residual growth rates is more or less symmetric, and unimodal (with a modal value of around zero). There are, however, quite significant departures from normality in each case.

Now the above facts (that the distributions of residual growth rates are not normal, and that if the firms are grouped by size, the characteristics of the residuals are significantly different for firms of different sizes), point to the following conclusions, which are not mutually exclusive. First, one can conclude from this that no simple chance process such as the law of proportionate effect is at work. Secondly, it is possible that there are other systematic influences on growth, apart from profitability, and once these are removed as well, the residuals may well obey the law of proportionate effect. Lastly, it is also possible that we have not properly taken into account the influence of profitability on growth, or to put it in econometric terms, there is a specification error in the simple linear and log-linear models we have employed in removing the influence of profitability. The last possibility will be examined below by comparing the distributions of actual growth rates with those of expected as well as residual growth rates from these models.

Table 7.10 **Distribution of Residual Growth Rates by Size of Firm**

Residual growth rates derived from the regression equation:

Growth $= a + b$ (Post-tax Rate of Return of Equity Assets) $+ \epsilon$

Industry	04, Engineering			11, Clothing and Footwear			12, Food		
	Residual Growth (%)			Residual Growth (%)			Residual Growth (%)		
Whole Period (1948-60)	Number of firms	Mean	Standard Deviation	Number of firms	Mean	Standard Deviation	Number of firms	Mean	Standard Deviation
Size (£'000)									
<250	39	−0.69	3.34	21	−0.39	3.87	20	−0.45	5.94
<500	40	−0.70	3.14	16	0.36	3.88	19	−1.12	6.15
<1,000	55	0.45	3.83	18	−0.66	1.68	8	0.36	4.17
<2,000	40	0.13	3.53	7	−0.17	1.32	7	−0.72	2.20
>2,000	39	0.64	3.86	6	2.56	3.95	19	1.70	3.37
Total	213	0.00	3.61	68	0.00	3.35	73	0.00	5.10
Sub-period 2 (1954-60)									
<250	29	−2.17	3.20	17	1.168	7.648	16	1.59	13.75
<500	39	−0.45	4.67	16	1.035	6.626	24	−1.68	7.32
<1,000	55	0.43	5.01	26	−1.441	2.942	12	1.22	5.12
<2,000	53	0.14	4.61	10	−1.520	3.365	16	−2.20	4.20
>2,000	85	0.58	5.64	8	2.030	5.514	22	1.64	4.50
Total	261	−0.00	5.01	77	−0.000	5.615	90	0.00	7.90
Sub-period 1 (1948-54)									
<250	50	0.27	4.22	30	−0.36	5.07	32	−0.54	6.65
<500	55	−1.26	3.58	19	0.90	7.95	29	0.003	5.76
<1,000	68	0.06	4.30	20	−0.38	2.04	13	1.33	5.64
<2,000	45	0.69	4.50	9	−0.95	1.61	11	−0.76	8.16
>2,000	40	0.52	3.07	7	1.41	2.68	23	0.36	3.07
Total	258	−0.00	4.06	85	0.00	5.05	108	0.00	5.37

Table 7.11. Univariate distribution of residual growth rates

The residual growth rates are obtained from the following regression model (explained in the text):

$$G = a_1 + b_1 \, P' + b_2 \, P'D_1 + b_3 \, P'D_2 + a_2 \, D_1 + a_3 \, D_2 + \epsilon$$

Where P' = Post-tax rate of return on equity assets

(The meaning of the equation is explained in the text, page 160)

The population consists of continuing companies in the Clothing and Footwear, Food, and Engineering industries.

Growth Rate Range (% p.a.)	Number of firms in each range		
	Sub-Period 1 (1948-54)	Sub-Period 2 (1954-60)	Whole Period (1948-60)
< -20.0	-	-	-
< -15.0	1	1	-
< -10.0	6	3	1
< - 7.5	7	6	5
< - 5.0	17	32	15
< - 2.5	77	112	61
< 0.0	164	125	123
< 2.5	86	52	75
< 5.0	48	37	37
< 7.5	20	19	17
< 10.0	10	15	14
< 15.0	8	16	6
< 20.0	6	4	-
< 25.0	1	4	-
< 30.0	-	-	-
< 35.0	-	1	-
< 40.0	-	1	-
> 40.0	-	-	-
Total	451	428	354

Specification error in the regression models

The distributions of the expected values of growth rates from the dummy variables equation given above are presented in Table 7.12 for sub-period 1 (1948-54) and sub-period 2 (1954-60) respectively. For purposes of comparison, we also present in this table, the corresponding distributions of actual growth rates.

Although the distributions of actual and expected growth rates appear broadly similar, there are some important systematic differences between them. The tables show that both in sub-period 1 and sub-period 2 below a certain growth rate (2.5% in the period 1948-54, 5% in period 1954-60), the actual frequency of firms is far too high compared with the predicted frequency. In the middle range of growth rates (ranging from about 5% to 15%), the predicted frequency is much greater than the actual one, and at the top of the scale the reverse is again true. Essentially the same result, with only minor modifications as to the cut-off points, was obtained, when, instead of comparing the actual growth rates with the predictions from the linear equation, the predicted growth rates from the log-linear equation in growth and profitability were used.[1]

The comparison of the distributions of actual and predicted growth rates strongly points to the possibility of a specification error in the models used. The specification error could either arise from the fact that there is a complex non-linear relationship between growth and profitability, as opposed to a simple linear or a log-linear one, or it could be due to the fact that the errors are heteroscedastic in these models.

These possibilities can be examined, at least in a tentative way, by arranging the residual growth rates according to the order of magnitude of the predicted growth rates. This is done in Tables 7.13a and 7.13b where for each range of predicted growth rates, the mean residual growth rate and the standard deviation of residual growth rates are given. Both the predicted and the residual growth rates have been derived from the linear, dummy variables, equation in profitability and growth, used above.

Considering the question of heteroscedasticity first, Table 7.13a shows that although the standard deviations of the residual growth rates are considerably larger for very low or for very high levels of predicted growth rates, the error term is fairly homoscedastic for most levels of predicted growth rates, in sub-period 1. In sub-period 2 (Table 7.13b) there is stronger evidence of heteroscedasticity. The standard deviation of the residual growth rates appears to be higher for the above average level of predicted growth rates than for those which are below average.

However, more importantly, Tables 7.13a and 7.13b also seem to support the suggestion of a complex non-linear relationship between growth and profitability. Both in sub-period 1 and sub-period 2, at very low predicted growth rates ($< 5\%$), the average residual growth rate is positive. From about -5% to 7.5% (the latter is approximately the level of average growth), the average residual growth rates are consistently negative. At above the level of average predicted growth

172

Table 7.12. Distribution of actual and predicted growth rates

The Growth Rates have been predicted from the equation:

$$G = a_1 + b_1 \, P' + b_2 \, P'D_1 + b_3 \, P'D_2 + a_2D_1 + a_3D_2 + \epsilon$$

(The meaning of this equation is explained in the text, page 160)

Growth Rate Range	Sub-Period 1 (1948-54)		Sub-Period 2 (1954-60)		Whole Period (1948-60)	
	Predicted % of firms	Actual % of firms	Predicted % of firms	Actual % of firms	Predicted % of firms	Actual % of firms
<-5.0	1.3	2.2	1.9	2.8	1.4	1.4
<-2.5	0.4	1.3	0.7	1.4	0.3	1.1
<0	1.1	4.6	1.6	6.5	1.7	2.0
<2.5	3.8	9.3	3.5	12.7	2.0	8.4
<5.0	12.2	10.8	13.8	16.3	9.0	15.1
<7.5	21.1	17.2	30.6	17.7	28.0	21.7
<10.0	24.8	17.9	27.6	14.4	31.9	16.9
<15.0	29.3	21.9	18.0	15.7	22.9	23.9
<20.0	4.7	9.7	1.6	7.6	2.2	7.0
>20.0	1.3	5.1	0.7	4.9	0.6	2.5
Number of firms	451	451	428	428	354	354

Table 7.13a. The mean and standard deviation of residual growth rates arranged in the order of magnitude of predicted growth rates*

All firms (except Tobacco), sub-period 1 (1948-54)

Predicted Growth Rates (%)	Residual Growth Rates (%)		
	Average	Standard Deviation	Number of Firms
< - 5.0	3.1	9.8	6
< - 2.5	-0.5	2.2	2
< 0	-5.7	5.4	5
< 2.5	-1.5	2.2	18
< 5.0	-1.8	4.2	55
< 7.5	-0.4	4.0	98
< 10.0	1.0	4.8	110
< 15.0	0.6	4.1	131
< 20.0	-0.6	4.9	20
> 20.0	-1.0	8.0	6

Von Neumann Ratio	= 1.68
Von Neumann Ratio based only on signs of residuals (ignoring magnitudes)	= 1.7
Critical value of Von Neumann ratio at 10% level	= 1.90
Critical value of Von Neumann ratio at 5% level	= 1.87

*   The predicted and residual growth rates have been obtained from the following equation:

Growth = $a_1 + b_1 P' + b_2 P'D_1 + b_3 P'D_2 + a_2D_1 + a_3D_2 + \epsilon$

where P' = Post-tax rate of return on equity assets.

Table 7.13b. **The mean and standard deviation of residual growth rates arranged in the order of magnitude of predicted growth rates***

All firms (except Tobacco), sub-period 2 (1954-60)

Predicted Growth Rates	Residual Growth Rates		
	Average	Standard Deviation	Number of Firms
<- 5.0	6.4	12.1	8
<- 2.5	2.5	0.2	2
< 0	-2.2	3.0	8
< 2.5	-2.7	3.6	16
< 5.0	-0.9	4.7	59
< 7.5	-0.5	5.0	133
< 10.0	0.5	6.3	115
< 15.0	1.0	5.2	77
< 20.0	-1.6	5.4	7
> 20.0	-0.7	17.5	3

Von Neumann Ratio	= 2.1
Von Neumann Ratio based only on signs of residuals (ignoring magnitudes)	= 1.75 (approx.)
Critical value at 10% level	= 1.91
Critical value at 5% level	= 1.87

* The predicted and residual growth rates have been obtained from the following equation:

$$\text{Growth} = a_1 + b_1 P' + b_2 P'D_1 + b_3 P'D_2 + a_2 D_1 + a_3 D_2 + \epsilon$$

where P' = Post-tax rate of return on equity assets.

(from 7.5% to 15%), the residuals are consistently positive. At very high predicted growth rates ($> 15\%$), the average residual growth rate is again consistently negative. Since there is always a positive association between growth and profitability, this suggests the very stylized picture below of the regression model which would best describe the data.

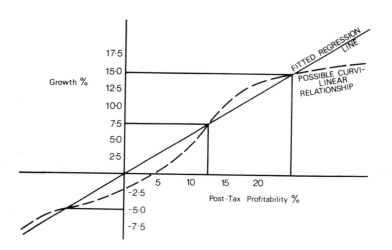

Such a picture of the relationship between growth and profitability is by no means unreasonable from an economic point of view. It suggests that growth responds in varying degrees to a given <u>change</u> in profitability, at different <u>levels</u> of profitability. For example, when the profits are average or above average, a given change in profitability may be expected to lead to a much larger change in growth than when the profits are much below average. When a firm is making good profits, it is likely to find it much easier to raise equity capital or sell fixed interest bearing securities than when it is making very low profits. However, if a firm is making exceptionally high profits it is quite reasonable to argue that the stock market does <u>not</u> expect it to <u>continue</u> to do so. In that case a given increase in its profitability may not lead to as much increase in its growth, as if it were a somewhat lower, but from the point of view of the stock market, a <u>sustainable</u> level of profitability. Thus, from an economic point of view, it is not at least unreasonable that there should be a different relationship between profitability and growth for firms in the different ranges of profitability.[1]

Now, whether the true relationship between profitability and growth in fact takes the form shown in the figure above, can be rigorously established only by fitting the appropriate polynomial to the data, and testing the significance of the regression coefficients pertaining to the higher order terms in profitability. Alternatively, it is possible to sub-divide the data into different categories of profitability and to estimate separately a relationship between growth and profitability for each of these categories. This could be done quite easily by introducing additional dummy variables for each of the categories into the dummy variables equation given above. One could then test the significance of the regression coefficients relating to the appropriate dummy variables in a manner similar to that followed in section 1 and section 2.

We have adopted the cruder method of testing for possible non-linearity (rather than of the specific kind depicted in the figure above), by computing the Von Neumann ratio from the residual growth rates and testing whether there is a positive serial correlation among the residuals.[1] The existence of the latter would confirm that the true relationship between growth and profitability is non-linear. This is tested by means of Theil-Nagar test, the results of which are given at the bottom of Tables 7.13a and 7.13b. The tests showed that in sub-period 1 (1948-54) the hypothesis of serial independence of the residuals is rejected at the 5% level in favour of the alternative of positive serial association between them. However, in sub-period 2 (1954-60), the null hypothesis is rejected at the 5% level if we ignore the magnitude of the residuals and consider only their signs. Thus, we conclude that there is a strong evidence of possible non-linearity in the relationship between growth and profitability in sub-period 1. The evidence in sub-period 2 is not quite so strong, but neither can it be ignored.[2]

To sum up, a comparison of the distributions of the actual, expected and residual growth rates suggests that the possibility of a complex non-linear relationship between growth and profitability deserves to be seriously investigated.[3] With a correctly specified model, which takes proper account of the influence of profitability on growth, it may yet be the case that the distribution of residual growth rates obeys the law of proportionate effect. These issues, however, cannot be pursued here; they will be taken up in subsequent work.

5.   First-order correlation coefficients

Another fruitful way of looking at the residuals is to consider the first-order correlation coefficients between growth and other variables, with profitability held constant.

In Chapter 3, we presented matrices of simple (zero-order) correlation coefficients between each possible pair of the fourteen economic and financial variables whose distributions were given in Chapter 2 of the book. The zero-order correlation matrices showed how growth was related to other variables such as size (Indicator 1), profitability (Indicators 5 and 6), liquidity (Indicator 11), gearing (Indicator 10), stock market valuation of the firm (represented by the valuation ratio, Indicator 14), and how the latter variables were related among themselves. To recall briefly the main conclusions of Chapter 3, we found that although there was a striking absence of any relationship between size and any of the other variables, a large number of these variables were related both to profitability and to growth. For instance, the correlation coefficients showed a considerable degree of positive association between the valuation ratio and growth as well as between the valuation ratio and either measure of profitability. Similarly, variables such as the dividend return (Indicator 7), retention ratio (Indicator 8), gearing and liquidity showed some association both with profitability and with growth. On the basis of the simple correlation coefficients, it is not possible to say whether there was an independent association between growth and these other variables, or whether the observed association between them was entirely due to the association of these variables with profitability. To shed some light on this question, the first-order correlation coefficients, (partial correlation coefficients), between growth and the other variables, with post-tax profitability on equity assets (Indicator 6) held constant,[1] for the different industries and time periods are given in Tables 7.14a, 7.14b and 7.14c.

An intuitive way of interpreting the first-order correlation coefficients between any two variables in Tables 7.14a to 7.14c is to regard them as the simple correlation coefficients between these variables for firms with the same level of profitability. In fact, these coefficients represent another way of looking at the nature of the residuals from the simple regression equation relating growth to profitability. The first order correlation coefficient between growth and (say) the valuation ratio, with profitability held constant, is merely the simple correlation coefficient between the residuals from the linear regression equation relating growth to profitability, and the residuals from the linear regression equation relating valuation ratio to profitability. The linear influence of profitability both on growth and on valuation ratios is removed when the residuals are calculated from the respective regression equations. The first order or the partial correlation coefficient between growth and valuation ratio, with profitability held constant, thus shows if there is an independent or net association between growth and the valuation ratio, over and above the association between them due to the influence of profitability.[2]

There are two important limitations of the concept of a partial correlation coefficient which are of some significance. First, it is a measure of net linear association between the two variables. When there is reason to believe that the relationship between any pair of variables may be non-linear, the partial correlation coefficient would be an inadequate tool of analysis.[3]

Secondly, analogous to the simple correlation coefficient, it is merely a measure of net association between the variables; it implies no cause and effect relationship. In the present context, however, we regard this limitation of partial correlation analysis as a virtue and the main reason why we chose this particular statistical tool rather than multiple regression analysis to separate out the relationships between growth and other variables for the same level of profitability. The regression coefficients of the multiple regression equation relating growth to, say, the valuation ratio and profitability would also give an indication of the

Table 7.14a. First-order correlation coefficients

(With Post-tax Profitability on Equity Assets held constant)

Sub-period 1 (1948-54)

Industry / Variables	Clothing and Footwear	Food	Non-Electrical Engineering	All (including Tobacco)
Growth and Valuation Ratio	.1182	-.2083*	.2422*	.1163*
Growth and Gearing	-.1016	-.0405	-.2442*	-.2348*
Growth and Retention Ratio	.0956	.3996*	.1511*	.1632*
Growth and Internal Finance	-.7414*	-.7287*	-.5768*	-.7303*
Growth and Liquidity	.0288	-.1215	.1382*	.0676
Growth and Dividend Return	-.0128	-.0882	.1804*	.0546

* Indicates significance at the 5% level.

Table 7.14b. First-order correlation coefficients

(With Post-tax Profitability on Equity Assets held constant)

Sub-period 2 (1954-60)

Industry / Variables	Clothing and Footwear	Food	Non-Electrical Engineering	All (including Tobacco)
Growth and Valuation Ratio	.1527	.5661*	.2235*	.2917*
Growth and Gearing	.2873*	-.0055	.1781*	.1441*
Growth and Retention Ratio	.1759	.0382	.2118*	.1027*
Growth and Internal Finance	-.7786*	-.7609*	-.7665*	-.7303*
Growth and Liquidity	-.3332*	-.4615*	-.0697	-.2294*
Growth and Dividend Return	-.2071	.2626*	-.3056*	-.1720*

* Indicates significance at the 5% level.

Table 7.14c. First-order correlation coefficients

(With Post-tax Profitability on Equity Assets held constant)

<u>Whole period (1948-60)</u>

Industry Variables	Clothing and Footwear	Food	Non-Electri-cal Engi-neering	All (includ-ing Tobacco)
Growth and Valuation Ratio	-	-	-	-
Growth and Gearing	.1769	-.1470	.0850	-.0076
Growth and Retention Ratio	.0296	.2446*	.2158*	.1837
Growth and Internal Finance	-.7575*	-.8376*	-.6731*	-.6849*
Growth and Liquidity	-.0209	-.3818*	-.0655	-.0378
Growth and Dividend Return	-.0442	.2750	-.3290*	.0563

*   Indicates significance at the 5% level.

net association between growth and the valuation ratio. However, to the extent that the causal relationship between growth and the valuation ratio is a two-way one (for the same level of profitability a high growth rate may cause a high valuation ratio and a high valuation ratio may in turn cause high growth rate), the regression coefficients of the multiple regression equation (as opposed to r^2) would tend to be biased (in the upward direction in this case). This is particularly true of the relationships between growth and other variables such as liquidity and gearing where it is even more likely that liquidity and gearing are determined by the growth rate rather than the other way round.

The question of causation is a problematical one and can only be treated satisfactorily in the context of a simultaneous equations model of the equilibrium of the firm. It seems reasonable to suppose that the firm, in the process of maximizing its profitability or, as some writers suggest, its growth, chooses the appropriate levels of financial variables such as gearing, liquidity, retention ratio etc., with the result that their optimum values are determined simultaneously with the optimum values of growth, profitability and stock market valuation of the firm.[1] However, there are very considerable theoretical and statistical problems in the application of such models to our type of data and they will not be considered here.[1] The partial correlation coefficients may not be an adequate guide to the underlying chain of causation, but they do tell us whether, for given profitability, there is any relationship between growth and the financial and stock market variables.

Turning to Table 7.14a, we find that for firms of the same level of profitability in the Engineering industry, there is a significant (at the 5% level) positive association between growth in the period (1948-54) and stock market valuation at the end of the period (i.e. in 1954). However, in the Clothing and Footwear industry, the first-order correlation coefficient between growth and valuation ratio is insignificant, though positive, and in the Food industry, it is significant and negative. A glance at Appendix G will show that the zero-order correlation coefficient between growth and valuation ratio in the latter two industries is in every case significant and positive. The observed association between these two variables, shown by the simple correlation coefficients, must, therefore, be due to the influence of profitability on both of them. Once the influence of profitability is eliminated, the association between growth and valuation ratio in these two industries becomes either negative or non-existent. Thus, in sub-period 1 (1948-54) it was only in the Engineering industry that there existed an independent positive association between the growth and the stock market valuation of firms.

In sub-period 2 (1954-60), Table 7.14b shows that for firms of the same level of profitability, there is a positive association between growth and valuation ratio at the end of the period, in each of the three major industries. The first-order correlation coefficient is significantly positive in the Food and Engineering industries, and it is particularly marked in the former industry. Now, with given profitability, a positive association between growth and valuation ratio at the end of the period may be expected if the stock market expects the high growth rate in this period to lead to higher profitability and higher dividends in the future. It seems, therefore, that in 1960 the stock market had a much more positive attitude to growth over sub-period 2 (1954-60) – the period which witnessed the stock market boom of 1959-60 – than its attitude in 1954 to growth during sub-period 1 (1948-54). Here it must be remembered that we are relating the growth achieved in the period 1954-60 to the valuation ratio in 1960. The causation is, therefore, likely to run from growth to valuation ratio rather than the other way round.

As for growth and gearing, the zero-order correlation coefficients always showed these variables to be negatively related. When profitability is held constant, there is still a negative relationship between these variables in sub-period 1 (1948-54), although the negative association is significant at the 5% level only in the Engineering industry. However, in sub-period 2 (1954-60), the partial correlation coefficients show that there is a significant positive association (at the 5% level) between growth and gearing in Engineering and in Clothing and Footwear. For given profitability, the firms with above average growth in these two industries tended to pay an above average proportion of their income in fixed interest and dividend payments.

The simple correlation coefficients showed growth and liquidity to be almost always positively associated, although there were a few cases when they were also negatively associated. For the same level of profitability there is no clear pattern in sub-period 1, but growth and liquidity tend to be negatively correlated in each industry in sub-period 2 (1954-60). The negative association is particularly pronounced in the Food industry, but it is also significant at the 5% level in the Clothing and Footwear industry during sub-period 2.

As is to be expected, the partial correlation coefficients between growth and retention ratio are always positive and in a number of cases significant at the 5% level. Similarly, with given profitability, there is in every case a very pronounced negative association between growth and internal finance of growth (Indicator 9). Thus we find that among firms with the same level of profitability those with an above-average rate of growth tend only only to retain an above proportion of their profits, but they require so much finance that they also tend to raise an above proportion of it from outside sources.

Growth and Dividend Return on Equity Assets (Indicator 7) were always significantly positively associated in terms of the simple correlation coefficients. However, for given profitability, we find that there is often a significant negative association between these variables – i.e. with given profitability, firms which pay out an above-average proportion of profits in dividends tend to have below-average growth rates. This is not a necessary logical consequence, since reliance on external finance could easily produce an opposite result, and in fact in the Food industry in sub-period 2, we find that growth and dividend return are, indeed, positively associated. The positive association may arise from the fact that with given profitability, the firms which pay out above average dividends, have above average valuation ratios, which enables them to have above average growth from external sources.

182

To sum up, the first-order correlation coefficients show whether there is any association between growth and the financial and stock market variables when profitability is held constant. For instance, we have found that the observed negative association between growth and gearing considered by themselves, or the positive association between growth and dividend return by themselves, is quite often due to the influence of profitability on these variables. For given profitability, the nature of the independent association between these variables is opposite to the ones observed when they are considered by themselves. Secondly, the partial correlation coefficients also give some indication of the attitude of the stock market to growth in the two periods, 1948-54 and 1954-60. We have found that the stock market reacted much more positively to growth in the latter period than in the period 1948-54.

6.   **The prediction of growth by other economic and financial variables**

So far in this chapter, we have studied the relationship between growth, profitability and other variables over the current time span. In this section, we wish to find out to what extent, with knowledge of the economic and financial characteristics of the firm during the recent past, it is possible to predict its rate of growth in the subsequent time-periods.

We have seen, earlier in this chapter, that current profitability has an important influence on the current growth of the firm. We also found, in Chapter 6, that past profitability is a good predictor of current profitability. It seems likely, therefore, that the simplest model for predictive purposes would be to make the growth of the firm in the second sub-period (1954-60) a function of its achieved profitability in the first sub-period (1948-54). Thus we have the predictive model:

$$G_t = a + b \, P'_{t-1} + \epsilon_t \, ,$$

where   G is the growth rate (Indicator 4)

P' is the post-tax rate of return on equity assets (Indicator 6)

The subscript 't' refers to the period (1954-60) and t-1 to the period (1948-54).

The results of fitting this model to the firms in the individual industries and in all industries together are given in Table 7.15. We find that, although the regression coefficient relating achieved profitability in one period to growth in the subsequent period is significant at a high level (1%) in two of the three major industries and in all industries together the results are rather disappointing for the purposes of prediction. Only in the food industry does the proportion of explained variance of subsequent growth reach 20 per cent; in Clothing and Footwear, it is nearly zero, and in the Engineering industry it is less than 10 per cent. In spite of this, it is worth noting that the past profitability seems to provide a better explanation of future growth than the past growth of the firm taken by itself. A comparison of Table 7.15 with the regression results given in Table 5.7, pertaining to the persistency of growth, will make this point clear.

Table 7.15. Regression results

$$G_t = a + b\ P'_{t-1} + \epsilon_t$$

Industry		Parameter Estimates	a	b	$\bar{R}^2$	No. of observations
04	Engineering	Value	4.3	.43	.08	162
		S.E.	±1.36	± .11		
		T.	3.14*	3.96*		
11	Clothing and Footwear	Value	6.95	.077	0	36
		S.E.	±2.20	± .172		
		T.	3.15*	.448		
12	Food	Value	1.1	.66	.18	45
		S.E.	±2.6	± .20		
		T.	.433	3.41*		
All	Including Tobacco	Value	4.1	.43	.08	246
		S.E.	±1.1	± .09		
		T.	3.624*	4.862*		

*   Indicates significance at the 5% level.

Note. $\bar{R}^2$ is R^2 adjusted for degrees of Freedom.

184

It is possible that the predictive power of the model may be improved by including additional explanatory variables. _A priori_ the most relevant variables, apart from past profitability, would appear to be the valuation ratio (Indicator 14) and the past growth of the firm. For the same level of profitability the higher the valuation ratio, the more a firm will be able to grow by raising new issue finance. Similarly, since as we saw in Chapter 5, there is some persistency of growth rates, it is possible that there is a type of firm which is growth-minded and which grows persistently faster than other firms for the same level of profitability. We could also include size as an explanatory variable, but we have accumulated enough evidence from the past chapters to indicate that the size of the firm has no influence on its growth rate. Thus we now have the following model to predict the growth of the firm:

$$G_t = a + b\ P'_{t-1} + c\ V_{t-1} + d\ G_{t-1} + \epsilon_t$$

where V_{t-1} is the valuation ratio (Indicator 14) at the end of the period, t-1.

Since profitability, valuation ratio and growth are highly inter-correlated the least squares estimators of b, c and d are not reliable. However, although it is not possible to estimate separately the influence of these variables on the future growth of the firm, the model, under certain assumptions, can still be used for predictive purposes.

The results, given in Table 7.16, show that in fact the second model is not much of an improvement over the earlier one. Only in the Food industry, is the $\bar{R}^2$ slightly higher for this model as compared with the first one.

Finally, more as an act of desperation than of _a priori_ justification, [1] we shall try a model which brings in most of the known economic and financial characteristics of the firm in the previous period. Thus we have:

$$G_t = a + b\ \log S_{t-1} + c\ V_{t-1} + d\ G_{t-1} + e\ P'_{t-1}$$
$$+ f\ R_{t-1} + g\ I_{t-1} + h\ N_{t-1} + i\ L_{t-1} + \epsilon_t$$

where   G, V and P' are as given above

          S = Closing Size (Indicator 2)

          R = Retention Ratio (Indicator 8)

          I = Internal Finance of Growth (Indicator 9)

          N = Gearing (Indicator 10)

          L = Liquidity (Indicator 11)

The results of fitting this model to the individual industries and to all industries together are given in Table 7.17. Again because of the inter-correlation between the variables, the estimates of the individual regression coefficients are not reliable. However, the last but one column of Table 7.17 shows a remarkable improvement in the predictive ability of this model as compared with the earlier ones. There is a marked improvement in the degree of explanation achieved in the Cloth-

Table 7.16. Regression results

$$G_t = a + b\, P'_{t-1} + c\, V_{t-1} + d\, G_{t-1} + \epsilon_t$$

Industry	Parameter Estimates	a	b	c	d	$\bar{R}^2$	n
04 Engineering	Value	3.95	.039	.129	.305	.07	162
	S.E.	±1.41	± .13	± .121	± .164		
	T.	2.797*	.292	1.065	1.858		
11 Clothing and Footwear	Value	6.27	.317	- .232	.298	0	36
	S.E.	±2.56	± .349	± .207	± .272		
	T.	2.447*	.908	-1.122	.110		
12 Food	Value	6.9	.17	- .33	.77	.21	45
	S.E.	±2.9	± .21	± .21	± .26		
	T.	.333	.828	-1.56	3.00*		
All Including Tobacco	Value	3.6	.15	- .019	.36	.08	246
	S.E.	±1.2	± .10	± .091	± .13		
	T.	3.07*	1.45	- .214	2.77*		

* Indicates significance at the 5% level.

Note. $\bar{R}^2$ is R^2 adjusted for degrees of Freedom.

Table 7.17 Regression Results

Equation: Growth $= a + b.y$ log opening size$_t$ $+ c.$ Valuation Ratio$_{t-1}$ $+ d.y$ Growth$_{t-1}$ $+ c.$ Post-tax Rate of Return on Equity Assets$_{t-1}$ $+ f.$ Retention Ratio$_{t-1}$ $+ g.$ Internal Finance$_{t-1}$ $+ h.$ Gearing$_{t-1}$ $+ i.$ Liquidity$_{t-1}$

Industry	Parameter	a	b	c	d	e	f	g	h	i	$\bar{R}^2$	No. of observations
04	Engineering Value	0.032	−0.0052	0.23	−0.25	0.50	0.12	−0.082	−0.10	−0.022	0.11	162
	SE	0.031	0.0045	0.18	0.17	0.23	0.048	0.028	0.082	0.021		
	T	1.03	−1.15	1.26	−1.43	2.14*	2.57*	−2.90*	−1.27	−1.06		
11	Clothing and Foot-wear Value	0.16	0.0067	0.042	−0.69	0.55	0.050	−0.13	−0.10	−0.049	0.17	36
	SE	0.64	0.012	0.45	0.23	0.41	0.092	0.038	0.12	0.062		
	T	2.50*	0.57	0.095	−2.94*	1.34	0.54	−3.40*	−0.86	−0.79		
12	Food Value	0.29	0.00019	−0.24	−0.75	1.1	−0.20	−0.075	−0.25	−0.14	0.54	45
	SE	0.081	0.0066	0.23	0.30	0.26	0.084	0.057	0.13	0.040		
	T	3.56*	0.028	−1.06	−2.50*	4.22*	−2.39*	−1.33	−1.92	−3.49*		
All	Including Tobacco Value	0.071	−0.0035	0.21	−0.35	0.66	0.048	−0.082	−0.0053	−0.044	0.16	246
	SE	0.027	0.0034	0.13	0.13	0.16	0.038	0.023	0.055	0.018		
	T	2.58*	−1.02	1.58	−2.74*	4.11*	1.27	−3.65*	−0.10	−2.46*		

* Indicates significance at the 5% level. Note: $\bar{R}^2$ is R^2 adjusted for degrees of freedom.

187

ing and Footwear industry and in the Food industry. Nevertheless, the results are still disappointing; the inclusion of 8 explanatory variables in the model still explains only 16% of the variance of growth in the next period for the firms in all industries taken together. Thus, it appears that knowledge of the economic and financial characteristics of the firm in one period is not a good guide to the prediction of its growth in the subsequent period.

It is, of course, possible to look at the above results in a more optimistic way. It can be argued that although the predictive models given above explain only a small part of the variance of the subsequent growth of the firms, for practical purposes it is still better than having no predictive model at all. In other words, if the past economic and financial record of the firm were known, then using the parameters of the above models, one would always be able to predict the growth of the firms better on an average than without the knowledge of the firm's record. However, this argument rests on the assumption that the parameters of the predictive models, estimated above by comparing the growth of the firm in 1954-60 with its record in the period 1948-54, are reasonably immutable. In fact, since as noted earlier there have been marked changes in the relationship between growth, profits and other variables over time, there is every reason to suspect that these parameters will be markedly different now from what they have been in the past. Thus, even in a limited sense, the above predictive models are unlikely to be helpful from a practical point of view in predicting the growth of the firms (say) in the period 1968-74.

Lastly, we should note that the above conclusions, and the results presented in Tables 7.15, 7.16 and 7.17 are based on a rather restrictive population of firms. The firms, which did not continue, which did not have valuation ratios in 1954 (i.e. a stock market quotation for ordinary shares was not available on Moodies Cards or in the Stock Exchange Year Book), which had negative average equity assets, or which grew by less than one per cent per annum in either period are excluded. Only the last restriction is a serious one, but it became necessary in order to include the Internal Finance of Growth (Indicator 9) in the model for which meaningful values are available only for the restricted population. However, as the results of Tables 7.15 to 7.17 are still based on an analysis of nearly 250 firms, the main conclusions of this section are unlikely to be altered to any significant degree even if the full population of firms were studied.

7.   Summary and conclusions

The main purpose of this Chapter has been to analyze the effect of systematic influences on the growth of firms. The major systematic influence on growth is that of profitability. The relationship between profitability and growth, which is of considerable theoretical as well as practical importance, has been examined in great detail in the first part of the Chapter.

We saw that the growth of a firm depends both on its willingness and its ability to grow. The profits provide the ability to finance growth, but the willingness to grow depends on a number of important factors other than profitability. Therefore, in an expanding economy, although we expect a close relationship between the proftiability and growth of firms, on a cross-section basis, we should not be surprised if the nature of this relationship is different in different industries at any particular time, or within a particular industry over different time periods. There is reason to believe that it may also tend to vary between firms of different sizes.

The main conclusions of our empirical investigation of the relationship between growth and profitability for firms in different industries are as follows. First, as expected, there was found to be a fairly strong positive association between growth and profitability, with profitability explaining on an average, about 50% of the variation in growth rates. A one percentage point increase in a firm's post-tax profitability on equity assets could be expected to lead on an average to a .7 percentage point increase in its growth rate. Secondly, it was found that the post-tax profitability on equity assets, rather than the pre-tax rate of return on net assets provided the best explanation of firm's growth. Thirdly, the empirical results showed that there were statistically significant differences in the regression coefficients relating profitability to growth in different industries. For example, in sub-period 2 (1954-60), whereas a 1 percentage point increase in the profitability of an Engineering firm led on an average to .7 percentage points increase in its growth rate, a similar increase in the profitability of a Clothing and Footwear firm, was associated with an almost equivalent (1 percentage point) increase in its growth rate. Fourthly, the regression coefficients relating growth to profitability in different industries were also found to vary significantly over time.

The relationship between growth and profitability was also examined separately for the largest firms (i.e. firms with opening net assets of greater than £2 million) in each industry. Although the regression coefficients for the largest firms varied considerably between industries and over time, the standard error of these coefficients was so high that very few of the inter-industry and inter-temporal differences were found to be statistically significant. In other words, for these large firms, and at least for the industries which we have examined, the available data do not reject the hypothesis that growth-profitability observations in different industries and over different time periods come from the same basic population or the same statistical structure. This finding lends support to a tentative conclusion of the last chapter that as far as the analysis of growth and profitability is concerned, the conventional industrial classification is less relevant for the largest firms. This also accords with a priori reasoning.

The relationship between growth and profitability for the largest firms was also compared with that observed for the smaller-sized firms. In spite of the high standard errors of the regression coefficients of the largest firms, these coefficients were found to be significantly different from those of smaller-sized firms in sub-period 2 (1954-60) and the whole period (1948-60). However, no conclusion could be arrived at with respect to the direction of the difference in these regression coefficients relating growth to profitability; in some industries, the largest firms had higher regression coefficients, whereas in others it was the smaller-sized firms which had the larger coefficients.

Next we analyzed the residuals of the growth rates from the linear and log-linear regression models. In previous chapters we had found that the crude distribution of growth rates is not generated by the simple stochastic process known as the law of proportionate effect. Here we tried to see whether, once the influence of a major systematic factor such as profitability is removed, the distribution of residual growth rates can be deemed to have been generated by the law of proportionate effect. The various distributions of residual growth rates were found to be incompatible with this hypothesis. However, a further analysis of the residuals showed that there is most likely a specification error in the linear and log-linear regression models used to obtain the residual growth rates. It appears that there is a more complex non-linear relationship between growth and profitability which needs further investigation.

The analysis of residuals was carried a stage further by computing the first-order correlation coefficients between growth and other economic and financial variables, with profitability held constant. The first-order correlation coefficients showed that, for firms with the same level of profitability, there was a much more consistent and a higher positive association between growth in the period 1954-60 and valuation ratio at the end of the period, than between growth in the period 1948-54 and valuation ratio in 1954. This indicates that in the economic environment of the latter period, the stock-market reacted much more favourably to growth than in the period 1948-54. We also found that a greater part of the observed (zero-order) correlation between growth and financial variables such as liquidity, gearing, dividend return, etc., was due to the fact that all these variables were also related to profitability. When the influence of profitability was removed, the relationship between growth and these variables either disappeared, or was opposite to that which the simple correlation coefficients purported to show. On the more positive side, it was found that in sub-period 2 (1954-60), among firms with the same level of profitability, firms which had above-average growth tended to have above-average stock-market valuation at the end of the period. They also tended to have above-average gearing, they retained an above-average proportion of their profits, and they operated at a below-average level of liquidity.

Finally, we attempted to find out to what extent it was possible to predict the growth of firms in the period 1954-60 on the basis of their performance in the period 1948-54. This analysis was carried out on a somewhat restricted population of firms and a number of different prediction models were tried. The results, however, were not found to be very encouraging. At least over the period which we have studied, knowledge of the economic and financial characteristics of the firm over one six-year period did not go far in predicting its growth over the next six years. Furthermore, we have no reason to believe that the relationship which held between growth in 1954-60 and the values of economic and financial variables in 1948-54 is likely to hold between later periods. However it does appear that the variable whose past value is most likely to explain future growth is profitability, and that past profitability is likely to be positively associated with future growth.

190

8   Summary and Conclusions

In the last four chapters, we have discussed in detail the relationship between the size, profitability and growth of firms. However, this discussion has been conducted within a particular analytical framework and it has also been concerned with a number of rather narrow methodological and theoretical issues. In this chapter, we attempt to draw together those conclusions of our analysis which are of general interest, and to assess their practical significance. This chapter is not, therefore, a summary of all the main conclusions of our analysis; it ignores specific analytical issues such as the Law of Proportionate Effect,[1] and it also treads rather lightly over many qualifications which should be attached to the results.

The discussion below follows approximately the order in which various subjects have been discussed in the previous chapters, rather than the order of their practical importance.

1.   Size in relation to growth and profitability

We have found that, in each of the industries examined, the average growth rate measured in terms of net assets (Indicator 4) is remarkably independent of the opening size of firms (Indicator 1). The same is also true of profitability, when it is measured in terms of either of our rates of return (Indicators 5 and 6). The relationship between size and growth is examined in Chapter 4 (see especially Tables 4.1 to 4.3) and that between size and profitability in Chapter 6 (see especially Tables 6.6 to 6.10).

It is of considerable theoretical interest to find this independence of profitability and of growth in relation to size, in each industry. The independence of profitability and size accords with contemporary theories such as those of Mrs. Penrose[2] and R.L. Marris,[3] which deny the existence of an optimum size to which all profit-maximizing firms should tend; the independence of growth and size goes further and shows that a firm's rate of growth is in fact more or less independent of its size.

Although the average growth rate does not vary significantly with the size of the firm, we have found that the variability of growth rates as between firms does change with size to a significant extent, and that the tendency is for it to decrease as size increases. The variability of profit rates also tends to decrease as size increases, and this tendency is more marked and more regular than that relating to growth rates. In other words, large firms have a more predictable rate of growth and rate of profit but not, on average, a higher one. The smaller firms studied include both the fastest growing and the fastest shrinking companies; they also include both the highly profitable and highly unprofitable companies. The largest firms rarely shrink in size or make losses but also they achieve less often spectacular growth rates or spectacular rates of profit.

This result seems very plausible on a priori grounds.

Firstly, large firms tend to be more diversified in the range of their activities, so that losses on one product are offset against exceptional profits on another. Similarly, declining output and investment in one activity will be offset against the growth of other activities. This may also explain the fact that inter-industry differences between average profit and growth rates are less for large firms than for small firms. The large firms tend to form a class on their own, with similar growth or profit rates, irrespective of industry, and this could well be because diversification does, in fact, make the industry classification relatively unimportant in this context.

Secondly, large firms may be less adventurous in their policies, which means that they avert the risk of making losses but lose the chance of making exceptional profits. This may be partly a function of the market structure, since the larger firm is more likely to be in an oligopolistic or monopolistic situation. It is also possibly due to the nature of the management of a larger company, which may be more bureaucratic perhaps more rational, and also perhaps less flexible and therefore less adventurous.[1]

However, it seems that the reward of being a large firm is not a higher prospective rate of profit or rate of growth, but the greater certainty that there will be somewhere near the average rate of profit and somewhere near the average rate of growth. This again has interesting implications for the theory of the firm, in relation to the interests of shareholders and of managers.

From the shareholder's point of view, it may be preferable to have greater certainty of profitability if he is averse to risk, although if he has a speculative or gambling psychology he might prefer the same probable profitability with a greater chance of variability, which is offered by a smaller firm. Of course, a shareholder can usually offset risks to some extent by investing in a range of companies, but the greater predictability of large companies still enables him to achieve a greater security from their shares than from a similar range of shares in small companies.

Even more than the shareholders the obvious beneficiaries of the relative stability of large companies are the employees, including management. They, unlike shareholders,[2] are committed to one firm and are likely to be averse to risk, since they stand to lose far more by loss-making and the shrinkage of the company than they stand to gain by exceptional profitability or expansion. It seems, therefore, that the more modern 'managerial' theories of the firm are right to emphasize the attraction of size as a means to security for the managers of companies.

2.   Mobility

In the first two sections of Chapter 5, we examined the question of mobility of firms within industries. By mobility we mean the degree to which firms change their ranking order between two dates, when they are ranked by size. This is a dynamic measurement of the rigidity of the structure of an industry and provides a valuable supplement to the information given by the static measure of industrial concentration which show the degree to which the larger firms dominate the industry <u>at a point in time.</u>

The results of our study of mobility are of limited interest in the present context. We have studied only three industries, so that we are unable to generalize about which type of industry is most mobile, or what are the conditions of profitability and growth which lead to the greatest degree of mobility. However, we have found at least two features worth recording.

Firstly, the slowest-growing industry was the most mobile. This, although it is clearly possible, is contrary to what might be expected. Our result may be due to the fact that the more dynamic firms tend to seek much the same growth rate, whichever industry they are in, and this growth will carry them further up the ranking order in a slow-growing industry. On the other hand, the result would also be consistent simply with the idea that, in the slow-growing Clothing and Footwear industry, the relative success of firms depends on a great and variable factor, such as the importance of striking the right fashion.

Secondly, the largest companies are less mobile than the others. This latter result does conform with what would be expected, in view of the fact, already mentioned, that the dispersion of growth rates is less for the larger firms; the fact that the variation of size is greatest among large firms also supports this expectation, since the larger gaps between company sizes mean that more growth is needed to change the order.

3.   The persistency of growth

In Chapter 5 (Section 3), we examined the persistency of growth of net assets. We found that those firms which had above-average growth rates in the period 1948-54 also tended to have above-average growth rates in the following period, 1954-60, in two of our three major industry groups.

This result was achieved by rank correlation analysis, which we chose, for technical reasons, as being the most appropriate statistical tool for the purpose. It can be seen from the rank correlation results (Table 5.8) that, although the positive association between growth in 1948-54 and growth in 1954-60 was statistically significant (at the 5% level) for firms in Engineering and in Clothing and Footwear, it was nevertheless rather weak. The Kendall rank correlation coefficient is equal to +1 when there is identical ranking in the two distributions compared, (i.e. in this case, each company came in identical order, when ranked by growth, in 1954-60 as in 1948-54), -1 when the ranking orders are opposite, and 0 when the ranking orders bear a completely random relationship to one another, i. e. as many pairs retain their ranking orders as change them. The value of the rank correlation coefficient obtained for Non-electrical Engineering, $r_k = 0.25$ (See Table 5.8) indicates that, of all possible pairs of continuing companies in this industry, five eighths[1] had the same relative ranking by growth in 1954-60 as by growth in 1948-54, whereas the other three eighths changed ranks.

Regression analysis, which is a cruder tool of analysis for the present purpose, but which has a clearer intuitive meaning, yielded a statistically significant positive association between growth in 1948-54 and in 1954-60 in our largest industry, Non-Electrical Engineering, but not in the other two large industries. In the Engineering industry, a growth rate of one percentage point above (or below) average in 1948-54 was associated, on average, with a growth rate of 0.37 percentage points above (or below) average in 1954-60 (see column 1 of Table 8.1). However, only 11.5 per cent of the inter-firm variation in growth rates for the period 1954-60 was explained by the growth rate of the preceding period ($r^2 = 0.115$ in Table 5.7).

Thus, although within two industries there was a tendency for certain firms to grow persistently faster than others, there were powerful factors other than the level of past growth, which affected the future growth of the firm, relative to other firms in the same industry. Some of these factors are considered in the sections of Profitability and Growth and the Prediction of Future Growth (Sections 5 and 8 of this chapter).

4.　　　The persistency of profitability

In Chapter 6 (Section 5), we examined the persistency of profitability. We found that those firms with above-average profit rates in the period 1948-54 also tended to have above-average profit rates in the subsequent period (1954-60). The association was much stronger than that for growth rates and was statistically significant (at the 5 per cent level) for each of our three large industry groups, even when the relatively crude method of regression analysis was used. Of the two measures of profitability used, the pre-tax Rate of Return on Net Assets was more persistent than the post-tax Rate of Return on Equity Assets. The greatest degree of persistency of profitability was found, as in the case of persistency of growth, in the Non-Electrical Engineering industry. In this industry 53% of the inter-firm variation in pre-tax Rate of Return on Net Assets (46% when post-tax Rate of Return on Equity Assets is used) in the period 1954-60 was explained by profitability in the preceding period (1948-54). A net asset return of 1 percentage point above average in 1948-54 was associated with a return 0·58 percentage points above average in 1954-60, as is shown by the value (0.58) of the coefficient b in column (2) of Table 8.1. (See also Tables 6.12 and 6.13).

It will be seen that the regression coefficients relating profitability to past profitability vary between industries. This makes generalizations about the persistency of profitability difficult. It is also likely that the relationship between past and future profitability will be different as between different periods of time, so that it would be dangerous to

Table 8.1: Values of the regression coefficient for inter-period regressions

The values of the regression coefficient, b, are estimated from the equation: $X_t = a + b\,X_{t-1} + \epsilon$

where: a is a constant

b is the regression coefficient, given in the table.

ϵ is the error term.

The subscript t indicates the value of X in 1954-60

The subscript $t-1$ indicates the value of X in 1948-54

$$X = \begin{cases} \text{Growth (Indicator 4) in column 1} \\ \text{Rate of Return on Net Assets (Indic. 5)} \\ \text{in col. 2} \\ \text{Post-tax Rate of Return on Equity} \\ \text{Assets (Indicator 6) in column 3.} \end{cases}$$

Industry		Values of the Regression Coefficient, b		
		(1) Growth	(2) Net Asset Return	(3) Equity Return
Clothing and Footwear	(11)	-0.26	0.44*	0.10
Food	(12)	0.07	0.26*	0.52*
Non-electrical Engineering	(04)	0.37*	0.58*	0.66*
All (including Tobacco) (04 + 11 + 12 + 14)		0.19*	0.49*	0.49*

*   Indicates statistical significance at the 5% level.

Source: Table 5.7 and Tables 6.12 and 6.13.

Interpretation: A value of b = 0.49 (as for All Industries, both rates of return, at the foot of columns (2) and (3)) indicates that a company whose value of the relevant indicator was 10 percentage points above average in 1948-54 would tend to have a value 4.9 percentage points above average in 1954-60.

Note: The rank correlation coefficients presented in Tables 5.8 and 5.9 and Tables 6.14, 6.15 and 6.16 are in this context a better method of measuring the inter-period persistence of profitability and growth than the regression analysis presented above, and the reader is referred to these tables and to the text of Chapter 5 for further information. The Clothing and Footwear Industry has a significant positive persistency of growth in terms of rank correlation.

attempt to predict, say, profitability of a firm in the period 1966-72 from profitability in 1960-66 on the basis of our estimates of the relationship between 1954-60 and 1948-54. However, we can say with reasonable confidence that the association is likely to be positive. We can also observe that the regression coefficient b was, in every industry group, substantially greater than zero and substantially less than unity, i.e. a rate of profit of (say) 10 percentage points above the average for the industry in 1948-54, implied, on average, that the profit rate in 1954-60 would be above average, but not by as much as 10 percentage points.

If we assume that this type of relationship holds permanently, it is of considerable interest and practical use for the investor. It means that if he aims to select companies which will have above-average profit rates in the future, he should select those which have had above-average profit rates in the past. This arises simply from our discovery of a positive association between past and future profit rates.

Our discovery that the regression coefficient is less than unity enables us to take the argument a stage further. The investor is not usually as interested in the future profit rate on the assets of the company (at book value) as in the return on the price which he pays for his share. The price which he pays for the share is usually different from the book value of the underlying assets and this difference is expressed in our Valuation Ratio (Indicator 14: the ratio of the stock market's valuation to the book value of a firm's shares).

If the stock market fully discounts any above-average past profits, so that the past rate of return on market valuation is the same for all firms (i.e. the Price/Earnings ratios are identical), then the investor who wishes to maximize the future return on his investment (i.e. on the stock market price of shares) should buy the shares of companies which have had a below-average return on the book value of their assets. This is because the regression coefficient is less than unity, i.e. above average past profitability will not be achieved to the same extent in the future, whereas the market, by fully discounting the above-average past profit rate, has assumed that it will be fully maintained in the future.

If, on the other hand, the stock market does not discount past profits at all, so that market valuation bears the same relationship to the book value of the underlying assets for all firms (i.e. their Valuation Ratios are equal), then the investor who wishes to maximize future profits per pound of his outlay should buy shares of firms which have had above-average past rates of return on the book values of assets, since they will achieve above-average returns in the future and the market has not anticipated these returns.

It will be realized that we have given two limiting cases above and that the assessment of future profitability, the determination of the share-price in the stock-market, and the aims of the individual shareholder have, in fact, been over-simplified for the purposes of exposition. However, intermediate cases can easily be worked out and assumptions can be dropped in order to suit particular cases. The essence of our result is that it enables us to predict with reasonable confidence that a random selection of companies with above-average past profitability will, taken together, achieve above-average future profitability, but that the future profitability will not be as far above average as was past profitability. It should be remembered that in the case of any individual firm, this need not be so, as we have established only an average relationship which explains less than half of the total variation in profitability.

There are two possible explanations for the observed persistency of the profitability of firms. One explanation could be that profitable firms tend to have good management. The continuity of good management would ensure the persistency of high profitability. Alternatively, it can be argued that high profitability could be due to monopoly power. In this case, the persistency of high profitability would be due not to the continuity of good management, but to the continuity of monopoly power.

5.   Profitability and growth

In Chapter 7 we investigated the relationship between profitability and growth. The results are given in Tables 7.1 to 7.9 and some are summarized in Tables 8.2 and 8.3. In every industry and period we found a highly significant positive correlation between these two variables, which we expected in view of the results obtained by previous researchers, and because of the obvious a priori theoretical arguments for such a correlation. Correlation is, of course, neutral as to causation. It may indicate that growth determines profitability or that profitability determines growth, or, perhaps more plausibly, that they react mutually upon one another. We have not attempted to test a comprehensive model in which growth and profitability are simultaneously determined by each other and by other financial variables, but we have chosen rather to confine our attention to the simple relationship which assumes that profitability explains growth, because it seems a priori to be the most interesting and relevant one.

We found that the Post-tax Rate of Return on Equity Assets usually explains a greater proportion of the variance of Growth than the (pre-tax) Rate of Return on Net Assets. In general, a Post-tax Rate of Return on Equity Assets which is 10 percentage points above average tends to be associated with a growth rate which is 7 percentage points above average (the regression coefficient $b = 0.7$, as for all industries together, in each sub-period, see Table 8.2). Also, at a zero level of profitability, the growth rate tends to be very low or, in some cases, negative. This is shown by the value of the constant term, a, in Tables 7.1 and 7.2. In most cases, something less than half of the variance of Growth was explained by profitability.

However, the regression coefficients vary between industries. This can be seen by comparing the coefficients given in Table 8.2 for different industries in the same period. It seems, for example, that a Clothing and Footwear firm which had a post-tax equity return of 10 percentage points above the average for the industry in 1948-54 would tend to have growth of 5.7 percentage points above average ($b = 0.57$ in column (2) of Table 8.2), whereas a similarly placed Engineering firm would have a growth of 8.4 percentage points above the industry average.

The regression coefficients also vary over time within the same industry. For example, our Clothing and Footwear firm, had it maintained an

197

Table 8.2: Regression coefficients relating profitability to growth

	(1)	(2)	(3)	(4)
Sub-period 1: 1948-54				
Industry 11, Clothing and Footwear	0.44	0.57	0.45	0.57
Industry 12, Food	0.36	0.55	0.86	0.53
Industry 04, Non-Electrical Engineering	0.41	0.84	1.13	0.82
All four industries (including Tobacco)	0.42	0.70	-	-
Sub-period 2: 1954-60				
Industry 11, Clothing and Footwear	0.61	0.98	1.40	0.97
Industry 12, Food	0.35	0.35	0.88	0.28
Industry 04, Non-Electrical Engineering	0.36	0.70	0.49	0.79
All four industries (including Tobacco)	0.41	0.72	-	-
Whole period: 1948-60				
Industry 11, Clothing and Footwear	0.16	0.30	1.00	0.78
Industry 12, Food	0.36	0.08	0.81	0.71
Industry 04, Non-Electrical Engineering	0.35	0.72	0.82	0.23
All four industries (including Tobacco)	0.29	0.27	-	-

Source: Table 7.1 (Col. 1), 7.2 (Col. 2), 7.7 (Col. 3) and 7.8 (Col.4).

Interpretation: Column (1) relates Growth to Rate of Return on Net Assets for all firms.

Column (2) relates Growth to Post-tax Rate of Return on Equity Assets for all firms.

Column (3) is as for column (2), but only for firms with opening size $>$ £2 million.

Column (4) is as for column (2), but only for firms with opening size $<$ £2 million.

Table 8.3: r^2 for the linear regression of growth on profitability

	(1)	(2)	(3)
Sub-period 1: 1948-54			
Industry 11, Clothing and Footwear	0.44	0.55	0.07
Industry 12, Food	0.45	0.40	0.53
Industry 04, Non-Electrical Engineering	0.54	0.61	0.63
All four industries (including Tobacco)	0.52	0.55	-
Sub-period 2: 1954-60			
Industry 11, Clothing and Footwear	0.43	0.68	0.10
Industry 12, Food	0.15	0.09	0.29
Industry 04, Non-Electrical Engineering	0.28	0.35	0.13
All four industries (including Tobacco)	0.24	0.35	-
Whole period: 1948-60			
Industry 11, Clothing and Footwear	0.20	0.64	0.03
Industry 12, Food	0.30	0.05	0.59
Industry 04, Non-Electrical Engineering	0.39	0.48	0.20
All four industries (including Tobacco)	0.29	0.19	-

Source: Tables 7.1 (col. 1), 7.2 (col. 2) and 7.6 (col. 3).

Interpretation: r^2 indicates the proportion of the variance of Growth which can be explained by a simple linear association with Profitability.

> Column (1) relates Growth to Rate of Return on Net Assets for all companies.
> Column (2) relates Growth to Post-tax Rate of Return on Equity Assets for all companies.
> Column (3) relates Growth to Post-tax Rate of Return on Equity Assets for large companies only (i.e. opening net assets > £2 million). The values of r^2 in this column (but not in the other columns) are adjusted for degrees of freedom.

equity return of 10 percentage points above average in 1954-60 would then have tended to grow at a rate 9.8 percentage points above the industry average. This variation over time in the relationship makes it difficult to generalize about what the relationship might look like over, say, the subsequent period 1960-66.

The proportion of the variance of Growth explained by profitability also varied between industries and between time periods. This can be seen by comparing the various values of r^2 given in Table 8.3.

6. The profitability and growth of large companies

In an earlier chapter (Chapter 6) we had found important differences in the growth and profitability experience of large firms (defined as firms with opening net assets of more than £2 million) as opposed to that of small firms. Not only did large firms, as mentioned above, have lower variability of profitability and growth as compared with small firms, but we also noticed that the average profitability and average growth of large firms was remarkably alike in different industries. The dispersion of profitability and growth of large firms was also found to be very similar in different industries. This suggested that inter-industry classification may not be as relevant for large firms as for small firms, at least in the range of industries we have studied. In view of the a priori reasons given earlier (the diversification of large firms, similarities in the management structure, etc.), this finding is certainly not implausible.

In Chapter 7, we tried to find out to what extent the relationship between profitability and growth for the large firms is different from that observed for the smaller-sized firms. In particular, we tried to find out to what extent, if at all, the inter-industry and inter-temporal differences in the regression coefficients relating growth to profitability which exist for all firms, also exist when the largest firms alone are considered. We therefore studied the relationship between profitability and growth amongst large companies and smaller companies, taken as two separate populations. The regression coefficients relating profitability to growth among large companies in each industry are given in column (3) of Table 8.2 and those for the smaller companies are given in column (4).

The results show that there are important differences in the relationship between profitability and growth for large companies in different industries. For example, column (3) of Table 8.2 shows that in the period 1954-60, a 1 percentage point increase in the profitability of a large firm, tended to be associated with a 1.4 percentage point increase in its growth rate in the Clothing and Footwear industry, to a 0.88 percentage points increase in growth rate in the Food industry. There are also differences in the relationship within each industry over different time periods. However, the standard errors of the regression coefficients in column (3) are so high that we cannot rule out the possibility that the observed differences in the regression coefficients of large firms (between industries and over time) have arisen from chance. It was found impossible to reject the hypothesis that the growth-profita-bility observations relating to large firms in different industries and over different time periods do not come from the same basic population or the same statistical structure. However, in the case of inter-industry and inter-period differences in the regression coefficients of smaller-sized firms (column (4)), such a hypothesis is ruled out with 95% probability.

In spite of the high standard errors of the regression coefficients of large companies, it was found that in sub-period 2 (1954-60) and the whole period (1948-60), these coefficients were significantly different from that observed for the relationship between growth and profitability of smaller-sized firms. However, as a comparison of column (3) and column (4) shows, it is not possible to establish that the regression coefficients of large firms are always higher or lower than those of small firms. All we can say is that they are different, but no generali-zation can be made as to the direction of the difference.

Thus, the results of Chapter 7, lend support to two suggestions: firstly that as far as the analysis of growth and profitability is concerned, the conventional inter-industry classification is less relevant for the largest firms; secondly, that the distinction between large and small firms is significant. If this were universally true, it would be a powerful con-clusion, but we must warn the reader that it is based on an analysis of effectively three industries only. It will be interesting to see whether the same conclusion holds when this analysis is extended to the other industries.

7.   First-order correlation coefficients

In Part I of the book, we found, by means of simple correlation coeffi-cients, that there was some association between growth and other eco-nomic and financial variables such as the valuation ratio (Indicator 14), gearing (Indicator 10), liquidity (Indicator 11) etc. However, the simple correlation coefficients also showed that all these variables were asso-ciated with profitability. In view of the fairly close association between growth and profitability, we tried to find out in Chapter 7 if there was any independent association between growth and the financial policy variables, over and above the association which may exist between them due to their mutual association with profitability. This was done by calculating the first-order correlation coefficients between growth and each of these variables, with profitability held constant. A first-order correlation coefficient between growth and another variable may be interpreted intuitively as a simple correlation coefficient between the two variables for firms with the same level of profitability.

The first-order correlation coefficients showed that in a number of cases the nature of independent association between growth and the financial policy variables for the same level of profitability, is radically different from that shown by the simple correlation coefficients in Chapter 3. For example, the zero-order order correlation coefficients show that growth and gearing are negatively related, in each of the nine cases. This is because companies with high profitability tend to have low gearing (which is to be expected, since our measure of gearing is expressed as proportion of profits) and a high growth rate. The first-order correlation coefficients, on the other hand, show that there is a positive association between gearing and growth when profitability is held constant. In other words, if two companies have the same level of profitability, the one with the higher gearing (defined in terms of fixed dividend and interest payments) will tend to have a higher growth rate.

On the more positive side, the first-order correlation analysis showed that at least in the period 1954-60, among firms with the same level of profitability, those with above average growth tended to have above average stock market valuation at the end of the period. They also tended to pay out an above-average proportion of their profits in fixed dividend and interest payments, and a below-average proportion of their profits in ordinary dividend payments. Such firms also tended to operate at a below-average level of liquidity. Finally, this analysis showed that the stock market put a higher premium on past growth of net assets in 1960 than in 1954.

9.   **Prediction of growth rates**

Finally, we attempted to relate the relative growth of companies in the period 1954-60 to the values of various indicators in the first period.

The results reported in Table 7.17 show that 16% of the variance of growth rates amongst all the companies studied in the period 1954-60 could be predicted from the past values of various indicators. This was double the proportion explained by past profitability alone (this being a priori the most likely variable to explain future growth), and very much greater than the amount explained by past growth alone (see Table 5.7), but it still leaves a very large proportion of future growth unexplained. Past profitability, taken by itself, always had a positive association with future growth and explained a greater proportion of the variance of growth than any single one of the other historical indicators which we tested.

There is, of course, no reason to believe that the parameters relating growth in 1954-60 to the values of various economic and financial indicators in 1948-54 would be of any use in predicting growth in 1966-72 from data for 1960-66. However, it seems that if one wished to predict growth over such periods, the most sensible working hypothesis to start with would be to assume that future growth would be higher, the higher past profitability.

Appendix A   The Data and their Limitations

The data used in this study come from two sources. The first and most important is the standardized series of company accounts prepared by the National Institute of Economic and Social Research and the Board of Trade. The second source is the estimate of the average annual stock exchange price of each company's ordinary shares, which is described in Part II of this Appendix. Part I of the appendix will be devoted to the accounting data.

Part I. Accounting data

(1) Introduction

The 1948 Companies' Act introduced fairly detailed minimum requirements as to the specific items to be shown in company accounts, and made consolidated accounts virtually compulsory. These requirements are stated in the Eighth Schedule to the Act. Thus, for the first time, it was possible to draw up a standard form to which most public companies' group accounts would conform. The National Institute of Economic and Social Research initiated a project to standardize the consolidated accounts of all companies with share capital quoted on United Kingdom stock exchanges, other than companies engaged primarily in business activities abroad or in banking, insurance, finance, shipping and agriculture.[1] This was done for the five years following the Companies' Act and the aggregate results were published in 'Company Income and Finance, 1949-53' which contains, in addition, an excellent account of the data. A dis-aggregated analysis of the same data was also undertaken and published in 1959 as a symposium 'Studies in Company Finance', edited by Brian Tew and R. F. Henderson.

The National Institute were assisted by the Statistics Division of the Board of Trade, who extended the series on largely the same basis to 1960. From 1961 onwards, the analysis was restricted by excluding some of the smaller companies.[2] Analyses of the extended series have been published by the Board of Trade in articles in Economic Trends and in their Company Assets and Income series.[3] All of these analyses have been either on a highly aggregated level or for very short periods because of the vast data processing problems involved in the analysis of the full series.

The Board of Trade have generously supplied the full series from 1949 to 1960 on punched cards to the Department of Applied Economics, Cambridge. It is hoped to transfer all the data to magnetic tape for use on a high speed electronic computer which provides the only feasible means of carrying out detailed dis-aggregated analysis. The present study is the first product of this project and covers four of the twenty-

Table A.1. Industrial classification* of companies studied

Description		Pre-1958 S.I.C. number		Post-1958 S.I.C. number	
Group	Sub-group	Group	Sub-group	Group	Sub-group
Non-electrical Engineering	Shipbuilding and marine engineering	4	1	37	1
	Machine tools and engineers' small tools	4	2	33	1
	Textile machinery	4	3	33	2
	Other non-electrical engineering	4	4, 5	33	3
Clothing and Footwear	Clothing	11	1	44	1
	Footwear	11	2	44	2
Food	Grain milling	12	1	21	1
	Baking, etc.	12	2	21	2
	Sugar	12	3	21	3
	Confectionery	12	4	21	4
	Fruit and vegetable products	12	5	21	5
	Other Food	12	6	21	6
Tobacco	Tobacco	14	1	24	1

* The classification is based on the <u>Standard Industrial Classification</u> (S.I.C.), which is published by H.M.S.O.

Table A. 2 (a) Statistics of the companies studied, 1948-60

	Non-electrical Engineering	Clothing & Footwear	Food	Tobacco	Total
Continuing companies (1948-60)	214	70	73	7	364
Births (1948-60)	115	34	43	2	194
Deaths (1948-60)	73	28	57	7	165
Less Double counting*	16	4	12	1	33
Total companies in the population	386	128	161	15	690
Including					
Non-quoted companies**	8	-	2	1	11
Privately controlled companies+	3	2	3	-	8
Foreign-owned companies†	13	1	3	3	20

*   Double counting refers to companies which were born and also died within the period.

**   Most of the non-quoted companies are foreign-owned and are also included in the latter category.

ǀ   Privately controlled companies are companies in which United Kingdom companies outside the population have a controlling interest. This covers ownership, for example, by quoted financial companies such as investment trusts as well as ownership by non-quoted companies. As with foreign ownership, the information may be incomplete because there is no legal obligation on the controlled or the controlling company to declare the existence of the interest to any readily accessible public source. Even the company's list of shareholders filed at the Companies' Registry is rendered less useful by the existence of nominee holdings.

†   Foreign-owned means that a company registered abroad has a controlling interest in the company concerned. There may be other companies which are foreign-owned and which are not recorded here because the fact is not recorded in the basic sources of information, namely the companies' annual report and accounts, and entries in the Stock Exchange Official Year Book.

Source: A card index of all companies in the full N. I. E. S. R. and B. O. T. population, copied from the card indices kept by the N. I. E. S. R. and Board of Trade respectively.

Table A. 2 (b) Number of continuing companies over the two sub-periods

	Non-electrical Engineering	Clothing & Footwear	Food	Tobacco	Total
Sub-period 1, 1948-54	259	86	108	11	464
Sub-period 2, 1954-60	262	79	91	7	439

one industries (under the pre-1958 industrial classification) in the series. A brief account of the computing processes involved is given in Appendix B.

(2) The companies included in this study

This study is confined to companies which satisfied the following conditions:

    (1) They were U.K. quoted companies.

    (2) They were not consolidated subsidiaries of other U.K. quoted companies.

    (3) They were mainly engaged in one of four major industrial groups which we have chosen.

    (4) They continued to fulfil the above conditions throughout at least one of two six-year periods, 1948-54 and 1954-60.

These conditions will now be examined in detail.

The accounting data used in this study are the consolidated accounts of quoted public companies, i.e. the group accounts where the quoted company is a holding company. Quoted companies controlled by other companies in the quoted population and included in the consolidated accounts of such companies are, therefore, excluded from the population. Nevertheless, the companies included in the population are not all independent. Some are controlled by private companies, a few are controlled by one or more other companies in the quoted population but are not consolidated by them, and a considerable number are controlled by foreign companies. Our definition of a 'quoted' company includes all companies whose shares (ordinary, or preference, or both) are quoted on stock exchanges in the United Kingdom. It also includes companies whose loan stock only is quoted, provided that information for them is available. In addition to the quoted companies, a small number of very large non-quoted companies are included in the population. Statistics of private and foreign ownership and of the number of non-quoted companies included in our population are given in the second part of Table A.2 (a).

The present study is confined to four industries, one of which (Tobacco) is very small in terms of numbers of companies, although not in terms of output or assets. Of the other three, one (Non-Electrical Engineering) is a capital goods industry, and two (Clothing and Footwear, and Food) are consumer goods industries. We chose these particular industries in order to given an approximate balance, in terms of number of firms, between the two types of manufacturing industry, and because several earlier company finance studies, both in Britain and the United States, have been based on samples from these industries.

Table A.1 lists the industries included in the present study. The classification is based on the Standard Industrial Classification, which was revised in 1958. We have used the old classification throughout, because it was in operation for the greater part of the period, and because for our purposes the only major difference between the two classifications is that Shipbuilding becomes a separate group rather than a sub-group, in the new classification. Since the number of continuing companies for the full period in Shipbuilding was only 26, we did not consider that it was worth separating the group out as a separate industry. We have adopted the practice of treating a company which changed industry group during the period as belonging to its original group. This is a purely arbitrary convention whose only virtue is the important one of consistency.

The classification of quoted companies to industrial groups is bound to be arbitrary, especially where a company has many heterogeneous subsidiaries. Cases such as that of Vickers, classified as non-electrical engineering, but including important steel and aircraft producing subsidiaries, spring immediately to mind. An extreme case was that of the Amalgamated Tobacco Corporation (now London and Midland Industrials), classified as a tobacco company, which acquired Golders Green Crematorium. Nevertheless, the study carried out by the National Institute and the Board of Trade showed that, in 1951, 87% of the employees of manufacturing companies in the population were in establishments belonging to the industry group of the employing company.[1] This figure refers only to employment in the United Kingdom, which draws attention to another defect in the demarcation of our population, namely that, although companies operating primarily overseas are excluded from the population, many companies operating primarily in the United Kingdom have branches overseas or overseas subsidiaries which are included in the consolidated accounts.

Within the four industries chosen for analysis, we have followed Tew and Henderson in confining our attention to continuing companies. A continuing company is, for our purposes, one which remained in the population throughout the period under observation, which may be either a 6-year sub-period or the full 12-year period. The main reason for concentrating on continuing companies is the severely practical one that long-run indicators, i. e. ones calculated over a period, can be obtained on a comparable basis only for such companies. It is intended to remedy this omission later by studies of the whole population, including a special study of take-over bids.

The definitions of birth, death and continuity of companies are clear in principle but arbitrary at the margin. A birth means that a company has entered the population by fulfilling all the requirements, e. g. by the achievement of a stock exchange quotation, and a death means that it has been removed from the population by ceasing to fulfil all the requirements, e. g. because it has been acquired by another company in the population. A continuing company is one which is neither born nor dies but remains undisturbed in the population. There are, however, marginal cases which are treated arbitrarily. For example, if company A and company B merge, then if both A and B are taken over by a newly-formed holding company, C, the transaction results in the 'death by acquisition' of both A and B, whilst C is 'born' into the population. If, on the other hand, it is decided to make B the new holding company, then A will 'die' by acquisition, but B will be a continuing company. This arbitrariness of treatment reflects the fact that the legal entity of the company, to which accounting data relate, does not necessarily constitute an economic entity, in the sense of a financial or industrial undertaking, which may continue under a variety of different legal guises.

Table A. 2 gives some statistics of the population covered by the present study. The number of continuing companies for the whole period in the industries studied (364) should be compared with the total of approximately 1900 continuing companies in the full population. Thus, it seems that the industries selected cover something short of a fifth of the full population. Table A. 3 gives evidence relating to total net assets and gross profit, and this seems to confirm the general impression that we are dealing with a little less than a fifth of the total population. An interesting feature of this table is the change in relative importance of the different industries when assets or profits are the criterion. Tobacco becomes much larger, particularly relative to Clothing and Footwear, and Non-electrical Engineering. This is due largely to the fact that it contains two giant companies, Imperial Tobacco (ranked third on net assets out of the full population in 1960) and Gallaher (ranked 26th).

Table A. 4 gives a breakdown of births and deaths by cause. These are obviously important, as continuing companies constitute little more than half of our population by number, although by size they would be expected a priori to be more important. The analysis of births by cause is perhaps less interesting than that of deaths, because the different causes of birth tend to reflect the legal convention chosen rather than the economic nature of the operation. There is, for instance, no reason why a birth by incorporation should imply that the company entering the population is a new undertaking in the economic sense; it may merely imply that the company previously conducting the under-taking was, for purely legalistic reasons, not readily suitable for con-version to public company status or for fulfilling the requirements for a stock exchange quotation.

The cause of death is more interesting. The predominance of death by acquisition by a company in the population is striking, but not entirely unexpected. The substantial number of acquisitions by companies outside the population is less expected, although it should be remembered that the latter include companies in industries not covered by the larger population (banking, finance, etc.,) as well as non-quoted companies and companies operating primarily overseas. Liquidation, which is usually associated with complete financial failure, is a comparatively rare occurrence. It seems that if there were unprofitable companies, whose independent existence was not justified, they attracted buyers who acquired the company as a going concern, rather than allowing it to go into liquidation. The fact that losses could be carried forward against future taxation, and therefore had a considerable monetary value which would be lost if the legal person of the company were liqui-dated, may also have had something to do with this.

(3) The form of the standardized accounting data

This section describes the standardized quantitative accounting data in principle rather than in detail. A full list of the 67 individual items in the standard form together with definitions, will be found in Appendix

Table A. 3 Indicators of the size of the industries studied
relative to the full quoted company population, in 1960*

Industry (post-1958 Industry no. in brackets)	Pre-Tax Profit**		Net assets+		Number of companies	
	%	£'000's	%	£'000's	%	
Food (21)	4.7	96,026	4.5	608,886	3.8	100
Tobacco (24)‡	2.6	52,740	2.6	354,472	0.4	9
Non-electrical Engineering‡‡ (33 & 37)	9.2	187,076	9.5	1,276,456	12.3	323
Clothing and Footwear (44)	1.6	33,411	1.3	178,031	3.5	92
Total	18.1	369,253	17.9	2,417,845	20.0	524
All Industries (Manufacturing & Distribution)	100.0	2,043,389	100.0	13,495,458	100.0	2,618

Notes;

* Figures relate to companies in the population in 1960 (which was 'year 12' of the combined N.I.E.S.R. and B.O.T. series). This includes many companies which did not continue over a sub-period and are not, therefore, included in the present study.

** Pre-tax Profit is defined here as Trading Profit, plus Income from Investments, plus Other Income, less Depreciation and Other Provisions.

+ Net Assets are defined here as Fixed Assets, plus Current Assets, less Current Liabilities.

‡ Imperial Tobacco and Gallaher together acount for 83% of Net Assets in Tobacco.

‡‡	Non-electrical Engineering comprises:	Gross Profit	Net Assets	Number of Companies
		£'000's	£'000's	
	(33) Non-electrical engineering	169,428	1,105,342	294
	(37) Shipbuilding	17,648	171,114	29

Source: Income and Finance of Public Quoted Companies, 1949-60. Board of Trade, Statistics Division, London, 1962.

Table A.4 Causes of birth and death (1948–1960)

Cause of Birth	Engineering	Clothing & Footwear	Food	Tobacco	Total
Conversion from private company	48	11	20	1	80
Permission to deal on a stock exchange	25	1	8	-	34
Incorporation*	40	20	12	-	72
Hived off from company in the population	1	-	-	-	1
Not stated	1	2	3	1	7
Total	115	34	43	2	194
Cause of death					
Acquired by company in population	56	19	42	3	122
Acquired by company not in population	7	4	6	2	19
Liquidation	6	2	4	1	13
Conversion to Investment or Property co.	2	2	1	-	5
Accounts not available	1	1	2	-	5
Not Stated	1	-	2	1	4
Total	73	28	57	7	168

(column grouping: Industry)

* Incorporation does not necessarily imply the creation of a new enterprise, e.g. it may merely imply the transfer of an existing enterprise from a private company to a newly formed public company.

Source: The card index used for Table A.2.

C. All numbers in brackets in the text of this section are the numbers
of the accounting items referred to, as they appear in the Appendix C
list. Less detail is available in the sequence than in either the Board
of Trade (1954-60, approximately) or the National Institute data (1948-
53), but in order to obtain a comparable series for the full period we
were obliged to accept the maximum amount of information common to
all periods and reject additional details, however valuable, which were
available for only part of the period.

The basic data consist of a Balance Sheet, a Sources and Uses of Funds
Statement, and an Appropriation of Income Statement for each company
for each year. The source of this information is the annual report and
accounts of each company. Company accounts have well known defects,
some of the more obvious of which are dealt with in Section 6 of this
appendix. The minimum standard form itself is more detailed than
the minimum disclosure required by the Companies' Act, but most
companies do in fact publish all the information contained in our Balance
Sheet and Appropriation of Income Statement, so that errors of estimation are unusual here, although they are sometimes important.[1]

The Balance Sheet is the most comprehensive part of the accounting
information. It shows the stock of assets, liabilities and proprietors'
interest in the group at the end of each accounting year. The information given is fairly detailed and the defects of the balance sheet are in
the methods of valuation used (discussed further in Section 6 of this
appendix) rather than in a basic lack of disclosure.

The Appropriation of Income statement, on the other hand, is very
inadequate. The title indicates that it is not a full Profit and Loss
Account or Trading Account, and such basic elements as total sales,
wages, and purchases of raw materials are absent. Instead, we start
with a figure for Operating Profit (50), which is the trading profit of
the group for the period under review, after deducting all expenses
other than depreciation. Other sources of income are then added, to
give the pre-tax and pre-depreciation profit of the group (66=50 + 51 + 52
Interest on long-term loans is then deducted. The value of showing
this item separately is reduced by the fact that interest on bank overdrafts is deducted in calculating Operating Profit, so that a figure for
total interest payments is not available. The remainder of the Appropriation Statement shows how the Total Profit (66) is appropriated to
tax (54), Dividends (55 & 56), and Minority Interests (57). The remaining balance (67) is carried over to the Sources of Funds Statement,
where its various allocations to reserves and provisions (32, 33, 34,
& 35) appear separately. It should be noted that the depreciation and
other provisions are treated here as sources of funds because they are
retained in the business, but, since they are made in respect of actual
liabilities incurred in the course of trading, they should be deducted
from the Total Profit (66) if this is to represent profit in the conventional sense.

The Sources and Uses of Funds Statement is derived from the other
two accounts. Basically, it consists of the changes in individual
Balance Sheet items over the period, i. e. in its simplest form, it is
the closing Balance Sheet, less the opening Balance Sheet. Because

certain appropriations of profit, such as depreciation provisions and retentions, explain changes in balance sheet figures, these appropriations (32, 33, 34 and 35) are carried over from the Appropriation Statement to the Sources of Funds statement, as explained in the previous paragraph. This adds a certain amount of detail to the simple changes in balance sheet figures. For example, instead of a net change in the Provisions figures in the Balance Sheet (4), we have the increase in Provisions allocated from the Appropriation Statement (34) as a Source of Funds, and Expenditure out of Provisions (42) as a Use of Funds.

There is no generally accepted standard form of Sources and Uses statements. Most of the variations on the basic theme of changes in the individual balance sheet items are aimed at providing a greater or lesser degree of aggregation. For example, it is common to set off Increase in Credit Received (28) against Increase in Credit Given (41), leaving a single amount of net credit received or given. This may be valuable if it removes unnecessary detail and emphasizes the points at issue in a particular problem, but, in general, each balance sheet item can vary independently of other individual items. For example, it is possible to take more trade credit without giving any. It is therefore preferable to have as much detail as possible if the Sources and Uses Statement is to give an accurate picture of how the company's financial structure is changing. The Sources and Uses Statement in the data examined here is of the latter kind.

The value of the Sources and Uses Statement is, however, diminished in the present case by the large degree of estimation involved in its calculation. These special limitations are discussed in the next section.

(4) Special adjustments to the Sources and Uses of Funds Statement − 'book' transactions and adjustments on acquisition of subsidiaries.

(a) Book transactions. The first qualification which should be applied to the Sources and Uses Statement in the present data is that so-called 'book' transactions are omitted. A 'book' transaction is defined as one which does not involve a direct flow of funds to or from the outside world. The obvious case of such a transaction is a scrip issue. In such a case, our Sources and Uses Statement will show no change in either Reserves (35) or Share Capital (23), whereas an unadjusted Statement would show a decrease in reserves and an increase in share capital. The adjustment in this case is valuable because the book transaction is purely of a nominal kind, but in other cases the value of eliminating book transactions is less certain.

A second example, that of revaluation of fixed assets, should illustrate this. A Sources and Uses Statement which was a mere collection of changes in balance sheet items would show revaluation as an increase in "Expenditure, less receipts, on fixed assets" (37, 38 or 39) on the Uses side, and an increase in Reserves (35) on the Sources side. After elimination of 'book' items, the revaluation does not affect any items in the Sources and Uses Statement. This may be entirely valid insofar as the revaluation refers to appreciation which took place prior to the commencement of the period under consideration, for such a transaction merely corrects an error in the opening balance sheet, and not

213

a change which took place between two balance sheet dates. If, however, we are considering a 12-year period during which there was fairly persistant and rapid inflation, which is the case here, then a large part of any revaluation must represent appreciation of the money value of fixed assets during the period. This is a source of capital funds in money terms, and the fact that most firms hold it in the form in which it accrues, i. e. retain it as fixed assets, does not prevent it from being an important source of finance in an inflationary period.

In practice, however, it could be argued that the inclusion of revaluation as a source of funds would be misleading because not all firms revalue, and those which revalue do so at irregular intervals. Thus comparisons both between different companies and between different periods for the same company would be of doubtful significance. On the other hand, the practice of ignoring revaluations avoids understating capital appreciation by the drastic method of leaving it out altogether. This is a basic limitation of accounting practice which we are forced to accept.

Another 'book' transaction whose elimination is in some ways regrettable is the conversion of debenture stock to ordinary or preference shares. In an unadjusted Sources and Uses Statement, this would involve an Issue of Share Capital (23 or 24) and a reduction of long-term loans (26). In our adjusted Statement, it has no effect. To the extent that the redemption of debentures would otherwise have involved raising funds from another source, it seems reasonable to say that, although the transaction is a 'book' item, involving no cash payment, it is nevertheless a flow of funds. If the debentures were redeemed by cash paid out of the proceeds of a new issue made on the open market, rather than to debenture holders, this would be an identical operation as far as the company's financial structure was concerned, and the transaction would appear in our Sources and Uses Statement as a flow of funds.

(b) Adjustments on acquisition of subsidiaries. The other type of special adjustment applied to the Sources and Uses Statement, and that which gives rise to the greatest amount of estimation, is the adjustment which is made when a company acquires a new subsidiary.

The accounts used in the present study are, as stated earlier, the consolidated accounts of the group, where a quoted company has subsidiaries. Consolidated accounts are derived as follows. Suppose the Balance Sheet of a holding company H, with a subsidiary S, to be (in stylized form) that shown below.

Balance Sheet of H Ltd., at time t

	£		£
Ordinary Share Capital	50	Tangible Fixed Assets	100
Reserves	50	Shares in subsidiary, S	50
Liabilities and Provisions	100	Current Assets	50
	200		200

Suppose that the Balance Sheet of subsidiary, S, is as follows;

214

Balance Sheet of S. Ltd., at time t

	£		£
Ordinary Share Capital	30	Fixed Assets	50
Reserves	20		
Liabilities and Provisions	50	Current Assets	50
	100		100

If the entire share capital of the subsidiary had been bought at book value, the Consolidated Balance Sheet would appear as follows:

Consolidated Balance Sheet of H and its subsidiary, at time t

	£		£
Ordinary Share Capital	50	Fixed Assets (100 + 50)	150
Reserves	50		
Liabilities and Provisions (100 + 50)	150	Current Assets (50 + 50)	100
	250		250

It will be noted that 'book value' is taken to mean that the shares were acquired at their nominal value plus the value of the reserves which they represent. Thus, the asset, 'Shares in Subsidiary' in H's Balance Sheet, is offset against the items 'Ordinary Share Capital' and "Reserves" in S's Balance Sheet, on consolidation. Any surplus over book value paid for the share capital and accumulated reserves of the subsidiary would appear in the consolidated Balance Sheet as an intangible asset, described as "Goodwill". A surplus of book value over cost would give rise to a capital reserve in the consolidated Balance Sheet. If only part of the subsidiary's share capital is acquired, the book value of the portion not acquired, together with any reserves attributable to it, appears as 'Minority Interest in Subsidiary' on the capital and liabilities side of the consolidated Balance Sheet.

The consolidated procedure has important implications for the Sources and Uses Statement for a year in which a new subsidiary is consolidated. If, in the example quoted above, H had acquired S for cash during the year ending at time t, the Sources and Uses Statement of H for the year t-1 to t would be distorted by the addition of S to the consolidated Balance Sheet. The abnormal Sources and Uses due to the acquisition of S would be as follows:

Sources of Funds		Uses of Funds	
	£		£
Liabilities and Provisions of Subsidiary	50	Fixed Assets of Subsidiary	50
		Current Assets of Subsidiary	50
	50		100

215

The net use of funds here, £50, is the actual cash payment (which reduces the cash balance (49)) made by H for the shares in S. (If this payment were made in shares of the parent company, rather than in cash, there would of course be another entry in the Statement, i.e. Sources of Funds; Issue of Shares £50).

The procedure adopted in preparing the Sources and Uses Statement in the data used here was to eliminate, where possible, the effect of the acquisition, showing the net impact of the transaction as one Use of Funds, 'Expenditure on Acquisition of Subsidiaries' (included in 39). In the example quoted above, this would involve deducting £50 from the crude figures (i.e. consolidated Balance Sheet figure for t minus value at t-1) of changes in Fixed Assets, Current Assets and Liabilities and Provisions, respectively, and inserting a new figure of £50 spent on acquiring the new subsidiary. Unfortunately, the necessary information (i.e. the separate Balance Sheet of the acquired subsidiary at the date of acquisition) is not always available, and the adjusted figures are often partial, or subject to estimation. The net amount left unexplained in such cases appears as the Consolidation Adjustment (44). If, in the present case, only the changes in assets due to the acquisition were identifiable, this would leave a £50 Source of Funds (actually included in the increases in Liabilities and Provisions) unadjusted, and this would be balanced on the other side of the Statement by a positive £50 Consolidation Adjustment. (The adjustments in this case would be: reduce Fixed Assets and Current Assets each by £50, and increase 'expenditure on subsidiaries' by £50. There would thus be an unexplained reduction of £50 in Uses of Funds, which would appear as a Consolidation Adjustment to balance the Statement. If full information had been available, this amount would have been deducted from the increase in Provisions and Liabilities).

The adjustment on acquisition of new subsidiaries therefore has two important implications for the Sources and Uses of Funds Statement. Firstly, it means that most of the items can be subject to estimation (all items, in fact, other than issues of shares, 23 and 24) whenever there is a consolidation adjustment. Secondly, it means that the Statement does not show the total changes in the group's asset and liability structure over a period, since the initial effect of adding new subsidiaries is ignored. This means, for example, that a measure of the growth of net assets derived from the Statement, such as that used by Tew and Henderson, ignores growth which is due to the addition of the minority interests and long-term loan capital of newly-acquired subsidiaries.[1]

(6) Comparability over time

(a) The time period. Our data extend over a period of twelve years. The years are fiscal years rather than calendar years, i.e. they begin on 6 April and end on 5 April. Since companies are allowed to choose their own accounting dates, they exhibit little conformity, although a large number choose 31 December and a lesser, but significant number, choose 31 March.[2] The convention adopted in preparing the data was to classify the accounts of a company up to the accounting date in any particular fiscal year as being the accounts for that year.[3]

216

The precise period covered by the data is the fiscal year 1948/9 to the fiscal year 1960/61, i. e. all accounts dated between 6 April, 1948 and 5 April, 1961. The fiscal year 1948/49 is described as 'year 0' because it provides the opening Balance Sheet for the series. It does not have flow accounts (Sources and Uses Statement and Appropriation Statement) because these would relate to the <u>period</u> ending in 1948/49. The other years, 1 (1949/50) to 12 (1960/61) have balance sheets and flow accounts which apply to the year ended on the balance sheet date.

The full series, therefore, comprises twelve sets of annual flow accounts and thirteen annual balance sheets. Because the median accounting date is 31st December, the actual time periods may be regarded as being calendar years, in which case, the period covered would be 1949 to 1960, inclusive.

(b) <u>Linking</u>. The present data were originally prepared with the object of producing aggregate figures for each industry which would be comparable on a year-to-year basis. For year-to-year aggregate comparison it was necessary firstly that the population should be the same in each year and secondly that the time period covered by data for each company should be the same in each year. The first requirement meant that strict comparability was possible only between pairs of adjacent years, which is why many of the series published by the National Institute and the Board of Trade are of this type. This involves their being two populations over any period, one for comparison with the preceding period and one for comparison with the following period.[1] Companies which died in the following year are in the "backward linked" population (comparable with the preceding year). Companies which were born in the current year are in the "forward linked" population (comparable with the next year). Births and deaths do not really concern us here, as we include every company provided that it continued over the relevant period and ignore it if it did not. What do concern us are the cases where one company has two sets of data for one year, one comparable with the next year (forward linked) and one with the preceding year (backward linked).

The events which give rise to this situation are of two types, change of accounting date and change of industry group. When a company changes accounting date, the flow items refer to a period greater than or less than one year. Put briefly and perhaps over-simply, the procedure in such a case is to apportion off part of these items (where the period is greater than one year) or add a proportion of their value for adjacent accounting periods (where the period is less than one year). Certain adjustments can also be made to the Balance Sheets (e. g. a new issue known to have taken place at a specific time can be allowed for) preceding and at the changed date, in order to make them more comparable with the new and old dates respectively. It will be observed that there is a choice between making the figures for the period leading to the date change comparable either with the following year or with the preceding year. In our data, both alternatives have been calculated and we have arbitrarily chosen the backward-linked data where such a choice arises. The same applies to an industry group change. Here, for the year of the change there will be two sets of figures, one in the old industry group (backward linked) and one in the new industry group (forward linked).

The reasons why we have always chosen backward-linked data are two. Firstly, there is no reason to believe that either backward or forward linked data provide the better estimates when we are trying to obtain a series for an individual company over a sequence of years: in the case of a date change, either involves counting one period twice or ignoring one period. Secondly, the process of establishing a forward link always starts with a forward linking opening Balance Sheet, without any of the flow statements. The reason for this is obvious; the opening Balance Sheet is for comparison with the future and its associated flow statements would relate to the past period, which is not comparable with the future. Thus, the first set of forward linked data does not provide us with the flow statements which are necessary if we are building up a series for the individual company, and it is therefore convenient, in the absence of any other objection, to choose the backward-linked data.

It will be observed that the adjustment for change of accounting date adds a further degree of estimation to the Sources and Uses Statement (and to the Appropriation Account) and provides another reason why it may not amount to the crude changes in balance sheet items between two accounting dates. It is obviously a desirable adjustment from our point of view since, in comparing individual companies over the period, we require all the figures to relate to twelve years exactly, rather than eleven and a half for some and twelve and a half for others, which could arise if crude balance sheet differences were taken.[1]

(7) The defects of company accounts

The most obvious defects of company accounts are those of omission. The lack of a proper Profit and Loss Account has already been mentioned and a cursory glance at our list of standardized variables (Appendix C) will reveal many items whose dis-aggregation would be desirable for some purposes. The lack of dis-aggregation in such cases is usually due to the lack of detail in company accounts, since our standardized form, with very few exceptions, comprises the maximum amount of detail which is obtainable on a comparable basis for all companies. No attempt will be made here to list the additional details which might be desirable. The reader who is interested in such matters is referred to the Bibliography at the end of this appendix. Neither will an attempt be made to present a comprehensive critique of the information which is available. Instead, it is proposed to concentrate on one important aspect which is of fundamental importance, the valuation of assets.

Assets are divided into two classes in the Balance Sheet, fixed assets and current assets. The latter present the least difficulty, although they are not without their ambiguities. Cash (21), for example, seems to be a fairly unequivocal concept, whose measurement presents no difficulty. It includes, of course, cash in bank current accounts as well as cash in hand, and deposit accounts at banks and building societies and holdings of Treasury Bills are also included where possible. The main ambiguity arises out of the fact that a liability item "Bank

Overdrafts and Loans" (9) appears on the other side of the balance sheet, and different companies vary in the degree to which they net out the liability against the asset. Some show both items gross, whilst others offset overdrafts against the asset figure whenever there is a legal right to offset the liabilities (i. e. where both the asset and the liability represent accounts with the same bank and could at law be offset against one another to determine the net amount in credit between the company and the bank).

Marketable Securities (19) are a case where the actual valuation of an item presents an ambiguity. All companies are required to show the market value, at balance sheet date, of quoted marketable securities, but this often appears by way of note. The securities commonly appear in the books (and therefore in our data) at cost, although some companies write them up or (more often) down to market value, where they consider that the change of value is permanent and the revaluation is expedient. The 1948 Companies Act (Eighth Schedule, para. 11 (7)) requires companies to disclose whenever the balance sheet valuation of a current asset is, in the opinion of the directors, greater than its reรlisable value.

Stocks and Work in Progress (17) is an even more difficult item to handle. Here there is neither an objective cost nor an objective market valuation. The convention here is 'cost or market value, whichever is the lower', since it is deemed prudent to anticipate losses, but not profits. Unfortunately, market value is usually more difficult to determine than in the case of marketable securities, which are highly saleable, homogeneous commodities, for which a reliable quotation is probably available. The cost, which is the usual basis of stock valuation. is fraught with difficulties of allocating overheads and joint costs, and, as a result, is very unreliable as between companies, although it may be rather more reliable as between different years for the same company, when the valuation conventions are not changed. It should be noted that, in a period of inflation such as is covered by the present data, stock appreciation is a considerable source of profit which is not separated out in the conventional Profit and Loss Appropriation Account.

Turning to fixed assets, the item 'Trade Investments' (16) is usually valued in the same way as Marketable Securities (19), except that it probably includes a greater proportion of unquoted investments and a current market valuation of quoted investment is not required to be disclosed where it is different from the amount shown in the Balance Sheet. Also, since trade investments are usually held for a long period, the market value will often diverge widely from the balance sheet value, where the latter represents the original cost, without any revaluation.

Intangible Assets (15) are the most ambiguous of all balance sheet items. This classification includes two distinct types of asset. One is expenditure of a capital nature which is designed to produce a permanent trading advantage to the company. Examples of this kind are expenses of acquiring patents and trade marks or advertizing expenditure necessary to launch a new brand, which would probably be described as 'goodwill'. A rather different type of asset, but one which is also described as 'goodwill', is the amount paid for a subsidiary company in excess of the book value of its shares. This is sometimes eradicated by revaluing the assets of the subsidiary at the date of acquisition, and this is probably the most realistic treatment of the operation in most cases, since the excess of purchase consideration over book value often reflects the fact that book value tends to be less than current market value, although there are cases where it reflects genuine "goodwill" in the sense of the excess of the value of the business as a going concern over the value of its physical assets. The most common treatment, is, however, the very conservative one of treating the excess payment as an intangible asset, "goodwill", and writing it off as quickly as possible. Other intangible assets, of the patent and trade mark variety, are also usually shown at historical cost, less a very rapid annual write-off. Thus, intangible assets, are a heterogeneous collection of items which are probably undervalued in many company accounts, and which are often omitted entirely.

Tangible Fixed Assets (14) are a major item in the majority of company accounts, and one which is usually undervalued. The most common valuation convention is historic cost less depreciation to date, although a revaluation sometimes replaces historic cost and certain assets, particularly freehold land and buildings, are often not depreciated, since the Companies' Act does not make depreciation compulsory. The historical cost basis means that many fixed assets are very much undervalued, because fixed assets, by definition, last for a long time, and prices are liable to change more over a longer period. During the period 1948 to 1960, which is covered by our data, the L. C. E. S. price index for capital goods rose from 66 to 100,[1] although not all capital goods last for twelve years, and those which do are constantly depreciating and being replaced (with the notable exception of freehold land) or being added to. Therefore, the average age of fixed assets, and consequently the degree of under-valuation, may be less than might superficially seem to be the case. On the other hand, the fact that companies have fixed capital stocks of varying age composition which may be revalued from time to time or may be valued at historic cost, less depreciation, means that inter-firm comparisons need to be made with caution, even when similar accounting conventions are being used. Since depreciation is based on the book value of fixed assets, an under-valuation of the asset will also tend to lead to an under-statement of depreciation.

Some of the defects of asset valuation described above are, of course, reflected in the Sources and Uses of Funds Statement since this reflects the changes in the balance sheet figures. However, since the Sources and Uses Statement reflects current changes in Balance Sheet figures, it avoids some of the problems of historic cost valuation. The Sources and Uses Statement is less useful than it might otherwise be because details of sales and expenditure on fixed assets do not appear in the accounts. Instead the change in the balance sheet figures of fixed assets at cost or valuation is used. This nets out acquisitions and disposals and hides the gross amount of new investment undertaken. Furthermore, in order to obtain a consistent series, we have been forced to deduct the profit on disposal of fixed assets from 'Expenditure, less receipts, on Fixed Assets – tangible' (37), which wrongly assumes that all capital profits are attributable to tangible fixed assets rather than trade investments or intangible assets. Thus, the uses of funds items referring to fixed assets (37, 38 and 39) should be treated with caution, especially when consolidation of a new subsidiary adds another degree of estimation.

The profit figures are also affected by the asset valuations, especially as regards capital profits. Some capital profits, e. g. those on fixed assets which have appreciated but have not be revalued, are not shown in the accounts at all, whilst others, such as those due to stock appreciation, are included in the operating profit. On the other hand, user depreciation is understated where the asset concerned has appreciated in value.

Enough has been said to indicate that the basic accounting data are unsatisfactory, particularly as regards asset valuation. It remains to say that although these defects are important, they need not vitiate the significance of the data for particular purposes. The most important feature of accounting valuation conventions is that they all work in the same direction, i. e. it is considered almost criminal to over-value and prudent to under-value. It is not surprizing, to learn that a recent study by the Board of Trade[1] bears out the predicition that companies under-value their assets. It is also probable that differences in valuation conventions between companies will be less within industry groups, where type of assets held are likely to be similar.

The length of life of fixed tangible assets, for example, is an important factor determining the average age of assets, and therefore the degree of error in historical cost valuation, and this is likely to depend on the technology of the industry.[2] Furthermore, a company which has grown slowly will tend to have a lower proportion of new assets, which will probably mean that it undervalues its assets relative to a fast growing firm of similar asset structure

Finally, it should be remembered that, although the accounting information is imperfect, it is, in many respects, the best information available to management and (more so) to shareholders. From some points of view, therefore, it may explain economic variables, such as the share price, better than would theoretically sounder information which was not available to the actual decision makers.

Bibliography

Publications of the N. I. E. S. R. and the Board of Trade, using the data studied in this book.

Company Income and Finance 1949-53, National Institute of Economic and Social Research, London, 1956.

A Classified List of Large Companies Engaged in British Industry, National Institute of Economic and Social Research, London, 1956.

Studies in Company Finance, edited by Brian Tew and R. F. Henderson, Cambridge University Press, 1959.

Income and Finance of Public Quoted Companies, 1949-60, Statistics Division, Board of Trade, London 1962.

Company Assets and Income in 1957, H.M.S.O., London, 1960

Company Assets, Income and Finance in 1960, H.M.S.O., London, 1962

Company Assets, Income and Finance in 1963, H.M.S.O., London, 1965

Articles in Economic Trends, February 1958, February 1959, December 1959, December 1960, November 1961, April 1962, April 1963, December 1963, November 1965.

Articles on the subject have also appeared from time to time in the Board of Trade Journal.

An article on non-quoted companies appeared in Economic Trends for February 1965.

Company Law and Accounts.

> The Companies Act, 1948, H.M.S.O., London
>
> Modern Company Law, by L.C.B. Gower, Stevens and Sons, London, 1957.
>
> Report of the Company Law Committee, (the Jenkins Committee Report), Cmnd. 1749, H.M.S.O., London, 1962.
>
> Disclosure in Company Accounts, by Harold Rose, Eaton Paper 1, Institute of Economic Affairs, London, 1965.
>
> Business Finance, by F.W. Paish, Pitman, London, 1965.

Accounting and Economic Theory

> Studies in Accounting Theory, edited by W.T. Baxter and S. Davidson, Sweet and Maxwell, London, 1962.
>
> Accounting for Economists, by R.L. Mathews, Melbourne, 1963.
>
> Accounting for Inflation, by L.A. Wilk, Sweet and Maxwell, London, 1960.
>
> The Accountant in a Golden Age, by G.C. Harcourt, Oxford Economic Papers, Vol.17, No.1, March 1965.

Part II. Share prices data

Computation of valuation ratios

We shall now describe the data used and the method of computing average valuation ratios for the calendar years 1954 and 1960, discussed in Section 7 of Chapter 2. As defined in Chapter 2:

the valuation ratio, $V = \dfrac{\text{market value of a firm's equity}}{\substack{\text{book value of the firm's capital} \\ \text{owned by equity shareholders}}}$

$= \dfrac{\substack{\text{Number of ordinary shares} \times \text{market price} \\ \text{of one share}}}{\substack{\text{Book value of the firm's capital owned by} \\ \text{equity shareholders}}}$

222

As it stands, the valuation ratio is a stock concept and it has a definite magnitude on the date of the balance sheet. However, since there are large short run fluctuations in the market price of the shares, the average value of 'V' over a longer period is a more suitable tool of analysis for a number of purposes. We have considered here the time period of a year; in particular, we have tried to compute the average valuation ratio for the calendar year 1954 and the calendar year 1960, respectively, for each firm.

It has been demonstrated elsewhere that the mid-range of the firm's highest and lowest share prices is a reasonably accurate measure of a firm's average share price during the year.[1] Moodies cards, provided by Moodies Services Ltd. to their subscribers in the U.K., give the highest and lowest share price during a calendar year for every quoted firm. These cards also give information on the capital structure of the firm. By making certain other assumptions, described presently, the numerator of the average valuation ratio for the year has been computed from the information given in Moodies cards. The following information was in fact collected for each firm.

1. Identification of the firm.

2. Accounting date of the firm.

3. Nominal value of Ordinary Capital.

4. Nominal value of an Ordinary share.

5. Details of the capital changes in the past accounting year.

6. Highest share price for the calendar year.

7. Lowest share price for the calendar year.

The denominator of the valuation ratio is Equity Assets, which has been obtained from the Company accounts described in Part I of this Appendix.[2] In order to obtain the average valuation ratio for the year, it is further assumed that the change in equity assets and the nominal value of ordinary capital[3] from one balance sheet date to the next balance sheet date is linear. Since the shares issued (which are a factor in the numerator) and the assets acquired (which are a factor in the denominator) have been treated in exactly the same way, the above assumption is by no means an unreasonable one. However, although in principle it may seem quite easy to compute valuation ratios from the data given in Moodies cards and in Company accounts, there remain a number of practical difficulties in the computation of these ratios. The more important of these problems are discussed in the next section.

Accounting Date. The accounting date raises the most serious practical problems. The conceptual problem is quite simple: we wish to obtain the average valuation ratio for the calendar year, mainly because the highest and lowest share prices are available on Moodies cards only for the calendar year. However, on the simple assumption of linear change made in the last section, the average number of shares in issue and the average level of equity assets during the year can only be calculated for the accounting year. If the accounting year and the calendar year coincide, e. g. the balance sheet date is 31 December, there is no problem at all, but to the extent that they differ, some adjustments have to be made. The nature of these adjustments for the following mutually exclusive and collectively exhaustive categories is shown below.

(a) For firms with accounting dates between 1 January and 5 April of (say) the calendar year 1954. To fix ideas the following line diagram may be kept in mind:

```
Dec. 31, 1952    July 1    Dec. 31, 1953    July 1    Dec. 31, 1954
├────────┬─────────┬──────────┬─────────┬────────┬──────┤
       April 5    Oct. 1      April 5    Oct. 1   April 5, 1955
```

As explained in Part I, section 6, of the Appendix, the accounting year 1953 means the company's accounting year ending between 1 January and 5 April 1954; and the accounting year 1954 similarly extends from the accounting date in the period 1 January to 5 April, 1954 to the corresponding date in 1955.

In computing the average valuation ratio for 1954, the average of the book value of equity assets for the accounting years 1953 and 1954 (i. e. average of the balance sheet figures in 1954 and 1955) has been used in the denominator, the average share price of the calendar year 1954 has been used in the numerator as well as the average number of shares in issue at the end of the accounting years 1953 and 1954. It is clear from the diagram that this procedure would still lead to an inevitable small bias which would increase in magnitude the closer the accounting date of a particular firm is to the end of the first quarter. But this appears to be the best one can do.

(b) For firms with accounting dates between 6 April and 30 September of (say) the year 1954. Here we have used the book value of the accounting year, 1954, (e. g. book value on the balance sheet date 30 June, 1954), the average share price for the calendar year 1954 and the average number of shares in issue at the end of the accounting year 1954.

(c) For firms with accounting dates between 1 October and 31 December of (say) the year 1954. The procedure adopted here is exactly analogous to that for firms with accounting dates in the first quarter, i. e. in computing the average valuation ratio for 1954, the average book value of equity assets, as well as the average number of shares in issue at the end of the accounting years 1953 and 1954, and the average share price for the calendar year 1954 have been used. If the accounting date is 31 December, there is no bias at all; the bias increases the nearer the accounting date is to 1 October.

It is clear from the above discussion that the procedures adopted for adjustment for the accounting date may make inter-firm comparisons with different accounting dates somewhat hazardous. Properly speaking, the inter-firm comparisons of valuation ratios should be restricted to firms for which the accounting dates fall within the same quarter of the calendar year. Fortunately about half of the firms have their accounting dates falling within the last quarter (the largest number of these have 31 December as the accounting date), and something like

224

eighty per cent have accounting dates either in the first or the last quarter.

New Issues. As suggested above it is assumed here that the change in the nominal value of ordinary capital, due to new issues between the two balance sheet dates, is linear. Whereas this assumption resolves most of the difficulties for firms with accounting dates in the first and last quarter, some difficulties still remain for a small class of firms with accounting dates in the middle two quarters.

The difficulties which arise here may be illustrated by taking the case of a firm with balance sheet date as 30 June, 1954

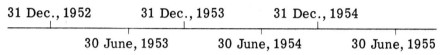

| 31 Dec., 1952 | 31 Dec., 1953 | 31 Dec., 1954 |
| 30 June, 1953 | 30 June, 1954 | 30 June, 1955 |

If the new issue takes place between 1 January, 1954 and 30 June, 1954, it is taken into account in the balance sheet of 30 June, 1954. However, if the issue takes place between 30 June, 1954 and 31 December, 1954, the shares issued and the assets acquired would not be reflected in the balance sheet of 30 June, 1954, although they may affect the share prices of the firm in the latter half of 1954. But the number of firms for which this problem arises is very small indeed, and wherever possible an appropriate adjustment was made.

Bonus issues. Fortunately, bonus issues do not pose any difficulty since Moodies adjust the highest and lowest share price for any bonus issue made during the year.

Rights issues. Rights issues have had to be treated in the same way as new issues in view of the fact that Moodies make no adjustment for them. The effort involved in adjusting for rights issues for such a vast number of firms was much too great to be undertaken for the present work.

In the end, we may again note that on the basis of the simple assumptions made previously, proper inter-firm comparisons of the average equity assets with average stock market valuation for the calendar year can only be made for those firms which have a balance sheet date of 31 December. On this date both the calendar year and the accounting year coincide. For other data, the comparisons would suffer from various degrees of bias. However, to the extent that, in the procedures we have adopted, the numerator and the denominator of the valuation ratio are treated in exactly the same way, this bias is unlikely to be important.

Appendix B   A Note on Computing

The main body of company finance data was received from the Board of Trade punched on eighty-column Hollerith cards. These were converted to eight-channel I. B. M. paper tape, using an I. B. M. 870 machine made available to us by the Cambridge University Department of Chemical Engineering. Our early program development was carried out on the EDSAC II and, TITAN computers at the University Mathematical Laboratory, Cambridge, using paper tape input. Unfortunately paper tape input was found unsatisfactory for such a large volume of data and we encountered difficulties in storing the data on magnetic tapes, so we decided to find a computer specifically designed for large-scale data processing. We were fortunate in obtaining the use of the I. B. M. 7090 computer at Imperial College, London, which, with high speed card input and reliable magnetic tape facilities, has proved ideal for the job.

Our data processing system, as it has finally emerged, is as follows:

1. Sorting

The Board of Trade Hollerith cards for one industry are sorted into time series sequence for each individual company, using an I. C. T. counter-sorter at the Department of Applied Economics. Companies which were reclassified to other industries are brought back into their original industry, to obtain a continuous time series. This is done by reference to our card index of company numbers, names and history, prepared from the records of the N.I.E.S.R. and the Board of Trade.

2. Testing for missing cards and correct sequence

There can be from 4 to 22 or more punched cards for each company for each year. Their correct sequence is determined by numbers punched in the first 24 columns of the card (hereafter referred to as the indicative section). The sequence is tested by running the cards through the small H. E. C. 1202 computer which the Department of Applied Economics shares with the Cambridge Language Research Unit.

3. Copying the punched cards on to magnetic tape

The cards are input to the I. B. M. 7090 computer at Imperial College (the actual input unit being part of a 1401 Satellite computer). The card images are written up on magnetic tape and the original cards become superfluous at this stage, except as evidence of what was originally input.

226

4. Testing and rearranging the indicative section

The indicative section of each card, which contains information about the history and activities of the company, is input from magnetic tape and subjected to rigorous logical tests, e.g. if a company is indicated as being 'born' in a certain year, it should have only four data cards for that year. In addition, the indicative section is reduced to a standard format, which eliminates the many changes which took place during our 12-year period, and eradicates duplicate cards, arising out of the linking procedure, which are not required. The tested and rearranged card images are stored on magnetic tape. Details of any errors are printed out by the line printer, and appropriate corrections are made at a later stage.

5. Testing and rearranging the quantitative information

The card images from the previous stage are input from magnetic tape. The actual accounting information is subject to consistency tests, e.g. all balance sheets are tested to ensure that they balance, and all summary items are reconciled with the total of their components. The accounting information is then put into the standardized format, described in Appendix C. This standardized form is stored on magnetic tape, and any errors are printed out and dealt with at a later stage. In addition, certain summary statistics are printed out for each company for each year. These are designed to provide information for more specialized studies which are being undertaken into take-over bids, trade credit, and other topics.

6. Correction of errors

All errors which are reported at stages 4 and 5 are investigated, usually by reference to the company's published accounts as recorded on Moodies' Cards, or, in more difficult cases, by reference to the Board of Trade's original work-sheets. The errors are then corrected by deleting the faulty data from the magnetic tape and writing up corrected data (from punched cards) in its place.

7. Calculations on the standardized data

The fully standardized and tested data are then input from magnetic tape and the economic indicators described in Appendix D and Chapter 2 are calculated, for continuing companies, over each sub-period and the full period. The indicators are punched on cards, there being one card per company per period, together with certain indicative information (company number, period number, industry number, etc.). The cards can then be sorted on our counter-sorter and are an easily rearranged or sub-divided form of input for further computing. The card images are also stored on magnetic tape and are output in printed form. The print-out also includes reports about any company which has a freak value for some indicator, e.g. because the net assets are computed to be negative: such cases are then excluded from statistical analysis involving these indicators, e.g. the frequency distributions of Chapter 2, or the correlations of Chapter 3.

8. Final calculations

Correlation and regression analysis are carried out by the 7090 computer using the cards obtained in 7 above as input. The cards are also sorted by the counter-sorter and printed out to provide information such as that given in Appendix F, further calculations being performed by desk calculating machines. Some of the printed information was also punched on paper tape for regression analysis, using the Department of Applied Economics standard regression program ('Reg X') on the Cambridge University Mathematical Laboratory's TITAN computer.

Appendix C   List of Standardized Variables in the Basic Accounting Data

List of standardized variables in the basic accounting data

Variable number	Title
	Capital and Reserves
1	Issued Capital – Ordinary
2	" " – Preference
3	Capital and Revenue Reserves
4	Provisions
5	Future Tax Reserves
	Memorandum
6	Contracts for capital expenditure outstanding
	Liabilities
7	Interest of Minority Shareholders in Subsidiaries
8	Long-term liabilities
9	Bank overdrafts and loans
10	Trade and other creditors
11	Dividends and Interest liabilities
12	Current Taxation liabilities
	Memorandum
13	Total Depreciation
	Assets
14	Fixed Assets: Tangible, net of depreciation
15	" " Intangible
16	" " Trade Investments
17	Stocks and work in progress
18	Trade and other debtors
19	Marketable securities
20	Tax reserve certificates
21	Cash
	Summary
22	Total Net Assets

Variable number	Title
	Sources of Funds
23	Issue of Shares – Ordinary
24	" " " – Preference
25	Increase in liability to minority interests
26	Issue of long-term loans
27	Bank credit received
28	Trade and other credit received
29	Increase in dividend and interest liabilities
30	" " current tax liabilities
31	" " future tax reserves
32	Balance of Profit-Depreciation provision
33	" " " -Provision for amortization
34	Balance of Profit – Other provisions
35	" " " – Retained in reserves
36	Other receipts
	Uses of Funds
37	Expenditure, less receipts, on fixed assets – tangible
38	Expenditure, less receipts, on fixed assets – intangible
39	Expenditure, less receipts, on fixed assets – trade investments and investments in subsidiary companies
40	Increase in value of stocks and work in progress
41	Increase in credit given – trade and other debtors
42	Expenditure ex Provisions
43	Sundry expenditure
	Adjustments
44	Consolidation adjustment
45	Conversion "
46	Residual "
	Balance
47	Change in securities
48	" " tax reserve certificates
49	" " cash
	Appropriation of Income
50	Operating profit (before depreciation)

Variable number	Title
51	Dividends and interest received (gross of income tax)
52	Other income
53	Interest paid on long-term liabilities, gross
54	Tax on current profit
55	Dividend, net of income tax, Ordinary
56	" " Other
57	To minority interest in subsidiaries (net of taxation)
58	Prior year adjustments – Tax
59	" " " – General

Summary

60	Total capital and reserves (Items 1 to 6)
61	" liabilities (Items 7 to 12)
62	" fixed assets, net of depreciation (Items 14 to 16)
63	" current assets (Items 17 to 21)
64	" sources (Items 23 to 36)
65	" uses (Items 37 to 43)
66	" profit (Items 50 to 52)
67	" balance of profit (Items 32 to 35)

Notes. Items headed 'Memorandum' do not have any arithmetic consistency with other items, e.g. 'total depreciation' has already been deducted from the value of 'tangible fixed assets'.

Items headed 'Summary' are the sums of groups of other items.

The following are the basic accounting equalities underlying the data:

(1) Balance Sheet:
Capital and Reserves (60) + Liabilities (61) = Fixed Assets (62) + Current Assets (63)

(2) Sources and Uses of Funds Statement:
Total Sources (64) = Total Uses (65) + Adjustments (44 to 46) + Balance (47 to 49)

(3) Appropriation Statement:
Total Profit (66) = Interest paid (53) + Tax on current profit (54) + Dividends (55 & 56) + Minority Interest (57) + Prior year adjustments (58 & 59) + Balance of Profit (67).

Notes on specific items

The following notes refer to those items which, by virtue of the peculia-
rities of accounting conventions or of their treatment in the present
analysis, are likely to be misleading or ambiguous. The reader who
is unfamiliar with accounting terms and concepts in general is referred
to the Bibliography at the end of Appendix A, Part I.

The Sources and Uses of Funds Statement has some special limitations
resulting from the methods used to calculate it. These are described
in Section 4 of Appendix A, Part I.

Reserves (3) and provisions (4)

The distinction between reserves and provisions, as defined by the 1948
Companies Act (Eighth Schedule, Part IV), is that a provision is an
appropriation to meet a known liability, the amount of which cannot be
accurately determined, whereas a reserve is an amount retained out
of profits to meet future contingencies. Revenue reserves are available
for distribution as dividends, but capital reserves and provisions are not.

The amounts included in provisions here do not include accruals of current operating expenses, which are treated as current liabilities. The
type of provisions which are included under the heading 4 and the corresponding Sources of Funds item (34), are those relating to longer term
liabilities, such as those for pensions and deferred repairs.

Future tax reserves (5)

Company income tax (Schedule D) was assessed throughout this period
on the 'preceding year' basis. This means that the tax liability for
any fiscal year (6 April to 5 April) was based on the profits of the company accounting year ended in the previous fiscal year. Thus, in the
case of a company preparing accounts to 31st December 1959, the
income tax based on the profit of that year would not become a legal
liability until the fiscal year 1960/61 and would be correctly shown in
the 1959 accounts as a reserve, not a liability or a provision. It would
become a current liability in the 1960 accounts.

Interest of minority shareholders in subsidiaries (7)

Where a subsidiary company is not wholly owned by its parent, the consolidated accounts will show the proportion of the subsidiary's capital
and reserves attributable to shareholders outside the group. In the
case of preference shares, this will be simply the nominal value of the
shares, but in the case of ordinary shares, it will include in addition
the proportion of capital and revenue reserves attributable to minority
shareholders. Dividends due to minority shareholders are not included
in the minority interest, but are added to item 11, dividend and interest
liabilities.

Long-term liabilities (8)

The definition of 'long-term' is decided by reference to the length of
the original loan rather than by the time of redemption. Thus, deben-

232

ture stock redeemable within months of the balance sheet date will be classified as 'long-term'.

Current taxation liabilities (12)

This will include foreign taxes and United Kingdom profits tax on the current year's profits and United Kingdom income tax on the preceding year's profits, less amounts already paid in respect of such liabilities.

Intangible assets (15)

This includes such items as preliminary expenses of forming the company, the cost of patents and trade marks, and advertising expenditure capitalized as goodwill, but its most important component in consolidated accounts is the goodwill consisting of the excess of the price paid for shares in a subsidiary over the net book value of the assets which they represent.

Stocks and work in progress (17)

Progress payments received for work in progress are deducted from the value of this item.

Issue of shares and long-term loans (23, 24 and 26)

The costs of issue have been deducted from gross receipts in respect of these items.

Other receipts (36)

This includes receipts of a capital nature, other than profits on the sale of fixed assets (see below). An example which was fairly common in the early years of the period was the receipt of excess profits tax post-war refunds.

Expenditure, less receipts, on fixed assets (37, 38 and 39)

The receipts deducted here include profits on the sale of fixed assets which will therefore reduce the net figure. Conversely, losses on sale will increase the net figure.

For purchases of tangible fixed assets, the expenditure used here is the gross amount (i.e. expenditure before deducting depreciation), because depreciation written off in the year of purchase is included as a source of funds on the other side of the Statement.

Expenditure ex provisions (42)

This is expenditure charged against provisions included under headings 4 and 34. An example would be a pension payment for which a provision had been made.

Sundry expenditure (43)

This is expenditure of a capital nature which could not be classified to any other Uses of Funds category. The most important example of this type of expenditure is a capital distribution to shareholders.

Consolidation adjustment (44)

This is the net amount left unexplained after the Sources and Uses Statement has been adjusted to remove the effects of acquiring a new subsidiary company, under the procedure described in Section 4 of Appendix A.

Conversion adjustment (45)

This represents the change in the net difference arising on conversion of overseas assets from foreign currency to pounds sterling. The difference arises because the parent's interest always appears in sterling in its own books, but in the subsidiary's (or branch) books it appears in a foreign currency which will fluctuate in sterling value.

Residual adjustment (46)

This consists of any change in a balance sheet item which cannot be explained sufficiently well for it to be classified to another Sources and Uses heading. The amounts involved are usually very small.

Operating profit (50)

This is the trading profit of the group after deducting all expenses (including directors' remuneration and audit fees) but before deducting depreciation, other provisions, interest on long-term loans, or taxation.

Tax on current profit (54)

Includes all taxes which will be assessed at some time on the profit of the current year. It therefore includes U.K. Profits tax and foreign taxes for the current year and U.K. income tax for the following year.

To minority interest in subsidiaries (57)

The share of the current profits, net of taxation, attributable to minority shareholders, including a portion of reserves, as well as dividends.

Appendix D   List of Indicators Calculated[1]

Indicators 1 to 13 inclusive are calculated for each continuing company for each sub-period and the period as a whole.

Terminology

m = last year of a period or sub-period.

p = first year of a period or sub-period.

o = year p <u>minus</u> one year.

n = number of years in a period or sub-period.

  = m-o

y = standard rate of income tax:

         9/20 for years 0,1,2

        19/40 "   "   3,4

         9/20 "   "   5,6

        17/40 "   "   7,8,9,10

        31/80 "   "   11,12

Values of m, p. o, and n are as follows:

    Full period : $m = 12$, $p = 1$, $o = 0$, $n = 12$

    Sub-period 1: $m = 6$, $p = 1$, $o = 0$, $n = 6$

    Sub-period 2: $m = 12$, $p = 7$, $o = 6$, $n = 6$

In subsequent definitions, numbers preceded by "Q" refer to the number of a variable in our standardized company-year data sequence given in Appendix C, e.g. Q1 is "Issued Capital-Ordinary".

Definitions

<u>Net assets:</u>

$(Q60 + Q7 + Q8 - Q4)$

<u>Aggregate net assets:</u>

$$\{[(\text{Net Assets})_m + (\text{Net Assets})_o] \div 2\} + \{\sum_{p}^{m-1} (\text{Net Assets})\}$$

This concept gives half weight to opening and closing values in order

---

[1] The indicators are described and explained verbally in Chapter 2.

to obtain an average figure which is comparable with flows, e.g. profits, on the arbitrary assumption that the change in net assets from one balance sheet date to the next is linear. See Chapter 2, note 6, page 22. The numerators of Indicators 11, 12 and 13 are also weighted in this way, to give the average for the 12-year period covered by our flow measures, rather than for a 13-year period which would not be strictly comparable.

Indicators

(1) Net assets — opening:

$$(\text{Net Assets})_o$$

(2) Net assets — closing:

$$(\text{Net Assets})_m$$

(3) Net assets — average:

$$(\text{Aggregate Net Assets}) \div n$$

(4) Growth of net assets:

$$\sqrt[n]{\frac{\sum_p^m (Q23 + Q24 + Q31 + Q35 + Q36 - Q43) + (Q7 + Q8)_m + (Q60 - Q4)_o}{(\text{Net Assets})_o}} - 1$$

The numerator of this indicator consists of Closing Size, estimated by using actual closing figures for Minority Interests and Long-term liabilities, and Sources and Uses figures added to opening figures for the remaining components. This is because the Sources and Uses figures, which are adjusted for accounting date changes where accounts cover a period other than one year, were considered more accurate for many of the components of growth, but Minority Interests and Long-term liabilities are under-stated in the Sources and Uses Statement, to the extent that it excludes changes in these items due to the consolidation of a new subsidiary company. This is explained in Appendix A (pp. 214-16).

(5) Rate of return on net assets:

$$\frac{\sum_p^m [Q66 - (Q32 + Q33 + Q34) + Q59]}{(\text{Aggregate Net Assets})}$$

(6) Post-tax rate of return on equity assets:

$$\frac{\sum_p^m (Q35 + Q55)}{\{[(Q60 - Q4 - Q2)_o + (Q60 - Q4 - Q2)_m] \div 2\} + \{\sum_p^{m-1} (Q60 - Q4 - Q2)\}}$$

In the denominators of this and the following indicator, our Equity Assets concept, (Q60 - Q4 - Q2), is aggregated over the period in the same way as Aggregate Net Assets (Definition 1)

(7) Dividend return on equity assets:

$$\frac{\sum_{p}^{m}[Q55 - (1 - y)]}{\{[(Q60 - Q4 - Q2)_o + (Q60 - Q4 - Q2)_m] \div 2\} + \{\sum_{p}^{m-1}(Q60 - Q4 - Q2)\}}$$

(8) Retention ratio:

$$\frac{\sum_{p}^{m}(Q35)}{\sum_{p}^{m}(Q35 + Q55)}$$

(9) Internal finance of growth:

$$\frac{\sum_{p}^{m}(Q31 + Q35 + Q36 - Q43)}{\sum_{p}^{m}(Q23 + Q24 + Q31 + Q35 + Q36 - Q43) + (Q7 + Q8)_m - (Q7 + Q8)_o}$$

Growth in the denominator of this indicator is defined in the same way as in the numerator of Indicator 4.

(10) Gearing:

$$\frac{\sum_{p}^{m}[Q53(1 - y) + Q56]}{\sum_{p}^{m}[Q53(1 - y) + Q55 + Q56 + Q35]}$$

(11) Liquidity:

$$\frac{[(\text{Liquid Assets})_m + (\text{Liquid Assets})_o] \div 2 + \sum_{p}^{m-1}(\text{Liquid Assets})}{(\text{Aggregate Net Assets})}$$

where Liquid Assets = $(Q19 + Q20 + Q21 - Q9 - Q11 - Q12)$

(12) Net trade credit given:

$$\frac{\{[(Q18 - Q10)_m + (Q18 - Q10)_o] \div 2\} + \{\sum_{p}^{m-1}(Q18 - Q10)\}}{(\text{Aggregate Net Assets})}$$

(13) Stocks:

$$\frac{[(Q17)_m + (Q17)_o] \div 2 + \sum_{p}^{m-1}(Q17)}{(\text{Aggregate Net Assets})}$$

(14) Valuation ratio:

$$\frac{(\text{Market Valuation of Equity Capital})}{(Q60 - Q4 - Q2)_m}$$

Appendix E   Transition Matrices for the Individual Industries

The transition matrices for the three major industries for sub-period 1 (1948-54), for sub-period 2 (1954-60) and the whole period (1948-60), are given in Tables E. 1 to E. 9. As indicated in Chapter 5, these matrices show the proportion of firms in different size classes at the beginning of the period which have gone into various size classes at the end of the period. The transition matrices for the firms in all industries (including Tobacco) combined were given in Tables 5. 1 to 5. 3.

Apart from their usefulness in analysing a number of other important aspects of the growth process of firms, these matrices form the basis of probability calculations for the comparisons of relative mobility in different industries in Section 1 of Chapter 5.

Table E.1 Sub-Period 1, 1948-54, Industry 04, Non-Electrical Engineering

Indicators 1 & 2, Opening Size and Closing Size

Opening Size (£)	Closing Size (£) <62,500	<125,000	<250,000	<500,000	<1,000,000	<2,000,000	<4,000,000	<8,000,000	<16,000,000	<32,000,000	>32,000,000	Total number of firms
<62,500	33.3	33.3	33.3	—	—	—	—	—	—	—	—	3
<125,000	5.3	26.3	57.9	5.3	5.3	—	—	—	—	—	—	19
<250,000	—	—	13.8	72.4	13.8	—	—	—	—	—	—	29
<500,000	—	1.8	1.8	20.0	70.9	5.5	—	—	—	—	—	55
<1,000,000	—	—	1.5	—	22.1	60.3	16.2	—	—	—	—	68
<2,000,000	—	—	—	—	—	20.0	71.1	8.9	—	—	—	45
<4,000,000	—	—	—	—	—	—	23.1	76.9	—	—	—	26
<8,000,000	—	—	—	—	—	—	—	57.1	42.9	—	—	7
<16,000,000	—	—	—	—	—	—	—	—	80.0	20.0	—	5
<32,000,000	—	—	—	—	—	—	—	—	—	100.0	—	1
>32,000,000	—	—	—	—	—	—	—	—	—	—	100.0	1
Total number of firms	2	7	18	33	59	53	49	28	7	2	1	259

Proportionate Growth

Size in 1954/Size in 1948	1/4	1/2	1	2	4	8	Total number of firms
Number of firms	2	2	61	169	24	1	259
Proportion of firms	0.8	0.8	23.5	65.2	9.3	0.4	

239

Table E. 2 Sub-Period 2, 1954-60, Industry 04, Non-Electrical Engineering

Indicators 1 & 2, Opening Size and Closing Size

Opening Size (£)	Closing Size (£)											Total number of firms
	<62,500	<125,000	<250,000	<500,000	<1,000,000	<2,000,000	<4,000,000	<8,000,000	<16,000,000	<32,000,000	>32,000,000	
<62,500	50.0	50.0	—	—	—	—	—	—	—	—	—	2
<125,000	—	37.5	50.0	12.5	—	—	—	—	—	—	—	8
<250,000	5.0*	—	50.0	45.0	—	—	—	—	—	—	—	20
<500,000	—	—	2.6	43.6	43.6	10.3	—	—	—	—	—	39
<1,000,000	—	—	—	—	43.6	47.3	9.1	—	—	—	—	55
<2,000,000	—	—	—	—	—	43.4	47.2	9.4	—	—	—	53
<4,000,000	—	—	—	—	—	—	37.0	56.5	4.3	2.1	—	46
<8,000,000	—	—	—	—	—	—	—	34.5	55.2	6.9	3.4	29
<16,000,000	—	—	—	—	—	—	—	—	—	100.0	—	7
<32,000,000	—	—	—	—	—	—	—	—	—	50.0	50.0	2
>32,000,000	—	—	—	—	—	—	—	—	—	—	100.0	1
Total number of firms	2	4	15	27	41	53	47	41	18	11	3	262

* Includes company with opening size <250,000 and closing size <0.

Proportionate Growth

Size in 1960/size in 1954	1/4	1/2	1	2	4	8	Total number of firms
Number of firms	1	1	107	132	19	2	262
Proportion of firms	0.4	0.4	40.8	50.4	7.2	0.8	

Table E.3 Whole Period, 1948-60, Industry 04, Non-Electrical Engineering

Indicators 1 & 2: Opening Size and Closing Size

Closing Size (£)

Opening Size (£)	<62,500	<125,000	<250,000	<500,000	<1,000,000	<2,000,000	<4,000,000	<8,000,000	<16,000,000	<32,000,000	>32,000,000	Total number of firms
<62,500	—	33.3	33.3	33.3	—	—	—	—	—	—	—	3
<125,000	7.1	14.3	50.0	14.3	—	14.3	—	—	—	—	—	14
<250,000	—	—	4.5	40.9	40.9	9.1	4.5	—	—	—	—	22
<500,000	2.4*	—	2.4	9.8	43.9	31.7	9.8	—	—	—	—	41
<1,000,000	—	—	—	—	3.6	38.2	41.8	14.5	1.8	—	—	55
<2,000,000	—	—	—	—	—	10.0	25.0	52.5	10.0	2.5	—	40
<4,000,000	—	—	—	—	—	—	16.0	32.0	40.0	8.0	4.0	25
<8,000,000	—	—	—	—	—	—	—	14.3	42.9	42.9	—	7
<16,000,000	—	—	—	—	—	—	—	—	—	80.0	20.0	5
<32,000,000	—	—	—	—	—	—	—	—	—	100.0	—	1
>32,000,000	—	—	—	—	—	—	—	—	—	—	100.0	1
Total number of firms	2	3	10	16	29	42	42	38	18	11	3	214

* Includes company with opening size <500,000 and closing size <0.

Proportionate Growth

Size in 1960/size in 1948	1/8	1/4	1/2	1	2	4	8	16	Total number of firms
Number of firms	1	—	2	20	81	83	21	6	214
Proportion of firms	0.5	—	0.9	9.3	37.8	38.8	9.8	2.8	

Table E.4 Sub-Period 1, 1948-54, Industry 12, Food

Indicators 1 & 2: Opening Size and Closing Size

Opening Size (£)	Closing Size (£)											Total number of firms
	<62,500	<125,000	<250,000	<500,000	<1,000,000	<2,000,000	<4,000,000	<8,000,000	<16,000,000	<32,000,000	>32,000,000	
<62,500	—	—	—	—	—	—	—	—	—	—	—	—
<125,000	—	62.5	25.0	12.5	—	—	—	—	—	—	—	8
<250,000	—	—	41.7	45.8	12.5	—	—	—	—	—	—	24
<500,000	—	3.4	—	48.3	37.9	10.3	—	—	—	—	—	29
<1,000,000	—	—	—	7.7	38.5	53.8	—	—	—	—	—	13
<2,000,000	—	—	—	—	—	63.6	27.3	9.1	—	—	—	11
<4,000,000	—	—	—	—	—	10.0	20.0	70.0	—	—	—	10
<8,000,000	—	—	—	—	—	—	—	28.6	71.4	—	—	7
<16,000,000	—	—	—	—	—	—	—	—	33.3	66.6	—	3
<32,000,000	—	—	—	—	—	—	—	—	—	33.3	66.6	3
>32,000,000	—	—	—	—	—	—	—	—	—	—	—	—
Total number of firms	—	6	12	27	19	18	5	10	6	3	2	108

Proportionate Growth

Size in 1954/size in 1948	$\frac{1}{4}$	$\frac{1}{2}$	1	2	4	Total number of firms
Number of firms	1	2	47	50	8	108
Proportion of firms	0.9	1.8	43.5	46.3	7.4	

Table E.5 Sub-Period 2: 1954-60, Industry 12, Food

Indicators 1 & 2: Opening Size and Closing Size

Opening Size (£)	Closing Size (£)											
	<62,500	<125,000	<250,000	<500,000	<1,000,000	<2,000,000	<4,000,000	<8,000,000	<16,000,000	<32,000,000	>32,000,000	Total number of firms
<62,500	—	—	—	—	—	—	—	—	—	—	—	—
<125,000	50.0	—	25.0	—	25.0	—	—	—	—	—	—	4
<250,000	8.3	41.7	33.3	16.7	—	—	—	—	—	—	—	12
<500,000	—	4.2	62.5	25.0	—	4.2	4.2	—	—	—	—	24
<1,000,000	—	—	—	—	38.5	46.1	15.4	—	—	—	—	13
<2,000,000	—	—	—	—	12.5	43.7	37.5	6.3	—	—	—	16
<4,000,000	—	—	—	—	—	—	—	50.0	—	50.0	—	2
<8,000,000	—	—	—	—	—	—	—	25.0	62.5	12.5	—	8
<16,000,000	—	—	—	—	—	—	—	—	33.3	50.0	16.7	6
<32,000,000	—	—	—	—	—	—	—	—	—	33.3	66.6	3
>32,000,000	—	—	—	—	—	—	—	—	—	—	100.0	3
Total number of firms	3	6	20	8	8	14	9	4	7	6	6	91

Proportionate Growth

Size in 1960/size in 1954	½	1	2	4	8	Total number of firms
Number of firms	4	42	33	9	3	91
Proportion of firms	4.4	46.1	36.3	9.9	3.3	

243

Table E. 6 Whole Period, 1948-60. Industry 12, Food

Indicators 1 & 2: Opening Size and Closing Size

Opening Size (£)	Closing Size (£) <62,500	<125,000	<250,000	<500,000	<1,000,000	<2,000,000	<4,000,000	<8,000,000	<16,000,000	<32,000,000	>32,000,000	Total number of firms
<62,500	—	—	—	—	—	—	—	—	—	—	—	—
<125,000	—	25.0	25.0	—	50.0	—	—	—	—	—	—	4
<250,000	—	—	18.7	56.2	25.0	—	—	—	—	—	—	16
<500,000	—	—	5.3	36.8	21.0	21.0	15.8	—	—	—	—	19
<1,000,000	—	—	—	—	25.0	50.0	25.0	—	—	—	—	8
<2,000,000	—	—	—	—	—	28.6	42.9	28.6	—	—	—	7
<4,000,000	—	—	—	—	—	—	—	28.6	42.9	28.6	—	7
<8,000,000	—	—	—	—	—	—	—	—	33.3	50.0	16.7	6
<16,000,000	—	—	—	—	—	—	—	—	33.3	33.3	33.3	3
<32,000,000	—	—	—	—	—	—	—	—	—	—	100.0	3
>32,000,000	—	—	—	—	—	—	—	—	—	—	—	—
Total number of firms	—	1	5	16	12	10	8	4	6	6	5	73

Proportionate Growth

Size in 1960/size in 1948	½	1	2	4	8	Total number of firms
Number of firms	1	16	29	19	8	73
Proportion of firms	1.4	21.9	39.7	26.0	11.0	

Table E.7 Sub-Period 1, 1948-54. Industry 11, Clothing and Footwear

Indicators 1 & 2: Opening Size and Closing Size

Opening Size (£)	Closing Size (£)											Total number of firms
	<62,500	<125,000	<250,000	<500,000	<1,000,000	<2,000,000	<4,000,000	<8,000,000	<16,000,000	<32,000,000	>32,000,000	
<62,500	50.0	50.0	—	—	—	—	—	—	—	—	—	2
<125,000	14.3	42.9	42.9	—	—	—	—	—	—	—	—	7
<250,000	4.5	4.5	59.1	31.8	—	—	—	—	—	—	—	22
<500,000	5.3	—	—	31.6	47.4	15.8	—	—	—	—	—	19
<1,000,000	—	—	—	5.0	75.0	20.0	—	—	—	—	—	20
<2,000,000	—	—	—	—	—	77.8	22.2	—	—	—	—	9
<4,000,000	—	—	—	—	—	—	60.0	40.0	—	—	—	5
<8,000,000	—	—	—	—	—	—	—	—	—	—	—	—
<16,000,000	—	—	—	—	—	—	—	—	50.0	50.0	—	2
<32,000,000	—	—	—	—	—	—	—	—	—	—	—	—
>32,000,000	—	—	—	—	—	—	—	—	—	—	—	—
Total number of firms	4	5	16	14	24	14	5	2	1	1	—	86

Proportionate Growth

Size in 1954/size in 1948	1/8	1/4	1/2	1	2	4	Total number of firms
Number of firms	1	1	3	49	29	3	86
Proportion of firms	1.2	1.2	3.5	57.0	33.7	3.5	

Table E. 9 Whole Period, 1948-60. Industry 11, Clothing and Footwear

Indicators 1 & 2: Opening Size and Closing Size

Opening Size (£)	Closing Size (£)											Total number of firms
	<62,500	<125,000	<250,000	<500,000	<1,000,000	<2,000,000	<4,000,000	<8,000,000	<16,000,000	<32,000,000	>32,000,000	
<62,500	50.0	50.0	–	–	–	–	–	–	–	–	–	6
<125,000	16.7	33.3	33.3	16.7	–	–	–	–	–	–	–	6
<250,000	13.3	6.7	26.7	20.0	33.3	–	–	–	–	–	–	15
<500,000	6.2	–	–	12.5	50.0	31.2	–	–	–	–	–	16
<1,000,000	–	–	–	–	44.4	55.6	–	–	–	–	–	18
<2,000,000	–	–	–	–	14.3	–	71.4	14.3	–	–	–	7
<4,000,000	–	–	–	.	–	–	–	75.0	25.0	–	–	4
<8,000,000	–	–	–	–	–	–	–	–	–	–	–	–
<16,000,000	–	–	–	–	–	–	–	–	–	50.0	50.0	2
<32,000,000	–	–	–	–	–	–	–	–	–	–	–	–
>32,000,000	–	–	–	–	–	–	–	–	–	–	–	–
Total number of firms	5	4	6	6	22	15	5	4	1	1	1	70

Proportionate Growth

Size in 1960/size in 1948	$\frac{1}{8}$	$\frac{1}{4}$	$\frac{1}{2}$	1	2	4	Total number of firms
Number of firms	1	2	3	17	33	14	70
Proportion of firms	1.4	2.9	4.3	24.3	47.1	20.0	

Table E.8 Sub-Period 2, 1954-60. Industry 11, Clothing and Footwear

Indicators 1 & 2: Opening Size and Closing Size

Opening Size (£)	Closing Size (£)											
	<62,500	<125,000	<250,000	<500,000	<1,000,000	<2,000,000	<4,000,000	<8,000,000	<16,000,000	<32,000,000	>32,000,000	Total number of firms
<62,500	50.0	25.0	—	25.0	—	—	—	—	—	—	—	4
<125,000	40.0	40.0	—	20.0	—	—	—	—	—	—	—	5
<250,000	—	10.0	50.0	20.0	20.0	—	—	—	—	—	—	10
<500,000	6.2	—	6.2	25.0	50.0	12.5	—	—	—	—	—	16
<1,000,000	—	—	—	—	61.5	38.5	—	—	—	—	—	26
<2,000,000	—	—	—	—	10.0	40.0	50.0	—	—	—	—	10
<4,000,000	—	—	—	—	—	—	20.0	80.0	—	—	—	5
<8,000,000	—	—	—	—	—	—	—	—	100.0	—	—	1
<16,000,000	—	—	—	—	—	—	—	—	—	—	100.0	1
<32,000,000	—	—	—	—	—	—	—	—	—	100.0	—	1
>32,000,000	—	—	—	—	—	—	—	—	—	—	—	—
Total number of firms	5	4	6	8	27	16	6	4	1	1	1	79

Proportionate Growth

Size in 1960/size in 1954	1/8	1/4	1/2	1	2	4	8	Total number of firms
Number of firms	1	—	5	35	31	6	1	79
Proportion of firms	1.3	—	6.3	44.3	39.2	7.6	1.3	

247

Appendix F The Relationship between Average Values of Various Indicators

Introduction

This appendix gives the mean values of each indicator for different groups of companies classified by the ranges of selected indicators, i.e. it shows how the average values of other indicators change as each of the selected indicators rises in value.

The key indicators selected are as follows:

Tables	Indicator	
	Number	Description
1 and 2	1	Opening Size
3 and 4	4	Growth
5 and 6	5	Rate of Return on Net Assets
7 and 8	8	Retention Ratio
9 and 10	9	Internal Finance
11 and 12	10	Gearing
13 and 14	11	Liquidity
15 and 16	14	Valuation Ratio

The time periods covered by the tables are 1948-60 (the Whole Period) and 1954-60 (Sub-period 2) except in the case of the Valuation Ratio, where 1948-54 (Sub-period 1) is substituted for 1948-60.

The industrial groupings used are Consumer Goods (Clothing & Footwear, Food, and Tobacco; industries 11, 12 and 14) and Non-Electrical Engineering (industry 04). The former is rather unsatisfactory, as the analysis in the text has shown that these industries are heterogeneous, but space and time do not permit a more detailed break-down.

The companies included in these tables are all the companies which continued over the period, less certain rejects. The rejects for each indicator are given below. Companies which had a rejected value of the key indicator are excluded from all columns of the relevant table, but additional rejects may be made from individual columns because of unusual values of the particular indicator to which the column relates.

248

Criteria for the rejection of observations

Indicator 1, Opening Size   No cases arise

Indicator 2, Closing Size   No cases arise

Indicator 4, Growth

(1) Negative average Equity Assets (indicating that the size is trivial throughout most of the period).

(2) Annual average growth greater than 99.9% or less than minus 99.9%.

Indicator 5, Rate of Return on Net Assets

(1) Negative average Equity Assets (indicating that average Net Assets are either negative, rendering the ratio meaningless, or very low, making the ratio extreme in value).

(2) Annual average rate of return above 99.9% or below minus 99.9%.

Indicator 6, Post-tax Rate of Return on Equity Assets

As for Indicator 5.

Indicator 7, Dividend Return

As for Indicator 5.

Indicator 8, Retention Ratio

*(1) Negative retentions

(2) Negative post-tax equity profits (i.e. retentions plus net equity dividend is negative)

(3) Average retention ratio exceeding 999.9%.

*In fact (1) should automatically preclude (2) and (3)

Indicator 9, Internal Finance of Growth

(1) Growth (Indicator 4) less than 1.0% per annum.
(Very low values of Growth, the denominator, would lead to high values of the whole ratio.)

(2) Internal Finance greater than 999.9% or less than −999.9% of Growth,

Indicator 10, Gearing

(1) Negative denominator, i.e. [Retention + Ordinary Dividends (net) + Preference Dividends (net) + Debenture interest (net)] is negative.

(2) Values greater than 99.9% (Negative values do not arise).

Indicators 11, 12, and 13, Liquidity, Trade Credit, Stocks

(1) Average Equity Assets is negative, i.e. the denominator is either negative or very small.

Indicator 14, Valuation Ratio

(1) Negative Equity Assets (denominator) for the relevant year.

(2) No quotation for the ordinary shares available on Moodies' cards.

The number of observations for the key indicators is given in the tables below.

Number of Observations of Key Indication

Indicator 1, Opening Size

Range (£'000's)	1948-1960			1954-1960		
	Consumer Goods	Engineering	All	Consumer Goods	Engineering	All
<125	12	17	29	13	10	23
<250	31	22	53	22	20	42
<500	35	41	76	40	39	79
<1,000	27	55	82	39	55	94
<2,000	15	40	55	28	53	81
<4,000	12	25	37	8	46	54
>4,000	18	14	32	27	39	66
Total	150	214	364	177	262	439

Indicator 4, Growth

Range (%)	1948-1960			1954-1960		
	Consumer Goods	Engineering	All	Consumer Goods	Engineering	All
< −5.0	5	1	6	8	3	11
< −2.5	1	1	2	4	1	5
< 0	6	1	7	15	12	27
< 2.5	20	10	30	31	27	58
< 5.0	32	24	56	28	43	71.
< 7.5	32	47	79	27	50	77
< 10.0	21	39	60	22	39	61
< 15.0	20	65	85	13	55	68
< 20.0	9	17	26	15	18	33
> 20.0	2	8	10	10	13	23
Total	148	213	361	173	261	434

Indicator 5, Rate of Return on Net Assets

Range (%)	1948-1960 Consumer Goods	Engineering	All	1954-1960 Consumer Goods	Engineering	All
< 0	5	3	8	10	5	15
< 5.0	5	2	7	10	7	17
<10.0	16	18	34	26	31	57
<15.0	41	36	77	39	53	92
<20.0	40	50	90	40	54	94
<25.0	20	48	68	28	55	83
<30.0	13	30	43	13	33	46
<35.0	5	16	21	3	12	15
<40.0	3	6	9	4	8	12
>40.0	—	5	5	2	4	6
Total	148	214	362	175	262	437

Indicator 8, Retention Ratio

Range (%)	1948-1960 Consumer Goods	Engineering	All	1954-1960 Consumer Goods	Engineering	All
< 20.0	4	2	6	9	8	17
< 30.0	8	2	10	10	8	18
< 40.0	12	7	19	22	15	37
< 50.0	25	17	42	22	26	48
< 60.0	32	41	73	27	57	84
< 70.0	27	74	101	41	85	126
< 80.0	19	53	72	14	42	56
<100.0	5	12	17	7	11	18
>100.0	1	—	1	3	—	3
Total	133	208	341	155	252	407

Indicator 9, Internal Finance of Growth

Range (%)	1948-1960			1954-1960		
	Consumer Goods	Engineering	All	Consumer Goods	Engineering	All
< 0.0	5	2	7	3	7	10
< 20.0	7	3	10	9	7	16
< 40.0	12	21	33	13	28	41
< 60.0	16	28	44	18	19	37
< 80.0	14	32	46	7	22	29
<100.0	17	52	69	15	37	52
=100.0	40	55	95	46	91	137
<120.0	12	10	22	16	20	36
<140.0	2	1	3	3	2	5
>140.0	2	2	4	3	—	3
Total	127	206	333	133	233	366

Indicator 10, Gearing

Range (%)	1948-1960			1954-1960		
	Consumer Goods	Engineering	All	Consumer Goods	Engineering	All
0	29	46	75	39	62	101
< 2.5	9	43	52	10	49	59
< 5.0	15	40	55	23	45	68
< 7.5	20	30	50	16	29	45
<10.0	9	16	25	15	20	35
<15.0	22	13	35	20	20	40
<20.0	11	10	21	11	11	22
<30.0	11	4	15	13	4	17
<40.0	6	4	10	8	10	18
>40.0	11	5	16	9	7	16
Total	143	211	354	164	257	421

Indicator 11, Liquidity

| Range (%) | 1948-1960 | | | 1954-1960 | | |
	Consumer Goods	Engineering	All	Consumer Goods	Engineering	All
<−20.0	25	24	49	30	27	57
<−10.0	17	26	43	22	28	50
< −5.0	13	19	32	17	26	43
<0	21	24	45	25	31	56
< 5.0	10	25	35	15	28	43
< 10.0	17	20	37	14	35	49
< 20.0	19	36	55	16	38	54
< 30.0	11	19	30	19	31	50
< 40.0	9	10	19	8	8	16
> 40.0	6	11	17	7	10	17
Total	148	214	362	173	262	435

Indicator 14, Valuation Ratio

| Range | 1948-1954 | | | 1954-1960 | | |
	Consumer Goods	Engineering	All	Consumer Goods	Engineering	All
<0.50	19	36	55	10	23	33
<0.70	39	44	83	14	27	41
<0.90	35	53	88	23	29	52
<1.00	10	21	31	11	25	36
<1.10	17	12	29	12	14	26
<1.30	15	26	41	18	37	55
<1.50	11	14	25	11	24	35
<2.00	23	14	37	26	30	56
<2.50	5	5	10	14	13	27
>2.50	2	1	3	10	10	20
Total	176	226	402	149	232	381

Table F. 1 Means of other Indicators classified by Opening Size (Indicator 1): 1948-1960.

Indicator	1, Opening Size			2, Closing Size			4, Growth		
Range* \ Industry Group	Consumer Goods	Engin-eering	All	Consumer Goods	Engin-eering	All	Consumer Goods	Engin-eering	All
< 125	76. 4	80. 8	79. 0	253. 8	303. 6	283. 0	7. 0	9. 3	8. 4
< 250	179. 5	188. 5	183. 3	359. 6	700. 0	500. 9	4. 3	9. 6	6. 5
< 500	362. 0	355. 0	358. 2	929. 8	1, 080, 0	1, 010. 8	6. 2	8. 1	7. 2
<1, 000	683. 4	729. 5	714. 3	2, 050. 3	2, 665. 7	2, 463. 1	5. 7	10. 0	8. 6
<2, 000	1, 353. 3	1, 406. 4	1, 391. 9	2, 697. 2	5, 291. 9	4, 584. 3	5. 0	9. 8	8. 5
<4, 000	2, 641. 7	2, 566. 5	2, 590. 7	9, 937. 3	10, 075. 6	10, 030. 8	10. 1	10. 0	10. 0
>4, 000	17, 067. 4	11, 217. 3	14, 508. 0	42, 116. 7	28, 168. 3	36. 014. 3	7. 7	6. 9	7. 3
Total	2, 645. 5	1, 577. 8	2, 017. 8	6, 799. 4	4, 997. 1	5. 739. 8	6. 1	9. 3	8. 0

Indicator	8, Retention Ratio			9, Internal Finance			10, Gearing		
< 125	40. 4	58. 1	47. 6	76. 0	85. 2	81. 8	12. 7	4. 8	8. 1
< 250	51. 0	62. 4	56. 2*	84. 2	77. 0	80. 6	16. 2	6. 0	11. 7
< 500	51. 0	59. 5	55. 9	63. 3	76. 5	70. 8	13. 9	7. 6	10. 4
<1, 000	53. 4	63. 7	60. 4	69. 8	77. 9	75. 5	13. 1	6. 2	8. 5
<2, 000	62. 0	66. 0	65. 0	95. 1	77. 4	81. 9	14. 7	5. 9	8. 2
<4, 000	61. 4	65. 5	64. 2	68. 4	69. 5	69. 1	9. 1	7. 2	7. 8
>4, 000	63. 2	64. 8	63. 9	66. 9	82. 8	73. 9	11. 7	5. 5	9. 0
Total	54. 3	68. 0	59. 6	73. 3	77. 4	75. 9	13. 5	6. 3	9. 2

* Expressed in £'000's.

Table F. 2 Means of other Indicators classified by Opening Size (Indicator 1): 1954-1960

Indicator	1, Opening Size			2, Closing Size			4, Growth		
Range* \ Industry Group	Consumer Goods	Engin-eer-ing	All	Consumer Goods	Engin-eer-ing	All	Cons-umer Goods	Engin-eer-ing	All
<125	74. 4	94. 1	83. 0	195. 8	158. 3	179. 5	13. 6	8. 3	11. 1
<250	198. 1	182. 7	190. 8	288. 7	251. 6	271. 0	2. 7	4. 9	3. 7
<500	367. 7	368. 6	368. 1	574. 7	632. 8	603. 4	4. 9	7. 4	6. 2
<1, 000	723. 3	674. 9	695. 0	1, 096. 6	1, 170. 1	1, 139, 6	5. 9	8. 4	7. 4
<2, 000	1, 444. 1	1, 422. 3	1, 429. 8	2, 748. 4	2, 435. 5	2, 543. 5	6. 8	7. 8	7. 4
<4, 000	3, 338. 5	2, 736. 4	2, 825. 6	6, 439. 8	4, 960. 4	5, 179. 5	7. 8	8. 9	8. 7
>4, 000	20, 209. 9	10, 508. 5	14, 477. 3	33, 583. 2	17, 365. 2	23, 999. 8	9. 0	8. 7	8. 8
Total	3, 734. 8	2, 546. 5	3, 025. 6	6, 270. 4	4, 313. 5	5, 102. 5	6. 5	8. 0	7. 4

Indicator	9, Internal Finance			10, Gearing			11, Liquidity		
<125	89. 6	91. 6	90. 6	11. 6	3. 8	7. 5	−19. 0	3. 4	−8. 9
<250	77. 2	89. 5	84. 3	18. 1	6. 0	12. 2	9. 6	4. 0	6. 9
<500	77. 8	82. 5	80. 3	16. 4	13. 1	14. 7	6. 8	−1. 0	2. 9
<1, 000	75. 0	76. 2	75. 8	13. 7	6. 9	9. 7	−0. 3	−1. 2	−0. 8
<2, 000	87. 9	79. 5	82. 1	7. 6	8. 4	8. 1	2. 9	5. 7	4. 8
<4, 000	79. 5	75. 1	75. 8	10. 2	7. 7	8. 0	−2. 4	6. 2	4. 9
>4, 000	75. 3	69. 8	72. 0	11. 0	5. 2	7. 5	−3. 9	7. 1	2. 6
Total	79. 2	77. 8	78. 3	13. 2	7. 8	9. 9	1. 2	3. 3	2. 5

* Expressed in £'000's.

254

5, Rate of Return (Net Assets)			6, Post-tax Rate of Return (Equity Assets)			7, Dividend Return		
Consumer Goods	Engineering	All	Consumer Goods	Engineering	All	Consumer Goods	Engineering	All
19. 6	24. 6	22. 6	9. 6	11. 8	11. 0	10. 9	8. 8	9. 6
15. 9	22. 2	18. 6	7. 5	11. 4	9. 2	7. 1	7. 6	7. 3
16. 3	19. 0	17. 8	7. 6	9. 4	8. 6	7. 7	6. 5	7. 0
14. 3	20. 7	18. 6	6. 0	10. 7	9. 1	6. 1	6. 8	6. 6
16. 8	20. 8	19. 7	4. 8	11. 0	9. 3	6. 6	7. 1	7. 0
20. 5	18. 4	19. 1	11. 5	9. 4	10. 1	7. 5	5. 7	6. 3
15. 1	15. 4	15. 2	9. 1	8. 2	8. 7	5. 7	4. 9	5. 4
16. 4	20. 3	18. 7	7. 6	10. 3	9. 2	7. 2	6. 8	6. 9

11, Liquidity			12, Trade Credit			13, Stocks		
− 6. 5	1. 6	−1. 6	−1. 5	13. 2	7. 4	57. 1	42. 8	48. 4
6. 7	− 0. 3	3. 8	−0. 3	8. 5	3. 4	46. 5	50. 4	48. 2
2. 8	− 0. 9	0. 8	2. 6	10. 7	7. 0	47. 5	50. 4	49. 1
− 4. 3	0. 1	−1. 4	4. 2	11. 6	9. 2	54. 5	49. 3	51. 0
7. 9	7. 8	7. 8	4. 8	3. 8	4. 1	44. 3	48. 6	47. 4
0. 0	5. 2	3. 5	3. 3	9. 2	7. 2	44. 9	44. 5	44. 6
−10. 8	14. 8	0. 1	−1. 0	9. 8	3. 7	54. 0	37. 8	46. 9
0. 3	3. 0	1. 9	1. 8	9. 4	6. 3	49. 5	47. 6	48. 4

5, Rate of Return (Net Assets)			6, Post-tax Rate of Return (Equity Assets)			7, Dividend Return			8, Retention Ratio		
Consumer Goods	Engineering	All	Consumer Goods	Engineering	All	Consumer Goods	Engineering	All	Consumer Goods	Engineering	All
12. 0	22. 3	16. 9	7. 4	11. 3	9. 3	7. 5	8. 9	8. 2	55. 3	50. 5	52. 8
10. 7	17. 2	13. 8	4. 9	8. 3	6. 5	5. 8	7. 2	6. 5	44. 6	50. 4	47. 8
14. 7	18. 5	16. 6	7. 3	9. 7	8. 5	7. 4	6. 7	7. 1	48. 4	53. 7	51. 1
16. 3	18. 4	17. 6	9. 2	9. 9	9. 6	7. 2	6. 3	6. 7	50. 6	58. 9	55. 5
17. 0	17. 5	17. 4	9. 1	9. 4	9. 3	7. 2	6. 2	6. 5	55. 8	61. 9	59. 9
16. 6	20. 0	19. 5	8. 9	11. 1	10. 8	5. 9	7. 6	7. 4	60. 2	57. 2	57. 6
16. 7	16. 6	16. 7	10. 2	9. 2	9. 6	6. 5	6. 0	6. 2	61. 4	59. 7	60. 4
15. 1	18. 3	17. 1	8. 2	9. 8	9. 2	6. 9	6. 7	6. 8	52. 9	57. 6	55. 8

12, Trade Credit			13, Stocks			14, Valuation Ratio		
−11. 9	13. 4	0. 2	65. 9	46. 2	56. 5	1. 69	1. 13	1. 44
1. 6	10. 1	5. 6	47. 3	48. 9	48. 0	0. 96	1. 10	1. 03
2. 8	8. 7	5. 7	41. 9	51. 0	46. 4	1. 36	1. 27	1. 32
5. 4	12. 6	9. 7	49. 9	46. 1	47. 7	1. 13	1. 21	1. 18
5. 5	9. 7	8. 3	41. 5	45. 0	43. 8	1. 48	1. 29	1. 35
0. 5	7. 9	6. 8	50. 5	45. 9	46. 6	1. 68	1. 17	1. 23
0. 7	8. 5	4. 7	47. 8	42. 3	44. 6	1. 51	1. 11	1. 28
2. 0	9. 9	6. 7	47. 1	46. 2	46. 6	1. 34	1. 20	1. 26

Table F.3 Means of other Indicators classified by Growth (Indicator 4): 1948-1960

Indicator	4, Growth			1, Opening Size			2, Closing Size		
Range (%)	Consumer Goods	Engineering	All	Consumer Goods	Engineering	All	Consumer Goods	Engineering	All
<−5.0	−8.3	−8.3	−8.3	210.0	1,502.0	425.3	86.8	1,361.0	299.2
<−2.5	−2.8	−2.7	−2.8	166.0	259.0	212.5	257.0	211.0	234.0
<0	−1.4	−1.6	−1.4	675.5	1,309.0	766.0	493.5	1,602.0	651.9
<2.5	1.0	1.2	1.0	410.5	801.7	540.9	484.6	1,063.0	677.4
<5.0	3.6	4.0	3.7	2,017.5	2,041.8	2,027.9	3,085.6	3,508.8	3,267.0
<7.5	6.4	6.3	6.3	6,023.4	1,476.0	3,318.0	5,895.6	3,490.8	4,464.9
<10.0	8.4	8.7	8.6	3,493.2	2,755.1	3,013.4	10,054.6	7,554.0	8,429.2
<15.0	12.1	12.2	12.2	1,293.3	1,206.5	1,226.9	5,633.8	5,135.5	5,258.8
<20.0	16.8	16.4	16.5	2,840.0	932.9	1,593.1	19,206.8	6,296.9	10,765.7
>20.0	26.9	22.4	23.3	519.5	769.9	719.8	11,168.5	8,979.1	9,417.0
Total	6.1	9.3	8.0	2,679.8	1,583.8	2,033.1	5,538.9	5,020.6	5,233.1

Indicator	8, Retention Ratio			9, Internal Finance			10, Gearing		
<−5.0	—	—	—	—	—	—	0.0	—	0.0
<−2.5	—	35.9	35.9	—	—	—	50.0	47.7	48.9
<0	20.7	—	20.7	—	—	—	33.7	17.4	31.0
<2.5	39.3	55.1	43.7	96.8	54.0	80.8	31.7	15.9	26.8
<5.0	51.6	59.8	55.3	83.8	85.9	84.7	12.6	10.0	11.4
<7.5	58.1	61.0	59.8	82.0	84.8	83.6	9.5	6.4	7.6
<10.0	65.4	62.7	63.6	70.2	82.1	78.0	9.1	5.2	6.6
<15.0	56.5	67.0	64.5	63.3	74.3	71.7	6.2	4.4	4.9
<20.0	53.0	61.1	58.3	41.6	59.6	53.3	8.0	4.0	5.3
>20.0	68.2	68.9	68.7	17.5	66.8	57.0	5.3	4.1	4.3
Total	53.9	63.0	59.5	74.8	77.4	76.4	13.6	6.3	9.3

5, Rates of Return (Net Assets)			6, Post-tax Rate of Return (Equity Assets)			7, Dividend Return		
Consumer Goods	Engineering	All	Consumer Goods	Engineering	All	Consumer Goods	Engineering	All
2.9	−2.5	2.0	−4.7	−6.8	−5.1	4.9	2.0	4.4
3.9	11.2	7.6	0.2	5.8	3.0	2.7	6.6	4.7
9.6	4.9	8.9	−6.3	1.1	−5.2	7.6	3.7	7.0
9.9	8.1	9.3	4.5	2.6	3.9	5.0	3.1	4.4
14.0	12.8	13.5	5.1	6.4	5.6	6.5	4.6	5.7
19.1	17.6	18.2	9.8	8.9	9.3	7.6	6.1	6.7
18.1	21.6	20.4	10.2	11.0	10.7	6.4	7.1	6.9
23.4	23.5	23.4	12.9	12.2	12.4	9.3	7.2	7.7
22.0	28.6	26.3	13.4	15.1	14.6	10.5	10.9	10.8
22.3	32.4	30.3	14.9	17.7	17.1	10.3	9.5	9.7
16.4	20.4	18.7	7.6	10.4	9.3	7.2	6.8	7.0

11, Liquidity			12, Trade Credit			13, Stocks		
−28.5	−25.0	−27.9	−14.8	12.0	−10.3	97.6	49.2	89.6
10.4	84.1	−36.9	2.4	0.2	1.3	29.8	101.5	65.7
9.8	1.9	8.7	2.1	13.4	3.7	46.0	51.1	46.7
−3.9	−11.2	−6.3	6.1	3.8	5.4	48.3	62.7	53.1
3.1	−3.4	0.3	6.1	9.4	7.5	48.5	52.9	50.4
3.5	8.0	6.2	3.0	8.9	6.5	45.2	46.6	46.0
2.3	9.8	7.2	−2.9	12.3	7.0	47.5	39.6	42.3
3.4	3.1	3.2	−2.0	9.0	6.4	46.9	47.7	47.5
3.6	−0.1	1.2	0.6	8.1	5.5	57.2	52.1	53.8
−31.9	−0.4	−6.7	6.6	10.5	9.7	60.9	42.2	45.9
1.0	3.1	2.2	1.8	9.3	6.3	49.5	47.7	48.4

Table F.4 Means of other Indicators classified by Growth (Indicator 4): 1954-1960.

Indicator	4, Growth			1, Opening Size			2, Closing Size		
Industry Group Range (%)	Consumer Goods	Engin- eer- ing	All	Con- sumer Goods	Engin- neer- ing	All	Con- sumer Goods	Engin- eer- ing	All
< −5.0	−13.0	−7.6	−11.5	545.1	1,143.0	708.2	298.5	1,058.0	505.6
< −2.5	−3.3	−3.7	−3.3	624.8	394.0	578.6	586.0	403.0	549.4
<0	−1.2	−0.9	−1.1	370.7	1,142.1	713.6	368.3	1,081.3	685.2
<2.5	1.2	1.1	1.1	1,465.5	1,668.1	1,559.8	1,633.7	1,852.5	1,735.6
<5.0	3.7	3.8	3.8	8,742.5	2,823.0	5,157.4	11,136.0	3,716.2	5,642.4
<7.5	5.8	6.2	6.1	4,941.9	2,422.2	3,305.8	7,479.0	3,568.6	4,939.7
<10.0	8.8	8.6	8.7	5,851.1	5,443.3	5,590.3	10,365.6	8,713.3	9,309.2
<15.0	12.1	11.9	12.0	1,050.8	1,756.0	1,621.2	2,100.5	3,680.1	3,378.1
<20.0	18.0	17.8	17.9	3,599.4	1,432.0	2,417.2	10,207.1	3,956.2	6,797.5
>20.0	33.7	23.4	27.9	2,647.9	2,101.6	2,339.1	12,480.6	8,608.5	10,292.0
Total	6.5	8.0	7.4	3,808.8	2,555.7	3,055.2	6,404.1	4,330.0	5,156.8

Indicator	9, Internal Finance			10, Gearing			11, Liquidity		
<−5.0	—	—	—	—	100.0	100.0	−12.4	−42.6	−20.6
<−2.5	—	—	—	7.7	—	7.7	6.9	5.4	6.6
<0	—	—	—	28.1	25.0	26.7	9.4	−3.0	3.9
<2.5	102.5	86.4	94.7	22.6	10.6	16.9	−0.2	4.6	−2.0
<5.0	97.9	83.3	89.0	10.0	10.7	10.4	5.6	−0.3	2.1
<7.5	93.5	94.3	94.0	5.6	4.6	5.0	2.8	6.0	4.9
<10.0	70.5	78.1	75.3	7.9	4.3	5.6	1.2	4.8	3.5
<15.0	65.9	69.9	69.1	4.7	5.6	5.4	−0.7	6.6	5.2
<20.0	45.7	67.1	57.4	8.6	3.9	6.0	−9.6	7.5	−0.2
>20.0	18.0	34.3	27.2	13.4	6.5	9.3	−21.7	−4.9	−12.1
Total	77.7	77.8	77.8	12.6	7.8	9.6	−0.3	3.3	1.9

5, Rate of Return (Net Assets)			6, Post-tax Rate of Return (Equity Assets)			7, Dividend Return			8, Retention Ratio		
Consumer Goods	Engineering	All	Consumer Goods	Engineering	All	Consumer Goods	Engineering	All	Consumer Goods	Engineering	All
−8.8	−0.5	−6.5	−12.1	−5.1	−10.2	1.1	2.5	1.5	—	—	—
3.6	−3.9	2.1	0.6	4.2	−0.4	3.2	0.3	2.6	19.4	—	19.4
9.0	7.0	8.1	4.3	3.1	3.7	5.9	4.5	5.3	30.5	20.3	25.6
10.9	10.7	10.8	5.6	5.6	5.6	5.8	5.2	5.5	40.0	45.2	42.5
15.9	14.2	14.8	9.0	7.3	8.0	7.1	5.5	6.1	55.0	55.3	55.2
19.5	20.8	20.4	10.9	11.2	11.1	7.8	8.3	8.1	59.2	59.8	59.6
19.5	20.2	20.0	11.1	10.8	0.9	7.1	7.0	7.1	60.9	61.9	61.5
23.2	22.4	22.6	13.0	12.2	2.4	8.6	6.7	7.1	59.6	66.1	64.8
22.8	27.9	25.6	14.3	15.1	14.8	9.6	8.2	8.8	58.8	67.1	63.3
15.5	21.2	18.8	10.6	13.4	12.2	9.0	8.7	8.8	57.1	61.1	59.6
15.1	18.5	17.1	8.2	9.9	9.2	6.9	6.7	6.8	52.6	58.1	56.0

12, Trade Credit			13, Stocks			14, Valuation Ratio		
−4.7	6.4	−1.7	59.2	70.7	62.3	1.35	0.58	1.14
3.3	−35.6	−4.5	45.8	76.0	51.8	0.70	—	0.70
3.4	3.8	3.6	38.5	54.2	45.5	0.77	0.68	0.73
6.6	8.7	7.6	51.4	49.2	50.4	0.91	0.77	0.84
3.7	16.4	11.4	42.9	46.3	44.9	1.22	0.83	1.00
3.2	8.4	6.6	46.3	45.1	45.5	1.34	1.12	1.19
2.4	11.3	8.1	44.1	43.4	43.7	1.38	1.38	1.38
1.5	9.0	7.6	44.7	43.9	44.0	1.45	1.32	1.34
−4.7	6.2	1.2	46.5	39.6	42.8	2.31	1.88	2.07
15.6	10.6	12.8	62.9	49.4	55.3	2.22	1.94	2.06
3.3	9.9	7.3	47.1	45.9	46.4	1.34	1.20	1.25

Table F.5 Means of other Indicators classified by Rate of Return on Net Assets (Indicator 5): 1948-1960

Indicator	5, Rate of Return (Net Assets)			1, Opening Size			2, Closing Size		
Range (%) Industry Group	Consumer Goods	Engin- eering	All	Consumer Goods	Engin- eering	All	Consumer Goods	Engin- eering	All
<0	−3.8	−4.2	−4.0	334.8	857.0	530.6	306.2	678.0	445.6
<5.0	3.4	4.8	3.8	760.4	784.5	767.3	710.6	1,002.5	794.0
<10.0	7.8	8.2	8.0	2,376.0	1,193.8	1,750.1	3,482.7	2,047.4	2,722.8
<15.0	12.6	12.5	12.6	2,409.2	3,710.2	3,017.5	6,525.3	10,122.8	8,207.3
<20.0	17.5	17.2	17.3	5,245.7	1,520.8	3,176.3	12,494.9	4,591.5	8,104.1
<25.0	22.7	22.4	22.5	1,308.1	1,263.7	1,276.8	5,799.8	4,791.7	5,088.2
<30.0	27.2	27.4	27.3	1,167.8	801.2	912.0	4,888.2	3,611.2	3,997.3
<35.0	31.9	32.3	32.2	282.6	647.3	560.5	1,030.2	3,040.7	2,562.0
<40.0	36.9	36.5	36.6	585.0	796.2	725.8	2,341.7	4,741.2	3,941.3
>40.0	—	49.1	49.1	—	518.8	518.8	—	3,809.8	3,809.8
Total	16.4	20.3	18.7	2,679.8	1,577.8	2,028.4	6,891.0	4,997.1	5,771.4

Indicator	8, Retention Ratio			9, Internal Finance			10, Gearing		
<0	—	—	—	−134.9	—	−134.9	—	—	—
<5.0	53.0	—	53.0	58.9	−78.5	13.1	60.1	27.8	49.4
<10.0	35.7	50.3	44.3	34.3	45.9	41.7	37.6	19.5	28.0
<15.0	54.7	63.7	59.1	65.9	66.6	66.1	14.7	10.7	12.8
<20.0	59.1	65.5	62.7	82.6	80.1	81.2	9.0	5.5	7.0
<25.0	51.3	66.2	61.9	83.8	81.8	82.4	4.1	4.1	4.1
<30.0	56.7	64.6	62.2	83.1	91.7	89.7	2.8	1.4	1.8
<35.0	52.6	60.2	58.4	84.7	85.2	85.1	0.8	1.8	1.5
<40.0	57.7	63.5	61.6	91.5	87.5	88.8	1.7	0.8	1.1
>40.0	—	46.2	46.2	—	96.7	96.7	—	0.4	0.4
Total	53.9	63.0	59.5	71.6	77.4	75.2	13.6	6.3	9.3

4, Growth			6, Post-tax Rate of Return (Equity Assets)			7, Dividend Return		
Consumer Goods	Engineering	All	Consumer Goods	Engineering	All	Consumer Goods	Engineering	All
−4.6	−4.0	−4.4	−18.4	−8.5	−14.7	2.6	1.4	2.1
−0.3	−2.0	−0.2	−10.7	1.0	−7.4	4.3	2.9	3.9
2.8	4.0	3.5	3.4	4.4	3.9	4.5	3.8	4.1
5.2	7.1	6.1	6.7	6.7	6.7	5.5	4.3	4.9
6.9	8.3	7.7	9.6	9.2	9.4	7.0	5.4	6.1
8.2	10.4	9.7	12.1	11.6	11.7	10.0	6.8	7.7
10.1	11.4	11.0	14.2	13.4	13.7	10.6	8.3	9.0
13.0	13.6	13.5	15.7	16.1	16.0	13.2	11.3	11.7
12.8	17.8	16.1	19.3	18.5	18.7	13.9	11.7	12.4
—	17.0	17.0	—	25.5	25.5	—	25.3	25.3
6.1	9.3	8.0	7.6	10.3	9.2	7.2	6.8	6.9

11, Liquidity			12, Trade Credit			13, Stocks		
−21.6	−28.4	−24.1	−16.7	14.2	−5.1	84.9	60.1	75.6
0.8	11.5	3.8	5.9	−1.9	3.7	40.5	55.2	44.7
−19.1	−19.6	−19.3	0.9	5.6	3.4	69.1	62.9	65.8
−4.9	−1.5	−3.3	−0.7	6.0	2.4	49.9	47.0	48.6
4.3	6.4	5.5	6.0	9.5	7.9	46.0	45.6	45.8
10.5	6.2	7.5	0.7	11.5	8.3	44.4	47.5	46.6
11.2	11.1	11.1	7.0	12.8	11.1	36.5	39.4	38.5
6.2	7.4	7.1	0.3	16.5	12.6	52.2	41.1	43.7
29.3	13.0	18.4	−1.7	−3.3	−2.8	29.8	48.9	42.5
—	−7.5	−7.5	—	−0.6	−0.6	—	77.6	77.6
0.2	3.0	1.9	1.8	9.4	6.3	49.5	47.6	48.4

Table F. 6 Means of other Indicators classified by Rate of Return on Net Assets (Indicator 5): 1954-1960

Indicator / Range (%)	5, Rate of Return (Net Assets) Consumer Goods	Engi-neer-ing	All	1, Opening Size Consumer Goods	Engi-neer-ing	All	2, Closing Size Con-sumer Goods	Engi-neer-ing	All
<0	−8.1	−6.6	−7.6	584.5	847.4	672.1	350.8	807.8	503.1
<5.0	2.3	3.1	2.6	1,597.6	716.3	1,234.7	1,625.9	771.7	1,274.2
<10.0	7.7	7.5	7.6	1,430.5	3,589.9	2,604.9	2,598.8	4,715.6	3,750.0
<15.0	12.6	12.5	12.5	4,424.6	4,770.9	4,624.1	7,013.0	8,067.3	7,620.4
<20.0	17.2	17.4	17.3	8,129.7	1,811.1	4,499.9	12,803.2	3,116.2	7,238.4
<25.0	22.1	22.1	22.1	2,158.3	2,132.8	2,141.4	5,132.9	3,740.5	4,210.2
<30.0	27.2	27.1	27.1	2,908.8	1,310.2	1,762.0	6,142.5	3,104.2	3,962.9
<35.0	31.2	31.5	31.4	459.3	1,440.8	1,244.5	680.7	2,667.0	2,269.7
<40.0	37.3	36.6	36.8	704.3	1,457.9	1,206.7	1,589.8	3,504.3	2,866.1
>40.0	42.6	47.7	46.0	882.0	1,621.3	1,374.8	2,440.0	2,615.8	2,557.2
Total	15.0	18.3	17.0	3,777.0	2,546.5	3,039.2	6,341.9	4,313.5	5,125.8

Indicator	9, Internal Finance			10, Gearing			11, Liquidity		
<0	−60.4	−27.2	−43.8	—	—	—	−15.9	−21.4	−17.8
<5.0	46.5	−29.2	8.7	85.6	50.0	69.0	−11.5	−10.3	−11.0
<10.0	43.6	40.5	41.6	18.1	22.4	20.4	0.2	−8.6	−4.5
<15.0	86.6	68.8	76.0	13.3	7.9	10.2	0.2	−0.1	0.1
<20.0	71.4	82.4	77.7	8.8	4.9	6.5	−2.9	8.4	3.6
<25.0	85.1	90.0	88.3	4.0	3.2	3.4	6.4	7.1	7.1
<30.0	85.9	85.7	85.7	1.7	2.3	2.1	10.4	6.3	7.5
<35.0	100.0	92.1	93.6	0.0	1.5	1.2	35.4	11.1	16.0
<40.0	90.6	91.1	90.9	1.3	1.2	1.2	21.3	14.2	16.6
>40.0	83.3	101.4	95.4	2.6	0.3	1.1	9.7	−1.5	2.2
Total	77.0	77.8	77.5	13.3	7.8	9.9	0.8	3.3	2.3

4, Growth			6, Post-tax Rate of Return (Equity Assets)			7, Dividend Return			8, Retention Ratio		
Consumer Goods	Engineering	All	Consumer Goods	Engineering	All	Consumer Goods	Engineering	All	Consumer Goods	Engineering	All
−7.7	−3.2	−6.4	−14.1	−9.4	−12.4	1.3	1.2	1.3	—	—	—
0.2	1.4	0.7	0.2	1.0	0.5	1.2	2.0	1.6	69.6	20.5	38.9
5.2	3.6	4.3	4.3	3.8	4.0	4.6	3.6	4.1	36.6	45.2	41.4
4.4	6.3	5.5	7.7	7.0	7.3	5.7	5.2	5.4	54.2	55.1	54.7
9.1	7.8	8.3	10.5	9.9	10.1	7.3	6.3	6.7	57.0	61.6	59.6
8.7	8.9	8.9	12.3	11.7	11.9	9.6	6.9	7.8	52.4	65.1	60.8
12.7	12.6	12.6	14.8	14.5	14.6	10.8	9.0	9.5	55.9	63.3	61.2
6.4	12.3	11.1	15.0	17.0	16.6	14.7	11.7	12.3	42.9	58.9	55.7
16.2	14.9	15.3	20.4	18.8	19.3	13.8	10.4	11.5	59.5	67.7	64.9
20.3	12.3	15.0	28.9	26.1	27.0	17.7	27.2	24.0	63.0	42.0	49.0
6.4	8.0	7.4	8.2	9.8	9.2	6.9	6.7	6.8	52.6	58.3	56.1

12, Trade Credit			13, Stocks			14, Valuation Ratio		
−7.0	3.5	−3.5	57.0	64.5	59.5	1.60	2.26	1.76
−4.1	7.4	0.6	65.5	59.5	63.0	0.62	0.56	0.59
5.9	7.5	6.8	48.9	53.6	51.5	0.82	0.65	0.72
−0.4	9.3	5.2	50.2	45.6	47.5	1.02	0.88	0.94
5.1	10.7	8.3	46.3	43.2	44.5	1.30	1.04	1.15
3.6	11.6	8.9	39.1	44.9	42.9	1.70	1.30	1.44
2.7	13.0	10.1	37.3	39.5	38.9	1.91	1.65	1.72
6.9	11.1	10.2	34.0	42.8	41.0	1.75	2.00	1.94
−1.1	7.1	4.3	38.0	43.0	41.4	2.88	2.47	2.57
3.9	−12.9	−7.3	34.3	84.1	67.5	3.97	3.79	3.85
2.2	9.9	6.8	46.9	46.2	46.5	1.34	1.20	1.26

Table F.7 Means of other Indicators classified by Retention Ratio (Indicator 8): 1948-1960

Indicator	8, Retention Ratio			1, Opening Size			2, Closing Size		
Industry Group / Range (%)	Consumer Goods	Engin- eering	All	Consumer Goods	Engin- eering	All	Consumer Goods	Engin- eering	All
<20.0	10.0	16.0	12.0	334.5	442.5	370.5	327.5	820.0	491.7
<30.0	24.3	22.1	23.9	259.3	793.0	366.0	343.0	4,269.5	1,128.3
<40.0	35.4	35.9	35.5	515.4	840.9	635.3	1,810.6	2,343.7	2,007.0
<50.0	45.2	44.5	44.9	6,358.6	722.1	4,077.1	14,431.4	1,954.7	9,381.3
<60.0	54.4	55.5	55.0	1,501.6	993.2	1,216.1	3,690.1	3,170.9	3,398.5
<70.0	64.8	65.2	65.1	3,917.2	2,473.1	2,859.1	11,332.4	7,352.0	8,416.1
<80.0	73.9	73.7	73.7	1,636.9	1,397.4	1,460.6	4,164.8	5,346.3	5,034.5
<100.0	86.8	85.1	85.6	7,194.2	1,242.0	2,992.6	24,530.4	3,988.2	10,030.0
>100.0	100.0	—	100.0	35.0	—	35.0	39.0	—	39.0
Total	54.3	63.0	59.6	2,928.5	1,602.5	2,119.7	7,612.4	5,120.6	6,092.5

Indicator	7, Dividend Return			9, Internal Finance			10, Gearing		
<20.0	4.4	4.8	4.5	0.0	2.6	1.3	33.6	28.2	31.8
<30.0	9.6	41.9	16.1	79.5	91.8	83.6	12.8	0.9	10.4
<40.0	8.2	9.0	8.4	55.4	67.5	59.1	17.2	11.4	15.1
<50.0	10.1	10.7	10.3	64.5	74.5	68.9	8.0	4.2	6.4
<60.0	8.3	7.4	7.8	86.0	73.9	79.1	8.2	7.1	7.6
<70.0	6.5	6.7	6.6	76.4	79.7	78.9	9.5	4.9	6.2
<80.0	4.3	5.1	4.9	96.8	83.6	87.1	9.5	5.0	6.2
<100.0	1.9	2.0	2.4	76.2	86.0	83.0	19.2	9.2	12.1
>100.0	—	—	—	260.0	—	260.0	0.0	—	0.0
Total	7.4	6.9	7.1	79.0	78.9	78.9	10.8	6.0	7.9

4, Growth			5, Rate of Return (Net Assets)			6, Post-tax Rate of Return (Equity Assets)		
Consumer Goods	Engineering	All	Consumer Goods	Engineering	All	Consumer Goods	Engineering	All
0.3	3.9	1.5	6.9	7.6	7.1	2.8	3.2	2.9
1.7	14.8	4.3	14.3	55.7	22.6	7.2	31.1	12.0
6.2	4.6	5.6	14.4	17.0	15.3	7.2	8.0	7.5
8.9	8.0	8.5	20.1	22.7	21.1	10.5	11.0	10.7
6.6	8.2	7.5	20.1	18.4	19.1	10.4	9.6	9.9
8.7	10.4	9.9	19.0	21.7	21.0	10.8	11.1	11.0
6.4	10.9	9.7	16.6	21.5	20.2	9.5	11.2	10.7
11.3	8.4	9.3	13.1	17.0	15.8	9.0	10.0	9.7
—	—	—	—	—	—	—	—	—
7.1	9.6	8.6	17.8	20.8	19.7	9.6	10.7	10.3

11, Liquidity			12, Trade Credit			13, Stocks		
-21.2	-20.8	-21.0	6.7	24.0	12.5	69.5	60.2	66.4
26.9	-36.9	14.2	3.2	-7.8	1.0	28.8	109.5	44.9
-9.8	-10.8	-10.2	-2.5	7.4	1.1	65.9	57.6	62.8
-2.3	0.4	-1.2	3.8	13.1	7.6	51.1	43.0	47.9
7.3	-1.9	2.1	1.9	10.9	7.0	42.1	51.1	47.1
1.4	6.0	4.8	3.9	10.5	8.7	47.9	45.6	46.2
2.5	7.7	6.3	1.4	7.6	6.0	43.6	47.1	46.2
-7.6	11.3	5.8	11.2	2.9	5.4	55.5	34.4	40.6
—	—	—	—	—	—	—	—	—
1.8	3.5	2.8	2.8	9.5	6.9	47.9	47.4	47.6

Table F. 8 Means of other Indicators classified by Retention Ratio (Indicator 8): 1954-1960

Indicators	8, Retention Ratio			1, Opening Size			2, Closing Size		
Range (%) \\ Industry Group	Consumer Goods	Engi-neering	All	Con-sumer Goods	Engi-neering	All	Con-sumer Goods	Engi-neering	All
<20.0	11.5	5.5	8.7	393.0	727.3	550.3	560.0	981.1	758.2
<30.0	26.2	24.7	25.5	1,045.9	1,945.4	1,445.7	1,259.2	2,303.3	1,723.2
<40.0	35.9	35.9	35.9	1,246.9	1,665.2	1,416.5	2,172.5	2,216.5	2,190.3
<50.0	45.1	45.8	45.5	8,725.1	2,024.3	5,095.5	11,712.2	2,998.3	6,992.1
<60.0	55.1	55.7	55.5	4,726.7	3,703.1	4,032.1	9,610.2	5,890.6	7,086.2
<70.0	64.6	64.9	64.8	3,915.8	2,795.0	3,159.7	7,033.4	5,128.9	5,748.6
<80.0	73.8	73.9	73.9	2,764.6	2,125.7	2,285.4	5,432.3	4,151.3	4,471.6
<100.0	83.0	84.8	84.1	11,093.1	1,986.2	5,527.8	17,223.3	3,442.5	8,801.7
>100.0	100.0	—	100.0	550.3	—	550.3	7,313.3	—	7,313.3
Total	52.9	58.3	56.2	4,126.2	2,614.2	3,190.0	7,029.0	4,450.1	5,432.2

Indicators	9, Internal Finance			10, Gearing			11, Liquidity		
<20.0	3.4	25.7	20.2	15.0	14.3	14.7	8.8	5.5	2.1
<30.0	70.8	23.5	47.2	11.2	13.4	12.2	18.5	—4.6	8.2
<40.0	80.2	87.4	83.5	10.5	9.3	10.0	2.3	1.1	1.8
<50.0	70.9	68.7	69.9	4.8	14.8	10.2	—1.0	—1.9	—1.5
<60.0	72.5	75.0	74.2	10.5	4.9	6.7	—0.1	6.3	4.3
<70.0	87.7	83.1	84.6	9.0	3.8	5.5	2.4	4.2	3.6
<80.0	86.7	83.0	83.9	11.9	5.4	7.0	—0.7	9.0	6.6
<100.0	91.6	95.6	94.0	10.8	9.6	10.1	—18.9	15.1	1.9
>100.0	187.3	—	187.3	19.1	—	19.1	—12.8	—	—12.8
Total	81.5	79.2	80.0	9.9	6.7	7.9	1.4	4.6	3.4

4, Growth			5, Rate of Return (Net Assets)			6, Post-tax Rate of Return (Equity Assets)			7, Dividend Return		
Consumer Goods	Engineering	All	Consumer Goods	Engineering	All	Consumer Goods	Engineering	All	Consumer Goods	Engineering	All
2.9	1.4	2.2	9.5	13.3	11.3	4.9	7.1	5.9	7.4	11.3	9.2
0.6	0.7	0.6	15.5	10.7	13.4	7.6	5.0	6.4	9.6	6.4	8.2
5.6	4.6	5.2	14.5	19.9	16.7	7.6	10.4	8.7	8.3	11.1	9.4
9.0	4.4	6.5	19.8	12.7	16.0	11.1	6.8	8.8	10.3	6.2	8.1
7.7	8.7	8.4	17.8	19.1	18.7	9.9	10.1	10.0	7.5	7.6	7.6
8.5	9.4	9.1	19.7	20.7	20.4	11.8	11.2	11.2	7.0	6.7	6.8
8.9	11.7	11.0	18.5	22.0	21.1	11.5	12.5	12.2	5.1	5.5	5.4
13.2	9.0	10.6	15.4	20.3	18.4	12.9	11.3	11.9	3.6	3.0	3.3
20.3	—	20.3	5.0	—	5.0	6.7	—	6.7	0.0	—	0.0
7.7	8.3	8.1	17.3	19.1	18.4	10.0	10.4	10.2	7.5	6.9	7.1

12, Trade Credit			13, Stocks			14, Valuation Ratio		
1.9	−10.0	−3.7	47.4	70.2	58.1	0.92	0.92	0.92
8.2	17.6	12.4	39.6	48.6	43.6	1.16	0.82	1.02
3.9	12.2	7.3	42.2	46.4	43.9	1.28	1.28	1.28
4.4	10.7	7.8	46.2	45.3	45.7	1.55	0.85	1.17
3.4	14.1	10.6	42.9	41.5	41.9	1.23	1.35	1.31
3.4	10.5	8.2	44.8	46.5	46.0	1.55	1.24	1.34
5.3	6.3	6.0	40.0	42.7	42.0	1.31	1.27	1.28
−8.3	5.8	0.3	73.8	36.4	51.0	1.17	0.41	0.88
−16.4	—	−16.4	83.2	—	83.2	0.47	—	0.47
3.2	10.1	7.5	45.5	45.0	45.2	1.35	1.20	1.25

Table F.9 Means of other Indicators classified by Internal Finance (Indicator 9): 1948-1960

Indicator	9, Internal Finance			1, Opening Size			2, Closing Size		
Range (%) \ Industry Group	Consumer Goods	Engin- eering	All	Consumer Goods	Engin- eering	All	Consumer Goods	Engin- eering	All
<0	−69.0	−72.8	−70.1	419.4	228.0	364.7	748.6	329.5	628.9
<20.0	12.3	9.2	11.4	1,902.1	599.7	1,511.4	7,288.7	1,175.7	5,545.8
<40.0	29.5	30.6	30.2	1,179.1	3,986.8	2,965.8	7,760.1	13,456.6	11,385.1
<60.0	48.8	50.7	50.0	5,152.9	1,863.5	3,059.6	15,374.0	7,301.4	10,236.9
<80.0	67.6	69.7	69.1	1,222.4	1,035.1	4,135.6	23,767.9	3,828.7	9,897.1
<100.0	90.7	91.6	91.4	3,891.1	2,087.3	2,531.7	10,699.7	6,008.3	7,164.1
=100.0	100.0	100.0	100.0	586.8	700.9	652.9	1,263.5	2,029.0	1,706.7
<120.0	106.2	107.1	106.6	1,027.6	455.8	767.7	2,435.9	1,312.4	1,925.2
<140.0	127.1	128.9	127.7	7,814.5	794.0	5,474.3	11,845.5	1,086.0	7,925.7
>140.0	210.7	155.9	183.3	476.0	3,229.5	1,852.7	493.0	4,191.0	2,342.0
Total	73.3	77.4	75.9	3,052.4	1,602.8	2,155.7	7,968.2	5,147.3	6,223.2

Indicator	7, Dividend Return			8, Retention Ratio			10, Gearing		
<0	5.1	3.4	4.6	0.0	—	0.0	39.0	39.4	39.1
<20.0	5.4	3.7	4.9	41.8	30.2	38.3	23.4	24.6	23.7
<40.0	9.1	5.3	6.7	46.0	58.8	54.4	13.4	14.8	14.3
<60.0	7.4	6.0	6.5	58.5	63.9	61.9	9.0	8.5	8.6
<80.0	7.5	6.7	6.9	59.0	65.6	63.6	10.7	4.7	6.5
<100.0	7.0	8.1	7.9	66.6	64.2	64.8	5.9	0.2	3.9
=100.0	8.3	7.3	7.7	54.0	64.5	60.1	9.2	3.4	5.8
<120.0	5.6	7.6	6.5	62.1	65.3	63.6	8.3	1.7	5.3
<140.0	4.7	3.6	4.4	61.1	59.4	60.5	23.0	5.0	17.0
>140.0	2.5	5.5	4.5	86.4	59.2	72.8	3.5	11.7	7.6
Total	7.4	6.9	7.1	56.5	63.4	60.8	11.1	6.1	7.9

4, Growth			5, Rate of Return (Net Assets)			6, Post-tax Rate of Return (Equity Assets)		
Consumer Goods	Engineering	All	Consumer Goods	Engineering	All	Consumer Goods	Engineering	All
5.1	1.7	4.1	3.2	5.4	3.8	−12.0	1.5	−8.1
11.6	6.4	10.1	9.5	7.0	8.7	6.3	3.1	5.3
12.8	11.9	12.2	16.9	13.3	14.6	9.6	7.3	8.1
10.3	11.2	10.8	17.4	17.1	17.2	10.1	9.8	9.9
8.1	11.6	10.5	18.5	21.5	20.6	10.8	11.4	11.2
8.1	9.7	9.3	21.7	24.0	23.5	11.8	12.3	12.2
5.4	8.1	6.9	20.5	23.5	22.3	10.2	11.6	11.0
5.0	7.9	6.3	16.5	23.5	19.7	9.1	11.8	10.3
2.3	2.0	2.2	11.0	9.5	10.5	7.0	5.0	6.3
1.2	2.2	1.9	12.5	14.4	13.8	5.0	7.4	6.6
7.6	9.7	8.9	17.8	20.9	19.7	9.1	10.8	10.1

11, Liquidity			12, Trade Credit			13, Stocks		
−6.7	−0.8	−5.0	−7.6	−8.3	−7.8	41.3	57.4	45.9
−28.9	−13.7	−24.3	−0.3	10.6	3.0	79.0	50.7	70.5
−14.4	−7.8	−10.2	−5.4	8.6	3.5	59.9	51.5	54.6
−3.4	−7.4	−5.9	−0.8	11.5	7.0	44.2	52.1	49.2
−9.6	−2.3	−4.5	2.9	9.0	7.2	51.6	49.8	50.4
4.9	7.9	7.1	−0.9	10.2	7.4	49.9	45.5	46.6
10.7	14.0	12.6	7.2	9.0	8.2	45.4	41.9	43.4
8.6	12.3	10.3	5.0	7.6	6.2	36.1	47.6	41.3
−3.8	−5.2	−4.3	−9.2	11.4	−2.4	30.3	51.8	37.5
7.2	11.1	9.8	12.8	22.8	19.5	35.4	18.4	24.1
0.1	4.0	2.6	2.0	9.5	6.7	48.4	46.8	47.4

Table F. 10 Means of other Indicators classified by Internal Finance (Indicator 9):1954-1960

Indicator / Range (%)	9, Internal Finance Consumer Goods	Engineering	All	1, Opening Size Consumer Goods	Engineering	All	2, Closing Size Consumer Goods	Engineering	All
<0	−23.7	−20.2	−21.2	320.7	1,487.0	1,137.1	808.0	2,161.4	1,755.4
<20.0	12.5	9.8	11.3	1,957.1	2,536.0	2,210.4	6,356.2	8,368.1	7,236.4
<40.0	31.6	32.3	32.1	4,376.3	6,617.1	5,906.6	11,420.2	12,087.2	11,875.7
<60.0	49.4	51.6	50.6	6,130.6	3,925.9	4,998.4	12,997.6	6,939.6	9,886.8
<80.0	73.1	67.4	68.8	3,979.4	2,424.5	2,799.8	6,911.3	4,249.6	4,892.1
<100.0	91.2	91.6	91.5	16,222.8	3,285.1	7,017.1	23,216.6	5,295.8	10,465.2
=100.0	100.0	100.0	100.0	1,140.4	1,327.0	1,264.3	1,707.7	2,057.8	1,940.0
<120.0	104.4	104.7	104.6	5,062.3	2,396.3	3,581.2	7,181.4	3,658.8	5,224.4
<140.0	128.6	127.5	128.1	7,650.7	3,388.0	5,945.6	9,454.3	3,864.0	7,218.2
>140.0	219.5	—	219.5	4,638.7	—	4,638.7	5,984.0	—	5,984.0
Total	79.2	77.8	78.3	4,716.8	2,739.8	3,458.2	8,108.7	4,727.8	5,956.3

Indicator / Range (%)	8, Retention Ratio Consumer Goods	Engineering	All	10, Gearing Consumer Goods	Engineering	All	11, Liquidity Consumer Goods	Engineering	All
<0	—	18.6	18.6	15.5	38.3	52.6	−27.7	−29.5	−29.1
<20.0	41.4	30.0	45.2	10.0	29.5	18.5	−22.5	−4.2	−14.5
<40.0	32.2	57.6	55.9	11.2	10.4	10.6	−10.9	−5.5	−7.2
<60.0	63.8	64.4	64.1	10.1	7.2	8.6	−13.6	−2.3	−7.8
<80.0	58.7	64.9	63.4	3.6	5.2	4.8	−0.5	4.7	3.5
<100.0	62.5	62.7	62.7	4.0	2.8	3.2	3.3	0.3	7.5
=100.0	52.7	62.3	59.2	7.3	3.2	4.6	10.6	9.1	9.6
<120.0	65.1	58.1	61.2	10.8	3.3	6.6	1.3	4.7	3.2
<140.0	54.3	54.9	54.6	5.9	3.5	4.9	16.8	−7.1	7.2
>140.0	71.8	—	71.8	10.6	—	10.6	0.5	—	0.5
Total	56.9	60.7	59.3	9.5	6.3	7.4	−0.3	4.0	2.4

4, Growth			5, Rate of Return (Net Assets)			6, Post-tax Rate of Returns (Equity Assets)			7, Dividend Return		
Consumer Goods	Engineering	All	Consumer Goods	Engineering	All	Consumer Goods	Engineering	All	Consumer Goods	Engineering	All
24.0	6.5	10.4	−2.6	5.2	3.5	−13.8	0.6	−2.6	4.3	3.2	3.5
26.1	13.7	20.7	14.2	8.4	11.7	9.6	4.7	7.5	8.8	3.7	6.5
13.7	13.9	13.8	16.1	14.8	15.2	9.8	8.7	9.1	7.9	6.1	6.7
14.0	13.2	13.6	16.8	18.9	17.9	11.7	11.5	11.6	6.7	6.6	6.6
9.9	11.2	10.9	20.8	19.9	20.2	13.2	11.1	11.6	8.2	6.4	6.9
9.4	8.5	8.8	24.4	22.6	23.1	13.9	11.9	12.4	9.0	7.3	7.8
4.8	7.0	6.3	19.1	21.8	20.9	10.2	11.5	11.1	8.1	7.3	7.6
5.8	6.5	6.2	19.1	22.3	20.9	11.1	12.6	11.9	6.5	9.7	8.3
3.1	4.5	3.7	15.4	19.3	17.0	8.9	11.5	9.9	7.1	8.7	7.7
2.7	—	2.7	12.9	—	12.9	7.4	—	7.4	5.0	—	5.0
9.5	9.1	9.3	18.3	19.8	19.3	10.6	10.7	10.7	7.7	7.0	7.3

12, Trade Credit			13, Stocks			14, Valuation Ratio		
−38.2	13.4	1.9	38.5	66.8	60.5	2.66	1.59	1.83
−6.1	4.0	−1.7	59.8	39.7	51.0	1.75	0.67	1.29
−3.2	12.7	7.7	51.1	47.3	48.5	1.36	1.21	1.25
−0.7	10.4	5.0	49.2	51.2	50.2	1.61	1.34	1.46
6.4	7.4	7.1	55.3	46.3	48.4	1.15	1.21	1.20
8.5	13.9	12.4	45.0	39.1	40.8	1.82	1.47	1.56
3.8	10.7	8.4	42.8	43.0	42.9	1.21	1.13	1.16
4.4	7.9	6.3	42.0	46.3	44.4	1.60	1.47	1.53
5.0	11.9	7.8	31.2	53.5	40.1	1.72	0.85	1.50
−45.2	—	−45.2	88.2	—	88.2	0.80	—	0.80
1.2	10.8	7.3	46.9	44.9	45.6	1.46	1.26	1.33

Table F.11 Means of other Indicators classified by Gearing (Indicator 10): 1948-1960

Indicator	10, Gearing			1, Opening Size			2, Closing Size		
Range (%) / Industry Group	Consumer Goods	Engin-eering	All	Consumer Goods	Engin-eering	All	Consumer Goods	Engin-eering	All
0	0.0	0.0	0.0	457.4	653.5	577.7	1,164.1	2,344.7	1,888.2
<2.5	1.3	1.3	1.3	1,637.3	1,600.4	1,606.8	3,751.9	5,483.1	5.183.5
<5.0	3.9	3.7	3.7	1,587.0	1,464.4	1,497.8	4,896.7	5,578.6	5,392.6
<7.5	6.3	6.0	6.2	5,466.3	1,610.3	3,152.7	15,748.4	5,074.5	9,344.1
<10.0	8.7	8.5	8.6	1,965.8	1,367.9	1,583.2	8,145.9	3,767.4	5,343.7
<15.0	12.0	12.4	12.2	6,833.2	6,742.1	6,799.4	14,300.5	16,607.1	15,157.2
<20.0	17.4	17.2	17.3	1,747.0	1,293.7	1,531.1	9,614.3	5,513.3	7,661.4
<30.0	25.3	24.4	25.1	2,659.7	460.0	2,073.1	3,995.4	1,617.5	3,361.3
<40.0	34.0	34.6	34.2	1,934.7	416.0	1,327.2	3,150.5	1,229.5	2,382.1
>40.0	65.1	50.0	60.4	372.1	669.2	464.9	458.9	1,128.0	668.0
Total	13.5	6.3	9.2	2,750.6	1,588.1	2,057.7	7,115.6	5,058.5	5,889.5

Indicator	7, Dividend Return			8, Retention Ratio			9, Internal Finance		
0	9.2	9.2	9.2	47.2	58.9	54.6	93.1	95.4	94.6
<2.5	8.5	8.2	8.2	61.0	62.2	62.0	84.7	86.1	85.8
<5.0	9.1	6.7	7.4	57.3	66.3	63.8	75.6	73.5	74.1
<7.5	6.7	5.7	6.1	62.4	68.4	66.0	89.1	77.8	82.4
<10.0	7.7	4.4	5.6	63.5	66.8	65.7	63.7	66.6	65.6
<15.0	6.8	5.6	6.4	58.0	61.0	59.1	73.2	75.8	74.2
<20.0	6.6	3.7	5.2	50.1	61.5	55.3	64.7	53.6	60.0
<30.0	5.0	3.9	4.7	46.9	53.8	48.8	74.5	45.2	65.5
<40.0	5.0	4.3	4.7	53.9	58.9	55.7	42.0	6.8	26.3
>40.0	4.8	3.5	4.4	32.6	54.2	42.2	41.6	17.1	31.8
Total	7.3	6.9	7.0	54.3	63.0	59.6	76.4	77.4	77.0

4, Growth			5, Rate of Return (Net Assets)			6, Post-tax Rate of Return (Equity Assets)		
Consumer Goods	Engineering	All	Consumer Goods	Engineering	All	Consumer Goods	Engineering	All
6.0	9.4	8.1	20.8	26.1	24.1	9.3	12.5	11.3
9.0	10.6	10.3	24.3	24.0	24.1	12.1	12.1	12.1
10.3	11.3	11.0	22.9	22.2	22.4	12.7	11.7	12.0
6.9	9.9	8.9	18.5	19.1	18.9	10.1	10.4	10.3
9.8	8.7	9.1	18.6	15.1	16.4	11.3	8.4	9.4
7.1	6.5	6.9	15.5	14.5	15.1	9.6	8.5	9.2
6.7	5.9	6.3	13.2	9.9	11.6	7.7	5.4	6.6
3.0	6.5	3.9	10.4	9.2	10.1	5.5	4.8	5.3
5.5	7.1	6.1	12.1	8.1	10.5	5.9	5.5	5.8
0.8	3.3	1.6	7.3	10.7	8.4	2.3	4.5	3.0
6.6	9.4	8.3	17.2	20.6	19.2	9.0	10.6	10.0

11, Liquidity			12, Trade Credit			13, Stocks		
12.0	6.8	8.8	2.7	12.4	8.7	46.5	44.0	45.0
12.4	9.4	9.9	3.0	8.8	7.8	36.5	45.4	43.9
−8.0	7.5	3.2	3.6	12.0	9.7	55.1	41.6	45.3
6.7	5.7	6.1	−2.3	6.6	3.0	42.9	49.3	46.7
3.2	2.9	3.0	1.1	6.6	4.6	41.9	49.1	46.5
0.2	−5.2	−1.8	5.6	10.4	7.4	46.8	47.9	47.2
−6.0	−6.9	−6.5	3.4	3.1	3.3	60.9	56.3	58.7
−10.7	−34.8	−17.1	2.5	5.3	3.3	52.4	87.4	61.7
−1.7	−18.7	−8.5	−1.6	−4.6	−2.8	41.6	64.4	50.7
−11.5	−31.3	−17.7	3.1	13.3	6.3	57.6	63.2	59.3
1.2	3.4	2.5	2.4	9.3	6.5	48.3	47.5	47.8

Table F. 12 Means of other Indicators classified by Gearing (Indicator 10): 1954-1960

Range (%) / Industry Group	10, Gearing			1, Opening Size			2, Closing Size		
	Consumer Goods	Engineering	All	Consumer Goods	Engineering	All	Consumer Goods	Engineering	All
0	0.0	0.0	0.0	892.3	1,164.6	1,059.4	1,508.6	1,929.4	1,766.9
<2.5	1.2	1.3	1.3	2,234.5	3,042.4	2,905.5	3,345.1	5,215.7	4,898.6
<5.0	3.7	3.7	3.7	5,524.8	2,228.5	3,343.4	10,150.8	4,280.6	6,266.1
<7.5	6.4	6.2	6.2	5,056.6	2,707.6	3,542.8	10,289.2	4,901.1	6,816.8
<10.0	8.5	8.6	8.5	5,880.3	3,168.1	4,330.5	10,822.1	4,334.1	7.114.7
<15.0	11.7	12.6	12.2	10,067.1	7,779.0	8,923.0	12,875.9	11,942.5	12,409.2
<20.0	16.4	17.4	16.9	4,857.6	2,285.2	3,571.4	11,764.5	6,058.3	8,911.4
<30.0	23.5	22.9	23.4	1,788.5	411.0	1,464.4	2,970.8	401.7	2,366.3
<40.0	33.1	37.2	35.4	987.7	1,045.8	1,020.0	1,358.4	1,307.8	1,330.3
>40.0	94.9	72.9	85.3	1,646.6	953.3	1,343.2	1,789.8	1,327.4	1,587.5
Total	13.2	7.8	9.9	3,988.2	2,579.5	3,128.3	6,739.3	4,381.7	5,300.1

Range (%)	8, Retention Ratio			9, Internal Finance			11, Liquidity		
0	45.5	55.4	51.8	99.5	95.8	97.0	14.9	7.4	10.3
<2.5	54.7	60.6	59.6	82.6	88.6	87.6	1.2	8.2	7.0
<5.0	61.6	62.9	62.4	81.1	79.2	79.8	2.0	9.6	7.0
<7.5	55.8	64.0	61.1	61.5	69.8	66.8	−8.0	1.8	−1.7
<10.0	59.5	61.7	60.7	78.9	79.3	79.1	−0.6	5.7	3.0
<15.0	50.1	57.1	53.5	81.2	51.7	64.1	−4.2	−4.9	−4.6
<20.0	63.1	37.5	59.9	82.1	42.6	64.3	−6.0	−7.5	−6.8
<30.0	41.8	47.0	43.1	62.8	100.0	67.4	−7.2	1.2	−5.2
<40.0	46.1	26.9	35.4	60.6	17.0	36.4	−7.2	−24.1	−16.6
>40.0	64.8	63.2	64.0	47.7	17.9	32.8	−6.3	−22.9	−14.0
Total	52.9	58.3	56.2	80.1	78.3	78.9	0.8	3.4	2.4

4, Growth			5, Rate of Return (Net Assets)			6, Post-tax Rate of Return (Equity Assets)			7, Dividend Return		
Consumer Goods	Engineering	All	Consumer Goods	Engineering	All	Consumer Goods	Engineering	All	Consumer Goods	Engineering	All
5.4	7.4	6.6	19.1	22.9	21.4	9.5	11.5	10.7	8.8	8.2	8.4
8.9	9.3	9.2	23.7	23.2	23.3	12.7	12.3	12.4	9.1	8.5	8.6
10.5	10.1	10.2	23.0	21.5	22.0	13.4	12.1	12.5	8.4	7.2	7.6
13.6	9.6	11.0	16.1	16.6	16.5	10.2	9.7	9.9	7.4	5.7	6.3
8.8	7.7	8.2	17.9	16.2	16.9	10.8	9.8	10.2	7.2	6.1	6.8
6.2	7.6	6.9	13.5	11.7	12.6	9.4	6.8	8.1	6.9	4.8	5.9
7.0	8.6	7.8	13.8	10.4	12.1	8.8	6.6	7.7	5.7	4.6	5.2
4.0	0.9	3.3	9.6	7.6	9.1	6.1	4.4	5.7	5.2	3.4	4.8
4.4	3.0	3.6	11.9	6.8	9.0	6.3	3.2	4.6	5.2	3.7	4.3
2.7	3.0	2.8	5.0	7.7	6.3	2.2	2.1	2.2	2.9	2.4	2.7
7.4	8.2	7.9	16.7	18.8	18.0	9.6	10.2	9.9	7.3	6.8	7.0

12, Trade Credit			13, Stocks			14, Valuation Ratio		
3.3	11.6	8.4	40.4	43.9	42.6	1.29	1.28	1.28
5.9	9.7	9.0	40.0	43.1	42.6	2.02	1.39	1.50
4.2	10.0	8.0	40.5	40.9	40.8	1.57	1.43	1.48
−3.5	9.6	4.9	55.1	49.2	51.3	1.35	1.17	1.23
7.2	10.3	8.9	39.3	43.9	41.9	1.57	1.00	1.22
2.8	10.2	6.5	54.3	48.0	51.2	1.23	0.83	1.02
3.3	6.6	5.0	49.2	47.4	48.3	0.98	0.83	0.90
3.4	8.1	4.5	51.5	44.1	49.8	0.99	0.61	0.91
9.0	6.9	7.8	44.6	74.2	61.0	1.02	0.66	0.82
−4.9	8.9	1.6	55.8	59.6	57.6	0.83	0.73	0.78
3.1	10.0	7.3	45.9	45.9	45.9	1.33	1.19	1.24

Table F. 13 Means of other Indicators classified by Liquidity (Indicator 11): 1948-1960

Indicator	11, Liquidity			1, Opening Size			2, Closing Size		
Industry Group / Range (%)	Consumer Goods	Engin-eering	All	Consumer Goods	Engin-eering	All	Consumer Goods	Engin-eering	All
<−20. 0	−35. 7	−37. 9	−36. 8	6, 370. 5	634. 8	3, 561. 2	14, 703. 6	1, 818. 1	8, 392. 4
<−10. 0	−14. 5	−14. 5	−14. 4	4, 258. 1	1, 175. 7	2, 394. 3	12, 311. 2	6, 139. 4	8, 579. 4
<−5. 0	−7. 5	−7. 5	−7. 5	4, 498. 1	1, 000. 2	2, 421. 2	10, 965. 2	2, 800. 2	6, 117. 2
<−0	−2. 1	−2. 5	−2. 3	1, 168. 6	973. 3	1, 064. 5	3, 656. 0	3, 710. 9	3, 685. 3
<5. 0	2. 0	2. 4	2. 3	3, 180. 5	1, 582. 0	2, 038. 7	9, 520. 9	5, 815. 0	6, 873. 8
<10. 0	6. 8	7. 1	7. 0	1, 082. 3	4, 128. 6	2, 729. 0	2, 724. 2	11, 023. 6	7, 210. 4
<20. 0	14. 9	14. 7	14. 7	723. 7	1, 946. 7	1, 524. 2	2, 069. 1	5, 192. 9	4, 113. 8
<30. 0	24. 3	24. 4	24. 4	1, 122. 0	872. 0	963. 7	2, 914. 2	2, 673. 7	2, 761. 9
<40. 0	34. 7	35. 1	34. 9	319. 6	2, 364. 7	1, 395. 9	790. 1	3, 664. 1	3, 881. 7
>40. 0	52. 9	52. 6	52. 7	461. 2	1, 551. 8	1, 166. 9	609. 3	4, 874. 4	3, 369. 1
Total	0. 3	3. 0	1. 9	2, 679. 8	1, 577. 8	2, 028. 4	6, 891. 0	4, 997. 1	5, 771. 4

Indicator	7, Dividend Return			8, Retention Ratio			9, Internal Finance		
<−20. 0	6. 1	7. 0	6. 5	55. 0	54. 5	54. 7	49. 3	54. 7	52. 1
<−10. 0	6. 7	7. 1	6. 9	51. 0	64. 4	59. 2	70. 6	64. 2	66. 6
<−5. 0	6. 0	5. 2	5. 5	58. 5	62. 0	60. 6	58. 8	74. 5	68. 2
<−0	7. 0	7. 2	7. 1	54. 2	60. 6	57. 7	51. 4	71. 4	62. 3
<5. 0	6. 5	7. 1	6. 9	54. 3	65. 5	62. 2	64. 5	77. 9	74. 2
<10. 0	7. 8	7. 2	7. 4	56. 3	61. 2	59. 1	83. 1	81. 9	82. 4
<20. 0	7. 6	7. 2	7. 3	51. 1	64. 0	59. 8	96. 5	92. 3	93. 6
<30. 0	9. 2	6. 8	7. 7	56. 0	63. 3	60. 1	97. 3	140. 7	121. 2
<40. 0	8. 1	4. 6	6. 3	56. 4	75. 6	66. 5	95. 7	88. 0	91. 6
>40. 0	8. 8	6. 8	7. 5	42. 3	66. 7	58. 1	104. 3	93. 6	95. 9
Total	7. 2	6. 8	6. 9	53. 9	63. 0	59. 5	71. 9	80. 6	77. 2

4, Growth			5, Rate of Return (Net Assets)			6, Post-tax Rate of Return (Equity Assets)		
Consumer Goods	Engineering	All	Consumer Goods	Engineering	All	Consumer Goods	Engineering	All
5.3	6.5	5.8	10.7	15.5	13.1	2.5	7.6	5.0
6.5	11.8	9.6	15.1	19.7	17.9	8.5	10.5	9.7
7.8	7.6	7.7	14.8	15.6	15.3	6.9	8.4	7.8
7.2	10.8	9.1	15.1	20.6	18.0	6.4	10.6	8.6
7.2	10.9	9.8	16.1	21.7	20.1	8.9	11.5	10.7
6.2	9.6	8.0	18.5	21.4	20.0	9.2	10.8	10.0
4.7	8.1	6.9	18.5	22.2	20.9	9.5	11.1	10.6
6.2	8.9	7.9	22.4	22.0	22.1	11.3	10.6	10.9
6.5	10.0	8.3	22.2	21.1	21.6	10.7	10.9	10.8
3.1	9.5	7.2	18.6	23.4	21.7	8.9	11.8	10.8
6.1	9.3	8.0	16.4	20.3	18.7	7.6	10.3	9.2

10, Gearing			12, Trade Credit			13, Stocks		
22.2	14.9	18.5	4.4	11.6	7.9	81.5	74.7	78.2
18.0	10.3	13.4	0.4	9.7	6.0	60.6	61.5	61.1
12.9	8.8	10.4	−8.7	9.4	2.0	58.7	57.5	58.0
11.9	5.4	8.3	−0.0	12.2	6.5	48.9	47.0	47.9
7.4	3.8	4.9	1.4	10.5	7.9	45.9	45.3	45.4
11.2	4.0	7.3	5.7	12.4	9.3	38.1	40.5	39.4
12.0	3.7	6.6	4.0	10.3	8.1	36.9	41.1	39.6
8.3	4.0	5.5	3.0	5.8	4.8	28.3	38.2	34.6
3.2	4.3	3.8	4.4	4.7	4.5	29.4	21.1	25.1
9.1	2.4	4.8	1.4	−2.9	−1.4	14.9	20.5	18.5
12.9	6.3	9.0	1.8	9.4	6.3	49.5	47.6	48.4

Table F.14 Means of other Indicators classified by Liquidity (Indicator 11): 1954–1960

Indicator	11, Liquidity			1, Opening Size			2, Closing Size		
Range (%) / Industry Group	Consumer Goods	Engin-eering	All	Consumer Goods	Engin-eering	All	Consumer Goods	Engin-eering	All
<−20.0	−34.6	−38.3	−36.4	7,294.9	867.2	4,250.2	11,856.4	1,205.4	6,811.2
<−10.0	−14.4	−15.5	−15.0	6,182.1	1,995.4	3,837.6	10,976.6	4,656.0	7,437.1
<−5.0	−7.0	−7.3	−7.1	5,010.3	2,849.4	3,703.7	8,667.2	4,624.1	6,222.6
<0	−2.3	−2.6	−2.6	2,981.0	4,711.1	3,938.7	5,375.8	7,599.2	6,606.6
<5.0	2.3	2.9	2.7	2,904.3	2,187.2	2,437.3	5,023.5	3,741.8	4,188.9
<10.0	7.5	7.4	7.4	862.1	2,680.4	2,160.9	1,062.8	4,732.8	3,684.2
<20.0	15.2	14.6	14.8	3,564.1	2,379.4	2,730.4	5,659.5	3,720.0	4,294.7
<30.0	24.9	25.3	25.2	1,076.5	2,554.0	1,992.6	1,771.4	4,042.6	3,179.6
<40.0	35.4	34.6	35.0	945.6	3,327.9	2,136.7	1,274.9	5,563.5	3,419.2
>40.0	49.5	56.0	53.3	527.9	1,649.4	1,187.6	621.6	2,981.5	2,009.8
Total	−0.3	2.9	1.7	3,808.8	2,546.5	3,048.5	6,404.1	4,313.5	5,144.9

	8, Retention Ratio			9, Internal Finance			10, Gearing		
<−20.0	56.7	49.2	53.1	53.4	54.4	53.9	18.7	23.0	20.9
<−10.0	56.6	57.6	57.2	56.9	63.5	60.8	25.2	12.0	17.8
<−5.0	57.0	55.4	56.0	71.6	66.6	68.6	11.6	8.1	9.4
<0	52.9	57.8	55.6	75.6	61.2	67.7	9.3	5.9	7.4
<5.0	61.1	59.8	60.2	86.2	86.2	86.2	12.6	9.4	10.5
<10.0	42.7	60.2	55.4	103.7	85.2	88.5	6.7	4.0	4.7
<20.0	52.1	57.9	56.4	91.7	91.6	91.6	6.7	3.8	4.6
<30.0	49.3	59.4	55.7	98.3	90.8	93.5	8.0	4.1	5.5
<40.0	41.5	70.6	56.1	97.2	96.0	96.5	5.2	2.8	4.0
>40.0	41.6	65.8	55.9	104.2	91.5	96.6	8.0	2.2	4.6
Total	52.6	58.3	56.1	77.9	77.8	77.8	12.6	7.8	9.6

4, Growth			5, Rate of Return (Net Assets)			6, Post-tax Rate of Return (Equity Asset)			7, Dividend Return		
Consumer Goods	Engineering	All	Consumer Goods	Engineering	All	Consumer Goods	Engineering	All	Consumer Goods	Engineering	All
8.6	4.2	6.5	8.7	11.9	10.2	3.8	5.5	4.6	5.0	5.4	5.2
11.0	10.3	10.6	14.5	16.7	15.7	9.2	9.6	9.4	6.4	6.3	6.3
5.2	8.1	7.0	11.2	17.8	15.2	6.4	9.9	8.5	5.4	7.9	6.9
7.2	10.4	9.0	17.0	18.1	17.6	9.7	9.9	9.8	7.6	6.4	7.0
6.2	7.9	7.3	16.4	18.5	17.8	10.1	9.6	9.8	7.1	6.6	6.8
2.2	8.2	6.5	14.5	18.9	17.6	7.3	10.2	9.4	6.7	6.7	6.7
5.7	7.3	6.8	18.9	20.7	20.2	9.6	11.0	10.6	7.6	7.5	7.5
4.1	6.1	5.3	19.5	18.9	19.1	10.1	9.9	10.0	8.5	6.5	7.3
3.5	10.9	7.2	18.0	23.9	21.0	10.0	13.1	11.6	9.1	6.5	7.8
4.3	9.9	7.6	22.5	24.2	23.5	11.0	12.3	11.7	10.1	6.7	8.1
6.5	8.0	7.4	15.1	18.3	17.0	8.2	9.8	9.2	6.9	6.7	6.8

12, Trade Credit			13, Stocks			14, Valuation Ratio		
1.1	13.8	7.1	73.8	73.8	73.8	1.34	1.05	1.20
1.0	11.4	6.8	56.4	57.5	57.0	1.44	1.17	1.29
−2.8	7.1	3.2	50.2	55.2	53.2	1.18	1.16	1.17
−0.7	11.6	6.1	47.6	51.5	49.8	1.34	1.19	1.25
1.8	12.4	8.7	46.4	42.6	43.9	1.31	1.48	1.41
11.0	10.6	10.7	38.2	43.0	41.6	1.05	1.23	1.18
2.1	12.1	9.1	31.7	35.8	34.6	1.74	1.20	1.37
6.7	7.8	7.4	31.2	30.6	30.8	1.17	1.08	1.11
1.5	−4.1	−1.3	27.9	34.8	31.4	1.25	1.53	1.39
1.4	−4.1	−1.8	14.3	19.9	17.6	1.50	1.29	1.37
2.0	9.9	6.7	47.1	46.2	46.6	1.34	1.20	1.26

Indicator	14, Valuation Ratio			1, Opening Size			2, Closing Size		
Range \ Industry Group	Consumer Goods	Engineering	All	Consumer Goods	Engineering	All	Consumer Goods	Engineering	All
<.50	0.44	0.41	0.42	2,856.3	1,993.5	2,254.9	3,289.4	2,390.5	2,662.9
<.70	0.62	0.61	0.61	498.4	7,156.0	4,882.7	480.0	10,297.4	6,945.1
<.90	0.80	0.81	0.80	2,279.4	1,843.5	2,036.3	2,909.5	2,940.3	2,926.7
<1.00	0.94	0.94	0.94	2,736.0	2,150.0	2,329.1	4,133.0	3,819.7	3,915.4
<1.10	1.05	1.04	1.04	4,031.0	2,433.7	3,170.9	6,812.7	4,668.9	5,658.3
<1.30	1.19	1.20	1.20	2,129.7	1,203.0	1,506.3	3,826.1	2,062.4	2,639.6
<1.50	1.41	1.38	1.39	16,765.3	2,384.5	6,904.2	21,908.9	5,093.9	10,378.6
<2.00	1.71	1.67	1.69	3,405.9	2,800.5	3,081.6	7,486.6	5,538.2	6,442.8
<2.50	2.20	2.23	2.22	4,576.1	1,514.3	3,101.9	7,422.5	4,089.8	5,817.9
>2.50	3.28	3.54	3.41	3.937.2	1,205.9	2,571.6	11,013.3	2,974.3	6,993.8
Total	1.34	1.20	1.26	3,900.5	2,576.9	3,094.6	6,391.4	4,425.7	5,194.4

Indicator	8, Retention Ratio			9, Internal Finance			10, Gearing		
<.50	58.4	53.8	55.2	94.9	62.2	69.1	36.4	23.4	27.6
<.70	44.7	59.3	55.4	91.5	79.7	82.5	15.0	7.5	9.8
<.90	48.6	55.2	52.5	80.1	71.9	75.0	11.1	15.5	13.7
<1.00	60.3	56.4	57.3	85.0	71.6	74.6	10.8	6.1	7.3
<1.10	52.5	58.1	55.5	76.0	76.5	76.3	8.6	5.0	6.7
<1.30	50.2	54.2	52.9	75.6	77.8	77.1	8.4	4.9	6.1
<1.50	47.1	59.1	55.4	69.4	78.1	75.5	7.4	3.4	4.7
<2.00	57.2	63.0	60.9	76.9	84.0	80.9	8.9	2.9	5.6
<2.50	49.6	64.6	56.8	76.6	75.7	76.1	6.9	2.6	4.8
>2.50	56.3	58.1	57.3	51.1	65.7	58.8	4.0	3.3	3.6
Total	52.1	58.0	55.8	76.4	75.6	75.9	11.2	7.8	9.0

4, Growth			5, Rate of Return (Net Assets)			6, Post-tax Rate of Return (Equity Assets)			7, Dividend Return		
Consumer Goods	Engineering	All	Consumer Goods	Engineering	All	Consumer Goods	Engineering	All	Consumer Goods	Engineering	All
1.0	3.4	2.6	7.6	7.4	7.5	3.6	3.6	3.6	2.7	2.9	2.9
0.1	4.8	3.2	8.5	13.1	11.5	4.0	7.3	6.1	4.6	4.6	4.6
3.2	5.4	5.4	11.2	13.7	12.6	5.8	7.4	6.7	5.0	5.3	5.2
0.5	7.9	5.7	8.6	17.3	14.7	3.9	9.2	7.6	4.0	6.1	5.5
6.1	8.1	7.2	17.7	19.0	18.4	9.7	10.1	9.9	7.2	6.8	7.0
6.6	7.1	6.9	17.2	18.7	18.2	9.6	9.8	9.7	7.6	7.2	7.4
9.1	10.9	10.3	18.1	21.8	20.6	10.6	11.8	11.4	9.1	7.7	8.2
9.0	12.0	10.6	17.4	24.4	21.1	10.4	13.0	11.8	8.2	7.9	8.0
11.1	16.2	13.6	23.2	29.8	26.4	13.5	16.7	15.0	11.0	9.8	10.4
16.9	14.9	15.9	20.8	28.3	24.6	8.6	14.6	11.6	10.6	11.1	10.9
6.3	8.3	7.5	15.1	18.3	17.0	8.2	9.8	9.1	7.0	6.6	6.7

11, Liquidity			12, Trade Credit			13, Stocks		
-8.5	1.9	-1.2	13.0	5.8	8.0	68.2	43.3	50.8
5.9	3.5	4.3	7.0	11.1	9.7	41.8	43.5	42.9
-5.9	-7.0	-6.5	4.4	11.0	8.1	49.2	53.2	51.4
-0.3	5.9	4.0	7.0	7.9	7.6	38.0	44.9	42.8
3.9	3.5	3.7	5.7	11.5	8.8	43.0	50.7	47.1
2.6	-0.2	0.7	3.3	12.9	9.7	42.1	45.5	44.4
-4.8	12.6	7.1	-1.7	11.5	7.3	56.7	35.7	42.3
0.6	8.6	4.9	0.2	10.9	6.0	47.6	43.3	45.3
4.8	6.2	5.5	1.3	4.6	2.9	42.7	50.0	46.2
-7.4	-2.4	-4.9	-7.5	13.7	3.1	44.6	51.8	48.2
-0.6	3.2	1.7	3.1	10.3	7.5	46.9	45.5	46.1

Table F. 16 Means of other Indicators classified by Valuation Ratio (Indicator 14): 1948-1954

Indicator		14, Valuation Ratio			1, Opening Size			2, Closing Size		
Range	Industry Group	Consumer Goods	Engineering	All	Consumer Goods	Engineering	All	Consumer Goods	Engineering	All
<0.50		0.38	0.39	0.39	889.7	1,153.2	1,062.2	1,112.5	1,695.0	1,493.8
<0.70		0.58	0.61	0.60	1,975.2	1,372.1	1,655.5	2,870.8	2,141.5	2,484.2
<0.90		0.78	0.80	0.79	1,643.5	2,220.0	1,990.7	2,371.2	4,004.7	3,355.0
<1.00		0.96	0.96	0.96	2,269.5	1,442.6	1,709.3	2,718.0	2,911.9	3,171.9
<1.10		1.03	1.05	1.04	381.2	990.3	633.2	736.8	2,107.5	1.304.0
<1.30		1.18	1.18	1.18	898.7	1,265.7	1,131.5	1,293.7	2,931.9	2,332.6
<1.50		1.39	1.41	1.40	5,195.6	1,352.4	3,043.4	8,223.9	2,573.5	5,059.7
<2.00		1.67	1.70	1.68	5,974.4	840.4	4,031.8	8,997.3	1,964.1	6,336.1
<2.50		2.24	2.25	2.24	519.8	573.2	546.5	968.8	1,314.2	1,141.5
>2.50		2.75	4.30	3.26	1,666.0	269.0	1,200.3	2,544.5	111.0	1,733.3
Total		0.98	0.91	0.94	2,242.1	1,453.4	1,798.7	3,366.7	2,967.4	2,974.4

Indicator		7, Dividend Return			8, Retention Ratio			9, Internal Finance		
Range	Industry Group	Consumer Goods	Engineering	All	Consumer Goods	Engineering	All	Consumer Goods	Engineering	All
<0.50		3.8	3.7	3.7	56.5	68.4	64.8	80.6	90.6	87.9
<0.70		4.6	5.0	4.8	55.2	67.2	61.9	68.4	73.2	71.2
<0.90		5.4	5.8	5.7	61.7	67.9	65.6	82.8	86.3	85.0
<1.00		7.3	6.2	6.5	67.7	69.2	68.7	96.3	81.1	85.7
<1.10		9.2	7.8	8.6	57.2	65.5	60.6	76.2	80.9	78.1
<1.30		9.7	8.3	8.8	53.6	65.1	61.5	76.6	86.6	83.5
<1.50		9.8	10.3	10.1	52.6	61.3	57.5	83.5	89.4	86.8
<2.00		11.9	11.3	11.7	50.7	62.2	55.3	86.2	92.9	89.0
<2.50		17.1	15.2	16.2	57.6	54.3	55.9	100.9	78.4	89.7
>2.50		11.8	0.0	7.8	48.7	100.0	65.3	95.1	—	95.1
Total		7.4	6.6	6.9	56.7	66.6	62.5	80.9	84.3	82.9

4, Growth			5, Rate of Return (Net Assets)			6. Post-tax Rate of Return (Equity Assets)		
Con-sumer Goods	Engi-neer-ing	All	Con-sumer Goods	Engi-neer-ing	All	Con-sumer Goods	Engi-neer-ing	All
1.7	4.6	3.6	9.2	13.6	12.1	3.6	6.4	5.5
3.6	7.4	5.6	12.6	16.5	14.7	6.1	8.6	7.4
6.5	10.4	8.9	16.3	22.6	20.1	8.0	11.0	9.8
9.2	11.3	10.6	25.0	24.9	24.9	12.8	11.8	12.1
12.3	12.8	12.5	24.5	27.7	25.9	12.4	12.8	12.5
5.1	12.6	9.8	19.9	28.7	25.4	9.2	13.5	11.9
9.0	13.5	11.5	22.4	32.7	28.1	11.9	14.6	13.4
8.5	13.9	10.5	29.4	36.4	32.1	13.0	17.0	14.5
12.6	15.9	14.3	41.6	41.0	41.3	21.5	18.3	19.9
6.6	−6.3	2.3	26.4	1.4	18.1	12.4	3.6	9.4
6.5	9.8	8.4	19.2	22.9	21.3	9.2	11.0	10.2

10, Gearing			11, Liquidity			12, Trade Credit			13, Stocks		
Con-sumer Goods	Engi-neer-ing	All	Con-sumer Goods	Engi-neer-ing	All	Con-sumer Goods	Engi-neer-ing	All	Con-sumer Goods	Engi-neer-ing	All
21.0	8.4	12.6	−7.3	6.1	1.5	4.0	4.9	4.6	56.8	50.6	52.7
33.1	10.0	21.0	−2.9	−9.8	−6.6	0.8	7.4	4.3	53.3	57.1	55.3
12.7	3.9	7.3	3.3	8.9	6.7	2.0	7.3	5.1	43.3	47.0	45.5
4.8	3.6	4.0	17.4	8.1	11.1	6.2	9.9	8.7	36.1	45.6	42.5
6.2	1.6	4.3	12.5	11.1	11.9	0.9	8.6	4.1	46.7	46.4	46.6
16.0	2.4	7.2	3.0	4.4	3.9	1.0	9.9	6.6	42.9	50.3	47.6
8.0	1.8	4.5	−1.4	7.6	3.7	5.8	13.0	9.9	55.3	46.2	50.2
14.1	1.9	9.4	1.0	6.0	2.9	−5.7	10.4	0.4	58.4	53.7	56.6
3.7	1.7	2.7	−2.4	10.8	4.2	−1.8	20.7	9.4	48.4	38.1	43.2
3.2	0.0	2.1	13.2	−10.6	5.2	−4.0	8.1	0.1	24.7	69.4	39.6
16.9	5.1	10.2	1.8	4.1	3.1	1.1	8.4	5.2	49.5	50.0	49.8

Appendix G   Matrices of Simple Correlation Coefficients

The method of calculation and the interpretation of these simple (zero-order) correlation coefficients is described in Chapter 3, which contains the matrices of correlation coefficients for all four industries taken together (Tables 3.1 to 3.3). The following nine tables give separate correlation matrices for each of the major industries for each of the three periods.

Table G.1. Correlation coefficients

Industry 04: Non-electrical engineering, sub-period 1 (1948-54)

Indicators	1. Opening Size	2. Closing Size	4. Growth	5. Rate of Return [Net Assets]	6. Rate of Return [Equity Assets]	7. Dividend Return	8. Retention Ratio	9. Internal Finance	10. Gearing	11. Liquidity	12. Trade Credit	13. Stocks	14. Valuation Ratio
1. Opening Size	1.00	0.98	-0.04	-0.10	-0.07	-0.09	0.08	-0.13	0.04	0.09	0.00	-0.07	-0.05
2. Closing Size	0.98	1.00	0.05	-0.05	-0.04	-0.06	0.10	-0.15	0.02	0.08	0.01	-0.06	-0.02
4. Growth	-0.04	0.05	1.00	0.73	0.59	0.38	0.16	-0.24	-0.27	0.07	0.09	-0.04	0.34
5. Rate of Return [Net Assets]	-0.10	-0.05	0.73	1.00	0.60	0.71	-0.07	0.30	-0.40	0.16	0.20	-0.11	0.54
6. Rate of Return [Equity Assets]	-0.07	-0.04	0.59	0.60	1.00	0.42	0.02	0.22	-0.12	-0.07	0.05	-0.02	0.29
7. Dividend Return	-0.09	-0.06	0.38	0.71	0.42	1.00	-0.56	0.01	-0.23	-0.08	0.16	0.03	0.57
8. Retention Ratio	0.08	0.10	0.16	-0.07	0.02	-0.56	1.00	0.23	0.06	0.12	-0.07	-0.03	0.07
9. Internal Finance	-0.13	-0.15	-0.24	0.30	0.22	0.01	0.23	1.00	-0.05	0.34	-0.01	-0.16	-0.03
10. Gearing	0.04	0.02	-0.27	-0.40	-0.12	-0.23	0.06	-0.05	1.00	-0.29	-0.06	0.17	-0.33
11. Liquidity	0.09	0.08	0.07	0.16	-0.07	-0.08	0.12	0.34	-0.29	1.00	-0.11	-0.70	0.07
12. Trade Credit	0.00	0.01	0.09	0.20	0.05	0.16	-0.07	-0.01	-0.06	-0.11	1.00	-0.36	0.12
13. Stocks	-0.07	-0.06	-0.04	-0.11	-0.02	0.03	-0.03	-0.16	0.17	-0.70	-0.36	1.00	-0.03
14. Valuation Ratio	-0.05	-0.02	0.34	0.54	0.29	0.57	0.07	-0.03	-0.33	0.07	0.12	-0.03	1.00

Number of observations: Indicators 8 and 9 = 214; Indicator 10 = 251; Indicator 14 = 226, Other Indicators = 259

Table G.2. Correlation coefficients

Industry 04: Non-electrical engineering, sub-period 2 (1954-60)

Indicators	1. Opening Size	2. Closing Size	4. Growth	5. Rate of Return [Net Assets]	6. Rate of Return [Equity Assets]	7. Dividend Return	8. Retention Ratio	9. Internal Finance	10. Gearing	11. Liquidity	12. Trade Credit	13. Stocks	14. Valuation Ratio
1. Opening Size	1.00	0.97	-0.00	-0.09	-0.06	-0.06	-0.00	-0.17	0.06	0.04	0.03	-0.06	-0.08
2. Closing Size	0.97	1.00	0.13	-0.06	-0.01	-0.05	0.03	-0.25	0.06	0.03	0.02	-0.08	-0.03
4. Growth	-0.00	0.13	1.00	0.53	0.58	0.22	0.33	-0.49	-0.07	0.09	-0.00	-0.13	0.46
5. Rate of Return [Net Assets]	-0.09	-0.06	0.53	1.00	0.96	0.70	0.17	0.38	-0.46	0.26	0.01	-0.09	0.57
6. Rate of Return [Equity Assets]	-0.06	-0.01	0.58	0.96	1.00	0.69	0.24	0.27	-0.42	0.25	-0.02	-0.10	0.50
7. Dividend Return	-0.06	-0.05	0.22	0.70	0.69	1.00	-0.45	0.19	-0.29	0.04	-0.10	0.12	0.60
8. Retention Ratio	-0.00	0.03	0.33	0.17	0.24	-0.45	1.00	0.14	-0.12	0.16	-0.26	-0.05	0.07
9. Internal Finance	-0.17	-0.25	-0.49	0.38	0.27	0.19	0.14	1.00	-0.31	0.28	0.03	-0.11	0.05
10. Gearing	0.06	0.06	-0.07	-0.46	-0.42	-0.29	-0.12	-0.31	1.00	-0.28	-0.04	0.15	-0.24
11. Liquidity	0.04	0.03	0.09	0.26	0.25	0.04	0.16	0.28	-0.28	1.00	-0.21	-0.66	-0.01
12. Trade Credit	0.03	0.02	-0.00	0.01	-0.02	-0.10	-0.26	0.03	-0.04	-0.21	1.00	-0.27	0.02
13. Stocks	-0.06	-0.08	-0.13	-0.09	-0.10	0.12	-0.05	-0.11	0.15	-0.66	-0.27	1.00	0.09
14. Valuation Ratio	-0.08	-0.03	0.46	0.57	0.50	0.60	0.07	0.05	-0.24	-0.01	0.02	0.09	1.00

Number of observations: Indicators 8 and 9 = 208; Indicator 10 = 239; Indicator 14 = 232; Other Indicators = 262

286

Table G.3. Correlation coefficients

Industry 04: Non-electrical engineering, whole period (1948-60)

Indicators	1. Open-ing Size	2. Clos-ing Size	4. Growth	5. Rate of Return [Net Assets]	6. Rate of Return [Equity Assets]	7. Divi-dend Return	8. Reten-tion Ratio	9. Inter-nal Finance	10. Gear-ing	11. Liqui-dity	12. Trade Credit	13. Stocks
1. Opening Size	1.00	0.96	-0.05	-0.14	-0.11	-0.10	0.04	-0.11	0.04	0.08	0.02	-0.08
2. Closing Size	0.96	1.00	0.13	-0.07	-0.03	-0.06	0.08	-0.19	-0.01	0.06	0.02	-0.09
4. Growth	-0.05	0.13	1.00	0.64	0.70	0.36	0.17	-0.26	-0.24	0.08	0.04	-0.10
5. Rate of Return [Net Assets]	-0.14	-0.07	0.64	1.00	0.95	0.75	-0.06	0.43	-0.50	0.21	0.07	-0.06
6. Rate of Return [Equity Assets]	-0.11	-0.03	0.70	0.95	1.00	0.74	-0.02	0.34	-0.45	0.18	0.04	-0.07
7. Dividend Return	-0.10	-0.06	0.36	0.75	0.74	1.00	-0.56	0.17	-0.30	-0.06	0.04	0.13
8. Retention Ratio	0.04	0.08	0.17	-0.06	-0.02	-0.56	1.00	0.22	-0.23	0.22	-0.12	-0.16
9. Internal Finance	-0.11	-0.19	-0.26	0.43	0.34	0.17	0.22	1.00	-0.50	0.39	-0.01	-0.16
10. Gearing	0.04	0.01	-0.24	-0.50	-0.45	-0.30	-0.23	-0.50	1.00	-0.31	-0.08	0.21
11. Liquidity	0.08	0.06	0.08	0.21	0.18	-0.06	0.22	0.39	-0.31	1.00	-0.20	-0.66
12. Trade Credit	0.02	0.02	0.04	0.07	0.04	0.04	-0.12	-0.01	-0.08	-0.20	1.00	-0.27
13. Stocks	-0.08	-0.09	-0.10	-0.06	-0.07	0.13	-0.16	-0.16	0.21	-0.66	-0.27	1.00

Number of observations: Indicators 8 and 9 = 191; Indicator 10 = 207; Other Indicators = 214

Table G.4. Correlation coefficients

Industry 11: Clothing and footwear, sub-period 1 (1948-54)

Indicators	1. Opening Size	2. Closing Size	4. Growth	5. Rate of Return [Net Assets]	6. Rate of Return [Equity Assets]	7. Dividend Return	8. Retention Ratio	9. Internal Finance	10. Gearing	11. Liquidity	12. Trade Credit	13. Stocks	14. Valuation Ratio
1. Opening Size	1.00	0.97	0.03	-0.11	0.04	-0.16	0.29	-0.22	0.35	-0.00	-0.01	-0.15	0.05
2. Closing Size	0.97	1.00	0.13	0.05	0.11	-0.12	0.29	-0.27	0.31	0.02	-0.01	-0.17	0.13
4. Growth	0.03	0.13	1.00	0.66	0.74	0.37	0.16	-0.42	-0.33	0.32	-0.09	-0.16	0.34
5. Rate of Return [Net Assets]	-0.11	0.05	0.66	1.00	0.80	0.79	0.13	0.39	-0.63	0.26	-0.26	0.04	0.53
6. Rate of Return [Equity Assets]	0.04	0.11	0.74	0.80	1.00	0.51	0.44	0.29	-0.53	0.42	-0.04	-0.23	0.37
7. Dividend Return	-0.16	-0.12	0.37	0.79	0.51	1.00	-0.41	0.16	-0.47	0.06	-0.34	0.24	0.49
8. Retention Ratio	0.29	0.29	0.16	0.13	0.44	-0.41	1.00	0.21	-0.55	0.12	0.15	-0.16	0.15
9. Internal Finance	-0.22	-0.27	-0.42	0.39	0.29	0.16	0.21	1.00	-0.62	0.22	0.23	-0.13	0.17
10. Gearing	0.35	0.31	-0.33	-0.63	-0.53	-0.47	-0.55	-0.62	1.00	-0.13	0.05	-0.10	-0.10
11. Liquidity	-0.00	0.02	0.32	0.26	0.42	0.06	0.12	0.22	-0.13	1.00	0.34	-0.78	-0.14
12. Trade Credit	-0.01	-0.01	-0.09	-0.26	-0.04	-0.34	0.15	0.23	0.05	0.34	1.00	-0.63	-0.35
13. Stocks	-0.15	-0.17	-0.16	0.04	-0.23	0.24	-0.16	-0.13	-0.10	-0.78	-0.63	1.00	0.24
14. Valuation Ratio	0.05	0.13	0.34	0.53	0.37	0.49	0.15	0.17	-0.10	-0.14	-0.35	0.24	1.00

Number of observations: Indicators 8 and 9 = 56; Indicator 10 = 69; Indicator 14 = 75; Other Indicators = 86

Table G.5. Correlation coefficients

Industry 11: Clothing and footwear, sub-period 2 (1954-60)

Indicators	1. Opening Size	2. Closing Size	4. Growth	5. Rate of Return [Net Assets]	6. Rate of Return [Equity Assets]	7. Dividend Return	8. Retention Ratio	9. Internal Finance	10. Gearing	11. Liquidity	12. Trade Credit	13. Stocks	14. Valuation Ratio
1. Opening Size	1.00	0.91	0.12	0.07	0.10	0.03	0.05	-0.26	0.10	0.05	-0.08	-0.19	0.23
2. Closing Size	0.91	1.00	0.21	0.11	0.14	0.09	0.06	-0.28	0.05	0.03	-0.07	-0.17	0.29
4. Growth	0.12	0.21	1.00	0.67	0.82	0.48	0.45	-0.61	-0.02	-0.04	0.01	-0.03	0.29
5. Rate of Return [Net Assets]	0.07	0.11	0.67	1.00	0.91	0.80	0.13	0.17	-0.50	0.30	0.33	-0.33	0.37
6. Rate of Return [Equity Assets]	0.10	0.14	0.82	0.91	1.00	0.69	0.40	-0.09	-0.30	0.18	0.21	-0.24	0.25
7. Dividend Return	0.03	0.09	0.48	0.80	0.69	1.00	-0.38	0.05	-0.40	0.33	0.30	-0.28	0.53
8. Retention Ratio	0.05	0.06	0.45	0.13	0.40	-0.38	1.00	-0.12	0.07	-0.45	-0.19	0.37	0.17
9. Internal Finance	-0.26	-0.28	-0.61	0.17	-0.09	0.05	-0.12	1.00	-0.12	0.38	0.49	-0.12	0.17
10. Gearing	0.10	0.05	-0.02	-0.50	-0.30	-0.40	0.07	-0.12	1.00	-0.46	-0.08	0.26	-0.27
11. Liquidity	0.05	0.03	-0.04	0.30	0.18	0.33	-0.45	0.38	-0.46	1.00	0.21	-0.66	0.02
12. Trade Credit	-0.08	-0.07	0.01	0.33	0.21	0.30	-0.19	0.49	-0.08	0.21	1.00	-0.47	0.03
13. Stocks	-0.19	-0.17	-0.03	-0.33	-0.24	-0.28	0.37	-0.12	0.26	-0.66	-0.47	1.00	-0.07
14. Valuation Ratio	0.23	0.29	0.29	0.37	0.25	0.53	0.17	0.17	-0.27	0.02	0.03	-0.07	1.00

Number of observations: Indicators 8 and 9 = 52; Indicator 10 = 62; Indicator 14 = 68, Other Indicators = 79

Table G. 6. Correlation coefficients

Industry 11: Clothing and footwear, <u>whole period</u> (1948–60)

Indicators	1. Opening Size	2. Closing Size	4. Growth	5. Rate of Return [Net Assets]	6. Rate of Return [Equity Assets]	7. Rate of Dividend Return	8. Retention Ratio	9. Internal Finance	10. Gearing	11. Liquidity	12. Trade Credit	13. Stocks
1. Opening Size	1.00	0.79	0.11	-0.01	0.09	-0.08	0.23	-0.20	0.06	0.02	-0.09	-0.19
2. Closing Size	0.79	1.00	0.29	0.09	0.21	0.06	0.16	-0.22	-0.01	0.04	-0.07	-0.20
4. Growth	0.11	0.29	1.00	0.74	0.79	0.55	0.31	-0.43	-0.29	0.36	0.20	-0.44
5. Rate of Return [Net Assets]	-0.01	0.09	0.74	1.00	0.87	0.80	0.32	0.46	-0.62	0.60	0.41	-0.55
6. Rate of Return [Equity Assets]	0.09	0.21	0.79	0.87	1.00	0.72	0.46	0.28	-0.61	0.47	0.35	-0.54
7. Dividend Return	-0.08	0.06	0.55	0.80	0.72	1.00	-0.16	0.20	-0.41	0.41	0.26	-0.33
8. Retention Ratio	0.23	0.16	0.31	0.32	0.46	-0.16	1.00	0.30	-0.58	0.11	0.02	-0.14
9. Internal Finance	-0.20	-0.22	-0.43	0.46	0.28	0.20	0.30	1.00	-0.19	0.49	0.50	-0.25
10. Gearing	0.06	-0.01	-0.29	-0.62	-0.61	-0.41	-0.58	-0.19	1.00	-0.60	0.06	0.42
11. Liquidity	0.02	0.04	0.36	0.60	0.47	0.41	0.11	0.49	-0.60	1.00	0.34	-0.77
12. Trade Credit	-0.09	-0.07	0.20	0.41	0.35	0.26	0.02	0.50	0.06	0.34	1.00	-0.48
13. Stocks	-0.19	-0.20	-0.44	-0.55	-0.54	-0.33	-0.14	-0.25	0.42	-0.77	-0.48	1.00

Number of observations: Indicator 8 and 9 = 48; Indicator 10 = 60; Other Indicators = 70

Table G.7. Correlation coefficients

Industry 12: Food, sub-period 1 (1948-54)

Indicators	1. Opening Size	2. Closing Size	4. Growth	5. Rate of Return [Net Assets]	6. Rate of Return [Equity Assets]	7. Dividend Return	8. Retention Ratio	9. Internal Finance	10. Gearing	11. Liquidity	12. Trade Credit	13. Stocks	14. Valuation Ratio
1. Opening Size	1.00	0.99	-0.01	-0.11	-0.04	-0.19	0.21	-0.07	-0.04	-0.22	-0.08	0.17	-0.08
2. Closing Size	0.99	1.00	0.05	-0.07	0.00	-0.18	0.24	-0.12	-0.06	-0.23	-0.09	0.20	-0.07
4. Growth	-0.01	0.05	1.00	0.67	0.63	0.33	0.21	-0.45	-0.33	-0.05	0.01	0.21	0.27
5. Rate of Return [Net Assets]	-0.11	-0.07	0.67	1.00	0.88	0.77	-0.04	0.22	-0.45	0.16	0.10	0.05	0.62
6. Rate of Return [Equity Assets]	-0.04	0.00	0.63	0.88	1.00	0.61	0.10	0.15	-0.48	0.07	0.16	0.09	0.58
7. Dividend Return	-0.19	-0.18	0.33	0.77	0.61	1.00	-0.47	0.08	-0.30	0.12	0.04	0.03	0.69
8. Retention Ratio	0.21	0.24	0.21	-0.04	0.10	-0.47	1.00	0.08	-0.39	-0.06	0.04	0.02	0.03
9. Internal Finance	-0.07	-0.12	-0.45	0.22	0.15	0.08	0.08	1.00	-0.24	0.23	0.17	-0.21	0.25
10. Gearing	-0.04	-0.06	-0.33	-0.45	-0.48	-0.30	-0.39	-0.24	1.00	-0.24	-0.06	0.07	-0.25
11. Liquidity	-0.22	-0.23	-0.05	0.16	0.07	0.12	-0.06	0.23	-0.24	1.00	0.03	-0.62	0.14
12. Trade Credit	-0.08	-0.09	0.01	0.10	0.16	0.04	0.04	0.17	-0.06	0.03	1.00	-0.26	-0.04
13. Stocks	0.17	0.20	0.21	0.05	0.09	0.03	0.02	-0.21	0.07	-0.62	-0.26	1.00	-0.03
14. Valuation Ratio	-0.08	-0.07	0.27	0.62	0.58	0.69	0.03	0.25	-0.25	0.14	-0.04	-0.03	1.00

Number of observations: Indicators 8 and 9 = 80; Indicator 10 = 93; Indicator 14 = 93; Other Indicators = 108

Table G.8. Correlation coefficients

Industry 12: Food, sub-period 2 (1954-60)

Indicators	1. Opening Size	2. Closing Size	4. Growth	5. Rate of Return [Net Assets]	6. Rate of Return [Equity Assets]	7. Dividend Return	8. Retention Ratio	9. Internal Finance	10. Gearing	11. Liquidity	12. Trade Credit	13. Stocks	14. Valuation Ratio
1. Opening Size	1.00	0.98	0.08	0.04	0.09	-0.16	0.28	-0.14	-0.09	-0.15	-0.10	0.13	0.09
2. Closing Size	0.98	1.00	0.15	0.08	0.13	-0.12	0.29	-0.16	-0.10	-0.18	-0.12	0.12	0.16
4. Growth	0.08	0.15	1.00	0.38	0.29	0.38	-0.08	-0.62	-0.16	-0.33	-0.35	0.21	0.59
5. Rate of Return [Net Assets]	0.04	0.08	0.38	1.00	0.91	0.76	0.08	0.22	-0.51	0.39	0.03	-0.16	0.44
6. Rate of Return [Equity Assets]	0.09	0.13	0.29	0.91	1.00	0.66	0.21	0.14	-0.42	0.31	0.13	-0.12	0.24
7. Dividend Return	-0.16	-0.12	0.38	0.76	0.66	1.00	-0.48	-0.03	-0.36	0.29	-0.09	-0.11	0.59
8. Retention Ratio	0.28	0.29	-0.08	0.08	0.21	-0.48	1.00	0.22	-0.20	0.05	0.23	-0.15	0.02
9. Internal Finance	-0.14	-0.16	-0.62	0.22	0.14	-0.03	0.22	1.00	-0.07	0.60	0.37	-0.36	-0.00
10. Gearing	-0.09	-0.10	-0.16	-0.51	-0.42	-0.36	0.05	-0.07	1.00	-0.14	0.02	-0.03	-0.17
11. Liquidity	-0.15	-0.18	-0.33	0.39	0.31	0.29	0.05	0.60	-0.14	1.00	0.14	-0.59	-0.04
12. Trade Credit	-0.10	-0.12	-0.35	0.03	0.13	-0.09	0.23	0.37	0.02	0.14	1.00	-0.42	-0.22
13. Stocks	0.13	0.12	0.21	-0.16	-0.12	-0.11	-0.15	-0.36	-0.03	-0.59	-0.42	1.00	-0.08
14. Valuation Ratio	0.09	0.16	0.59	0.44	0.24	0.59	0.02	-0.00	-0.17	-0.04	-0.22	-0.08	1.00

Number of observations: Indicators 8 and 9 = 59; Indicator 10 = 74; Indicator 14 = 77; Other Indicators = 91

Table G.9. Correlation coefficients

Industry 12: Food, whole period (1948-60)

Indicators	1. Opening Size	2. Closing Size	4. Growth	5. Rate of Return [Net Assets]	6. Rate of Return [Equity Assets]	7. Rate of Dividend Return	8. Retention Ratio	9. Internal Finance	10. Gearing	11. Liquidity	12. Trade Credit	13. Stocks
1. Opening Size	1.00	0.96	0.07	-0.08	0.02	-0.27	0.34	-0.11	-0.07	-0.25	-0.10	0.14
2. Closing Size	0.96	1.00	0.19	-0.00	0.09	-0.21	0.36	-0.15	-0.10	-0.27	-0.11	0.15
4. Growth	0.07	0.19	1.00	0.55	0.43	0.43	0.01	-0.63	-0.41	-0.30	-0.16	0.22
5. Rate of Return [Net Assets]	-0.08	-0.00	0.55	1.00	0.77	0.74	-0.13	0.14	-0.55	0.26	0.11	-0.14
6. Rate of Return [Equity Assets]	0.02	0.09	0.43	0.77	1.00	0.50	-0.01	0.01	-0.48	0.10	0.06	0.01
7. Dividend Return	-0.27	-0.21	0.43	0.74	0.50	1.00	-0.60	-0.11	-0.26	0.17	-0.03	-0.16
8. Retention Ratio	0.34	0.36	0.01	-0.13	-0.01	-0.60	1.00	0.16	-0.26	-0.07	0.03	0.11
9. Internal Finance	-0.11	-0.15	-0.63	0.14	0.01	-0.11	0.16	1.00	-0.15	0.59	0.24	-0.36
10. Gearing	-0.07	-0.10	-0.41	-0.55	-0.48	-0.26	-0.26	-0.15	1.00	-0.06	0.01	-0.05
11. Liquidity	-0.25	-0.27	-0.30	0.26	0.10	0.17	-0.07	0.59	-0.06	1.00	0.13	-0.61
12. Trade Credit	-0.10	-0.11	-0.16	0.11	0.06	-0.03	0.03	0.24	0.01	0.13	1.00	-0.39
13. Stocks	0.14	0.15	0.22	-0.14	0.01	-0.16	0.11	-0.36	-0.05	-0.61	-0.39	1.00

Number of observations: Indicators 8 and 9 = 55; Indicator 10 = 67; Other Indicators = 73

References

CHAPTER 1

Page

17   1 The major theoretical writings in this area are those of
Edith Penrose: The Theory of the Growth of the Firm:
Oxford, 1959; R. L. Marris, Economic Theory of Mana-
gerial Capitalism, London 1964; Myron Gordon, The Invest-
ment, Financing and Valuation of the Corporation, Illinois,
1962; O. Williamson, The Economics of Discretionary
Behaviour; Managerial Objectives in a Theory of the Firm,
Englewood Cliffs, N. J. 1964; and J. Steindl, Random Pro-
cesses and the Growth of the Firm, London 1965.
The main empirical works, although by no means devoid
of theoretical interest, are those of P. Hart and S. Prais
'The Analysis of Business Concentration: A Statistical
Approach', Journal of the Royal Statistical Society, series
A, 1956, pp. 150-81; T. Barna, Investment and Growth
Policies in British Industrial Firms, Cambridge, 1962;
H. Simon and G. Bonini, 'The Size Distribution of Business
Firms', American Economic Review, September 1958,
pp. 607-17; S. Hymer and B. Pashigan, 'Firm Size and the
Rate of Growth', The Journal of Political Economy, Decem-
ber 1962, pp. 556-569; and E. Mansfield, 'Entry, Gibrat's
Law, Innovation and the Growth of Firms', American Econo-
mic Review, December 1962, pp. 1023-51.

18   1 We are grateful to Mr W. B. Reddaway for suggesting these
tables for non-statistical readers.

19   1 Cf. R. L. Marris, op. cit. and Chapter 7 of the present work.

19   2 For a limited number of exceptions, see Appendix A.

CHAPTER 2

21   1 B. Tew and R. F. Henderson, Op. cit., Preface.

22   1 The appropriate measure of size in the context of this study
is in terms of 'capital employed' by the firm, rather than
its turnover or employment. This is because this study is
concerned with the inter-relationship between certain
characteristics of firms, which relate, in one way or another,
to their use of economic and financial resources.

22   2 We have used here the book value of net assets to indicate
size. A very good case exists for the use of total assets
rather than 'net assets' which excludes current liabilities.
This is especially so since our indicators are long term
indicators averaged over a six-year period which would tend
to eliminate the main drawback of using total assets: namely
the atypical and stochastic character of current liabilities

at any moment of time. We are, however, obliged to use net assets since the gaps in information available (for example, in company accounts, profits are shown after deducting bank interest for which no separate figures are available) preclude the possibility of obtaining a rate of return on total assets. A similar measure of the size of the firm has been used by T. Barna, op. cit., and B. Tew and R. Henderson, op. cit.

22   3   Alternative procedures for valuing the assets of firms are to obtain an estimate of replacement cost, such as the fire insurance estimates, or to use the stock market valuation of the firm. The former information is very difficult to obtain for a large number of firms, whereas the latter procedure has serious drawbacks on theoretical grounds. Briefly, the main reason is that the stock market valuation of the firm is unlikely to represent the value of economic and financial resources embodied in the firm; if anything it is a reflection of the utilization of these resources and of the financial choices made by the firm. This issue is further explored in our discussion of Indicator 14 later on in this chapter.

22   4   Even this statement is strictly true only for firms with the same rate of growth. See the discussion in Chapter 6 about the relationship between size and profitability where this point assumes particular importance.

22   5   The bivariate distribution of opening and closing size for the two sub-periods are given in Appendix E. It should be noted that although the figures for opening size in sub-period 1 and the whole period pertain to balance sheets in the same accounting year, the tables pertain to different populations of firms.

22   6   Let A_{48} and A_{49} be Balance Sheet Assets at the end of 1948 and 1949 respectively. The mid-year Assets in 1949 are $\frac{1}{2}(A_{48} + A_{49})$. Average assets over sub-period 1 which extends from 1948 to 1954 are, therefore:

$$\frac{\frac{1}{2}A_{48} + A_{49} + A_{50} + A_{51} + A_{52} + A_{53} + \frac{1}{2} A_{54}}{6}$$

It is possible that a constant geometric rate of change is a more plausible assumption than the one we have adopted.

25   1   Various errors are introduced if growth of assets is measured from the opening and closing balance sheets. Firstly, in this period of inflation a firm which revalues its assets during the period would show a higher rate of growth, in general, than a firm which does not. Similarly, a firm may change its accounting date, as a result of which its growth will not be measured over the same time span as for other firms in the population which do not undergo accounting date changes. To avoid these problems, our calculation of growth of net assets is based only partly on the comparisons of Opening and Closing Balance Sheets;

Page

mainly, it is based on the Sources and Uses of Funds Statement where as far as possible these problems have been
eliminated.

This differs from Tew and Henderson who calculated the
growth of assets entirely on the basis of the Sources and
Uses of Funds Statement. We have found that, given the
way this Statement is constructed, especially in relation
to the consolidation of subsidiaries their procedure introduces errors of another kind, which we have tried to mini-
mize. See Appendix A for a further discussion.

25   2   Statistical tests of significance are not used in Part I of
the book. They are, however, extensively discussed in
Part II (Chapters 4 to 7).

25   In line with our definition of net assets, returns include
trading profits and investment and other income. They
are net of depreciation and charges for current liabilities
(e.g. bank interest), but are taken before taxation, long-
term interest payments and payments to minority interests
in subsidiaries. The denominator of this indicator is average
net assets (Indicator 3).

25   4   Cf. T. Barna, op. cit., Appendix B.

32   1   Equity Assets are derived from net assets by deducting
debentures, preference shares and minority interests from
the latter. Corresponding returns to equity assets are
obtained by deducting from the profits on net assets of the
company the following: interest on long-term liabilities,
share due to minority interests, preference dividend and
taxes. A similar averaging procedure was adopted to that
used to obtain the average rate of return on net assets
(Indicator 5).

39   1   This indicator was suggested to us by Lord Kahn.

48   1   T. Barna. Investment and Growth Policies in British Industrial Firms, Cambridge University Press, 1962.

56   1   The main focus of this book, as explained in Chapter 1, is
to examine the relationship between the growth, profitability and size of firms. The relationship of growth to
stock-market valuation of the firm is discussed here only
in a rudimentary way. The effect of growth, profitability
and other financial aspects of the firm on its stock-market
valuation is a complex and an important subject which
deserves a volume in its own right. The present work
provides the basic data and a preliminary analysis for a
fuller treatment of this subject to be taken up later on.

56   2   A similar problem arises in comparing the profits of different
firms. A relevant comparison of profits between firms can
only be made by removing the effect of size of the firm on
its profits. The solution to this problem is provided by
computing a rate of return for each firm.

56   3   In econometric studies on the explanation of share prices,
a number of investigators have used the book value of assets

to normalize share prices. See for instance, F. Modigliani
and M.H. Miller, 'Leverage, Dividend Policy and the Cost
of Capital', paper presented at December, 1960 meeting
of the Econometric Society.

56   4   Another helpful way of looking at this ratio is to regard the
book value of the firm as a proxy for its break-up value.
It is very difficult to know what the true break-up value of
the firm will be at any moment of time, but the book value
is one easily available approximation to it. In fact, Moodies
services, in their Investment Handbook refer to the book
value of assets per share as the 'break-up' value of assets
per share. In this sense, the valuation ratio is a ratio of
the market value of the firm as a going concern, to its
break-up value.

56   5   See for instance W. Gutman, 'Book value – market value
patterns', in E.M. Lerner, Readings in Financial Analysis
and Investment Management, Homewood, Illinois, 1963,
and S. Cottle and T. Whitman, Corporate Earning Power
and Market Valuation, 1935-55, Duke University Press,
1959.

56   6   The first economist to use this concept and to explore its
theoretical meaning was R.L. Marris, Economic Theory
of Managerial Capitalism, 1964. See also N. Kaldor,
'Marginal productivity and the macro-economic theories
of distribution', The Review of Economic Studies, 1966,
pp. 309-319.

59   1   See Appendix A, Part I, on this point.

59   2   We are indebted to W.B. Reddaway for this observation.

59   3   Moodies Industrial Share Price Index, with 1947 at 100,
stood at 92.9 in 1948, 85.5 in 1950, 85.7 in 1952, 88.1 in
1953 and 116.9 in 1954.

59   4   J.F. Wright, 'The Capital market and finance of industry'
in G.D.N. Worswick and P.H. Ady: The British Economy
in the 1950's, Oxford, 1962.

59   5   S. Cottle and T. Whitman, op. cit., page 71.

59   6   Cf. T. Barna, op. cit., Appendix B; J.F. Wright, op. cit.

59   7   1960 was the year when for the first time, a 'reverse yield
gap' appeared, i.e. the yield on ordinary shares at market
prices was less than that on gilt edged securities. Cf: The
British Economy, Key Statistics, 1900-64, Table g.

59   8   Board of Trade, Income and Finance of Public Quoted
Companies, Summary and Industrial Group tables, 1949-1960.

CHAPTER 3

61   1   As is well known, there is a link between the zero-order
correlation coefficient and the coefficient of determination
associated with a bivariate linear regression model. r can
also, therefore, be interpreted in a different way. The
coefficient of determination r^2 is equal to the square of the
correlation coefficient and gives the proportion of the variance

of the dependent variable, y, explained by the linear influence of the independent variable, x, for the regression model y = a + bx. Thus an r value of 0.5 indicates that the least squares regression of y on x accounts for 25% of the variance in y, and an r value of 0.9 similarly indicates that 81% of the variance in y is accounted for by the independent variable. However, because of the causality usually implicit in regression analysis, this interpretation of r must be used with particular care.

61 2 In the case of the Valuation Ratio, exclusions were due to the non-availability of a share price, usually because of the small number of transactions in the shares of the company concerned or because the shares were quoted only on provincial stock exchanges. In the case of the Retention Ratio, Internal Finance of Growth, and Gearing, certain values of these indicators are of dubious significance, as explained in Chapter 2. The companies excluded in correlating Retention Ratio and Internal Finance of Growth had one or more of the following characteristics: Negative Equity Assets: Negative Retentions: Negative Growth: Negative Internal Finance: Negative External Finance (i.e. Indicator 9 > 1.0). In correlating Gearing, the excluded companies had: Negative Equity Assets: Negative Growth: or Negative Post-tax Profits.

There were occasional odd values of other indicators but these were found to be so rare or so slight that they did not affect the correlation coefficients to any significant extent.

66 1 The values of 'r' given in the tables have not been adjusted for degrees of freedom.

67 1 It must be remembered that the average valuation ratio of the calendar year 1954 is being correlated here with the average of profitability, growth and other variables from 1948 to 1954; the valuation ratio for 1960 is similarly being correlated with the average of these variables from 1954 to 1960. The respective correlations are likely to be higher if a two- or three-year average of the latter variables rather than a six-year average is used, or if a weighted average with greater weights attached to the more immediate years, rather than an unweighted average is used.

67 2 The possible exception is with respect to the retention ratio (Indicator 8) for the Food and Clothing and Footwear industries for some time periods.

67 3 W.K. Gutman: 'Book value – market value patterns', in E.M. Lerner, op. cit.

67 4 It is, however, possible that size and valuation ratios may be related in a non-linear way.

68 1 It may be recalled that our definition of gearing is in terms of the proportion of a firm's total income which goes to service fixed interest securities, including preference capital. The negative association between gearing and profitability

is, in fact, what one would expect if gearing in capital term
was independent of the rate of return on total net assets,
because a high return would then lower the income gearing.
However, there are good reasons for preferring this income
measure over a capital measure of gearing. For instance,
the income measure of gearing is the most meaningful concept so far as concerns a constraint on the firm's ability
to raise money on fixed interest terms. It also avoids
various objections which apply to a capital measure such
as the limited validity of book values as a measure of total
assets.

68   2   In terms of Keynesian monetary theory, their precautionary
demand for cash is less.

68   3   Tibor Barna, op. cit., investigated the consistency of a rate
of return and a growth measure similar to ours. Growth
of dividend and earnings yields was studied by I. M. D. Little,
'Higgledy-Piggledy Growth', Bulletin of the Oxford Institute
of Economics and Statistics, November, 1962, and I. M. D.
Little and A. C. Rayner, Higgledy-Piggledy Growth Again,
Oxford, 1966. The inter-period consistency of growth is
considered further in Chapter 5 and of profitability in
Chapter 6.

CHAPTER 4

73   1   R. Gibrat, Les Inégalités Economiques, Paris, 1931, was
the first to propose this type of stochastic model.

73   2   The seminal study of the subject in the U.K. is that of
S. J. Prais and P. E. Hart, 'The Analysis of Business
Concentration: A statistical approach', Journal of the Royal
Statistical Society, Series A, vol. 119, part 2, 1956. See
also P. E. Hart, 'The Size and Growth of Firms', Economica,
1962, J. M. Samuels: 'Size and Growth of Firms', Review
of Economic Studies, 1965. The important studies in the
U.S. are those of H. A. Simon and C. P. Bonini, 'The Size
Distribution of Business Firms', American Economic Review,
1958; S. Hymer and P. Pashigan: 'Firm Size and Rate of
Growth', Journal of Political Economy, 1962; E. Mansfield,
'Entry, Gibrat's Law, Innovation and Growth of Firms',
American Economic Review, 1962; and Y. Ijiri and H. A.
Simon, 'Business Firm Growth and Size', American Econo-
mic Review, 1964. Also see J. Steindl, Random Processes
and the Growth of the Firm, London, 1965, for applications
of the law of proportionate effect to West German and
Austrian firms.

73   3   Some writers have stressed the implications of the law of
proportionate effect for the question as to whether or not
there are economies of scale. These implications seem to
us to be rather ambiguous, depending as they do on assumptions made with respect to market conditions and other

factors, cf. S. Hymer and P. Pashigan, op. cit. and the debate between these writers and H. Simon in Journal of Political Economy, 1964.

74   1   For example, suppose that at any point of time, the size of the largest firm in the population is £100 million and of the smallest firm, it is £10 million. Let us suppose that growth follows the law of proportionate effect and every firm has a chance of growing on an average by 50% every year. In that case, at the end of the first year, the size of the largest firm would be expected to be £150 million and of the smallest firm, it would be £15 million, which represents a greater dispersion in the size of the two firms than before.

However, if the law does not operate in the strong form stated above (for example, if as Kalecki suggested, the probability of growing by a given proportion declines with the size of the firm, or as Simon and Ijiri suggested that there is a particular way in which firms enter or leave the population) there might not be increasing industrial concentrations over time. Cf. M. Kalecki, 'On the Gibrat Distribution', Econometrica, 1945; and Y. Ijiri and H. Simon, op. cit.

74   2   Cf. J. Steindl, op. cit. and B. Mandelbrot, 'New methods in statistical economics', Journal of Political Economy, October, 1963.

74   3   The two requirements are necessary, though strictly speaking not sufficient, for the law to be valid.

75   1   It will be seen from Appendix D that growth as measured here is not precisely the same as growth measured by the ratio of closing size to opening size, which we use later.

75   2   The hypothesis of a linear relationship between size and growth was tested by means of first-order correlation coefficients in the last chapter. Since the usual significance tests for r are not very sensitive, equation (1) was tried to judge the significance of the regression coefficient b. However, b was not found to be significant for any of the fifteen populations for this equation, even at a higher than usual level of significance.

79   1   See A. C. Aspin and B. L. Welch, 'Tables for use in comparisons whose accuracy involves two variances separately estimated', Biometrika, vol. XXXVI, 1949, pp. 290-6. The results of the Welch-Aspin test are reported at the foot of Tables 4.1-4.3 and in Table 4.4.

80   1   It can be argued that our conclusion with respect to the variability of growth rates in individual industries may also be suspect for the same reason, i.e. it may also be merely due to the aggregation of different sub-industry groups within each industry. Our limited experiments with the sub-industry groups suggest, however, that this is not the case. It may also be noted that essentially similar relationships

between mean growth rate and size and the standard deviation of growth rates and size are obtained when many more than the five size-classes of Tables 4.1 to 4.3 are used. We obtained essentially the same results when eleven size-classes were used for each of the industries. See, however, note 80, 4 also.

80	2	For the significance test used, see, E.S. Hartley and K.S. Pearson, <u>Biometrika Tables for Statisticians</u>, vol. 1, table 31.
80	3	The only cases where the standard deviation was not significantly heterogeneous at the 5% level was in the Non-Electrical Engineering Industry in sub-period 2, in which case it was barely non-significant, and in the same industry in the whole period. However, even in these two cases, the standard deviation of growth rates was found to be significantly heterogeneous at a high level, when instead of the five size-classes used in Tables 4.1 to 4.3, firms were classified into eleven size-classes.
80	4	As noted in note 80, 1, indicator 4, which is the compounded annual rate of growth, is used as a measure of growth in this section. The conclusions of this section are unaltered if an alternative definition of growth (e.g. total proportionate growth observed for the period as a whole), which is free from the non-linear effects of compound interest, is used.
80	5	P.E. Hart, <u>Studies in Profit, Business Saving and Investment in the United Kingdom, 1920-1962</u>, Chapter 9, and Hart and Prais, <u>op. cit.</u>, J.M. Samuels, <u>op. cit.</u>
81	1	In terms of the transition matrices presented in the next chapter, this means that the frequency distribution along any row, column or diagonal should tend to be log-normal.

Testing the validity of the law of proportionate effect in terms of the logarithms of proportionate growth rates rather than the proportionate growth rates themselves has been justified by Hart on another ground as well. He argues that since the size distributions of firms at the beginning and the end of the period are log-normal the ratio of closing size to opening size, i.e. the proportionate growth rate, must also be log-normally distributed. However, we have no reason to assume that the size distribution of firms is in fact log-normal; most investigators have found that a Pareto-type distribution graduates the size distribution of firms better than the log-normal one. (Cf. Steindl, op. cit., Simon and Bonini, op. cit.) Furthermore, in order for Hart's argument to hold, it is necessary that the distribution of opening size and closing size are two parameter log-normal distributions, rather than three parameter ones which do not have the reproductive properties essential for Hart's argument.

81	2	See Appendix D.
81	3	We have not tested Hart's assumption that proportionate growth is log-normally distributed within each size class.

Page		
81	4	Samuels' study covered the period 1950 to 1959 and related to a sample of over 300 continuing companies quoted on the London Stock Exchange. He found that the mean of the logarithm of the proportional growth increased as the size of the firm increased. He also found homogeneous variances of growth rates between size-classes. The major source of difference between his results and ours is probably the fact that unlike us, he did not study the behaviour of firms within individual industries.
83	1	For a fuller discussion of this, see Hart op. cit. p.35 and Hart and Prais op. cit. p.172.
83	2	We have not tested the residual variance for homoscedasticity, but the tests in the preceding sections gave fairly conclusive evidence that the variance of proportionate growth rates are heterogeneous between size classes.
86	1	This is in spite of our rather technical definition of 'birth' and 'death' which means that a merger of two companies which involves the absorption of both by a third (new) company, appears as the death of the two old companies and the birth of the new company, which would be expected to be relatively large. The fact that the average size of births is greater than that of deaths in Table 4.10 is due entirely to the 'birth' of Reckitt & Colman (Holdings) Ltd. which was, in fact, due to a formal rearrangement of an existing group of companies.
90	1	See Simon and Bonini, op. cit.
90	2	The answer would depend partly on the statistical rules adopted to make their inclusion possible. Thus, in the case of a company born in, say, 1950, we clearly should not take zero as its 1948 size and show its growth rate as being infinite: apart from anything else, the company will probably have existed in 1948, but not been quoted. With sufficient research, we might have calculated its annual growth rate from 1950 to 1954 and assumed that this rate was appropriate for the full period, 1948-54, but this would have been an arbitrary and possibly a misleading assumption.
90	3	The measure of growth used for the regression analysis of section 1 of this chapter and for the analysis of means and standard deviations in section 2 was our own growth indicator (Indicator 4), which, as explained in Appendix D, omits the effect of revaluations in calculating growth. The analysis of section 3, however, used the ratio of closing net assets to opening net assets, calculated from balance sheet figures, and therefore included revaluations. The studies by Hart and Prais, op. cit., and Samuels, op. cit., also used this ratio.
90	4	Samuels, op. cit.
93	1	Since this finding relates only to continuing companies, and since births and deaths seem to have a greater incidence on the smaller companies, it is possible that the variance of growth rates would decline consistently with size if all companies were included.

302

<table>
<tr><td>93</td><td>2</td><td>If a large company was merely a group of smaller subsi-
diary companies operating independently in different markets,
so that the growth rates of the subsidiary companies were
independent of each other, then an elementary statistical
theorem shows that the variance of the holding company's
growth rate would be inversely proportional to its size.
In fact, the variance of the growth rates of the smaller
firms is heterogeneous, and that of the larger firms does
not decline with size as rapidly as would be predicted by
this theorem. This suggests that a large firm cannot be
viewed as an aggregation of independent smaller firms.</td></tr>
<tr><td>93</td><td>3</td><td>Hymer and Pashigan's sample consisted of the one thousand
largest American manufacturing companies divided by
industry, and growth was measured over the period 1946-
56. Their findings reported in the text are based explicitly
on all firms, but they suggest that these findings are not
altered if only continuing firms are considered.</td></tr>
<tr><td>93</td><td>4</td><td>Another important American study, that of Mansfield, found
for continuing companies that the mean of the lowest size-
class is a little higher than that of largest size-class.
He also found that variance declines with size, but the results
he presents on this point are not clear as to whether the
variance declines regularly with size. Mansfield's data
was not confined to the largest firms; it covered firms of
all sizes in a number of industries over an extended period
of time.</td></tr>
<tr><td>93</td><td>5</td><td>Cf. Y. Ijiri and H. Simon, op. cit.</td></tr>
</table>

CHAPTER 5

<table>
<tr><td>94</td><td>1</td><td>Prais and Hart, op. cit., page 161.</td></tr>
<tr><td>94</td><td>2</td><td>Cf. Simon and Bonini, op. cit.</td></tr>
<tr><td>94</td><td>3</td><td>This is, however, no more than a possibility since as was
noted in the last chapter, it is quite possible that the observed
distribution of growth rates for firms of various sizes is
compatible with a more complex stochastic process which
along with some other features of the law of proportionate
effect still retains the assumption of no serial correlation
in growth rates. It is perhaps worth noting in this context
that an alternative stochastic model proposed by Ijiri and
Simon, op. cit., to explain the pattern of homogeneous mean
growth rates and of declining variance of growth rates with
size, is in fact based on this existence of serial correlation
in growth rates. However, the degree of serial correlation
is assumed to vary inversely with time.</td></tr>
<tr><td>95</td><td>1</td><td>The transition matrices in fact represent an important
device for analyzing several aspects of the growth process
of firms. More complicated stochastic models of the growth
of firms can be formulated and tested by making various</td></tr>
</table>

assumptions about transition probabilities. For the application of this device to the problem of income distribution, see D. G. Champernowne, 'A model of Income Distribution', Economic Journal, 1953, pp. 318-351. S. J. Prais has investigated the problem of social mobility in these terms in, S. J. Prais, 'Measuring Social Mobility', Journal of the Royal Statistical Society, Series A, 1955. Similarly the characteristics of the equilibrium size distribution of firms in an industry can be studied if, along with some other postulates, it is assumed that transition probabilities remain constant over time. See for instance, I. Adelman, 'A stochastic analysis of the size distribution of firms', Journal of the American Statistical Association, 1958. See also, N. R. Collins and L. E. Preston, 'Size structure of industrial firms', American Economic Review, 1961. These issues will not be discussed here.

95   2   The transition matrices for the individual industries are exactly similar to those of Tables 5.1 to 5.3. To save space they are not reproduced here, but in view of their importance for other purposes, they are presented in Appendix E.

99   1   It should be noted that in making comparisons of relative mobility among different industries, the element in the reordering of size ranks which is solely due to the effect of the initial size distribution of firms (i.e. how closely packed together the size ranks happen to be in a particular industry at the beginning of the period) is, in fact, a spurious element of mobility from an economic point of view. In view of this, some investigators (Prais and Hart, op. cit), have used the variance of log ϵ as a measure of relative mobility, where log ϵ is the error term in the regression equation:

$$\log S_{t+1} = \alpha + \beta \log S_t + \log \epsilon$$

S_t denotes the opening and S_{t+1}, the closing size of the firm, α and β are parameters.
This measure of mobility is independent of the initial distribution of firm sizes. Unfortunately, however it has an unambiguous meaning as a measure of mobility only when the law of proportionate effect is valid. When the law of proportionate effect is not valid, and furthermore when log ϵ is not normally distributed, variance of log ϵ cannot be used as an indicator of relative mobility.

99   2   Our mobility measure is:

$$\frac{\text{Actual Number of catchings-up}}{\text{Maximum possible number of catchings-up}}$$

i.e. the proportion of actual to possible cases of companies catching up with or overtaking companies in the next higher size class. It equals 1 where every company catches up with every company in the next higher size classes, and it is zero where no companies catch up with companies in the next higher size classes, e.g. in the present case, if all firms exactly doubled in size.

For our purposes, 'catching-up' takes place when the firm enters a higher size class or the <u>same size class</u> as a firm from the next higher size class.

100   1   Mansfield, <u>op.cit.</u>, has used a variant of this measure in making inter-industry and inter-temporal comparisons of mobility. He takes the initially smaller firm to be .6 to .7 the size of the larger firm.

101   1   Kendall's rank correlation coefficient, r_k, is equal to

$$1 - \frac{2Q}{\frac{1}{2}n(n-1)} \; ,$$

where Q is the number of inversions, i.e. pairs of ranks which occur in different orders in the two rankings, n is the number of ranks.

101   2   Refer to note 99, 1.

103   1   Significance tests have not been used in this section to test the differences in the rank correlation coefficients. The main reason for this is that the tests which have been devised are notoriously insensitive in cases of comparisons where it is assumed that there is a parent correlation among the variables. Cf: M.G. Kendall, <u>Rank Correlation Methods,</u> London 1966, Chapter IV. However, it must be noted that although the differences among the rank correlation coefficients for the various industries are quite small, the same pattern of relative mobility is revealed for <u>all</u> the three time-periods. Furthermore, in drawing conclusions about relative mobility, we are using the rank correlation analysis in conjunction with the measure of mobility discussed in section I.

104   1   The discussion in Chapters 6 and 7 will show that the industrial classification, for a variety of reasons, is not particularly relevant when the largest firms alone are considered. It is not illegitimate, therefore to consider the size-ranks of firms across industries as is done in Tables 5.6a, 5.6b and 5.6c.

108   1   I.M.D. Little, 'Higgledy Piggledy Growth', <u>Bulletin of the Oxford Institute of Economics and Statistics,</u> November 1962.
I.M.D. Little and A.C. Rayner, <u>Higgledy Piggledy Growth Again</u>, Oxford, 1966.

108   2   For further discussion of this see Little and Rayner, <u>op.cit.</u>, p.31.

110   2   It is quite possible for instance that there is a positive serial correlation between growth rates for some of the sub-groups within the Food industry, and a negative serial correlation for others. Aggregation could obscure these relations and result in there being no apparent relationship between growth rates in the two sub-periods.

Page

110 1 The two companies concerned are J.H. Buckingham and Co. (the fastest growing company in the industry in the second sub-period and the fastest shrinking company in the first) and Selincourt and Sons. Both of these companies grew very rapidly through take-overs in the second period.

110 3 Since there are fewer firms in the sub-groups than in the industry, the rank correlation coefficients in the sub-groups are usually significant at a lower level of significance than they are in the industry as a whole.

110 4 The fifth sub-group contains approximately three-quarters of the companies in the industry and is extremely hetero-geneous in scope. To this extent, the attempt at dis-aggregation is not successful.

CHAPTER 6

114 1 Pre-Tax Rate of Return on Net Assets (Indicator 5) and Post-Tax Rate of Return on Equity Assets (Indicator 6).

114 2 Even in this sense, however, as is indicated in the dis-cussion in the next paragraph, the 'optimal size' of the firm cannot just be defined in terms of a single dimension of maximum average profitability. We must also consider variability of profits between firms of different sizes.

114 3 The size distribution of rates of return is sometimes used to draw conclusions about the 'economies of scale' or 'efficiency' of firms of different sizes. This is however, to say the least, a hazardous exercise in view of the problems posed by multi-product firms, firms operating in diverse geographical markets, monopoly power, etc., Cf. H.O. Steckler, Profit-ability and Size of Firm, Berkeley, 1963, Chapter 1.

115 1 We must, however, remember that although in Chapter 4, the average growth rates in the various size classes were not found to be significantly different from each other, average growth in the highest size classes tended to be somewhat larger than in other size classes especially in the second sub-period (1954-60).

119 1 Where, as in the Engineering industry, there are a suffi-ciently large number of cases in each size class, the assumption can be expected to be approximately true. There may, however, be some departures from normality for average profitability in the cases of Food and of Clothing and Footwear.

119 2 Cf. Section 2, Chapter 4, page 79.

119 3 Even in the Engineering industry, the variations between size classes become highly significant when the data is disaggregated into more than 5 size classes.

120 1 The additional exclusions for the log population were because of negative values of either growth, or one of the two rates of return, during the relevant period.

Page		

123   1   The highest proportion of inter-firm variation in the rates of return is 'explained' for Clothing and Footwear in 1948-54 (6% i.e. $r^2 = 0.06$); the average degree of explanation provided by the equation is about 1.5 per cent.

124   1   The linear equations and the semi-log equation which have the same dependent variable can be tested for goodness of fit in terms of r^2. However none of them can be compared in this way with the double log equation.

124   2   Steckler, op. cit., found that this equation gives a reasonably good fit to the American firms studied by him. However, he used grouped data rather than individual firm data for this purpose.

128   1   If size were related to retention ratio (Indicator 8), the operation of the differential profits tax which was in force throughout 1948-54 and for part of sub-period 2 (1954-60) would tend to make the tax burden differ between firms of different sizes. In fact, the zero-order correlation matrices in Chapter 3 show that there was some tendency in the individual industries for retention ratio to increase with the size of the firm. To the extent that this tendency exists and to the extent that the differential profits tax discriminated in favour of retained profits, it would make, the post-tax rate of return higher for the larger-sized firms for a given pre-tax rate of return. This phenomenon could account for the small difference in the strength of the inverse relationship between size and the two measures of profitability.

131   1   A similar tendency was noted in the last section.

131   2   The degree of aggregation involved in considering all firms with opening assets of more than £2 million as the 'largest' firms must be borne in mind. It is quite possible that within this group of largest firms, the most profitable ones may be the relatively small firms (say, those with net assets of between 2 million pounds and 4 million pounds) rather than the relatively large firms (say with assets greater than £10 million or £20 million).

133   1   P.S. Florence; The Logic of British and American Industry, Routledge, London, 1953.

133   2   An implication of the argument that large firms have to pay a greater attention to their performance on the stock market than small firms, is that they also perhaps ought to have a better performance in terms of profitability than small firms. This the large firms do in the sense that, even though their average profitability is not much different from that of small firms, the dispersion of profitability as between large firms is less than for the small firms. See a further discussion of this point in Chapter 8, pp. 191-2.

133   3   Cf. I.M.D. Little and A.C. Rayner, op. cit. Chapters 1 and 2.

134   1   A glance at Figure 6.4 indicates that if a regression model were used which minimized the effect of a small number of extreme observations relating to firms which were highly

unprofitable in either the period 1948-54, or the period 1954-60, the regression results would most likely show a statistically significant relationship between the rates of return in the two periods.

140   1   For a further discussion of the effects of the differential profits tax and of its abolition, on company behaviour, see A. E. Rubner, 'The irrelevancy of the British differential profits tax', Economic Journal, 1964, and of G. C. Harcourt and G. Whittington, 'The irrelevancy of the British differential profits tax, a comment', Economic Journal, June, 1965.

140   2   This issue is discussed further in Chapter 7.

140   3   As noted in the last chapter, (note 110, 3), the rank correlation coefficients in the sub-groups are usually significant at a lower level of significance than in the industry as a whole because of the smaller number of firms in the sub-groups.

141   1   The relevant tests showed that the observed persistency of the rates of return of the largest firms is not a spurious one either. It does not arise from the aggregation of large firms coming from different sub-groups.

141   2   For the 10 largest firms in the Food industry, the rank correlation coefficient between profitability in the two periods is considerably higher than that for the industry as a whole (.62 as opposed to .30). However, under the usual significance tests the former cannot be said to be significantly higher than the latter. This is because of the relative insensitivity of the tests of differences in the rank correlation coefficients when the hypothesis is, as in this case, that there is in fact a correlation among the variables in the two populations. Cf. M. G. Kendall, op. cit., Chapter 3.

141   3   We are most grateful to Mr. C. J. Bliss and Mr. R. E. Rowthorn for raising this point.

CHAPTER 7

149   1   R. L. Marris, Economic Theory of Managerial Capitalism, Chapters I and V. Also see Joel Dean and Winfield Smith, 'The Relationship between Profitability and Size', in W. W. Alberts and J. E. Segall, The Corporate Merger, Chicago, 1966.

150   1   R. L. Marris, Economic Theory of Managerial Capitalism, Chapter II; E. T. Penrose, The Theory of the Growth of the Firm.

150   2   Ideas put forward separately by R. L. Marris and E. Penrose, op. cit., have called attention to other aspects of the relationship between growth and profitability: not only does growth depend on profitability, but profitability itself is a function of growth. In fact, it is suggested that this converse functional relationship between growth and profita-

bility is a negative one: beyond a certain growth rate, the higher the growth the lower the level of profitability of the firm.

If this negative functional relationship between profitability and growth exists, it is possible in principle that it may be so strong as to completely outweigh the tendency for positive association between growth and profitability discussed in the text. In that case, if we examined a cross-section of firms, we might find that there was either no relationship between profitability and growth at all or that there was a negative relationship between these variables. However, there are a number of reasons why this tendency for a negative association between growth and profitability is unlikely to be a close one (Cf. R. L. Marris, 'Profitability and Growth in the Individual Firm', Business Ratios, Spring 1967), and therefore we should still expect to find a positive association between growth and profitability, as suggested in the text.

Apart from the fact that any converse relationship between growth and profitability is likely to be weak, it would be very difficult to estimate this relationship separately from the conventional relationship between growth and profitability using the same data. However, Marris has argued that there is a much greater variance of the error term in the former relationship as compared with the variance of the error term in the latter one. Therefore, we always identify the latter (i. e. the conventional relationship between growth and profitability), when we regress growth on profitability. (Cf. R. L. Marris, 'Incomes Policy and the Rate of Profit in Industry', Proceedings of the Manchester Statistical Society, 1964).

If this argument is correct, we are justified in confining our attention to only the conventional relationship between growth and profitability, i. e. growth depends on profitability, as is done in the text.

151   1   The total number of exclusions for the four industries was as follows (numbers in brackets are the number of companies in the full population): sub-period 1, 45(462); sub-period 2, 56(434); whole period 21(361).

151   2   The only exceptions were for the Food industry in the two sub-periods (1948-54 and 1954-60), when profitability was taken as Post-tax Rate of Return on Equity Assets. In both of these cases, the exclusion of negative growth and profit rates improves the degree of explanation because there is one freak case involving unusually high negative profit rates. See Figures 7.1 and 7.2, and note 159, 1. There were no comparable freaks in other industries.

151   3   In the Clothing and Footwear industry, which has an unusually large number of loss-making companies, another factor seems to contribute to the higher r^2 obtained for the full population. This is a strong tendency for loss-making com-

panies to shrink at a rate which is very closely associated with the rate of loss, since losses automatically reduce net assets. Thus, the scatter from the regression line is usually less for loss-making companies and these companies carry a higher-than-average weight, because extreme values contribute a large amount to the variance from the mean.

158   1   Strictly, the measure of goodness of fit (r^2) derived from equations (1) and (2) cannot be compared with that derived from equation (3), because the latter shows the proportion of the variance of the <u>logarithms</u> of growth rates which is explained, whereas the former give the proportions of the variance of the absolute values of growth rates which are explained.

158   2   The logarithmic equation could be tested on the full population by taking a base other than zero for the measurement of profitability and growth, e.g. if the base were minus 100, then a negative growth rate of 10% per annum would become +90.0 instead of -10.0. This procedure would, however, remove much of the special characteristic of logarithms, i.e. of giving less weight to extreme observations.

159   1   If these two observations are ignored, the results become:

1948-54 $r^2 = 0.50$, a = -0.45 (± 0.91), b = 0.78 (± 0.08)

1954-60 $r^2 = 0.34$, a = -1.22 (± 1.32), b = 0.83 (± 0.12)
It is interesting to explore these two unusual cases. The case of very high negative equity return in the first period is the Angus Milling Co. This company made heavy losses and, as a result of the accumulated loss and the fact that it had gearing, also had very low Equity Assets in relation to its total assets. The unusual case in the second period is Mellins Food, which actually managed to grow by acquiring subsidiaries whilst sustaining heavy losses. In the years for which a stock exchange quotation is available, the valuation ratio for this company was always greater than unity, despite the losses.
The first of these cases might be legitimately regarded as a freak of measurement, but the second seems to be an unusual, but perfectly legitimate, type of behaviour. We have not excluded either from our subsequent analysis, because this would raise the problem of appraising each individual company to decide whether it could qualify as a 'freak'. However, if we had decided on exclusion, the most sensible course of action would be to exclude the first case but include the second. This would not affect our subsequent conclusions about inter-industry and inter-temporal differences.

159   2   'Incomes Policy and the Rate of Profit in Industry', <u>Proceedings of the Manchester Statistical Society,</u> December 1964. Strictly, the Marris proposal relates to the regression of profitability on growth, not the regression of growth on profitability which is under consideration here. However,

we have regressed profitability on growth, and we find a
similar variation of the parameters over time.

159   3   It will be seen from Table 7.2 that for the four industries
taken together the regression coefficient is remarkably stable
between the two sub-periods. But in view of the differences
between the values for the individual industries, discussed
in the next section, we follow our normal practice in attach-
ing little importance to the results for the aggregate of four
arbitrarily chosen industries.

162   1   For the largest firms, considered by themselves the post-
tax rate of return on equity assets gave a much better
explanation of growth than the pre-tax rate of return on
net assets, in every case.

165   1   It should be emphasized that we are testing here for the
existence of differences between the regression coefficients
of large firms, as compared with those of small firms.
We are not testing for the existence of inter-temporal and
inter-industry homogeneity either in the group of large
firms or in the group of small firms.

165   2   Cf. G.C. Chow, 'Tests of Equality between sets of Coefficients in two Linear Regressions', Econometrica, July, 1960
and E. Kuh, Capital Stock Growth: A Microeconometric
Approach, North Holland Publishing Co. Amsterdam, 1963,
Chapters 5 and 6.

An alternative way of testing the differences between the
regression coefficients would have been to fit a dummy
variables regression equation to the data, where in addition
to the dummy variables for the individual industries, additional dummy variables for the size of the firm were also
introduced. This procedure is somewhat more cumbersome
than the one we have adopted.

168   1   For a somewhat similar approach to the problem of income
distribution, see T.P. Hill, 'An Analysis of the Distribution
of Wages and Salaries in Britain', Econometrica, 1959.
As far as we are aware, such an approach has never been
tried before in relation to the distribution of growth rates.

172   1   The tests for the log-linear equation were made only on
the Non-electrical Engineering industry, which is the biggest
of the three industries.

176   1   Parker hypothesises a similar, but not identical, relationship between growth and profitability. However, this curve
has the first turning point at the zero growth rate rather
than at the negative growth rate as shown in our diagram
(page 176). If the data is restricted to growing and profitable firms only, Parker's curve reduces to a log-linear one,
while we still get a third degree polynomial. Cf. J.E.S.
Parker, 'Profitability and Growth of British Industrial
Firms', Manchester School, 1965.

177   1   Cf. S.J. Prais and H.S. Houthakker, The Analysis of
Family Budgets, Cambridge, 1955, pp.51-55. Also
H. Theil and A.L. Nagar, 'Testing the Independence of Re-

Page		

gression Disturbances', The Journal of the American
Statistical Association, December, 1961.

177	2	In addition to testing the serial independence of residuals from the dummy variables equation pertaining to firms in all industries, we also computed the Von Neumann ratio from the residuals pertaining to the Engineering industry alone. The residual growth rates were obtained from the simple linear equation relating growth to post-tax profitability. In sub-period 1, the null hypothesis of serial independence of residuals arranged in the order of magnitude of profitability was rejected, in favour of positive serial association, at the 10% level if we ignored the magnitude of the residuals and considered only their signs. It was rejected at the 15% level if we considered both the sign and the magnitude of the residuals. In sub-period 2, just as in the case of firms in all industries, the null hypothesis could not be rejected at a high level of significance if we considered both the sign and magnitude of the residuals. However, if we considered only the sign of the residuals, the null hypothesis is rejected at the 10% level.
177	3	It should be clear from the text that the results of our analysis in this sub-section are necessarily tentative. We should like to emphasize that we are not implying that the relationship between growth and profitability is necessarily of the precise form given in the figure in the text for every industry. We do however, find evidence of some kind of non-linearity in the relationship between growth and profitability. We are persuaded that this non-linearity is more complicated than that implicit in a simple logarithmic equation.
178	1	Since the results are broadly similar, the first-order correlation coefficients with pre-tax rate of return on net assets (Indicator 5) held constant, are not reproduced here.
178	2	Analogous to the case of the simple correlation coefficient, a perfect positive net linear association between the two variables with the third variable held constant, will yield a value of the partial correlation coefficient of exactly + 1.0; a perfect negative linear association will yield a value of the partial correlation coefficient as - 1.0 and in cases where there is no net linear relationship between the variables, the partial correlation coefficient will be zero.
178	3	Following the analysis of section 4, to the extent that the relationship between profitability and growth may be a non-linear one, this particular limitation of partial correlation coefficients detracts from the subsequent analysis.
181	1	R.L. Marris presents some models of this type in Economic Theory of Managerial Capitalism.
181	2	For a pioneering attempt in the application of such a model, see, D.C. Mueller 'The firm decision process, an econometric investigation', Quarterly Journal of Economics, February, 1967.

312

185   1   An *a priori* case can be made for including some, but not all of these variables. For instance, an argument could be made for including Internal Finance of Growth on the grounds that there are certain firms which are used to making new issues on the stock market and, therefore, find it possible to grow faster, for the same level of profitability, than other firms which do not habitually make use of the stock market. Furthermore, we also know from the inter-period correlations in Chapter 3 that firms which have a low internal finance ratio in one period also tend to have a low internal finance ratio in the next period.

CHAPTER 8

191   1   For a summary of our conclusions with respect to this and the other theoretical and methodological issues, the reader is referred to the final sections of each of the Chapters 4 to 7.

191   2   Edith Penrose The Theory of the Growth of the Firm, op. cit.

191   3   R. L. Marris Economic Theory of Managerial Capitalism, op. cit.

192   1   We also suggest, in the context of inter-industry differences (Chapter 6) that large firms are possibly more sensitive than small firms to the stock market's appraisal of their performance relative to other firms, irrespective of industry.

192   2   Strictly, this argument applies to outside shareholders, as opposed to shareholders who have an interest in the management of the company.

Where management has a small stake in the ownership of the company, this will be of relatively minor importance relative to the benefits obtained from employment by the company. Where management has a large stake in the company, as in the case of family-controlled firms, it may well be different from most other shareholders in that a large portion of individual or family wealth is committed to the single concern, so that a greater premium is placed upon security. In most cases, therefore, the interests of outside shareholders are likely to be different from those who have a share in the management of the company.

194   1 $(0.25 + 1.0) \div 2 = 0.625$

APPENDIX A.

203   1   The exemptions were due partly to a desire to confine the analysis to a fairly homogeneous set of industries which could loosely be described as 'manufacturing and distribution', and also to the fact that banking and insurance companies were exempt from certain of the requirements of the 1948 Companies' Act. Shipping companies, which were also exempt from some of the provisions of the Act, and property companies, which were considered to resemble finance companies, were also excluded from the population when the Board of Trade extended the analysis. Thus, the basic population may be described as including companies engaged in manufacturing, distribution, construction, transport (excluding shipping) and non-financial services.

203   2   The companies excluded after 1960 were those with net assets of less than £0.5 million and income of less than £50,000 in 1960 (see Board of Trade Journal, 7 December 1962). The result was a fall in the number of companies from 2,618 to 2,241 (see also the table for Income and Finance of Quoted Companies, in the Annual Abstract of Statistics, which gives the data in aggregate, together with the number of companies per year).

203   3   These are listed in the Bibliography at the end of Part I of this Appendix.

208   1   Company Assets and Income, 1949-53, Appendix A.

212   1   For example, Imperial Chemical Industries Ltd., the largest company in the full population for most of the period under review, does not distinguish its current tax liabilities from 'provisions for other liabilities'.

216   1   Tew and Henderson, op. cit., pp. 15-17. Our own growth measure (Indicator 4), includes growth from these sources (see Appendix D). This has the disadvantage (relative to the Tew and Henderson measure) that a company may appear to 'grow' merely because it consolidates a subsidiary which was formerly treated as a trade investment. We are grateful to Professor Tew for pointing this out.

216   2   A table showing the distribution of accounting dates between companies will be found in Company Assets and Income, 1949-53, p. 9.

216   3   Cases where two sets of accounts (or no accounts) appear in one year because of a change of accounting date, are dealt with in part (b) of this section, on 'linking'.

217   1   It also involves there being no less than three aggregate balance sheets at any one date, as will be seen, for example, from the tables in Company Assets and Income, 1949-53. The first is the closing balance sheet for the comparable pair of years just ended, the second is the middle balance sheet for the current pair of comparable years, and the third is the opening balance sheet for the comparable pair of years which is just beginning.

Page		
218	1	This, of course is a strong point in favour of the Tew and Henderson growth measure referred to in note 216, 1.
220	1	The British Economy. Key Statistics, 1900-1964, published for the London and Cambridge Economic Service by The Times Publishing Company Ltd.
221	1	Board of Trade Journal, Vol. 190, No. 3595, 11 February 1966, pp. 313-4. It is estimated that, in 1963, the total assets of quoted companies were worth (at current prices) approximately 50 per cent more than their book value. In 1949, the difference was more than 100%.
221	2	This does not, of course, mean that our industry classification is ideal for the purpose. Examination of the depreciation rates allowed for tax purposes, which are settled on an industry basis, suggests that depreciation rates vary between some of our industrial sub-groups.
223	1	R. Marris and A. Singh, 'A measure of a firm's average share price', Journal of the Royal Statistical Society. Series A, 1966 and also C. Edwards and J. C. Hilton, 'High-Low Averages as an Estimator of Annual Stock Price', The Journal of Finance, 1966.
223	2	In terms of the notation used in Appendix C, equity assets are defined as: Q60 - Q4 - Q2.
223	3	We are referring here only to change due to a 'new issue', not due to a bonus issue. See further section 2.

Works Cited

Adelman, I. 'A Stochastic Analysis of the Size Distribution of Firms', Journal of the American Statistical Association, December, 1958.

Ady, P. and Worswick, G. D. N. The British Economy in the 1950's, Oxford, 1962

Alberts, W. W. and Segall, J. E. The Corporate Merger, Chicago, 1966.

Aspin, A. and Welch, B. L. 'Tables for use in comparisons whose accuracy involves two variances separately estimated', Biometrika, vol. XXXVI, 1949.

Barna, T. Investment and Growth Policies in British Industrial Firms, Cambridge, 1962.

Board of Trade, Income and Finance of Quoted Companies 1949-1960, London, 1962.

Bonini, C. and Simon, H. 'The Size Distribution of Business Firms', American Economic Review, September, 1958

Central Statistical Office, Annual Abstract of Statistics, H.M.S.O., London, published annually.

Central Statistical Office National Income Blue Book, National Income and Expenditure, H.M.S.O., London, published annually.

Champernowne, D. G. 'A model of Income Distribution', Economic Journal, June, 1953.

Chow, G. C. 'Tests of Equality between Sets of Coefficients in Two Linear Regressions', Econometrica, July, 1960.

Collins, N. R. and Preston, L. E. 'Size Structure of Industrial Firms', American Economic Review, 1961.

Cottle, S. and Whitman, T. Corporate Earning Power and Market Valuation 1935-55, Duke University Press, 1959.

Dean, Joel and Smith, Winfield. 'The Relationship between Profitability and Size' in Alberts, W. W. and Segall, J. E. The Corporate Merger, Chicago, 1966.

Edwards, C. and Hilton, J. C. 'High-Low Averages as an Estimator of Annual Stock Price', The Journal of Finance, 1966.

Florence, P. S. The Logic of British and American Industry, London, 1953.

Gibrat, R. Les Inégalités Economiques, Paris, 1931

Gordon, Myron. The Investment, Financing and Valuation of the Corporation, Illinois, 1962.

Gutman, W. 'Book value-market value patterns' in Lerner, E. M. Readings in Financial Analysis and Investment Management, Homewood, Illinois, 1963.

316

Harcourt, G. C. and Whittington, G. 'The Irrelevancy of the British Differential Profits Tax, A Comment', Economic Journal, June, 1965.

Hart, P. E. Studies in Profit, Business Saving and Investment in the United Kingdom, 1920-1962, London, 1965.

Hart, P. E. 'The Size and Growth of Firms', Economica, February, 1962.

Hart, P. E. and Prais, S. J. 'The Analysis of Business Concentration: A Statistical Approach', Journal of the Royal Statistical Society, Series A, 1956, vol. 119, part 2.

Hartley, H. O. and Pearson, E. S. Biometrika Tables for Statisticians, vol. 1, Cambridge, 1954.

Henderson, R. F. and Tew, B. Studies in Company Finance, Cambridge University Press, 1959.

Hill, T. P. 'An Analysis of the Distribution of Wages and Salaries in Britain', Econometrica, 1959.

Hilton, J. C. and Edwards, C. 'High-Low Averages as an Estimator of Annual Stock Price', The Journal of Finance, 1966.

Houthakker, H. S. and Prais, S. J. The Analysis of Family Budgets, Cambridge, 1955.

Hymer, S. and Pashigan, P. 'Firm Size and Rate of Growth', The Journal of Political Economy, December, 1962.

Hymer, S. and Pashigan, P. Reply to Simon, H. in Journal of Political Economy, 1964.

Ijiri, Y. and Simon, H. A. 'Business Firm Growth and Size', American Economic Review, 1964.

Kaldor, N. 'Marginal Productivity and the Macro-Economic Theories of Distribution', The Review of Economic Studies, 1966.

Kalecki, M. 'On the Gibrat Distribution', Econometrica, 1945.

Kendall, M. G. Rank Correlation Methods, London, 1948.

Kuh, E. Capital Stock Growth: A Micro-Econometric Approach, Amsterdam, 1963.

Lerner, E. M. Readings in Financial Analysis and Investment Management, Homewood, Illinois, 1963.

Little, I. M. D. 'Higgledy-Piggledy Growth', Bulletin of the Oxford Institute of Economics and Statistics, November, 1962.

Little, I. M. D. and Rayner, A. C. Higgledy-Piggledy Growth Again, Oxford, 1966.

London and Cambridge Economic Service. The British Economy, Key Statistics, 1900-64.

Mandelbrot, B. 'New Methods in Statistical Economics', Journal of Political Economy, October, 1963.

Mansfield, E. 'Entry, Gibrat's Law, Innovation and the Growth of Firms', American Economic Review, December, 1962.

Marris, R. L. Economic Theory of Managerial Capitalism, London, 1964.

Marris, R. L. 'Incomes Policy and the Rate of Profit in Industry', Proceedings of the Manchester Statistical Society, December, 1964.

Marris, R. L. 'Profitability and Growth in the Individual Firm', Business Ratios, Spring, 1967.

Miller, M. H. and Modigliani, F. 'Leverage, Dividend Policy and the Cost of Capital', paper presented at the Econometric Society, December, 1960.

Modigliani, F. and Miller, M. H. 'Leverage, Dividend Policy and the Cost of Capital', paper presented at the Econometric Society, December, 1960.

Moodies Services, Investment Handbook, published annually.

Mueller, D. C. 'The Firm Decision Process, an Econometric Investigation', Quarterly Journal of Economics, February, 1967.

Nagar, A. L. and Theil, H. 'Testing the Independence of Regression Disturbances', The Journal of the American Statistical Association, December, 1961.

Parker, J. E. S. 'Profitability and Growth of British Industrial Firms', Manchester School, 1965.

Pashigan, P. and Hymer, S. 'Firm Size and the Rate of Growth', The Journal of Political Economy, December, 1962.

Pashigan, P. and Hymer, S. Reply to H. Simon, in Journal of Political Economy, 1964.

Pearson, E. S. and Hartley, H. O. Biometrika Tables for Statisticians, vol. 1, Cambridge, 1954.

Penrose, Edith The Theory of the Growth of the Firm, Oxford, 1959.

Prais, S. J. 'Measuring Social Mobility', Journal of the Royal Statistical Society, Series A, 1955.

Prais, S. J. and Hart, P. E. 'The Analysis of Business Concentration: A Statistical Approach', Journal of the Royal Statistical Society, Series A, 1956, vol. 119, part 2.

Prais, S. J. and Houthakker, H. S. The Analysis of Family Budgets, Cambridge, 1955.

Preston, L. E. and Collins, N. R. 'Size Structure of Industrial Firms', American Economic Review, 1961

Rayner, A. C. and Little, I. M. D. Higgledy-Piggledy Growth Again, Oxford, 1966.

Rubner, A. E. 'The Irrelevancy of the British Differential Profits Tax', Economic Journal, 1964.

Samuels, J. M. 'Size and Growth of Firms', Review of Economic Studies, 1965.

Segall, J. E. and Alberts, W. W. The Corporate Merger, Chicago, 1966.

Simon, H. and Bonini, C. 'The Size Distribution of Business Firms', American Economic Review, September, 1958.

Simon H. and Ijiri, Y. 'Business Firm Growth and Size', American Economic Review, 1964.

Simon, H., Hymer, S. and Pashigan, P. Debate in Journal of Political Economy, 1964.

Smith, Winfield and Dean, Joel 'The Relationship between Profitability and Size', in Alberts, W. W. and Segall, J. E., The Corporate Merger, Chicago, 1966.

Steckler, H. O. Profitability and Size of Firm, Berkeley, 1963.

Steindl, J. Random Processes and the Growth of the Firm, London, 1965.

Tew, B. and Henderson, R. F. Studies in Company Finance, Cambridge, 1959.

Theil, H. and Nagar, A. L. 'Testing the Independence of Regression Disturbances', The Journal of the American Statistical Association, December, 1961.

Welch, B. L. and Aspin, A. C. 'Tables for use in comparisons whose accuracy involves two variances separately estimated', Biometrika, vol. XXXVI, 1949.

Whitman, F. and Cottle, S. Corporate Earning Power and Market Valuation 1935-55, Duke University Press, 1959.

Whittington, G. and Harcourt, G. C. 'The Irrelevancy of the British Differential Profits Tax, A Comment', Economic Journal, June 1965.

Williamson, O. The Economics of Discretionary Behavior, Managerial Objectives in a Theory of the Firm, Englewood Cliffs, N.J., 1964.

Worswick, G. D. N. and Ady, P. H. The British Economy in the 1950's, Oxford, 1962.

Wright, J. F. 'The capital market and finance of industry', in Worswick, G. D. N. and Ady, P. H., The British Economy in the 1950's, Oxford, 1962.

Index

and pre-tax profitability, 66-7, 148-59, 189-90, 197-200, 248-65
and profitability for largest firms, 162-8, 200-1,
and size, 25, 67, 73-93, 94-113, 115, 115n. 1, 185, 191-3, 248-65
and valuation ratio, 67, 177-82, 185-8, 248-65
and other indicators, 67-8, 185-8, 248-65
and mobility, see Mobility
ability to grow, 149, 168, 188-9
persistency of, 18, 94, 108-11, 113, 131, 141, 193-4
predicted, 172-7, 190, 202
residual, 168-77, 190
variance of, 81, 81n. 3, 92-3, 99
willingness to grow, 149, 168, 188-9

Heteroscedasticity, 81, 83n. 2, 93, 93n. 2, 120, 172

Industries studied, 19
Internal finance of growth, definition of, 39, 42, 237
    and growth, 67, 182, 248-65
    and other indicators, 67, 248-65
Inventory, see Stocks

Law of Proportionate Effect, the, 18, 73-93, 94, 99, 99n. 1, 108, 113, 168, 169,
Liquidity, definition of 45, 48, 237
    and growth, 67, 177, 178, 179, 180, 181, 190, 248-65
    and stocks, 68, 248-65
    and other indicators, 248-65
Log-normal distribution, 74

Management, 133, 140, 146-7, 149, 192, 192n. 2, 197
Mobility, internal, 18, 94-107, 111-13, 193
    of large firms, 104-7
    rank correlation, see Correlation coefficients
    relative mobility, over time, 103-4, 111, 113, 238-46
        of different size groups, 104
    spuriousness of, 99n. 1, 103-4

Net trade credit given, definition of, 45, 48, 53, 237
    and other indicators, 248-65
Non-linearity, 62, 67n. 4, 75, 120, 134, 144, 151, 172, 177, 177n. 3, 190

Pareto distribution, 74, 81n. 1
Population studied, births and deaths, 86-9
    statistics of, 19-20, 203-9
Profitability,
    Post-tax rate of return on equity assets, definition of, 32, 32n. 1, 236
        and growth, see Growth
        and size, 114-15, 119-20, 124, 128-33, 144-5, 191-2, 248-65
        persistency of, 133-44, 146-7, 191-7
            for large firms, 141, 146, 200-1
            spuriousness of, 141
    Pre-tax rate of return on net assets, definition of, 25, 25n. 3, 236
        and growth, see Growth

322